Precarious Secrets

BORDER HISPANISMS

Alberto Moreiras, Gareth Williams, and Gabriela Méndez Cota, Series Editors

ALSO IN THE SERIES

Nathaniel Wolfson, *Concrete Encoded: Poetry, Design, and the Cybernetic Imaginary in Brazil*

Paloma Duong, *Portable Postsocialisms: New Cuban Mediascapes after the End of History*

Robert McKee Irwin, ed., *Migrant Feelings, Migrant Knowledge: Building a Community Archive*

Juliana Martínez, *Haunting without Ghosts: Spectral Realism in Colombian Literature, Film, and Art*

Alberto Moreiras, *Against Abstraction: Notes from an Ex–Latin Americanist*

David E. Johnson, *Violence and Naming: On Mexico and the Promise of Literature*

R. Andrés Guzmán, *Universal Citizenship: Latina/o Studies at the Limits of Identity*

Eugenio Claudio Di Stefano, *The Vanishing Frame: Latin American Culture and Theory in the Postdictatorial Era*

Sergio Delgado Moya, *Delirious Consumption: Aesthetics and Consumer Capitalism in Mexico and Brazil*

Daniel Nemser, *Infrastructures of Race: Concentration and Biopolitics in Colonial Mexico*

Horacio Legrás, *Culture and Revolution: Violence, Memory, and the Making of Modern Mexico*

Samuel Steinberg, *Photopoetics at Tlatelolco: Afterimages of Mexico, 1968*

Charles Hatfield, *The Limits of Identity: Politics and Poetics in Latin America*

Precarious Secrets

A HISTORY OF THE LATIN AMERICAN POLITICAL THRILLER

Fabricio Tocco

University of Texas Press, *Austin*

Printed in the United States of America
First edition, 2025

Australian Academy of the Humanities

The author wishes to thank the Australian Academy of the Humanities for its support in the publication of this book.

♾ The paper used in this book meets the minimum requirements of ANSI/NISO Z39.48-1992 (R1997) (Permanence of Paper).

Library of Congress Cataloging-in-Publication Data

Names: Tocco, Fabricio, author
Title: Precarious secrets : a history of the Latin American political thriller / Fabricio Tocco.
Description: First edition. | Austin : University of Texas Press, 2025. | Includes bibliographical references and index.
Identifiers: LCCN 2025003246 (print) | LCCN 2025003247 (ebook)
ISBN 978-1-4773-3292-4 hardcover
ISBN 978-1-4773-3293-1 pdf
ISBN 978-1-4773-3294-8 epub
Subjects: LCSH: Thrillers (Motion pictures)—Latin America | Politics in motion pictures | LCGFT: Film criticism
Classification: LCC PN1995.9.S87 T63 2025 (print) | LCC PN1995.9.S87 (ebook) | DDC 791.43/6581098—dc23/eng/20250627
LC record available at https://lccn.loc.gov/2025003246
LC ebook record available at https://lccn.loc.gov/2025003247

doi:10.7560/332924

The University of Texas Press gratefully acknowledges the Joe R. and Teresa Lozano Long Endowment in Latin American and Latino Art and Culture for its support of this publication.

Para Caio Ástor, alegre estrella que me confió el viento

Contents

Precarious Secrets

Introduction

I will be accused of reading too much into the thriller.

JERRY PALMER, *THRILLERS* (1978)

SECRETS ARE OFTEN MORE INTRICATE THAN THEY appear. We tend to think about them in terms of information or content, but they are also closely linked to space and form. For the Romans, *secretus* stemmed from *secernere*: "to separate, to distinguish, to secrete,"[1] which is also connected to "discern." Secrets are at once content and containers, as they demand the fabrication of imaginary places where sensitive data can be concealed.

Throughout the twentieth century, much of Continental philosophy devoted time to examining secrecy and space in politics and culture. Jacques Derrida, for instance, reminds us that secrets are connected to "separation" and "isolation," in that they are information that must be insulated.[2] Although he does not explicitly mention it, he must be thinking of the twofold connotation of *secretus*. In turn, Gilles Deleuze and Félix Guattari note how even the disclosure of secrets is connected to space. Secrets are "certain contents," which "have a form, but that form is covered, doubled, or replaced by a simple container, envelope, or box." Secrets are "inseparable from two movements that can accidentally interrupt [their] course or betray [them], but are nonetheless an essential part of [them]: something must ooze from the box, something will be perceived through the box."[3] For them to exist in society, secrets must secrete: they always slip away. In other words, they must transpire through space: from the underground to the surface, darkness to light, inside to outside of the box.

Secrets, however, are not just about space. As sociologist Georg Simmel reminds us in his study devoted to secrecy, they are also inherently social.[4] Secrets are mechanisms of social bonding through space: when they are willingly disclosed among peers, they can generate positive affect. By contrast, when they are leaked to or seized by the enemy, they can change the course of history. As a social phenomenon, secrecy is also essential to politics: intelligence agencies work under the mandate of classified information, "state secrets" (*arcana imperii*), as studied by philosopher of law Norberto Bobbio: knowledge that the state keeps enclosed not only from its enemies but also from its friends, even from its own people, allegedly for their own security.[5]

Along with the growing colonization of life at the hands of technology, secrecy has become one of the main sources of anxiety that has been defining and redefining societies and politics for the last decades. This is why secrecy became a central philosophical problem for Derrida, Deleuze, Guattari, Simmel, Bobbio, and other prominent authors, such as Elias Canetti, who writes that "secrecy lies at the very core of power";[6] Michael Taussig, who talks about "public secrecy" in terms of fetishism;[7] and Silvia Federici, who discusses the ties between secrecy, gossip, and gender.[8]

The first quarter of this century provides numerous examples of how the leaking and the commodification of secrets have shaped international politics as well as private life on a global scale, affecting both the political and the personal: we need only think of the prosecution against Julian Assange, Edward Snowden, and Chelsea Manning in relation to the leaking of secrets. We could also cite Facebook–Cambridge Analytica's interference in the Brexit vote and Donald Trump's 2016 campaign, by means of breaching personal data privacy. The increasing role of encryption in our daily activities, the rise of cryptocurrencies and crypto scams, the concerns regarding who stores biometric information, and the consolidation of cybersecurity and "big data" all point to the renewed pivotal role that secrecy plays in our lives.

Secrets are also a condition of possibility for narrative: storytellers rely on hiding them and gradually revealing them to their audience. This is perhaps especially true for genre fiction. Ricardo Piglia, well aware of the spatial dimension of secrets (and its implications for the literary, the political, and even the economic), links it to the detective story in particular.[9] Although "every narrator always faces the problem of the secret [as] every story goes from not knowing to knowing," it is the detective story that "turns that transition into a theme."[10] As such, the slippery nature of secrecy is shaped not only by space but also by time, as it weaves through the unfolding sequence of events in a plot—whether in a novel or a film script.

Secrets are also one of the key ingredients in what Alberto Moreiras calls "the normative narrative structure of our time," the dominant cultural form to portray the world through fiction: the thriller.[11] Borrowing the detective story elements mentioned by Piglia, a distinct type of thriller has gradually yet steadily been developing for the past five decades in Latin America. This genre puts the political aspects of secrecy and space on center stage, juxtaposing society and politics, aesthetics and ethics, the political and the personal: the political thriller.

THE POLITICAL THRILLER AND THE THRILLER

Like secrets, thrillers are also linked to space, in that they are inherently slippery. There is something about their defining ingredients that is essentially precarious—something that always escapes (paraphrasing a friend of mine).[12] To begin with, despite what many critics claim, the thriller per se is not a genre.[13] In *Thrillers*, the most comprehensive study of the subject, Martin Rubin reminds us that thrillers are "too broad" to be considered at the same level as, say, science fiction or the western. Instead, thrillers are better understood as a "meta-genre."[14] Or, in Charles Derry's more illustrative terms, they are an "umbrella" covering several genres.[15] Throughout the twentieth century, critics have identified the detective, spy, psychological, police, crime, heist, legal, and political thriller, among many others.[16]

We could think of thriller genres as communicating vessels, constantly overflowing what Rubin calls the thriller's "amorphous boundaries."[17] This could be simply because all genres overlap. After all, as Janet Staiger notes regarding film genres, "Hollywood films have never been 'pure.'" Blending genres was always a strategy to reach diverse audiences. In turn, this heterogeneity was perceived to translate into more profit and greater originality.[18] So it is no wonder that genre hybridization was an inherent part of the film industry, along with the emergence of thrillers in the early twentieth century.[19] While Staiger is thinking about cinema, her claim could also be extended to genre fiction in literature.[20] Perhaps because of its highly commercial status, the thriller is nonetheless especially fluid, extremely prone to blending neighboring types.[21] Throughout the following pages, I allude here and there to other kinds of thrillers to strengthen a point. For the sake of brevity, I sometimes also describe a novel or a film simply as a "thriller." In most such cases, however, I am referring to the political thriller, which is the main topic of this book.

Because it is an elusive category, critics have struggled to provide concise definitions of the thriller-umbrella.[22] In a nutshell, thrillers are often defined as stories that involve the narrative exploration of a crime, through secrecy, unpredictability, vulnerability, and especially suspense.[23] Indeed, "thriller" has traditionally been translated in Spanish and Portuguese as *suspenso* and *suspense*, respectively. Through suspense, thrillers are designed to thrill us: to elicit affective reactions in the audience by displaying defenseless characters facing highly threatening situations.[24] It is Derry who offers the most persuasive definition of the political thriller. For him, the genre basically tells only two conspiratorial stories that create suspense: magnicides and state-sponsored plots. In other words, if thrillers in general tell the story of a crime, political thrillers in particular focus on political crimes, typically examining a planned assassination attempt or revealing the "conspiratorial nature of governments and their crimes against their people." This is done, in film at least, through very recognizable formal techniques: a "rhythmic soundtrack, much montage, a fast pace [and] a high-speed chase."[25] In literary political thrillers, we could add, a defining feature is the emphasis on plot over character study, which tends to be more typical, for instance, in dramas. While this book follows Derry, it also suggests that there is more to the genre than that.

Beyond the genre's themes, the point of view to explore political crimes can be comprehensive, which is perhaps what distinguishes the genre from other types of thrillers.[26] For instance, the detective thriller follows an investigator who tries to solve a crime or explore networks of criminality, while the crime thriller tends to commercialize the viewpoint of, say, serial killers or their victims. These crimes may or may not involve the political. By contrast, political thrillers can be told from all these perspectives, as long as the nature of the crime is explicitly political. Instead of detectives, we get journalists and human rights lawyers; instead of serial killers and their victims, we get state-sponsored criminals and survivors of their conspiracies, often including politicians. In short, political thrillers commodify and spectacularize political crimes by leveraging secrecy and suspense to examine the political from an angle that is never divorced from entertainment.

In addition to the explicit representations of the conspiracies mentioned by Derry, the Latin American political thriller, in particular, offers distinct themes and perspectives that constitute a unique contribution to the genre. Besides coups and magnicides, Latin American productions bring to the table the portrayal of massacres and genocides from the point of view of either perpetrators or survivors. Furthermore, the genre has a long history of thrillers that chronicle the armed struggle in the region, with guerrilla movements such as Brazil's Movimento Revolucionário 8 de Outubro (MR8) and Chile's Movimiento de Izquierda Revolucionaria (MIR). These thrillers sometimes do foreground magnicides or government conspiracies against the guerrillas, but not always. And this is because their point of view is radically different: they often tell the story from the perspective of guerrillas themselves. This book examines how Latin American political thrillers represent both conventional and innovative themes and perspectives.

Although the political thriller has been around since the emergence of the Cold War,[27] it is important to note that the "recognition of the political thriller" as a genre in its own right "has been slow," as Deena Bowman notes.[28] This is especially true in Latin America, where critics have tended to conflate political thrillers with other categories. They label them with catch-all names such as *género negro*, *el policial*, and *la policíaca* (words often used to describe hard-boiled fiction in Spain, Argentina, and Mexico, respectively) or the even broader *novela política* or *cine político*. It is true that some political thrillers showcase crime investigations, but not always.[29] Conversely, it is also true that Latin American hard-boiled fiction includes a large dose of political critique, as Mempo Giardinelli observes,[30] but this does not necessarily turn any detective story into a political thriller. Equally, as I explain later, not all political films are political thrillers.

Latin American authors and filmmakers have been engaging with the genre for more than fifty years, but the political thriller originated much earlier in Anglophone literature. Some Anglo-American journals and magazines have used the term to describe books and films ever since the 1950s. The words "political" and "thriller" first appeared together in British and American English in reviews of cultural works that are extremely heterogeneous.[31] The genre entered the scholarly conversation more centrally in the 1980s, but it took a few more years for it to consolidate as such.[32] Much of this conversation has revolved around the United States and Europe (specifically England and France), often excluding Latin American and other Global South productions.[33] Laura Podalsky is perhaps the sole critic to explicitly recognize the political thriller as a genre in its own right within the Latin American context.[34] Similarly, Elena Goity and David Oubiña as well as Constanza Burucúa acknowledge the genre, although they focus only on films made in Argentina—the country with the most prolific tradition of the genre in the region. They all label the films that they study as "political thrillers," going beyond conventional and imprecise catch-all terms. Building on their valuable research, this book tries to address this gap, offering a panoramic overview of the genre in the region.[35]

By no means should the works examined here be understood as the definitive account of the genre, as Latin American political thrillers have proliferated over the past decades—and they still do. Building on the existing literature on thrillers in general,[36] and on the political thriller in particular,[37] I offer a possible history of the genre through a few foundational novels in chapters 1 and 2 but focus mainly on film in chapters 3, 4, and 5. I should emphasize that this book is not about literature or film but about a genre. As such, I alternate between literary and cinematic examples, always trying to be mindful of the unique language of each medium. After all, despite our tendency to draw a sharp distinction between the two in discussions shaped by academic disciplines, authors have been profoundly influenced by filmmakers, and vice versa, since the twentieth century.

THE POLITICAL THRILLER AND THE POLITICAL

Foregrounding guerrillas, investigators, criminals, or victims of political crimes, the genre gradually becomes distinguishable from other types of thrillers for its complex relation with the political. This is because, as Pablo Castrillo and Pablo Echart observe, political thrillers are located at an intersection: they are simultaneously a type of thriller and a type of political text.[38] To be sure, not all stories about the political are thrillers: political dramas, documentaries, biopics of politicians or activists, political satires, films about election campaigns, war films, period dramas, docudramas, and even political comedies also foreground the political.[39] In fact, documentaries (and to a lesser extent left-leaning political dramas) rather than political thrillers have overwhelmingly been the dominant mode of engagement with the political in Mexico and Argentina, for example.[40] This is because the documentary was perceived to be a means to spark political change, especially during the Cold War, in times of military coups, armed struggle, and death squads, unlike film genres that were perceived to be a product of imperialism, as I examine in chapter 1.[41]

Some of these other types of political films, in Latin America and beyond, precede the political thriller itself. What distinguishes them is that thrilleresque ingredients (secrecy, suspense, vulnerability) tend to be less dominant if present at all, in Roman Jakobson's terms.[42] Walter Salles's biopic of Che Guevara's *Motorcycle Diaries* (2004), his recently acclaimed political drama *I'm Still Here* (2024), and Patricio Guzmán's documentary *Nostalgia for the Light* (2010) are clearly political films. But it would be far-fetched to read them as political thrillers because their use of such thrilleresque elements is more peripheral or absent.

In this sense, an analogous intersection is at stake: political thrillers are placed between pure entertainment (the thriller component) and the portrayal of grave issues (the political film dimension). For Castrillo and Echart, for example, American renditions of the genre picture the political not just as "the backdrop or setting" but as "inherently associated to the criminal source of conflict" that triggers the story.[43] But this has not always been consistent. Genres, after all, are historical expressions that change, however slowly, through time and space. It could be argued that American and European political thrillers, from the 1960s onward, included a higher degree of political content, increasingly turning the coupling of crime and the political into a central part of the text, not only of the context (as in the classic spy thriller) or the subtext (as in many films that allegorically speak about political issues).[44] But these post-1960s political thrillers always retained their forerunners' intention of entertaining more than constructing knowledge about cases of political crime.[45] This is perhaps what political thrillers have in common with other types of thrillers and not necessarily with other kinds of political films: their commitment to entertain the audience.[46]

In relation to the genre's entertainment aspect, Podalsky detects "a prevailing tendency among film scholars" to read "the political (if not depoliticizing) effects of . . . the thriller," which "tend[s] to emphasize its function as mindless entertainment." These scholars consider the Latin American documentary the "gold standard" against which to compare the degree of politicization of filmmaking.[47] But reading the political thriller as "mindless entertainment" is reductive, as there is a spectrum in terms of what the genre does with the political. Adam Barker, for instance, sees two poles: at one end are films featuring the "heroic quest" against a conspiratorial villain, the detective-like investigation where the political secret is revealed at the end of the story, offering a more or less happy ending—or at least a satisfying account of complex political events, as in Oliver Stone's *JFK* (1991). At the other end, Barker cites thrillers that are more common in the European context (such as the works of Costa-Gavras), which "opt for no happy endings and an enduring ambiguity about where the moral high ground lies."[48] In Latin America, the first pole has more typically been subverted, while the second has been more commonly reproduced, not without pushing its boundaries, to adapt it to the region's peculiarly turbulent history.

In this context, Latin American political thrillers had to address grave issues such as state-sponsored massacres committed against students and workers or transnational systematically orchestrated crimes against humanity. The ways in which they negotiate the depiction of such issues, through a genre that is part of the entertainment industry, are linked to their treatment of the political. In *Secretos precarios*, a documentary film that is the companion piece to this book, Enrique Buchichio, the director of the Uruguayan film *Zanahoria*, puts it eloquently: whereas Hollywood favors the "thriller," Latin American renditions of the genre lean toward the "political."[49] His claim could also be applied to many European models, especially Costa-Gavras, who is a central influence on the Latin American political thriller.

But the obvious question arises: is entertainment itself not also political? Certainly, it is. After all, going back to the ties between secrecy and the political already outlined, what is more entertaining than sharing or discovering a secret between friends and enemies? But as film historian Ana

María Amado notes in discussing the history of Argentine political film, linking "film and politics implies . . . the risk of falling into the trend of using them in a . . . vague way."[50] That is why this book understands the political in a narrower way. Several "intellectual tendencies" have leaned toward defining the "political" in extremely broad terms over the last quarter of the twentieth century, as political scientist Wendy Brown observes. Perhaps the most popular of these equations is the one that claims that "everything is political."[51] Chantal Mouffe, for instance, defines "the political" as "the dimension of antagonism that is inherent in all human society."[52] The political thriller challenges such axioms. Even though the genre explicitly engages with politics through entertainment, it also offers a paradox to think about the political, claiming that not everything in political thrillers is political. In fact, this is perhaps the genre's most important defining trait: sketching a threshold between what is political and what is not.

This threshold is deeply connected to the structure of the thriller-umbrella, as discussed by Rubin, who claims that thrillers always offer a "strong sense of *contrast* between two different dimensions." The first is the story's characters' daily life. The second is "those ingredients (a murder, a monster, a vital secret, supernatural forces) that invade the ordinary context, transforming it into something adventurous."[53] These two dimensions in the political thriller are the personal and the political, respectively. The political works as the extraordinary side. Or, to put it differently, the political is the monster.

That is not to say that political thrillers are inherently apolitical. The political as a monster, as it appears in thrillers, should not be equated with all politics per se. To be more precise, it is a monster defined by its lack of ethics, personifying the idea of power for power's sake. I elaborate on this in more detail in chapter 2, with a close reading of Rafael Bernal's novel *El complot mongol*. I do so by building on and expanding Moreiras's reading of thrillers as infrapolitical, in particular considering the connections with Kantian definitions of the political.[54] It suffices to say here that the genre constantly pictures the political as something that invades the ordinary life of the characters by piercing it, thrilling it. In this sense, the genre is placed at and hovers over the boundaries of the political. This can be seen in terms of space, in the myriad landscapes in which political thrillers are set: in palace-like buildings, like the White House, O Planalto, La Moneda, and La Casa Rosada, of course; but also in places that we would not immediately associate with the political, such as the Peruvian highlands, the Paraguayan woods, the Chilean desert, and Mexico City's Chinatown.

The genre repeatedly asks a question posed by philosopher Jean-Luc Nancy more than twenty years ago: "is everything political?"[55] For political thrillers, the answer to that question is negative, as it is for Nancy. At first glance, the genre seems to remain ambivalent about it, because, as Rubin notes, invasions are never fully at an end in thrillers.[56] But, as I hope to show throughout this book, the genre (while dwelling within the contours of this twofold world) mostly ends up siding against the absolute invasion of life by the political. As a response to this totalizing force, political thrillers offer alternative ways of understanding the political, sometimes eliciting affective reactions that invite us to inhabit the political otherwise or seeking to recover an ethical understanding of politics.

THE POLITICAL THRILLER AND LATIN AMERICA

The history of the political thriller in Latin America does not belong to Latin Americans only. It starts before the political thriller was adopted and produced locally. As such, it includes European and American filmmakers whose thrillers take place in Latin America, including Fritz Lang, Alfred Hitchcock, and John Huston but especially Costa-Gavras. Conversely, their thrillers are not solely American or European. They chose to set or in some cases film their productions in Latin America, which also makes them inseparable from the region. This speaks to the strong transnational ties that constitute the genre, which constantly breaches national borders within and beyond Latin America.

Like cinema,[57] the subway,[58] rock and roll,[59] and the internet,[60] political thrillers were imported to Latin America (perhaps unsurprisingly) through Mexico, Argentina, Chile, and Brazil. It is in these countries that the strongest traditions of the genre in the region were built. I give these central national film histories the importance they deserve, but I make sure to include, as much as possible, underrepresented countries that engaged with the genre, including Uruguay, Paraguay, Peru, and Bolivia. Although some of the productions of these smaller film industries could at times be derivative of the works of their bigger neighbors, others made central contributions to the genre.

I should clarify here that I do not examine a type of thriller that is very common in Colombia and Mexico: narco-narratives. I exclude them from this book because I consider them to be a separate genre. Even when they often showcase the liaisons that cartels maintain with the political, they do so from the perspective of the illegal drug-trade, privileging the depiction of its criminal brutality. In this sense, I see narco-narratives as an important Latin American contribution to the thriller-umbrella, but one that is actually more connected to the crime thriller.

The Latin American political thriller took off in the early 1970s. This was a time of political turmoil, with dictatorships in most of South America and repression of students and workers in Mexico. In other words, it was a historical moment in which the political was literally invading life on a daily basis. As a response to this, some filmmakers started timidly detaching part of their work from the overarching practice of the documentary to engage with genre fiction. This was still a marginal practice, but the choice was often justified in terms of impact: their aim was to reach a broader audience, beyond the intelligentsia and including the working class, which was, after all, the main subject of revolutionary movements.[61] In Argentina and Chile, in particular, the genre is founded on *clandestinidad*: it takes place in hiding, amid censorship, forced disappearance, and exile. Raymundo Gleyzer's *Los traidores* (1973), perhaps the first political thriller in Latin American cinema, never had a proper commercial release, for example. A black-and-white copy secretly circulated in clandestine networks, and it was only in the mid-1990s that the film could be screened in color.[62] Gleyzer, in turn, remains desaparecido since May 1976.

In this context, the role of the Latin American diaspora is fundamental to understanding the material history of the genre in the region. A few examples suffice to give an idea of the situation. One is Jorge Cedrón, who in desperation had to disguise the film cans of *Operación masacre* (1973) with fake labels while preparing to leave for Paris in 1977.[63] Other South American colleagues devoted to making political films (Raúl Ruiz, Pino Solanas, Patricio Guzmán, and Helvio Soto) also would be exiled there. Only three years later, Cedrón died after being stabbed in Paris, under circumstances that still remain unclarified.[64] Much like *Los traidores*, his film had been made and premiered in hiding at the end of the 1966–1973 Argentine dictatorship. Similarly, Helvio Soto's *Il pleut sur Santiago* (1975), the first political thriller about Augusto Pinochet's 1973 coup, was filmed in Bulgaria and France, mainly with European actors.[65] As for the diaspora within Latin America, the filming of Pablo de la Barra's *Queridos compañeros* (1979) was supposed to wrap on the same day that Pinochet staged his coup. The military halted it and destroyed the director's studio, including the film's audio. The negatives were preserved thanks to the Venezuelan embassy. De la Barra managed to complete the film only in exile in Caracas, six years later.[66]

These examples speak to the precarious conditions in which the political thriller emerged in Latin America as a local practice. The same historical circumstances that informed the birth of the genre quickly interrupted it: the volatility of the filmmakers' work and lives led to a halt.[67] Dictatorial and post-dictatorial censorship did the rest.[68] After their short-lived first appearance in the 1970s, Latin American political thrillers flourished only after the Cold War started to come to an end, within the broader context of what Podalsky calls "the return of genre film" in Latin American cinema, in the form of "an 'authorial vehicle' with political goals that include an interrogation of the past."[69] More precisely, political thrillers emerged as democratic administrations started to consolidate in the region in the 1980s and 1990s—however precariously and unevenly.[70] As censorship gradually waned between the 1980s and 1990s,[71] the intensification of transnational cinema in the 2000s and the emergence of online platforms in the 2010s contributed to the proliferation of local productions.[72] In short, the Latin American political thriller is a product of neoliberalism and globalization as much as it is of democratization and regional, trans-diasporic solidarity.

REALISM AND THE HISTORICAL

Anchored in Cold War anxieties, political thrillers typically foreground political conflicts by examining historical events through a realistic aesthetics. Bowman hits the mark when she locates the genre's key trait in its "cachet of authenticity."[73] Classic spy or detective thrillers, when they deal tangentially with politics, tend to be rife with McGuffins: fanciful secret plots whose main function is to trigger a storyline, only to become irrelevant later.[74] Their authenticity is not intrinsically important: by their very definition, McGuffins are only smoke and mirrors. Early political thrillers still used them, especially in the 1940s–1950s noir period. Nevertheless, from the 1960s onward, the genre gradually abandoned McGuffins or imbued them with an aura of historicity. This happened with different degrees of success, of course, as Hollywood productions sometimes explain historical events through conspiracy theories that can also seem like smoke and mirrors.[75] All in all, it is fair to say that political thrillers try to convince us of their realistic intentions, either by casting actors who closely resemble the politicians, activists, or guerrillas they play or by re-creating the historical atmosphere of the recent past, as opposed to period dramas that typically (though not always) go back further in time.

More than other types of thrillers, the genre tends to be rooted in the historical, whether its storylines are entirely fictional or based on real facts.[76] This is visually translated on the screen by tying historical processes to a specific time and place.[77] This convention is widely reproduced in Latin America. Intertitles such as "Santiago de Cuba, 1959," "Santiago de Chile, 1973," and "Ayacucho, 1980," for instance, crowd the Latin American political thriller. These dates are filled with connotations that become synonymous with the political episodes to which they refer: the Cuban Revolution, Pinochet's coup, the emergence of the Shining Path, and so forth. In this sense, political thrillers speak to postmodernist tensions, which, as Fredric Jameson notes, dwell between historical continuity and rupture by privileging "breaks" or "when-it-all-changed" events.[78]

Like their American and European counterparts,[79] Latin American political thrillers obsessively return to the past; because of the interruption brought by the 1970s political turmoil, however, they often feature a bigger historical gap between the films' release and the period they portray. Although they still feature what Ian Scott calls "domestic extensions" of the Cold War, they do not emphasize so much the paranoia and immediate anxieties of the present that we see in foreign cinematic models.[80] Most of the time, Latin American political thrillers focus on sharing the local theater of the Cold War, as clearly delineated by the places and dates mentioned in the inter titles.

This gap with the portrayed past is increasingly causing filmmakers to engage with representation through a memory and postmemory lens, in Marianne Hirsch's terms: "the relationship of the second generation to . . . traumatic experiences that preceded their births but that were nevertheless transmitted to them so deeply as to seem to constitute memories in their own right."[81] We can see this with Benjamín Ávila's *Infancia clandestina* (2012) and Diego Corsini's *Pasaje de vida* (2015). These filmmakers are effectively telling the story of their parents, who were involved in the armed struggle four decades earlier, in the 1970s. By contrast, American thrillers such as Sidney Lumet's *Fail-Safe* (1964) and Alan J. Pakula's *All the President's Men* (1976) premiered only two years after the historical events they were representing: the Cuban Missile Crisis and Richard Nixon's resignation, respectively.

Nevertheless, as Moreiras notes, "even though their ostensible topics are always and precisely concerned with nothing other than time and history . . . all good thrillers tend toward ontological eternity."[82] Beneath their apparently precise chronology, the genre's aim is to go beyond history, to deal with transhistorical topics, such as power and ethics, individual heroism and friendship, loyalty and betrayal, resentment and ambition, the political and the personal.

In relation to realistic depictions of historical events, Derry claims that political thrillers exhibit an "almost documentary sense of immediacy."[83] The "almost" is key here: I have mentioned that documentaries and political thrillers are not the same. This is because, at least in principle, the former offer a nonfictional testimony and the latter offer a story guided by rules of fiction, which tend to privilege verisimilitude over factuality. As Bowman notes, however, one of the ways in which political thrillers show their cachet of authenticity is by using real found footage, sometimes from documentaries, archival TV news, or video recordings of important politicians' speeches.[84] Though they are indeed different genres, political thrillers very frequently embed documentaries in their plots, to introduce or punctuate them. The proximity between these two types of political films could explain why some of the first Latin American directors to engage with political thrillers started their careers as documentary filmmakers: in Argentina (Raymundo Gleyzer), Brazil (Gustavo Dahl), and Mexico (Felipe Cazals). Equally, it could explain why so many critics have repeatedly misinterpreted political thrillers as documentaries in Latin America. In fact, Gleyzer was heavily criticized by his own colleagues for turning to genre film instead of pursuing his documentary work.[85] In relation to the political thriller's cachet of authenticity, I examine the use of screens (TVs, cinemas, smartphones, and tablets) in chapters 3, 4, and 5 as narrative devices that retell history through found footage.

Sticking to aesthetic realism, however, was never much of a choice for Latin American filmmakers (as it might have been for many of their models), but rather a result of the structural precarity that surrounds filmmaking in the region.[86] In Carlos Monsiváis's words, film budgets throughout the twentieth century were often *raquíticos* (too thin),[87] constraining what could be done in terms of *mise-en-scène* in genre film. To be sure, realistic storytelling frees producers from having to use expensive special effects or the complex creation of parallel worlds that are common in dystopian and sci-fi films. But reconstructing recent historical events can be pricey, too.[88] Films like Jorge Fons's *Rojo amanecer* (1989), for instance, manage to circumvent this by recreating the 1968 Tlatelolco massacre without ever leaving the interior of a middle-class family apartment. It is in this and other senses that I examine the genre through three central concepts: secrecy, space, and precarity.

SECRECY, SPACE, AND PRECARITY

The political thriller is constantly exploiting the connection between secrecy and space that I mentioned earlier. More precisely, to visually translate secrecy's movements through space, political thrillers feature what I call "a grammar of secrecy": a particular way of thinking about secrets, utilizing prepositions of space, such as "under" and "above," "inside" and "outside," "behind" and "in front of." If secrets are always stored somewhere, it is through these opposing pairs that the genre hides and, eventually, shows them. Political thrillers borrow these opposing pairs from the literary melodrama, as Peter Brooks reads it in his classic study.[89] Prepositions, in turn, point to a topography where secrets are distributed and concealed, waiting to be extracted, disclosed, or exposed: "under" and "above" point to depths and surfaces; "inside" and "outside" signal interiority and exteriority; and "behind" and "in front of" indicate invisibility and visibility. In turn, these prepositions imply movement and action, other important ingredients of the thriller.[90]

As mentioned earlier, political philosophers have explained secrecy in terms of movement and spatial transitions. Taussig, for example, defines "secrecy" as something that dwells between two "hypnotizing layers": depths and surfaces.[91] Through the grammar of secrecy, political thrillers foreground these two layers (sometimes literally, sometimes figuratively), typically placing secrecy "under" and "inside," waiting for a hero to bring it "above" and "outside."[92] The shifts between these layers are often conveyed through camera work in political thriller films, which offer a material representation of these transitions. Cameras can literally follow downward or upward trajectories, so film thrillers often feature a "multileveled labyrinthine world," with sites of depths working as a "primitive underworld of burrows, tunnels, alleys, and quarries," as Rubin notes, thinking about the thriller-umbrella.[93]

As for political thrillers in particular, these layers often symbolize the spatial placement of secrets that are related to power. We need only think of the central role that depths play in a canonical film that proved to be extremely influential not only in the United States but also in Latin America: *All the President's Men*. The prepositions "under" and "inside" are prominent in the film's underground parking lots: they play into Pakula's "fascination with that which is . . . buried deep by officialdom and bureaucracy," in Scott's words.[94] Deep Throat's secrets on Nixon's role in the Watergate scandal cannot be understood without space: the indoor, dark underground parking lot where he drip-feeds information to Bob Woodward and Carl Bernstein—the *Washington Post* journalists turned genre heroes. Pakula's treatment of space and secrecy is straightforward: the scenes between Woodward and the informer (whose alias already predisposes us to think of depths) are shot in the dark, with Deep Throat's face appearing only partially. Darkness, borrowed from classical film noir's "shadowy visual style,"[95] works as a topography of secrecy, where the disclosure of state secrets is a stable or "solid" transition with consequences. Bringing the state secret from darkness to light, ultimately, implies high stakes: Deep Throat's hidden information is transformative, as it changes the political fate of the United States. *All the President's Men* uses the grammar of secrecy to emphasize how the heroes unearth the truth, eventually causing the president's downfall. Political secrets, once buried deep down, are extracted from the depths to the surface, from invisibility to visibility, from interiority to exteriority.

Latin American political thrillers reproduce and sometimes subvert the grammar of secrecy's prepositions of space to offer something different. These subversions are less an act of resistance and more a resignification of the grammar of secrecy. For instance, they tend to showcase heroes and plotters set in plain sight, engaging in transactions that are literally and metaphorically superficial. Latin American political thrillers foreground secrets that are not solid, stable, or transformative. Building on Taussig's "public secrets" (which are "generally known, but cannot be articulated"),[96] I call them "precarious secrets," because they are informed by structural precarity. Characters in films such as *Matar a todos* (2007) and *Zanahoria* (2014), examined in chapter 4, trade in the appearance of knowledge that—instead of resulting in explosive underlying truths—all too often leads nowhere. Secrets in Latin American political thrillers are precarious because they are unstable and unsettling: they tend to leave us with no historical transformations at the end of the story. This results in a countertopography, in which both secrets and space are insubstantial, flimsy, and ephemeral: in short, precarious.

As this book reveals, precarity problematizes the use of prepositions, sometimes favoring "above," "outside," and "in front of" over "under," "inside," and "behind"; sometimes dissolving them altogether. Depths, surfaces, interiority, exteriority, darkness, and clarity all disintegrate in the presence of precarity. Whatever is supposed to be buried, enclosed, or shrouded in secrets in many Latin American political thrillers can be seen right in front of our noses. Precarity subverts one of the main genre conventions: the crystallization of high stakes into tangible transformations of the course of history that we see in *All the President's Men*.

As sociologist Maribel Casas-Cortés notes, "scholarly debates over precarity [have been] gaining unprecedented visibility across fields" in recent years. Most of these debates emphasize neoliberal precarity.[97] Throughout this book, however, I build on and go beyond the socioeconomic aspects of precarity to treat it in a polysemic way. After all, precarity predates neoliberalism by a great deal. In the following chapters, I instantiate the longevity of precarity through the Early Modern figure of the Hispanic *pícaro*. As such, I treat precarity itself as an elusive signifier, much like the slippery words "secrets" and "thriller." Precarity points to seemingly unrelated meanings: financial scarcity, to be sure, but also vulnerability, political instability, prosaicism, amateurism, parody, volatility, and linguistic unintelligibility, to name a few. All these connotations inform my readings.

CHRONICLING THE POLITICAL THRILLER IN LATIN AMERICA

In offering a panoramic overview of the political thriller in Latin America, this book follows a historical arc. It starts by tracing the genre's remote genealogy in Early Modern literature and concludes by sketching out very recent examples, with a deeper emphasis from the 1970s to 2010s. Within each chapter, however, the exploration of a series of major genre themes and their links to space, secrecy, and precarity at times supersedes the need for a strict chronological account.

Chapter 1, "Thrilling Gringos: Americans and Europeans Lost in Latin America," traces the genre's genealogy and its foundational ties with imperialism: specifically, the British adventure tale, the southern European *Crónicas de Indias*, and the Spanish picaresque. The chapter outlines the looming presence of Latin America in precursors of the genre written in English, such as Roy Rockwood's *Jack North's Treasure Hunt* (1904) and Guillermo Enrique Hudson's *The Purple Land* (1885), which both foreshadow the Latin American political thriller and destabilize the national boundaries of Anglo-American or Latin American literatures. In reading these texts, this chapter proposes two film clusters that construct Latin America as a site of thrilling adventure, constantly shifting into precarious secrecy, thwarted escape, and political threat. First, the 1940s "postwar thrillers": classical Hollywood productions set but not filmed in Argentina and Brazil, such as Edward Dmytryk's *Cornered* (1945), Charles Vidor's *Gilda* (1946), and Alfred Hitchcock's *Notorious* (1946). Second, the "Operation Condor thrillers": American and European films made in the 1970s–1990s that are set and filmed in the region, such as Costa-Gavras's *État de siège* (1972) and *Missing* (1982) as well as John Mackenzie's *The Honorary Consul* (1983) and Sérgio Toledo's *One Man's War* (1991). Chapter 1 suggests these two clusters should be read not only as a prehistory but as an important part of the genre's history in the region in and of itself. This brief chapter introduces overarching concepts that reappear in the history of the Latin American political thriller that I explore in much more detail in the following chapters of the book.

Chapter 2, "Botched Jobs: Coups and Magnicides as Precarious Conspiracies," explores Rafael Bernal's novel *El complot mongol* (1969). This is sometimes claimed to be Latin America's first hard-boiled novel, but chapter 2 examines Bernal's work within the tradition of the political thriller and concludes that it is also a foundational work of this genre. The chapter examines how Bernal reproduces and subverts genre conventions. Through a close reading of the novel, the chapter delves into Moreiras's notion of infrapolitics, which I engage with throughout the rest of the book but place particular emphasis on here. Chapter 2 examines this infrapolitical reading of the genre against the grain of more dominant hyperpolitical perspectives on literature and film. The chapter also examines how precarity appears linked to survival, parody, amateurism, and prosaicism in the novel, showing a continuity with the Spanish picaresque and some of the European and American political thrillers outlined in chapter 1.

Chapter 3, "Picturing the Slaughter: Massacres, Innocence, and the Political," analyzes a series of films that depict mass murders in the region, from Jorge Cedrón's *Operación masacre* (1973) in Argentina to Felipe Cazals's *Canoa* (1976) and Jorge Fons's *Rojo amanecer* (1989) in Mexico, concluding with a brief section on Francisco Lombardi's *La boca del lobo* (1988) in Peru. Chapter 3 analyzes the way all these films deal with political massacres through oppositions (interiority and exteriority, innocence and presumed guilt, apoliticism and politicization) that they ultimately expose as false dichotomies. This chapter also studies how these four films imagine massacres through sites of precarious secrecy.

Chapter 4, "Resisting and Investigating Genocide: Guerrilla Thrillers and Human Rights Thrillers," studies political thrillers from the Southern Cone and the Andes dealing with Operation Condor, linking them to Costa-Gavras's thrillers *État de siège* and *Missing* (set in Uruguay and Chile, respectively), introduced in chapter 1. Chapter 4 presents the history of two clusters, the "guerrilla thrillers" and the "human rights thrillers," with a common emphasis on the perspective of either the armed struggle or civilians before, during, and after the dictatorships that ravaged the region from the 1960s through 1980s. It then offers close readings of films made in Brazil (Toni Venturi's *Cabra-cega*, 2004) and Uruguay (Esteban Schroeder's *Matar a todos*, 2007, and Enrique Buchichio's *Zanahoria*, 2014).

Chapter 5, "Screening Oppression: Paramilitary, Accomplices, and Unemployed Thugs in Action," recounts the history of films that highlight the perspective of secret agents, accomplices, and thugs involved in Operation Condor, including the seamless continuation of their involvement after the transition to democracy. The chapter looks at films made in Argentina (Benjamín Naishtat's *Rojo*, 2018), Paraguay (Hugo Giménez's *Matar a un muerto*, 2019), and Chile (Andrés Wood's *Araña*, 2019). Chapter 5 pays special attention to how these films emphasize the "civic" side of the "civic-military dictatorship."

These last two chapters read films in which the transition to democracy is dramatized in triangles of characters, screens, and specters of the dictatorial past that in some cases haunt characters as they live through the left turn represented by the Pink Tide. These thrillers engage with forced disappearance, whose magnitude—and sometimes very existence—was never fully acknowledged by the perpetrators. These filmic representations of the desaparecidos and the unstable sites in which their bodies are located provide another instance of precarious secrecy.

The coda offers a series of concluding impressions on the topics discussed throughout the book, providing reflections on the future of the genre in the region.

Perhaps the different sites of secrecy that I examine in this book are all metonymies of Latin America itself. This is why there is no better way to start our journey through the genre's history in the region than by examining European and American political thrillers set south of the Río Bravo.

CHAPTER ONE

Thrilling Gringos

AMERICANS AND EUROPEANS LOST IN LATIN AMERICA

Captain Delgado: This is not America?

CHARLES VIDOR, *GILDA* (1946)[1]

THE SECRET LIAISONS BETWEEN LATIN AMERICA and the thriller go back a long way. Although thrillers have often been considered a relatively recent or rare phenomenon in the region,[2] the word "thriller" appears linked to Latin America as far back as 1906.[3] It does so almost timidly, within a footnote, on the inside flap of a Horatio Alger Jr. book. The footnote, a blurb, labels a forgotten American adventure novel called *Jack North's Treasure Hunt: Or Daring Adventures in South America* as a thriller. The novel, to be published the following year, was set in Chile and Peru. If we consider that the first recorded usages of the word hark back to the 1880s (used then as a synonym of "sensational story"),[4] the 1906 link between thrillers and the region is actually quite premature.

Authored by Roy Rockwood (one of Edward Stratemeyer's pen names), *Jack North's Treasure Hunt* is derivative of earlier British adventure tales, especially those set in Latin America and the Caribbean, like Robert Louis Stevenson's *Treasure Island* (1883).[5] Jack North is a young swindler from New England, a *pícaro* who is "too fertile in his resources to despair."[6] Like many others before and after him, North goes south, as he is sent to Chile on a business trip.

What distinguishes this novel from most of Stratemeyer's later work (and from Stevenson's) is space: *Jack North's Treasure Hunt* shifts the portrayal of Anglo-American imperialism from the Caribbean to the Andes.[7]

Nevertheless, the underlying political matrix for this and other adventure tales published by the Stratemeyer Syndicate (such as the series *Bomba, the Jungle Boy*) is similar: echoing, in fiction, Theodore Roosevelt's expansionist policies in Latin America.[8]

As soon as Jack arrives, the peripeteia typical of the adventure tale ensues, with its quest for survival and financial reward at the end of the story. First, a nemesis tries to drown Jack in the South Pacific Ocean. He is then cast away on a Robinson Crusoe island near the Chilean coast, explicitly citing the British adventure tale tradition and its ties with Latin America. Upon reaching the mainland, Jack discovers that the War of the Pacific (1879–1884) is erupting, involving Chile, Peru, and Bolivia. In his comings and goings, he learns about an Inca treasure island hidden in the Peruvian highlands. As in other adventure tales, the hero finds, extracts, and brings home the secret treasure, to bank it or invest it.[9]

Why were the adventure tale and the thriller so easily conflated in 1906? What did they have in common? For Martin Rubin, although the adventure tale precedes the thriller, they are overlapping sister forms. But they also feature prominent differences, especially in terms of space: thrillers are typically set in cities. Most commonly, they are situated in what Rubin calls the "trinity of American thrillers": San Francisco, LA, and New York.[10] Beyond the United States, thrillers often unfold in other urban trinities, such as their European (London, Berlin, and Paris) and Latin American (Acapulco, Buenos Aires, and Rio de Janeiro) counterparts.

In privileging urban spaces, thrillers juxtapose cities with the specter of "older . . . wilder, more marvelous . . . adventurous realms" that are often distant from them. As such, thrillers often retain and contain "earlier storytelling traditions," as Rubin notes, such as "the adventure tale" itself.[11] By contrast, the adventure tale is frequently set in exotic preindustrial spaces, which are perceived to be "primitive, and clearly removed from . . . the mundane . . . urban existence: the Amazon jungle, the Arabian desert,"[12] or islands in the Peruvian highlands. In short, whereas the adventure tale propels the hero and the reader outward to these exotic spaces, the thriller disrupts the reader's inner world within the confines of urban space.

Jack North's Treasure Hunt, then, would fall more closely in the adventure tale genre, in which heroes go to colonial territories more as "a proving ground" than as "a final destination," in Karen Sands-O'Connor's words.[13] The 1906 blurb selling the novel as a thriller could be understood in the context of the thriller's emergence in the early 1900s. At that time, thrillers were still in their infancy, far from becoming the more recognizable cultural form they would evolve into throughout the twentieth century.[14]

FROM THE ADVENTURE TALE TO THE POLITICAL THRILLER

What, however, are the links between the adventure tale and the political thriller in particular? It is evident that the adventure tale naturally leads to the heist thriller, as financial reward is central to both. But the ties with the political thriller seem less obvious. One ingredient they all share is the prominence of the Hispanic figure of the swindler or *pícaro,* the hero of one of the most important forerunners of the British adventure tale and a fundamental archetype for political thrillers: the picaresque novel.[15]

Ultimately, this is what *Jack North's Treasure Hunt* is about, the Bildungsroman of a sly young male character who grows up, much as any *pícaro* would, "through travel and adventure, wandering and getting lost," as Franco Moretti puts it.[16] What is distinctive about North's travel is that the *pícaro*'s growth is inseparable from learning how to navigate the political situation in Chile and Peru. In Early Modern Spain's picaresque novels, such as *Lazarillo de Tormes* and the like, the *pícaro*'s growth was linked to surviving in an extremely precarious environment. As I discuss throughout this book, precarity also plays a central role in the political thriller, especially in Latin America. In the picaresque novel the *pícaro*'s survival is about devising strategies to avoid hunger.[17] The hero in the political thriller is often a journalist, the relative of a victim of a political crime, a lawyer, or even a politician, disguised as a spy or a detective. Their survival, instead, is about acquiring the skill to read the intricacies of local politics, much as understanding the War of the Pacific is for Jack North.

Another prominent ingredient that adventure tales and political thrillers share is extraction. The hidden treasure in *Jack North's Treasure Hunt* is not so much gold (à la Stevenson) but other, less glamorous metals and minerals. Parallel to the quest for the hidden treasure is a second, more transparent, prosaic case of extraction: Jack becomes wealthy before finding gold, as a result of buying nitrate (one of the causes of the war) to sell in the United States.

Some political thrillers would later structure their narratives precisely around these elements: a path that involves gaining political awareness that is often connected to extracting secrets. In other words, political thrillers are rooted in adventurous aspects of politics: conspiracies, revealing classified information, breaching national intelligence, bringing hidden truths to the surface as if they were treasures, and so forth. Political thrillers translate gold or nitrate into another commodity that is less tangible but equally valuable and vital for many storylines: political power.

The ambivalence between these genres, then, could be a productive point of departure to trace the history of the political thriller in Latin America, where the demarcation—between what is mundane and what is adventurous, what is a mineral or metal and what is power, what is an adventure tale and what is a political thriller—often becomes blurry. In this chapter I outline a few European and American novels and films set in Latin America that, consciously or not, owe a debt to the imaginary played out in adventure tales like *Jack North's Treasure Hunt*.

These political thrillers are partially or entirely set outside of the urban centers in which they were written or filmed. Perhaps because of this discrepancy, they can easily disjoint and swap the mundane and adventurous realms that are perhaps more clearly demarcated in American and European political thrillers set in the United States or in Europe. For Rubin, the thriller hero features "a remarkable degree of passivity . . . a strong sense of being carried away."[18] By contrast, the foreign hero in thrillers set in Latin America (a European or American gringa or gringo) is lost on a confusing, thrilling subcontinent. These heroes are outsiders who personify their mundane, more developed city of origin. At the same time, they subvert what Rubin sees in the more "domestic" thriller hero, because they often become confident adventurers in a hostile environment.

The agent that disrupts the hero in these stories is the spatial incarnation of adventure: the Latin American territory. What is thrilling in *Jack North's Treasure Hunt* is Chile and Peru, not just because of the financial rewards that await the hero there but because of the physical obstacles to obtaining them. These obstacles are inseparable from the space, setting, and landscape of the stories. I am thinking in particular about both countries' natural and political landscapes. By "natural landscape" I mean the fascinating yet intimidating local fauna—including the jaguars, pumas, ocelots, and snakes that crowd the novel. The dangerous fauna mirrors the setting, to which I return later. By "political landscape" I mean the war, the thrilling dangers associated with the strife over nitrate fields and territorial borders. This is stressed in the novel through Jack's conflict with the "bush-raiders . . . bands of guérillas united to make war upon anybody and anything that crosses their path . . . [who] pretend to favor Chili" but who are actually just serving their own interest.[19] Linked to this scenario, where nothing is what it seems, deception becomes another key ingredient.

Both the picaresque novel and the adventure tale are rooted in imperialism.[20] So is the political thriller. In the 1970s Carlos Monsiváis explained what he considered to be scarce production of the thriller in Latin America by pointing to the very imperialistic dimension that the genre inherited from the adventure tale as well as emphasizing the region's dominated position in the history of imperialism. For Monsiváis, the thriller "implies development, industry, market ambition." Ultimately, it is "a literary imperialistic inquiry. . . . Or who would care to steal Ecuador's atomic secrets or to kidnap a Honduran scientist?"[21] Here Monsiváis is significantly overlooking the many American and European political thrillers set in the region, well before the 1970s. His claim, however, is partially true. After all, Latin America's presence in those early political thrillers was only possible as long as American or European geopolitical interests were at stake. Latin America, then "the turbulent periphery" (in the words of Roberto Russell and Fabián Calle),[22] is often ancillary to Washington's actual geopolitical interests, which Hollywood conveys through various archetypal villains: from Nazi Germany to the Soviet Union.

Political scientists Andrés Malamud and Luis Schenoni note that Latin America's "internal instability over the twentieth century" was one of the reasons why the region was then relevant for the United States, in stark contrast to our current century, in which it is gradually becoming more irrelevant.[23] In some cases, this relevance was due to the region's threatening proximity. Prominent twentieth-century events such as the handling of the Panama Canal or the Cuban Revolution and the Cuban Missile Crisis are central to American political thrillers such as Paul Guilfoyle's *Captain Scarface* (1953) and Alfred Hitchcock's *Topaz* (1969), respectively.[24]

But American and European political thrillers would also flourish in more distant Latin American countries (the Southern Cone). These films show how the region's relevance for Global North interests would often "bypass" these countries' remoteness. More than immediate risks escalating in the backyard of the United States, what is at stake here is anxiety about a hemispheric alignment in foreign policy. This anxiety can be clearly seen in what we could describe as two clusters: the 1940s "postwar thrillers" and the 1970s–1990s "Operation Condor thrillers." The first cluster features Argentina and Brazil as a Nazi haven: Edward Dmytryk's *Cornered* (1945), Charles Vidor's *Gilda* (1946), and Alfred Hitchcock's *Notorious* (1946). The second cluster imagines the Southern Cone as a site prone to Communist infiltration: Costa-Gavras's *État de siège* (1972) set in Uruguay and *Missing* (1982) set in Chile, John Mackenzie's *The Honorary Consul* (1983) set in the border between Argentina and Paraguay, and Sérgio Toledo's *One Man's War* (1991) set in Paraguay.

Whereas for Rubin the thriller's "primary conventional site of the exotic was Asia, in the stereotypical form of the Mysterious East,"[25] these two clusters suggest that the underlying spectral presence of Latin America is prominent in American and European thrillers.[26] As such, both clusters should be understood less as a prehistory of the Latin American political thriller and more as an important part of the genre's history in the region in its own right. This is especially true because they include films that are sometimes hard to distinguish from later local productions that either reproduce or subvert them. I return to these clusters (especially Costa-Gavras) in chapter 4.

Is it just a negligible anecdote, then, that *Jack North's Treasure Hunt* connects the thriller with Latin America so much earlier—even when it does so from an imperialistic perspective? Perhaps it is worth rereading imperialism against the grain, to better assess the role the region plays in the construction of the political thriller, even before Latin American authors and filmmakers themselves engaged with it. After all, when discussing cultural production that is marked by imperialism, it always takes two to tango: if Monsiváis's claim is only partially true, it is because he downplays the region's role in the configuration of the genre's imaginary.

At this point, Jack North's southbound journey could help us problematize Monsiváis's claim: in many ways, Latin America was not as "peripheral" as it seems—although it was certainly "turbulent." It could be argued that the region was as relevant for the genre (at least for its genealogy and emergence) as, say, the assassination and legacy of John F. Kennedy and the Watergate scandal.[27] To begin with, the region's centrality for the genre can be measured not only in the high number of productions but also in the prestige associated with some of the filmmakers, such as Hitchcock and Costa-Gavras or Fritz Lang and John Huston, among others.[28]

Latin America's looming presence in the adventure tale predates the twentieth century itself: we need only think of earlier examples such as Aphra Behn's *Oroonoko* (1688) and Daniel Defoe's *Robinson Crusoe* (1719). When Behn imagined African Prince Oroonoko arriving at Surinam only to become a slave, or when Defoe himself pictured the English sailor Crusoe cast away on a Caribbean Island, little did they know that they were setting the stage for later generations to imagine the region as an exotic, thrilling site, riddled with dangerous/exciting political/natural landscapes. And yet it is this unintended construction that made Rockwood's lesser-known novel be identified, centuries later, with the emerging cultural form of the thriller.[29]

Tracing the links between Latin America and the thriller, however, would require us to look much further back. It would not be far-fetched to argue that the equation between the region and thrilling adventure precedes the British adventure tale. I am thinking of the *Crónica de Indias*: the diaries, histories, and letters that accounted for the region's colonization, often following the style of the Spanish picaresque novel. Penned by southern European conquistadores and historians, from Christopher Columbus's letters in the 1490s until the seventeenth century, the *Crónicas* would often transplant mythological figures from ancient European literature (the cyclops, sirens, Amazons, and dragons) to blend them with Indigenous myths and ultimately construct the Latin American landscape that would oscillate between an appealing Edenic *locus amoenus* and a hostile, hellish *locus eremus*.[30] The transformation from one landscape to the other would recurrently feature in both adventure tales and political thrillers set in the region.

Gabriel García Márquez, for instance, reads works such as Antonio Pigafetta's *Relazione del primo viaggio intorno al mondo* (1524–1525) or Álvar Núñez Cabeza de Vaca's *Naufragios y comentarios* (1542) as a "rigorous chronicle which, nonetheless, seems like . . . fanciful adventure." For García Márquez, devoted to identifying the genealogies of magical realism, these chronicles work as "the seeds of our contemporary novels."[31] Whereas magical realism is all about an exotic world in which marvelous and mundane realities coexist without conflict, the opposite occurs in thrillers. But his claim works just the same for both. After all, these chronicles imagined Latin America not always as including supernatural creatures but almost invariably as presenting the ingredients that most political thrillers require: secrecy and revelation, risk and threats, escape and chases, glory and perdition.

The accounts of real expeditions led by colonizers who portrayed themselves or were frequently depicted as *pícaros*, seeking El Dorado (gold is one of the main nodes between the *Crónicas* and the adventure tale) or the Elixir of Life, are examples of this.[32] Latin America, from then onward, would become an alluring land, brimming with the promise of peripeteia and danger, financial reward and ruin, power and deception, freedom and oppression. The condensation of these opposing valences would later become a breeding ground for the political thriller.

Martin Green describes British adventure tales as "geographical romances": stories in which "the element of the dangerous derives from the events being so remote in *space*."[33] The same could be said about several of these *Crónicas de Indias*, even though they were not necessarily produced or read as fiction at the time.[34] Concealed risks and unexpected threats (slavery, shipwrecks, earthquakes, quicksand, rumors about human sacrifice and cannibalism, deadly fauna and flora) become plausible because of remoteness, laying the foundations for a series of ingredients that are central to the history of the political thriller in Latin America: secrecy, space, and precarity, as explored throughout this book.

Of course, the remoteness and exoticism mentioned by Green take us again to imperialism, as the audiences for these stories for the most part were located physically and culturally far from Latin America. So our question remains unanswered: can the secret liaisons between Latin America and the political thriller be understood solely as a passive by-product of imperialism? Perhaps we can address this by briefly examining an author born and raised in

Argentina, who imports and partakes in the British adventure tale set in the region, blending it with the preoccupations of the Spanish picaresque and the *Crónicas de Indias*: Guillermo Enrique Hudson.[35]

THE PURPLE LAND AND THE TRANSNATIONAL POLITICAL THRILLER

A rare author, halfway between Anglo and Latin America, Hudson was raised by two New England *estancieros* who moved to the outskirts of Buenos Aires in the 1830s.[36] Hudson himself settled in London in 1874, where he would write all of his work.[37] His first novel, *The Purple Land That England Lost*, problematizes the Latin American remoteness within the adventure tale, to the extent that some critics nowadays believe that it "stand[s] resistant to imperialism's integrative, exploitative force."[38] The novel tells the story of British traveler Richard Lamb and his teenaged Argentine wife, taking refuge in Uruguay because of their illicit relationship, amid political turmoil and scheming caudillos.

Here Latin America still appears as a thrilling site through the lens of a European character but now contaminated by what Jorge Luis Borges calls a process of *acriollamiento*.[39] Lamb, more or less willingly, becomes a Latin American, a criollo, a metamorphosis later portrayed in many American and European political thrillers. We need only think of Costa-Gavras's *Missing* (1982) and its main character: Ed Horman, a conservative New Yorker who travels to Chile looking for his son Charlie, a desaparecido under Augusto Pinochet's dictatorship. Horman slowly experiences a political *acriollamiento*, a narrative arc eerily reminiscent of Lamb's. They undergo a similar transformation, acquiring what I called earlier the skill to read the intricacies of local politics that the picaresque novel bequeaths to political thrillers via the adventure tale.

Published in London in 1885, *The Purple Land* was poorly received. It was only in 1904 (two years before *Jack North's Treasure Hunt* was labeled a thriller) that the novel was republished and gained more appreciation. Interestingly, this was thanks to another half-Anglo, half-foreign author, who also set one of his adventure novels in Latin America: Joseph Conrad, author of *Nostromo*. *The Purple Land* was republished in 1916 in New York, with a prologue by Theodore Roosevelt, who equated it with Herman Melville's adventure tales.[40] More importantly, the novel was not translated into Spanish until 1928.[41] In other words, it circulated as British literature (like Behn, Defoe, and Stevenson) to such a degree that by 1905 several British critics regarded Hudson as a member of a new generation of "emigrant novelists . . . seeking 'exotic romance,'" along with others such as Joseph Conrad and Rudyard Kipling, who were all returning to Behn and Defoe's treatment of the adventure tale.[42]

None of this impeded Borges (a half-Anglo, half-Latin author if there ever was one) to consider *The Purple Land* "essentially [*criolla*], native to South America."[43] But Borges's reappropriation of Hudson "is paradoxical only if we assume a literary model in which nationality, ethnicity, and language of writing and subject matter are always perfectly synchronized," as Richard Maxwell and Katie Trumpener point out.[44] Perhaps this is one of the foundational contributions that *The Purple Land* makes to the political thriller: its transnational dimension. As Miriam Haddu notes, the genre would later become a "transnational cinematic practice" in films aimed at audiences beyond a single nation through co-productions.[45] From literature (Hudson, Conrad, John Buchan) to film (Lang, Hitchcock, Preminger, Costa-Gavras), the genre's authors and filmmakers—many of whom were multilingual—all produced their works across countries and sometimes continents, combining a myriad of nationalities, settings, and languages in their stories. In short, Hudson foreshadows the way the political thriller eventually becomes a Babelesque genre.

The Operation Condor thrillers cluster includes clear instantiations of the genre's Babelesque dimension. For instance, Jack Lemmon portrays Ed Horman in *Missing*: an American father babbling in Spanish at the Estudios Churubusco, in a Mexico City that substitutes for Pinochet's Chile. Italian-born French actor Yves Montand plays Dan Mitrione in *État de siège*, an American official kidnapped by Uruguayan Tupamaros, while everyone speaks French on a Chilean set meant to represent Montevideo on the verge of its military dictatorship. Richard Gere plays Eduardo Plarr in *The Honorary Consul*, a Paraguayan doctor tormented by his father's forced disappearance. He reluctantly collaborates with guerrillas and becomes romantically involved with a woman who speaks Guarani—a love story set in Corrientes, Argentina, but actually filmed in Veracruz, Mexico. Welsh actor Anthony Hopkins plays Joel Filártiga in *One Man's War*, another Paraguayan doctor who hopelessly seeks justice for his murdered son during the most violent years of Alfredo Stroessner's dictatorship.

The transnational dimension, typical of thrillers, is rooted in precarity in Latin America: these constant spatial dislocations and linguistic dissonances speak to the vulnerable conditions of production, marked by military censorship as well as logistical, political, and financial constraints. In this context, the political thriller emerges in the region as a transnational practice that slowly becomes more and more appropriated, always informed by structural precarity.

Latin American literary and film productions would certainly mimic this plurilingual universe throughout the following decades by embedding several languages in addition to the region's most spoken ones, Spanish and Portuguese: for example, Chinese-accented Spanish in Mexico's Chinatown in films like *Distinto amanecer* (1943) and novels like *El complot mongol* (explored in chapter 2). English is commonly heard in characters who embody American interests in the region: in Raymundo Gleyzer's *Los traidores* (1973), Roberto Farias's *Pra frente, Brasil* (1982), Juan Carlos Desanzo's *En retirada* (1984), Bruno Barreto's *O que é isso, companheiro?* (1997), and Benjamín Naishtat's *Rojo* (2018), to name only films that I analyze in chapters 3, 4, and 5. French is spoken in Marco Bechis's *Garage Olimpo* (1999), in which a Francophone mother seeks help for her disappeared daughter. The frictional relation between Spanish and Indigenous languages such as Guarani is central in Hugo Giménez's *Matar a un muerto* (2019), examined in detail in chapter 5. There are many more examples. All this starts with *The Purple Land*, a story set in the Uruguayan Pampas through the lens of an *acriollado* Englishman born in Buenos Aires.

AFFECT AND THE POLITICAL THRILLER

If Maxwell and Trumpener are right in seeing Lamb as "an innocent . . . clueless, wanderer,"[46] in this sense, too, he predicts the typical vulnerability of the thriller hero, who experiences "a certain loss of control" that could easily be transmitted to the spectator.[47] Obviously, his surname reminds us of an animal traditionally linked to innocence: in particular, Lamb's drifting naiveté is inseparable from his obliviousness to local politics. Through Lamb's gradual loss of innocence, Hudson binds the adventurous realm of the thriller *avant la lettre* with a landscape that is no longer merely adventurous and exotic but prosaic and scarred by the particulars of Latin American political history.

Even for critics such as Ezequiel Martínez Estrada, who regrets that Hudson's novels address his political ideas only tangentially, *The Purple Land* is still "inspired by the passions of political struggle."[48] This is evident in the novel: Hudson's actual political stances are beside the point. It is now irrelevant whether Hudson supported Juan Manuel de Rosas in Argentina or sided with the Blancos or Colorados, the political parties portrayed in the novel as ravaging Uruguay throughout the nineteenth century. What remains important, however, is that Hudson's novel takes us through the typical journey of the political thriller: from apathetic indifference to awareness, from ignorance to ethical involvement, through what Moreiras calls "infrapolitical action," explored in more detail in chapter 2.[49]

The Purple Land pictures Lamb sipping mate with Uruguayan caudillos, gauchos, and *chinas* (the gauchos' female companions), repeatedly describing Montevideo as a "modern Troy," a "city of battle, murder and sudden death." His journey through rural Uruguay, from *estancia* to *estancia,* unfolds amid the civil war between Blancos and Colorados. Lamb becomes less of a lamb as he gradually gets closely acquainted with the intricacies of local politics. He says at the end of the novel that he will write his story and title it *The Purple Land,* "for what more suitable name can one find for a country so stained with the blood of her children?"[50] The political, here and in the political thriller, is not so much about ideas as it is about affect, the "passions" sensed by Martínez Estrada, punctuated by the encounters, in this case, between Lamb and local people and (more importantly) with the local fauna, much as in *Jack North's Treasure Hunt.*

The Purple Land portrays Uruguay through the centuries-long twofold landscape that emerged in the *Crónica de Indias*. Martínez Estrada eloquently sums up this landscape as a "[b]ucolic panorama filled with lightning."[51] Hudson himself notes in the appendix to the novel that "the heroic period in South American history . . . passed away. El Dorado, the Spaniard's New Jerusalem, has changed into a bank of malarious mist and a cloud of mosquitoes."[52] This ambivalent landscape, however, is not only tangible in the political strife between Blancos and Colorados but also in Lamb's affective encounters with the Uruguayan animals, the "malarious mist."[53] For instance, Lamb is at once mesmerized by the scintillating *luciérnagas* (fireflies) and terrified by the *vinchucas* (the blood-sucking kissing bugs that carry the Chagas disease). The two insects personify the opposing sides of the Latin American landscape: appealing and dangerous, Edenic and hellish.

By all means, it would be far-fetched and somewhat anachronistic to describe Hudson's adventure novel as a political thriller, a genre that only emerged more than half a century later with the Cold War, in the 1950s. Nevertheless, whereas *Martín Fierro* prophesized the birth of the tango for Borges,[54] perhaps *The Purple Land* could be read as a prophecy of the political thriller.

The most paradigmatic scene in the novel foreshadowing what political thrillers will exploit later is precisely the encounter between Lamb and a *vinchuca,* which pierces him, literally thrilling him. In the scene, Lamb is daydreaming about becoming a poet who would "astonish old *blasé* Europe," as he pictures himself writing about "remote semi-barbarous South American estancias."[55] Of course, the scene participates in a key dichotomy in nineteenth-century Argentine literature: civilization against barbarism. But it is also central to the genre studied here, as it juxtaposes the political with the thrilling affective sensation provided by the *vinchuca*. The sting, like any thrill, is "a bodily event" that "destabilizes individuals," as defined by Allan Hepburn.[56] In Hudson, as in *Jack North's Treasure Hunt*, the thrill is caused by the natural and political landscape, the fauna, and the civil war. Latin American political thrillers will later reimagine these thrills as invasions of the body, typically perpetrated by the militarized state, through scenes that put on center stage massacres, torture, forceful entries, and the legacy of forced disappearance.

As Rubin reminds us, the etymology of the Middle English word *thrill* means "to pierce": "a thrill is a sharp sensation, as if one had been pierced or pricked by a sharp instrument" . . . or a *vinchuca*,[57] the metonymy of a deceptive landscape that seems inviting at first but ends up invading you, thrilling you, stabbing you in the back before you notice it.

FROM SECRECY AND SPACE TO PRECARITY AND THE PICARESQUE

Whereas Rubin identifies the Amazon jungle as one of the adventure tale's preferred sites, Hudson paves the way for a different spatial lineage that privileges other natural landscapes in Latin America. The Uruguayan Pampas inaugurate an image of Latin American openness, an archetypal setting for the genre's history: the woods, the outdoors, and its different versions scattered throughout the region, beyond the Amazon. I refer to the multiple metamorphoses of this space with a Spanish word that defies translation: *la intemperie*, a vast labyrinthine site of secrecy and hideout, marked by precarity and defenselessness.

In *Jack North's Treasure Hunt* this site of secrecy is the Peruvian Andes, which the *pícaro* describes as an "intricate labyrinth."[58] It is not a coincidence that labyrinths work as "a key descriptive figure" of thrillers for Rubin.[59] Equally, it is not a coincidence that the word "intrigue" (one of the key ingredients of political thrillers) is etymologically linked to labyrinths.[60] In most European and American thrillers set in the United States and Europe, the labyrinth is primarily the modern city, with its claustrophobic multitudes, confusing alleys, elevated bridges, and sewer tunnels.[61] Throughout the past century, Latin American openness has featured multiple iterations that respond to the Global North's more conventional understanding of labyrinths: the Uruguayan and Argentine Pampas, the Paraguayan woods, the Atacama Desert, the Peruvian highlands, the Tlatelolco Square, a garbage dump in José León Suárez at the outskirts of Buenos Aires. They all work as paradoxical sites of precarious secrecy, emerging from the adventure tale to the political thriller, a genre filled with such oppositions. The paradox, of course, is that these instantiations of *la intemperie*—devoid of crowds, walls, depths, or layers—create a false sense of transparency, of visibility, in contrast to what we typically associate with a labyrinth. I go back to the role that precarity plays in the construction of these sites throughout this book.

In short, the Uruguayan Pampas are only the first of a series of sites that turn Latin America into a "floating signifier" in the genre, a term with highly shifting meanings.[62] *The Purple Land* announces this fluctuation by already portraying most of the roles that Latin America would later play in American and European political thrillers. As Lamb escapes from Buenos Aires to Montevideo after committing a crime (in his case, statutory rape), the region, encapsulated in the Uruguayan Pampas, sways from a site of adventure to a site of escape, from a refuge to a hideout, from a site of liberation to a site of political threat. All of these work as physical incarnations of the inseparable ties between secrecy and space, typical of thrillers. Some of these meanings are frequently contradictory, as the region promises something that it never quite delivers.

In this context, American and European political thrillers set in Latin America work as pretend hide-and-seeks, where gringas and gringos are thrilled as they try to escape to/from or hide in the region but eventually are caught by their pursuers and rarely achieve what they seek. The oxymoron is the paradigmatic trope of thrillers set in Latin America, a space rife with unsheltered refuges, conspicuous hideouts, confining escapes, and claustrophobic outdoors. This will later be translated in Latin American political thrillers by underlining the promise of high stakes that rarely materialize due to deception and precarity, two aspects that are strongly linked, once more, to the Hispanic tradition of the picaresque novel.

Deception and precarity are deeply embedded in the figure of the *pícaro*. This is evident even in Hitchcock's spy thriller *Secret Agent* (1936), a British film set entirely in Europe, which is one of the first thrillers to introduce a Latin American(ish) character: the "hairless Mexican general" Pompilio Montezuma de la Villa del Conde del Ombú. His long, pompous name is reminiscent of the *Crónica de Indias* and the adventure tale: it explicitly references Moctezuma, the Aztec emperor, while implicitly mocking the elaborate naming conventions of Spanish nobility (for example, the *cronista* Álvar Núñez Cabeza de Vaca). As the film itself quickly reveals, however, Pompilio is not bald or Mexican or a general but a hit man and a secret agent. This kind of deception would constantly inform the way Latin American political thrillers subvert the genre's horizon of expectations, with conspiracies, spies, detectives, and informants that are not conspiracies, spies, detectives, or informants at all. This sense of oxymoronic deception is already present in the sites of precarious secrecy described as *la intemperie*, with labyrinths that do not look like labyrinths in any way.

Pompilio is played by Lászlό Löwenstein, also known as Peter Lorre, a Jewish actor born in what was then the Austro-Hungarian Empire. Browner than his white Anglo counterparts, Löwenstein was often typecast as a sinister foreign thriller villain at the time, most famously as Lang's infanticidal serial killer *M* (1931). Löwenstein again plays the murderer of the story in *Secret Agent*, but Pompilio is also a Don Juan, a buffoon, an affected womanizer with a moustache, who wears an earring. In strongly Spanish-accented English, Pompilio frequently utters words in Spanish but also in French: he indistinguishably goes from *merde* to *caramba*, yet another instance of the Babelesque nature of the thriller. As he introduces himself, Pompilio always repeats his whole name, giving a comedic effect. He is literally described as a "swindler" in the film. Here Hitchcock lays another stepping stone in establishing the significant connection between the *pícaro* (known primarily for deceiving others) and the Latin American political thriller. As I explore in the following chapters, we can see *pícaros* from Mexico to Uruguay, from Bernal's *El complot mongol* to Buchichio's film *Zanahoria*.

In this context, the relevance of an Early Modern figure such as the *pícaro* for the contemporary political thriller and its links to precarity is evident. To begin with, the *pícaro* serves as an ideal example, illustrating that precarity is a constitutive phenomenon of modernity, far older than neoliberalism—contrary to the claims of several critics. In analyzing the political thriller, these critics often become entangled in using films to confirm their own political ideas. By contrast, as Jens Elze reminds us, the picaresque is a genre rooted in early capitalism, displaying a "predisposition to precarity," a "generic marker" notable for its "thematic, formal, and ethical continuity" throughout the genre's history, from Early Modern Spain until our days.[63]

Mikhail Bakhtin traces the origins of the picaresque to an even earlier historical period: ancient Greco-Roman times. In his reading of Apuleius's classical novel *The Golden Ass* (late second century AD), Bakhtin highlights the *pícaro*'s unique position as an outsider, a characteristic that remains central in the Spanish picaresque novel, the adventure tale, and the political thriller. Essentially, we should understand the *pícaro* as a spy, someone who is devoted to interpreting the way of the world. Swindlers engage in "eavesdropping on private life" without participating in it: they do not "occupy in it any defined fixed place, yet at the same time pass through that life and are forced to study its workings, all its secret cogs and wheels."[64] Much like the private life that spies observe, the world is literally foreign to the *pícaro*. The *pícaro* adopts a fluid role in the political thriller, personifying either the criminal like Pompilio—who wields power (or works under its command) and eventually goes rogue by perpetrating a political crime—or the hero. I examine the fluid nature of the *pícaro* in the Latin American political thriller in chapter 4, but I must first clarify some aspects of what I understand as "precarity," a concept that informs my reading throughout this book.

It goes without saying that "precarity" is not the same as "poverty." Precarity is about being impoverished in the face of an unequal environment rather than being structurally poor. In fact, precarity implies wealth: the abundance that is both trickled down to and vehemently pursued by the *pícaro*. Elze hits the mark in his reading of what he calls "the precarious picaresque" as a product of "imperial wealth."[65] *Lazarillo de Tormes* ultimately was written not only during a time of economic hardship for the Spanish population but also in a historical period marked by the onset of the Spanish Empire's rule in what is now Latin America and the financial gain it brought with it.

Elze notes how *Lazarillo* allows us to understand the distinction between precarity and poverty: the novel "not only points to the poverty that requires [Lazarillo] to steal . . . but also displays the utmost precariousness that *pícaros* experience when it comes to securing objects, property and identity."[66] In other words, poverty is only the trigger for the swindler's actions: this is why Claudia Delgado identifies hunger (a visceral reaction to poverty) as "the main driving force of the story."[67] Instead, precarity is the world in which the *pícaro* lives, where "all potential principles of property and security are undermined by the fact that objects may *always* be taken back or be withheld . . . always likely to collapse."[68] The political thriller transposes the *pícaro*'s precarious world by shifting the all-pervasive lack of solidity and the imminence of downfall to a political realm, emphasizing the ways in which it affects secrecy. For instance, the precarious control of the state is constantly besieged by the possibility of secret conspiracies: coups, magnicides, massacres, and genocide. I examine all these instances in the following chapters. Beyond space, I now turn to the genre's relationship with time.

THE POLITICAL THRILLER AND THE PAST

William Faulkner writes in *Requiem for a Nun* that in the southern United States "the past is never dead. It's not even past." He is mainly thinking of the region's tangible traces of slavery, almost a century after it was formally abolished.[69] Jon Beasley-Murray expands on Faulkner's idea to discuss Latin America's own history of slavery, which includes some of the last countries to abolish it: Cuba in 1886 and Brazil in 1888. Beasley-Murray brings in the example of anthropologist Miguel Barnet's 1966 *Biography of a Runaway Slave,* based on interviews with Esteban Montejo, a former slave who died in Havana in 1973. The short temporal distance between that year and our present is what leads Beasley-Murray to conclude that "slavery's legacies are still with us . . . sometimes the past is not even fully past."[70]

If we think about this sentence in Spanish, we can make visible its twofold, powerful meaning: *el pasado no ha pasado,* the past has not finished occurring yet. But also *el pasado no es (el) pasado,* the past is not what it is supposed to be. There is a gap here between the participle and the noun "past" as well as the verb "to pass": moving on a path to approach and continue beyond something. In short, the past is not past because we are still enduring it, because it is very much a part of what we call the present, and the threshold that divides the two is only a fragile mirage.

The idea that the past is not past is perhaps one of the most prominent, recurring, and transnational elements in the history of political thrillers in Latin America, up to our days. It centrally features in *Cornered, Gilda,* and *Notorious,* the postwar thrillers made in the mid-1940s. In fact, it is their basic premise: in all three films the past is not past. Even though World War II is over and Nazi Germany has surrendered, the war is very much not over in Latin America, as Nazis continue to secretly operate in Buenos Aires and Rio de Janeiro, where the films are set.

The obsessive trope of a past that cannot be overcome is resignified in the cluster of Operation Condor thrillers, especially *Missing, The Honorary Consul,* and *One Man's War,* where characters are tormented by mourning and grief over the desaparecidos. The Southern Cone political thrillers (both the "human rights thrillers" cluster examined in chapter 4 and the films analyzed in chapter 5) are all strongly influenced by the unsurmountable past that appears first in the Operation Condor thriller cluster. The Latin American renditions update—or rather make their own—the idea that the past is not past, due to the generalized impunity surrounding the perpetrators of forced disappearance.

In this context, Costa-Gavras's *État de siège* is a more peripheral example within the Operation Condor thrillers cluster. It shifts away from the victim's family and centers on the guerrillas, granting them "a very sympathetic treatment," as Derry notes.[71] Bequeathing a similar treatment to several Latin American productions, *État de siège* spawns in isolation the "guerrilla thrillers" cluster that I also discuss in chapter 4, especially in Brazilian films (from Toni Venturi's *Cabra-cega* to Wagner Moura's *Marighella)* and Argentine films (from *Infancia clandestina* to *Pasaje de vida*). In that cluster the "past is not past" trope is further resignified: through a postmemory lens, the guerrilla thrillers direct their gaze to the continuing legacy and validity of past guerrilla struggles in present democratic societies. These films, while often sharing Costa-Gavras's treatment of guerrillas (and in the case of *Infancia clandestina* even subtly hinting at a continuity of their agenda with recent progressive administrations), also problematize them.

The "past is not past" trope, however, is already central before the 1970s dictatorships. It can be seen in the first Latin American literary political thriller, published in 1969: Rafael Bernal's *El complot mongol* (see chapter 2). This novel is also haunted by the past: in this case, the flawed Mexican Revolution and its spectral legacies in light of the Tlatelolco massacre that took place one year before the novel's publication.

FINAL THOUGHTS

In addition to the "past is not past" trope, the American and European models outlined in this chapter bequeath to the Latin American political thriller another important convention that is still used nowadays: the inclusion in the story of at least one American or European character lost in Latin America: a thrilling gringo, like Jack North in the Peruvian Andes or Richard Lamb in the Uruguayan Pampas.

We can see this convention from the very beginnings of the genre's history, which, as noted, never ceased to welcome a plurilingual plot. *El complot mongol*, for instance, features clueless FBI and KGB agents in Mexico City. The American gringo is fundamental in Latin American political thriller films, where this convention quickly morphs to instantiate the complicity between American and Latin American states during Operation Condor. Gleyzer's *Los traidores* includes Mr. Crawford, an American unionist sent by the American embassy to train the working class to oppose Communist tendencies, a role also played by a character in *Pra frente, Brasil*. *En retirada*, *La historia oficial*, and *Rojo*, to name a few such films, all showcase American businessmen and their ties with the Argentine dictatorship. Closely following Costa-Gavras's *État de siège*, *O que é isso, companheiro?* foregrounds the story of Charles Elbrick, an American ambassador kidnapped by Latin American guerrillas.

This convention is still present in political thrillers in the twenty-first century that depict political intrigue in democratic times. An important scene in Santiago Mitre's *La cordillera* (2017) includes a long dialogue in English between a fictional US secretary of state and an equally fictional president of Argentina (played by renowned actors Christian Slater and Ricardo Darín, respectively). The scene suggests the seamless continuity of American geopolitical pressure in the region, in a somewhat different context.

Other European/Latin American co-productions set in Latin America update and reshape this convention to emphasize the ties between economic interests and political crimes. They fall within Derry's subcategory of political thrillers that became increasingly popular after the 1980s in Hollywood and were only belatedly and selectively imported to Latin America: "films which expand the basic concept of conspiracy to include institutions beyond the government," such as the banking system, the media, the penal system, or—less represented in Latin America—the pharmaceutical and nuclear industries.[72] For example, Ramón Termens's *Negro Buenos Aires* (2009) and Andreas Fontana's *Azor* (2021) tell the story of a naïve Catalan investor amid the Corralito 2001 crisis and a disoriented Swiss banker during the Argentine dictatorship, respectively, underscoring the continuities of the neocolonial ties of European financial powers with the region. In turn, the gringo's naïveté is also central to Jorge Ramírez Suárez's *Conejo en la luna* (2004), which features an English wife who becomes the typical victim-on-the-run of the thriller because of her gullibility.

To be sure, this inclusion of American and European characters in film is a consequence of the politics of co-production, often demanding a certain number of actors from the co-funding countries. But at the same time, even if involuntarily, it accentuates the transnational scale of the political thriller beyond the genre's imperialistic origins. We need only think of Gleyzer, a staunch leftist anti-imperialist filmmaker. The fact that he hired American producer Bill Susman, who effectively helped him to import the American genre conventions to Argentina (while working on an extremely domestic film), illustrates that political thrillers understand the political as something that can never be reduced to the nation-state. Perhaps more relevant to the point I hope to make in this chapter, Gleyzer illustrates how the transnational circulation of ideas or, more specifically, cultural genres should never be reduced to a hierarchical one-way direction. After all, much like secrets, genres can be extracted, spied on, infiltrated, reappropriated—in short, subverted—by anyone who chooses to engage with them.

CHAPTER TWO

Botched Jobs

COUPS AND MAGNICIDES AS PRECARIOUS CONSPIRACIES

Hay que construir un complot contra el complot.

RICARDO PIGLIA, "TEORÍA DEL COMPLOT"

CONSPIRACIES MAKE POLITICS THRILLING. AS MOST of the literature on the thriller over the last five decades has pointed out, sedition is a key ingredient for spectacularizing politics.[1] The portrayal of coups and magnicides imbues an otherwise routine activity with an extraordinary, captivating intensity. Latin American renditions of the genre are no exception to this, but they sometimes subvert the portrayal of conspiracies in interesting ways.

In addition to conspiracies, the critics have emphasized multiple times the role that suspense plays in thrillers.[2] Less attention, however, has been devoted to the ties between secrecy, spatiality, and precarity as central elements of the genre. The main contribution of the Latin American political thriller lies in the reshuffling of these ingredients and the ways in which it destabilizes the representation of conspiracies.

This reshuffling can be traced back to the origins of the genre, notably in Rafael Bernal's *El complot mongol* (1969), a novel that explores a fictional conspiracy while playing with depictions of both a magnicide and a coup. Because of the political thriller's belated visibility as a distinct form,[3] the novel was instead read in the light of neighboring genres: as the first Mexican hard-boiled/detective thriller,[4] for example, or even as a spy thriller.[5] But as Persephone Braham notes, "the novel mixes the hard-boiled and spy genres in a new and completely original way."[6] The result of that combination is the political thriller. Most critics have not fully explored Bernal's engagement with the genre itself.[7] In this context, chapter 2 is devoted to examining how

El complot mongol inaugurates the genre in Latin America, leaving behind a visible legacy that was at times overlooked and at others embraced. I offer a new reading of the novel, while analyzing its continuities and ruptures within the genre's tradition in both literature and film.

To begin with, it is worth noting that Bernal builds on two Mexican forerunners in both literary and cinematic works that deal with national politics: the novelist Martín Luis Guzmán and the filmmaker Julio Bracho. Their work was a modest yet still productive breeding ground that had been developing in Mexico over the previous decades, eventually shaping Bernal's work. On the one hand, the influence of Guzmán's *La sombra del caudillo* (1929), a novel that centers on political intrigue in the aftermath of the Mexican Revolution through a critical lens that challenges the postrevolutionary state, is evident in Bernal. On the other hand, Bracho's *Distinto amanecer* (1943), a political thriller *avant la lettre* that premiered during the Golden Age of Mexican cinema, also informs *El complot mongol*. His film combines intense melodramatic narratives with hints of the emerging political thriller during the 1940s film noir period. Bracho himself was in charge of a film adaptation of Guzmán's *La sombra del caudillo* in 1960 that was censored for more than three decades. By contrast, *Distinto amanecer* dodged censorship, perhaps due to its happy ending. It enjoyed a good reception, but without immediately spawning successors.[8]

Perhaps for all these reasons, the genre did not flourish in the region immediately after Guzmán and Bracho's works. Even though they were remarkably ahead of their time, their impact on the Latin American political thriller is difficult to establish, as the genre only bourgeoned over the last quarter of the twentieth century, several decades after the Mexican Revolution (1910–1920s) and the film noir period (1940s–1950s). Nevertheless, we can still see their trace in Bernal's 1969 novel, published at a time when the political thriller was becoming increasingly common in England and the United States.

To a certain extent, it is paradoxical that the Latin American political thriller originated in Mexico, "where filmmakers did not even produce a national cinema as politicized as the one from their South American counterparts," as Ignacio Sánchez Prado notes.[9] Of course, he is thinking here about Third Cinema, which, as noted in the introduction, tended to privilege politicized documentaries and political dramas, avoiding more commercial genres such as political thrillers.

Bernal's own previous literary career foreshadowed his pivotal role in the genre's tradition: before authoring *El complot mongol*, he had written lesser-known adventure novels, such as *Su nombre era Muerte* (1947) and *Tierra de gracia* (1963), both set in thrilling Latin American landscapes, like the Usumacinta River (in the jungle, near the Guatemalan border) or the Orinoco forests. In doing so, Bernal follows the genealogy that connects the adventure tale to the political thriller, as examined in chapter 1. I return to Bernal and his forerunners later. First, I outline several key aspects that shape my reading of his novel in relation to affect conspiracy, spatiality, secrecy, and precarity.

As Martin Rubin notes, "conspiracy" is always "a plural activity."[10] This is evident in the word's etymology: both "conspiracy" and "sedition" are inseparable from space, much like *secretus. Conspiratio* (common aspirations) implies a web of agents "breathing together," several plotters pushing toward a shared goal. By contrast, *seditio* emphasizes the opposite: separation, "going apart."[11] In both, the prominence of space is evident, as a given web of agents (revolutionaries, coup plotters, scheming civil servants, traitors) collectively goes to an imaginary place that others do not. Political thrillers tend to enhance these links between conspiracy and space. They often do so by telling a story in which a secret conspiracy is revealed, following spatial transitions of disclosure (from the inside to the outside, from the depths to the surface), amid the typical atmosphere of suspense.

In addition to space and suspense, it is important to bear in mind that the genre's portrayals of conspiracies are often imbued with affect. This may sound like a paradox, as political thrillers, in principle, are supposed to be about things we associate with politics more immediately, such as political ideas, parties, or politicians. Ian Scott, for example, reads American political films (including but not restricted to political thrillers) essentially as "all ideological," because in "Gramscian terms, Hollywood has a hegemonic set of values that reflects the conformities of American democracy."[12] Nevertheless, as they constantly elicit visceral reactions from their audiences, political thrillers can be better understood in terms of the posthegemonic intensities associated with political affect, rather than with ideas or beliefs.

After all, as Jerry Palmer acutely observes, ideology "constitutes only a superficial layer" in thrillers.[13] In fact, the very criticism against the genre, formulated in what was called "The Political Thriller Debate," was that it "did not encourage any kind of critical or active political thought in the spectator" because of "the use of genre conventions."[14] This is not to say, however, that political thrillers are never written for propaganda purposes or to offer clearly biased interpretations of specific historical events. It means rather that—in order to persuade us—thrillers must first and foremost somehow thrill us affectively and spatially.

As such, thrillers in general thrill us because they provoke "gut-level feelings rather than . . . cerebral, or emotionally heavy feelings, such as tragedy, pathos, pity, love, nostalgia," in Rubin's words.[15] Political thrillers in particular place these gut feelings in the context of political scenarios and historical events. They foreground the fear and anxiety but also the excitement and desire that the prospect of conspiracies (coups, magnicides, revolutions) can produce in the audience. Perhaps this is what is so compelling about conspiracies and why the genre keeps coming back to them over and over: because of the significant and tangible quantity of political affect they produce.

At first glance, political thrillers pretend to capture affect through language and events: they give us the impression that local idioms and jargon, as well as precise historical times and spaces, are fundamental to understanding the intricacies of the story. But they ultimately tend to privilege transhistorical and transnational topics, beyond the specificities of the nation-state they aim to portray in Latin America and beyond.

CONSPIRACIES, THE NATION-STATE, AND THE TRANSNATIONAL POLITICAL THRILLER

Because conspiracy and secrecy are so closely linked to space, we can think about them in terms of interiority and exteriority. This is why Norberto Bobbio distinguishes two types of conspiracy: *arcana dominationis* and *arcana seditionis* (secrets of domination and secrets of sedition). Whereas the former points to the internal secrets that belong to sovereign power, the latter alludes to the external counterpart that resides in the plotters who go against the state.[16] These ideas on sedition presume sites located inside and outside of the state. When he pictures internal sedition, Bobbio is thinking about ways in which sovereignty seeks to strengthen itself from within (such as self-coups or false-flag attacks). When he imagines external sedition, he is thinking about the Mafia, terrorist organizations, guerrilla movements, and so forth.

Political thrillers highlight and complicate these two types of conspiracy. The genre employs a trans-modal language, present across literature and film. This language can be analyzed by focusing on what I call the "grammar of secrecy"—a systematic way of thinking about secrets that privileges a specific class of words: prepositions of space. The grammar of secrecy conceives space through dialectics, using pairs of prepositions with opposite meanings: "under" and "above," "inside" and "outside," "behind" and "in front of." Prepositions, in turn, point to a topography where secrets are distributed and concealed, waiting to be extracted, disclosed, or exposed: "under" and "above" point to depths and surfaces; "inside" and "outside" signal interiority and exteriority; and "behind" and "in front of" indicate invisibility and visibility.

In relation to Bobbio's twofold conspiracy, the prepositions "inside" and "outside" are particularly relevant. They point to two layers of interiority and exteriority: outside and inside the state apparatus, outside and inside the nation-state territory. Through the grammar of secrecy, the genre represents conspiracies performed by either external plotters or internal civil servants as well as foreign or domestic threats. But beyond Bobbio's characterization, political thrillers also add a third layer of conspiracies that involve characters who may or may not belong to the political. In other words, the genre redefines interiority and exteriority as outside and inside of the political itself. In short, these layers examine three contours: the ones that delimit the state, the nation, and the political. *El complot mongol* is a paradigmatic example of how the genre reimagines these three layers in the Latin American context. The novel complicates the two types of conspiracy studied by Bobbio through a distinct treatment of space and precarity.

To better understand Bernal's innovative treatment of the genre, it is important to look at how he moves away from his transnational models. The novel was translated into English in 2013, respecting the original Spanish title: *The Mongolian Conspiracy*. The translation of the title makes clear the book's intertextual gesture toward its transnational models, as it explicitly parodies Richard Condon's political thriller *The Manchurian Candidate*, published in 1959, a decade before *El complot mongol*. Sánchez Prado, the only critic who takes notice of this gesture, observes how the novel engages in an "appropriation of cultural elements at the height of Cold War paranoia."[17] Some of these elements appear in the equation that several Anglo-American political thrillers establish between conspiracy and exteriority. One of Bernal's many "appropriations" has to do with eschewing this equation. Instead, as I elaborate later, he plays with space, diffusing the semantic strength of prepositions such as "outside" and "inside" and subsequently obscuring the boundary that separates *arcana dominationis* and *arcana seditionis*, which seem to be more clearly demarcated in Condon himself and, even more clearly, in Ian Fleming's James Bond series.

Both Condon's and Fleming's novels are particularly keen to associate exteriority (especially foreignness) with conspiring evil, which, in turn, is often personified by villainous characters who are typically of "non-Anglo-Saxon origin," as Palmer reminds us.[18] It is important to remember that both authors were extremely popular in the 1960s in the Spanish-speaking world, at the time Bernal was importing the genre to Latin America. *La novela de intriga*, a dictionary of genre fiction published in the early 1970s, describes Fleming as "the creator of the character that has produced the biggest impact in our times," amplified by the film adaptations.[19] In addition, Hispanic presses such as Círculo de Editores and Plaza & Janés published Spanish translations of Condon's 1959 novel (under the title *El mensajero del miedo*) as early as 1963, probably leveraging the success of John Frankenheimer's 1962 film adaptation starring Frank Sinatra. The significance of these novels makes Bernal's gesture even more important.

Condon's and Fleming's novels, along with other 1950s and 1960s Anglo-American political thrillers, tend to privilege *arcana seditionis* over *arcana dominationis*.[20] They frequently locate the threat of sedition overseas, outside of the state and the nation. Foreign characters, in turn, function as metonymies of their places of origin. *The Manchurian Candidate*, for instance, assigns the novel's conspiracy to an elite Chinese/Soviet commando, an embodiment of the Eastern bloc, who kidnaps and brainwashes American soldiers so that they will implement a Communist coup on American soil. Sedition starts overseas, then finally infiltrates the core of the state. In this context, Rubin explains that thrillers feature "exotic and foreign elements" in order to build a "mysterious, alluring, and exciting world," which is clearly demarcated from "the more solid, domestic world that the thriller transforms."[21] But what happens when thrillers are produced in a region that, far from projecting "solidity," is represented as structurally precarious? This is the case with Bernal's novel, which subverts exteriority and interiority through precarity.

Replicating and complicating *The Manchurian Candidate*, Bernal tells the fictional story of a magnicide attempt on the US president in Mexico, during an official visit at the peak of the Cold War in the late 1960s. Personifying the villainous dimension of exteriority, a group of Chinese or Mongolian plotters seems to have initiated the conspiracy. But one of the first clues that these personifications should not be taken too seriously is the way the book deliberately conflates China and Mongolia. This is intentional, of course, as Sánchez Prado reminds us that Bernal was "one of Mexico's most notable experts on Asia and the Pacific at large."[22] The novel features an apostrophe that acts as a leitmotiv, highlighting the criminals' foreign origin: *¡Pinches chales!* A colloquial and pejorative Mexican slur alluding to Asian migrants, *chale* is linked to *chalecos*, the vests that Japanese and Chinese people wore upon their arrival in Mexico throughout the first half of the twentieth century.

The slurs may give us a misleading first impression. We may think for a moment that Bernal is basically reproducing Anglo-American attitudes toward foreign characters and sedition. Some critics of the novel certainly follow this interpretation. They read this leitmotif as an expression of xenophobia and racism toward the Asian minority in the city.[23] But they miss the point of what Bernal is doing: mocking Anglophone genre conventions to import them to Latin America. Ultimately, by the end of the novel we find out that the *chales* have no clout in the conspiracy. Everything is domestic. Along with Sánchez Prado, Fernando Fabio Sánchez is one of the few critics to give the necessary weight to the fact that "the supposed international conspiracy is in fact a local plot."[24] What initially appeared to be rooted outside of the

Mexican territory was actually within it all along. Bernal, then, derides more than imitates Condon and Fleming's Cold War anxieties and their unshakable notions of interiority and exteriority: after a confusing investigation searching for plotters (involving the FBI, the KGB, and the rumor of Maoist China wanting to take control of Communist Cuba), the reader learns that it was all just a smoke screen to conceal an impending coup that involved only Mexican politicians and military men. In short, exteriority was never truly in play at all.

CONSPIRACIES, THE NATION-STATE, AND THE MEXICAN POLITICAL THRILLER

By contrast, the anxieties that are at stake in *El complot mongol* have less to do with the fears of foreign invasion that are so constitutive of many Anglo-American political thrillers and more to do with a transhistorical, Shakespearean topic: political succession. This issue, so prominent in most of Shakespeare's histories but also in his tragedies (*King Lear, Macbeth*, and *Hamlet*), is adapted for a Mexican context.

In Shakespeare, political succession is linked to usurpation, legitimacy, divine right, inheritance, and the consequences of unstable transfers of power. In the Mexican political thrillers, this last theme is perhaps the most prominent one, as it highlights precarity. Here political succession is linked to state-sponsored political crimes against the country's own population. Ultimately, this is more relevant for the country's political literature and film than the fears of foreign invasion. It is in this sense that Bernal seems to have a clear national model: Guzmán's *La sombra del caudillo* (1929), translated into English in 2017 as *The Shadow of the Strongman*. Bernal draws from Guzmán's treatment of succession in similar terms, as both texts view the continuity of executive power in Mexico in relation to the structural precarity that surrounds it.

Mexican Spanish speakers have a word for this precarious succession: *dedazo*, referring to a president's designation of a successor by pointing with a finger (*dedo*) when the incumbent's tenure is coming to an end. *Dedazos* were especially common before and during the Partido Revolucionario Institucional's seven decades of rule during the twentieth century. But, as Adolfo Arreola García notes, *dedazos* are not entirely gone in the twenty-first century.[25] *Dedazos* are considered authoritarian practices: hence the augmentative intensifier suffix *-azo*. They are conducted without any democratic consultation with the party's members, let alone their constituents. In addition, they often respond more to the incumbents' own interests, usually aligned with their economic backers. Guzmán and Bernal's novels demonstrate how the *dedazo* works as a shortcut to reduce anxieties toward the ever-present power vacuum that looms over the end of every *sexenio*, the six-year term prescribed by the Mexican constitution since 1928. Put differently, these novels represent *dedazos* as a force that renders visible the political precarity that informs sovereign power in Mexico, which can be seen as extending into several parts of Latin America. Thanks to Guzmán and Bernal, political succession will be key in the Mexican political thriller, as I outline in this chapter's final section.

The issue of succession in Guzmán's roman à clef, in particular, is significant because it involves the political wheeling and dealing in the aftermath of the Mexican Revolution during the 1920s.[26] It details the 1927 assassination of a political opponent, the fictional composite of General Francisco Serrano and other military men. It was feared that these men would dispute the country's leadership, then concentrated in the figure of the caudillo, a character in the novel loosely based on Álvaro Obregón (1920–1924) and his successor, Plutarco Elías Calles (1924–1928). Both politicians were among the leaders who emerged victorious after the revolution. The magnicide of Francisco Serrano would eventually result in a covert self-coup: the Maximato (1928–1934), deeply marked by an exacerbated case of *dedazo* before the consolidation of *sexenios*. When Obregón was also assassinated in 1928, Calles emerged as the PRI's *jefe máximo* (supreme leader), the caudillo who secretly wielded his influence over the interim presidents. *La sombra del caudillo* tells the story of the transitions that led to the Maximato.

Bernal deals with this same anxiety toward the continuity of power but subverts Guzmán's story: instead of depicting a magnicide that leads to a coup, he tells the story of a fictional domestic coup disguised as a magnicide with transnational repercussions that never actually comes to pass. Much as in the case of *El complot mongol*, most previous criticism has read *La sombra del caudillo* not as a political thriller but merely as another example of the *novela de la revolución mexicana* (novel of the Mexican Revolution) or an *avant la lettre* example of the *novela de dictador* (dictator novel) that would become popular in the 1970s—types of political novels not explicitly identified with thrillers.[27]

With these caveats, it is still possible to claim that *La sombra del caudillo* constitutes "the armature" of the Latin American political thriller. I borrow the term from Walter Benjamin, who once compared Poe's short story "The Man of the Crowd" (1840) to "an X-ray of a detective story," where the crime in and of itself is absent, but the genre's formal "armature remains: the pursuer, the crowd, and an unknown man": the detective, the victims/witnesses, and the criminal.[28] Something similar could be said about Guzmán's novel and the political thriller: before the genre would emerge in the Anglo-American context, *La sombra del caudillo* features a thematic (more than a formal) armature of the genre in the region. All the key themes commonly explored in the genre up to the present are already there: not only the representation of political wheeling and dealing but, more broadly, the portrayal of politics through secrecy, suspense, deceit, corruption, and violence. More specifically in the Latin American context, *La sombra del caudillo* features key themes that will be reproduced in several political thrillers: the inclusion of fake kidnappings; clandestine political executions of innocent characters in outdoor spaces (examined in chapter 3 in relation to a distinct type of landscape that I call *la intemperie*), through an assassination or the massacre of civilians; and, finally, the presence of a survivor (in Guzmán's case, the fictional congressman Axcaná González), who often (though not always) plays the role of the genre hero.

Beyond the novel, Bracho's 1960 film adaptation of *La sombra del caudillo* also anticipates the genre's classic uses of space that would appear only years later in Hollywood and Europe. Filmed and set in a palace-like landscape in the country's capital, the Chapultepec Castle, the movie prefigures many later American political thrillers where intrigue unfolds within Washington, DC, such as *Advise & Consent* (1962), *Seven Days in May* (1964), and *Fail-Safe* (1964), to name just a few important productions during the first half of the 1960s. In this regard, Bernal departs from *La sombra del caudillo*, as I examine later, by bringing intrigue to Mexico's Chinatown instead.

Perhaps it is thanks to Guzmán and Bernal that the foreign threat (although still present) sometimes vanishes entirely or at least loses its importance in later renditions of the genre in the region. Everything is often kept in the family: *arcana dominationis* and *arcana seditionis* frequently coexist within the boundaries of the nation and the state. In this sense, Latin American political thrillers follow the horizon established by Piglia in his "Theory of the Conspiracy." Much like Bobbio, Piglia sees inner forms of conspiracy, akin to *arcana dominationis*, in the form of "state intelligence, the secret services, whose main goals are to control people's movements as well as to camouflage and supervise the destructive effects of cash flow."[29] Building on Guzmán, Bernal isolates this internal side, ultimately detaching it from Cold War paranoia about foreign threats. In doing so, he problematizes the genre's conventions as well as the very existence of spaces such as interiority and exteriority in relation to the state. More broadly, *El complot mongol* prompts the question of whether there is an "inside" to the state, underlining instead the imaginary silhouette of its contours. Without exteriority, without Asian plotters, what room is there for interiority? In short, Bernal insistently seems to ask whether the state really has an interiority.

Through a specific treatment of the grammar of secrecy, then, *El complot mongol* problematizes interiority and exteriority, whose boundaries are reinforced in some of Bernal's foreign models. The novel disturbs what we could call the mirage of the state's interiority, which is quite common beyond the genre and the context in which the novel itself was published, as it still exists today. We need only think of current purveyors of political secrets and conspiracies or, more to the point, conspiracy theorists and their obsession with another topography of secrecy: the "deep state."

Conspiracy theorists often desperately need to believe in interiority because without it the very notion of the state would crumble. Similarly, as Julio Patán notes, "political thrillers need conspiracy theories," which he defines as "all-encompassing plots without fissures attributable to something known as the 'system' constituting an undefined entity."[30] More recent Mexican renditions of the genre somewhat forgot Bernal's lesson. Political thriller films such as Jorge Ramírez Suárez's *Conejo en la luna* (2004), Alfredo Gurrola's *Borrar de la memoria* (2010), and Carlos Bolado's *Colosio: el asesinato* (2012) exacerbate this ineffable "system," reinforcing the idea that something important is ultimately at stake, something solid behind the smoke-filled rooms where decisions are made.[31]

It is important to remember, however, that this belief in interiority is not exclusive to the political thriller or conspiracy theorists. It stems from key texts of political philosophy and European literature. Perhaps what they all have in common is the portrayal of conspiracy in terms of the grammar of secrecy and its topography, as interiority, darkness, and depths are typically used to describe sedition. Elias Canetti, for instance, defined "secrecy" in the 1950s as something that "lies at the very core of power," where "everything happens in the dark."[32] Several political thrillers would later feed on such commonplaces. Earlier instances can even be found in Honoré de Balzac's historical novel *Catherine de Medici* (1846), which claims that "all power . . . is a permanent conspiracy,"[33] and in the reflections of Ferdinand Bardamu, the main character of Louis-Ferdinand Céline's *Voyage au bout de la nuit* (1932), who thinks that "everything that's important goes on in the darkness."[34] Here private darkness is caused by a public event (the Great War): "we never know anyone's real inside story,"[35] Bardamu goes on to say, touching on the nocturnal obscurity caused by unprecedented technologies of warfare. By contrast, the master plan in Bernal's *El complot mongol* is crowded with unsolvable fissures: with precarity, not with solidity. Bernal's subversive reshaping of the thriller resonates with Michel Foucault's definition of the state as a heartless body, "not just in the sense that it has no feelings, either good or bad, but . . . in the sense that it has no interior."[36] Bernal dissolves both exteriority and interiority, exposing how the prepositions of space "outside" and "inside" resolve into pure fabrication.

A dialogue included in his novel, for instance, sounds like a distorted echo of Canetti, Balzac, and Céline's adages on the interiority and darkness of state power. Asked about Communist infiltrators in Mexico's Chinatown, one of the Chinese suspects responds: "Nobody know what deep in heart of man [*sic*]."[37] This answer, which initially seems to be a solemn definition of the human condition, should be read as parodic. But the parody is found not so much in its xenophobic mockery of Chinese accented language. What is parodic about it, Bernal seems to say, is that nobody knows what happens "in heart of man" (in interiority, darkness, and depths) not because knowledge is unattainable but because there really is nothing hidden to be known, unlike what many political thrillers would lead us to believe. Perhaps the secrets of the state, as shown in the sloppy coup represented in *El complot mongol,* are rather banal in the end: a precarious bungle, a disastrous attempt at taking the reins of power, a botched job. Latin American political thrillers like Bernal's seem to posit that perhaps depths, interiority, and darkness do not conceal anything interesting after all.

Canetti goes on to define secrecy as a bituminous "element of power," in that "every secret is explosive, expanding with its own inner heat," which he imagines as "the fiery suddenness of a volcano, unexpected and irresistible . . . an apotheosis."[38] Several Anglo-American political thrillers typically translate this explosive nature of secrecy and conspiracies by privileging one of the most important ingredients in the genre: high stakes. We need only think of 1950s–1960s Hollywood political thrillers that are important for Bernal's horizon of expectations, from Lewis Allen's *Suddenly* (1954) and Edward L. Cahn's *Three Came to Kill* (1960) to John Frankenheimer's adaptation of *The Manchurian Candidate* (1962) and *Seven Days in May* (1964). All engage with high stakes by picturing fictional coups or magnicides of domestic or international politicians in the United States.

Although the plotters are not always foreigners, these films all take the pervasive influence of exteriority in the interiority of the state at face value, reinforcing it. The accent in these political thrillers is not so much (or at least not only) on the continuity of power within the United States but on what Americans and many Europeans perceived to be no less than the leadership of the Western bloc: national stakes that were treated and conflated as global. In this context, Coyne notes that Frankenheimer's films in particular "closed with reassertions of the political status quo."[39] This is because the male hero, invoked to save the day by dealing with these high stakes, invariably foils the conspiracy in time. The dénouement of these films typically projects an image of solidity: coups and magnicides are averted and the imagined American democracy (and the Western bloc) remains solid at the end of the story.

In political thrillers made during the mid–1960s, the stakes grow even higher. For instance, Sydney Lumet's *Fail-Safe* (1964) and James B. Harris's *The Bedford Incident* (1965) foreground the hovering presence of full-scale mutual assured destruction as a result of the nuclear war between the United States and the Soviet Union. Deeply informed by the 1962 Cuban Missile Crisis, however, these films show a different treatment of conspiracy, which is no longer a simplistic product of foreign villainous forces but rather the result of a haphazard escalation within the Cold War. Lumet's and Harris's films are both much more radical than their forerunners: they go so far as portraying the actual materialization of mutual destruction. Yet they still show clear continuities with their forerunners. As Coyne claims, American exceptionalism is still at work here.[40] In *Fail-Safe*, especially, it is linked to the resolution of high stakes. New York and Moscow have to be destroyed by a nuclear bomb, always for the sake of the greater good, tied to even greater interests: avoiding the destruction of the whole planet.

El complot mongol subverts all of this by promising us similar high stakes (the assassination of the American president in Mexican territory), which are never truly delivered. Instead, as I explore later, the novel offers flimsy conspiracies with lower stakes that are about to implode like the impending coup: unlike Canetti's flammable apotheosis, however, they vanish. Bernal inaugurates the representation of the most important contribution of the Latin American political thriller, a response to high stakes: precarious secrets. Ephemeral and evanescent, precarious secrets are liable to sudden transformations that can quench the fire of conspiracies, which are nonetheless quickly absorbed by other equally erratic and improvised forms of sedition.

SECRECY AND PRECARITY

Before delving into *El complot mongol*'s use of precarious secrecy, I now offer some context in regard to intellectual debates on the meanings of precarity. I understand "precarious secrecy" as an aesthetic translation of precarity's ubiquity in Latin American life and culture. The most prominent theorists who discuss precarity do so precisely by emphasizing its all-pervasiveness, but at a global level. According to Pierre Bourdieu, for instance, precarity "is everywhere now."[41] For Zygmunt Bauman, it is "the most widespread . . . feature of contemporary life conditions."[42] Jacques Derrida, in turn, links it to "the fragility of nation-state sovereignty," describing precarity as "the principle of ruins that is working it over."[43] It is important to remember, however, that all these claims were made around the same time: in the late 1990s and the early 2000s, decades after Bernal's novel was published. Bourdieu and Bauman, specifically, are thinking about the generalized unemployment and underemployment that has affected some European societies ever since the 1990s. This is why Richard Nice (Bourdieu's translator) chooses "job insecurity" to convey the meaning of *précarité*.

But even though Derrida still sees it as a growing force, associated with "this phase of what is so obscurely called 'globalization,'" he acknowledges that precarity is "not . . . something absolutely new."[44] Bourdieu, in turn, detaches precarity from globalization, claiming that it is less the product of its "*economic inevitability*" and more the result of "a *political will*."[45] Bauman explicitly acknowledges that precarity is "experienced . . . all over the globe" but is "felt to be especially . . . depressing in the highly developed . . . part of the planet—for the reason of being . . . unprecedented."[46] To sum up, all three think about precarity by focusing on Europe and North America, as a "late-twentieth century transformation," which, as Sharryn Kasmir notes, is part of the shift from Fordism to post-Fordism that characterizes late capitalism.[47]

As I hope to show throughout this book, however, precarity in Latin American cultural production is very much not something new but rather structural: its impact transcends economic insecurity and overflows into the realm of nation-state sovereignty and cultural representation. This is what Constanza Burucúa and Carolina Sitnisky clearly establish, at least for the region's film history: precarity affects "every level of filmmaking," including "the spheres of production, distribution, and reception," ever since the origins of cinema at the beginning of the twentieth century.[48]

Post-Fordist neoliberal precarity certainly affected and accentuated economic inequality, job insecurity, and political instability in Latin America and beyond.[49] But precarity predates neoliberalism by a great deal. In this sense, it is more challenging to date precarity in the region in the same way that Bourdieu, Bauman, and Derrida confidently do with Global North democracies, when they tie it affirmatively or negatively to the 1970s neoliberal reorganization or the 1990s emergence of globalization. On the one hand, this is because, as Kasmir claims, "precarity has always been a feature of capitalist societies," but on the other because it "has perpetually characterized working people's lives" with a special emphasis "in the Global South." As she mentions, "the broader geographic and historical perspective on global capital accumulation shows . . . Fordist stability is the exception and precariousness the norm, as opposed to the obverse."[50] It is in this context of widespread, ever present, structural precarity that *El complot mongol* and other Latin American political thrillers portray precarious conspiracies, to examine ramifications that exceed both politics and economics, reaching language and aesthetics.

Bernal and his inheritors displace precarity to multiple levels, stressing what for Catherine S. Ramírez and others is the fact that "precarity goes beyond the workplace." It is not solely an economic issue but a more all-pervasive force that "links precarious work with precarious lives and livelihoods."[51] Or, to put it in Bauman's words, Latin American political thrillers understand precarity as "the preliminary condition of all the rest."[52] They do so by transforming the genre's grammar of secrecy by translating structural precarity through volatile images of truncated implosions, by using conspiracies to picture the fragile nation-states that conspirers aim to transform from within. Next I explore precarity as a source of parody in *El complot mongol* in particular.

PRECARITY AND PARODY THROUGH SPACE

Bernal's hero is Filiberto García. A former hit man (*sicario*) for one of Pancho Villa's generals during the Mexican Revolution, García is secretly hired to investigate the impending magnicide of the American president. Now a *pistolero* (a "gunslinger," in Amelia Simpson's words), García is an experienced but shoddy hit man disguised as an investigator,[53] who occasionally works for the state.

In this context, García belongs to what Bobbio calls the *sottogoverno*: the "sub-government" is an "invisible power that is constituted not only to fight against public power but also to obtain unlawful benefits" from it.[54] Bernal problematizes the location of secrecy in the construction of his hero by placing García at the same time "below" the state (the subgovernment) and (at least initially) inside of its secrets. As Derek Beaudry notes, García "does the dirty, illegal work that paradoxically upholds the law."[55] As such, he is aligned with Bobbio's *arcana dominationis* rather than *arcana seditionis*. Initially, the hit man does not conspire against the state but on its behalf, until (as I discuss later) the state starts prying into his own personal life.

As the novel has traditionally been read as the foundational hard-boiled novel in Latin America, García has been described as a cultural translation of two classic American detectives: Raymond Chandler's Philip Marlowe and Mickey Spillane's Mike Hammer.[56] In addition, Ilan Stavans brings in super-spy James Bond: for Stavans, Bernal mimics Fleming in that both "heighten suspense through a series of crucially important diplomatic events."[57] But do these events not serve as mere decoration in *El complot mongol*? Unlike any of Fleming's spy thrillers, the stakes are far from being high in the Mexican novel. In addition, the balance of these influences is uneven, favoring Marlowe over Bond. But, in any case, García is far more complex than a mere mix of Anglo-American detectives and spies.

Perhaps this is because García cites one of the heroes who can be found in the political thriller's genealogy: the Hispanic *pícaro*. This has gone unnoticed by most critics, except for Beaudry and Sánchez Prado.[58] Here, too, Bernal draws on Guzmán.[59] More than an American hard-boiled investigator or a British super-spy, García is a *pícaro* in that he is inseparable from precarity, as established in chapter 1: he is constantly tricking others for survival. In this sense, the novel's picaresque edge adds an original aspect to the Cold War's grave intricacies: parody.

Sánchez Prado reads *El complot mongol*'s use of parodic comedy as a response to "the absurdity of US genres when read against the backdrop of Latin American reality."[60] This use of parody, however, could also be understood not only as a reactive gesture but as an effective way to import the aesthetic universe of the political thriller into the Latin American cultural field. *El complot mongol*, in this sense, does to the political thriller what Antonio Helú's film *La obligación de asesinar* (1937) and Jorge Luis Borges and Bioy Casares's *Seis problemas para don Isidro Parodi* (1942) did with detective stories in Mexico and Argentina, respectively.[61] This is why Francisco Goldman links Bernal's novel to another Cold War parody, Stanley Kubrick's *Dr. Strangelove* (1964). He finds it "exquisitely comical that [Bernal] centers this international conspiracy threatening world peace in Mexico City's very tiny Chinatown, on Dolores Street, a few restaurants that serve poor people's Chinese food to poor people."[62] The Mexican Chinatown is one of Bernal's most parodic aspects in relation to space and precarity, which results in a constitutive site of precarious secrecy that will later be reproduced by several Latin American writers and filmmakers.

It is possible that Bernal borrows the link between political intrigue (secrecy) and Chinatown (space) from Bracho's *Distinto amanecer*, which had already foregrounded the same neighborhood, with a small Chinese restaurant where *defeños* (inhabitants of Mexico City) eat chop suey. Through Chinatown, Bracho "showcases the nation's *chiaroscuros*," in Maricruz Castro Ricalde's words.[63] Thus, he brings to the fore the exotic and captivating landscape of film noir, peppered with chases through the streets of Mexico City.

In addition, the film's story unfolds in a Chinatown apartment, which sets the stage for sites of precarious secrecy to come, highlighting an interiority deeply marked by precarity.[64] Instead, Bernal's Chinatown becomes parodic, because it appears after "the period of the thriller's development" (over the first half of the twentieth century), when "the primary conventional site of the exotic was Asia, in the stereotypical form of the Mysterious East," as Rubin observes.[65] *El complot mongol* mocks this very aura of orientalist mystery by juxtaposing it to Dolores Street. In doing this, Bernal reinforces and subverts what Bracho had already started doing through film in the 1940s—importing the labyrinthine imagery of the thriller to Latin America. Furthermore, considering that the novel was published in 1969, Bernal's parodic treatment of Chinatown could also be read as political criticism, mocking what Samuel Steinberg calls "the triumphant tones of Mexico's achieved modernity," marked by the "sadly ironic" coupling of the 1968 Olympic Games in Mexico City and the Tlatelolco massacre.[66]

Bernal's parody also stems from a British thriller set in Latin America that the critics have overlooked: Carol Reed's *Our Man in Havana* (1959), which tells the story of James Wormold, an amateur agent recruited by MI6 who submits fanciful reports to London merely for profit. Filmed during the last months of Fulgencio Batista's dictatorship, Reed's film laughs at political intrigue, treating it as pure fiction. This is exactly what Bernal would do one decade later. Whereas Wormold's plausibility relies on the distance that separates the Caribbean from England, Bernal, in turn, repurposes Reed's use of space to mock genre conventions in another way: through Dolores Street, he disguises Asian exotic remoteness in the form of urban proximity. Thus, Bernal sets the stage for global intrigue, much as it was in distant prerevolutionary Cuba for British spies. But what is original about *El complot mongol* is that international intrigue remains fanciful until the very end. By contrast, Wormold's façade in *Our Man in Havana* becomes a grave matter when his fictional reports and informants are intercepted by enemy spies, who take his "cell" at face value and end up eliminating the agents. What started as a playful treatment of political intrigue results in the representation of serious counterespionage at work. In Bernal, instead, there is only national Realpolitik.

Equally, the usage of Mexico's Chinatown is diametrically opposed to the tendency in other political thrillers (traditional and current) to locate collusions in palace-like buildings, such as the War Room at the Pentagon. As Scott notes, Washington, DC, in particular "becomes symbolic in many Hollywood films of solemnity, of theological contemplation, a place to seek sanctuary and find inspiration."[67] This is not only true of a myriad of twentieth-century political thrillers set in the US capital, such as Roger Donaldson's *No Way Out* (1987) and George Cosmatos's *Shadow Conspiracy* (1997), to name only a few. It is also true for political satires such as *Dr. Strangelove* itself and even more recent TV shows, such as Armando Iannucci's *Veep* (2012–2019), which struggle to detach themselves from the solemnity toward politics even when they are constantly mocking it.[68] Closer to Reed than to Kubrick, Bernal abandons all this gravity much more radically. This is fundamental to understanding how he offers a completely different relationship with secrecy and space: despite the initial impression of exotic remoteness, the ordinariness of Chinatown immunizes us against any sign of such solemnity.

Examples of this parodic tone can be seen repeatedly throughout the novel. For instance, they are evident in the parallelisms between the domestic and international characters, which point to the genre's grammar of secrecy: inside and outside of the Mexican nation-state's territorial boundaries. Whereas García is placed within interiority, the FBI and the KGB agents (the novel's own gringos lost in Latin America: Graves and Laski) are located within exteriority. The Asian characters, in turn, sway between these two topographies of secrecy.

Such parallelisms are often drawn through García's inner monologues, which offer comparisons between himself and his more glamorous foreign counterparts. An example of this can be found when García thinks of Graves, whose very surname evokes the high stakes of conspiracies, the solemnity toward politics: "*Pinches* gringos! They're always playing some part. Me, even if I wear that little hat and those glasses, I'd still look like what I am: a stiff factory." Elsewhere, García extends the comparison to Laski: "they're all in a different league—so professional . . . so international intrigue."[69] He even does the same with the suspected conspirers: "*Pinches* Chinamen! Sometimes it seems like they don't have a clue, but then it turns out they know everything. There I am pretending to be a big shot, and all the time they're seeing what a chump I am." García claims that in Mexico "we're not experts, we're just amateurs."[70] Far from being a "big shot" like Graves or Laski (or Bond), the *pistolero* is closer to Chandler's "common man,"[71] but with a more picaresque, parodic, and prosaic tone.

Another analogy between interiority and exteriority can be found in the hit man's leitmotivs. The constant curses, directed at the Asian characters as well as the Mexican revolutionary state and international politics, parallel another recurring phrase: *lo de Dallas*, "what happened in Dallas." The fresh memory of JFK's 1963 assassination in the 1969 book appears multiple times in this and other more elliptical ways. Here, again, space meets secrecy, in that the location alluded to works as the specter of a real magnicide with its international implications, allegedly involving the Soviet Union, Cubans, and Italian Americans. Kennedy's assassination serves as an iconic model for the impending magnicide in the novel that involves similar Cold War actors, now including Mexico in the mix. These iterations are part of the novel's parodic tone, as García jokingly muses: "tomorrow at this time we'll know if they whacked the president or not. But the gringos will have rolled out all their security. They're the experts. Like they were in Dallas."[72] Hence the parody: despite all the US technology, intelligence, professionalism, and sophisticated "wisdom," personified by Graves in the novel, JFK's assassination could not be stopped and the real identity of the masterminds behind the magnicide remains subject to speculation.

PRECARITY AS AMATEURISM AND PROSAICISM

El complot mongol sketches interiority and exteriority not only in terms of domestic and foreign agents but also in degrees of amateurism and professionalism, which could be understood as another instance of precarity: interiority is linked to García's (and Mexico's) amateurism, whereas professionalism is tied to international spies Graves and Laski. In fact, the words "expert" and "professional" reappear about fifty times throughout the novel.

Professionalism and amateurism are important to the thriller-umbrella. Palmer defines the genre's hero as "The Professional." By contrast, he identifies "The Amateur" with the passive, helpless, and incompetent female characters that feature in classic spy novels. "The Amateur," it could be added here, updates the medieval trope of the damsel in distress, who only complicates things for her savior—the male hero. Furthermore, Palmer builds on Umberto Eco's reading of Bond as an "improvisor" and his enemies as "programmers" or "planners" (conspirers). Palmer identifies the latter with the figure of "The Bureaucrat," such as Fleming's Dr. No.[73] Of course, the plans of Bond's nemeses always go wrong, as the MI6 agent eventually outwits them. Here, too, *El complot mongol* parodies and subverts tropes and conventions typical of the Anglo-American thriller: in Bernal's novel, García is the amateur, the villains are still bureaucrats but also improvisers, and the professionals (FBI and KGB) are essentially irrelevant. Bernal redefines "amateurism," which he links not to incompetence but to financial precarity and prosaicism.[74]

García, ultimately, is not the passive incompetent agent he claims to be. He eventually understands the intricacies of the real underlying conspiracy, even when he does so, parodically, by chance. His amateurism is more connected to the fact that he is a mundane *pistolero,* who lacks the resources that his North American and Soviet counterparts apparently have in abundance. Faced with Graves and Laski or the Asian suspects, García presents himself as nothing but an aging manufacturer of corpses ("a stiff factory") for an equally worn-out postrevolutionary state. This is what leads Braham to describe him as someone who "suffers from a lack of finesse in comparison to the other agents."[75] His exclusion from the top leagues is also an expression of the precarity surrounding Mexican society.

Palmer claims that "glamour . . . is essential to the enjoyment of the thriller," which he links to the luxury that we see especially in the Bond series.[76] Bernal, by contrast, puts on center stage the opposite: precarity and prosaicism. Perhaps the high stakes we see in Bernal's Anglo-American models are but a symbolic continuation of luxury and glamour: the wealthier nation-states whose conspiracies are perceived to be more important and central than anything that could ever happen in Dolores Street or, for that matter, in Asunción or La Paz. Through precarity, Bernal mocks Fleming's glamorization of political intrigue and his use of high stakes.

This is because, as noted, Bernal does not take at face value the equation between sedition and foreignness, unlike Condon or Fleming. Instead, his novel culturally translates to the Latin American context what Rubin calls the "anti-Bond" cycle: the British reaction against Fleming's work in 1960s literary and film political thrillers, themselves a product of secret agent Kim Philby's defection to the Soviet Union. Rubin is here thinking of John le Carré's early 1960s novels, which "explored the dark side of espionage," where the heroes feature a "relatively tangible drudgery" when compared to "Bond's leisure-class lifestyle."[77] In this sense, le Carré's Alec Leamas informs Bernal's García much more than Bond does, even more than Marlowe.

Within this cycle, Rubin also cites the beginning of Sidney Furie's film *The Ipcress File* (1965), with secret agent Harry Palmer "shuffling through his morning routine in a grubby flat: making coffee, reading the paper, getting dressed. He could be any ordinary civil servant preparing for the day's work."[78] In the film, Harry Palmer is described as "insubordinate, insolent, and a trickster." These words could very well define García. The use of prosaicism is particular to the anti-Bond cycle films, contrasting with the more mainstream Anglo-American political thrillers, which tend to rely on the glamorization of politics instead. Since Bernal, this anti-glamour aesthetics has become the mainstream way to practice the genre in Mexico and other Latin American national contexts.

Jerry Palmer reminds us that, for Eco, Bond outwits his enemies because of his ability to improvise.[79] By contrast, Bernal resignifies "improvisation": it is the bureaucrat-villains (the military plotters) who orchestrate a conspiracy that eventually becomes an improvised blunder. Ultimately, they are as amateur as García, concocting erratic plans that turn out to be catastrophic. Bernal also problematizes the more traditional understanding of the amateur in Martita, a Chinese-Mexican girl who serves as García's love interest. Martita remains ambiguous until the end of the story. With García, we are constantly hesitating in seeing her either as yet another damsel in distress or as a femme fatale. Here Bernal borrows from another American noir thriller set in Latin America: Orson Welles's *The Lady from Shanghai* (1947), whose titular female character (Elsa Bannister, played by Margarita Carmen Cansino, aka Rita Hayworth) also oscillates from one thriller trope to the other. But Martita ends up being the opposite of Elsa (a seemingly damsel in distress who turns out to be a femme fatale). I return to Martita later.

Amateurism is also linked to transparency and opacity in *El complot mongol*. Bernal portrays the perception of a mysterious wisdom to be found solely beyond Mexican borders, in Graves and Laski's coveted but unachievable expertise. This wisdom is opaque to García and, simultaneously, seems to allow his counterparts to read political intrigue transparently. Excluded from wisdom, Bernal defines García through unintelligibility, expressed in a colloquial Mexican idiom: *y yo sin agarrar la onda*. Katherine Silver's translation of García's comment on his inability to "catch the wave" is eloquent: "and I can't even make a play." It connects with the semantic universe that Bernal uses in the original to imagine political intrigue as something strictly playful. After all, Graves and Laski never show their wisdom, since there were no real international conspiracies at stake to begin with. All of this could be read as Bernal's strategy of exposing how his models portray politics in implausible and artificial ways. This reappears when García says that gringos such as Graves are always "playing some part."[80] Silver's translation here again is remarkably expressive, rendering the original colloquialism *hacer el teatro* (literally, "doing theater"). The semantic universe around artificiality confines intrigue to aesthetic representation—an imaginary play (in its twofold meaning of "drama" and "game") more than a factual reality.

At the end of the novel, García establishes yet another parallelism, again using a literary genre: this time not drama but tales (*cuentos*). He makes a correlation between present and past, Cold War intrigue and the Mexican Revolution, through prepositions of space and time: "outside" (international intrigue) and "inside" (the national revolution); "after" (the postrevolutionary order) and "before" (the revolutionary times). García notes that violence during the Mexican Revolution did not require people to "make up stories" (*no se anduvieron con cuentos*) about Outer Mongolia.[81] By treating international intrigue as pure aesthetic representation, Bernal portrays the political in the precarious terms of prosaicism, understanding the power dynamics of politics as less convoluted than some Anglo-American models imagine. By not taking secrecy seriously, *El complot mongol* manages to make the political thriller more palatable to Mexican readers and to blend the genre's transnational dimension with a more mundane territory.

If parody, as Linda Hutcheon would have it, is both a conservative and transformative power, preserving the model it mocks while at the same time "creating new syntheses,"[82] Bernal produces an innovative synthesis through parody, prosaicism, and amateurism by taking us from the Pentagon and the White House (and their aura of professionalism) to rudimentary, prosaic

Dolores Street, rife with petty criminals, poor people, and a shoddy, clueless *pistolero*.

PRECARITY AND THE THRILLER

Coyne notes that Hollywood legitimizes Washington through political thrillers, which work as visual platforms for national narratives, whose "supreme myth . . . is of a perfectible society." American renditions of the genre in the 1970s seem to question this myth, abandoning the self-congratulatory and idealistic tone of classic political dramas, such as Frank Capra's *Mr. Smith Goes to Washington* (1939), and instead crowding the screens with paranoid tales of sedition. As Coyne puts it, American exceptionalism nonetheless remains the normative principle, "even in those relentlessly pessimistic conspiracy narratives from the 1970s onwards." After all, they still express the "underlying message": "if liberty and democracy can be betrayed or subverted in America, then they can be destroyed *anywhere*." In this vein, Coyne discusses Alan J. Pakula's *All the President's Men*, which he sees as a Capraesque tale about American perfectibility, in which "sinister powers . . . are vanquished by the honest, tenacious little guys who still believe in Truth, Justice and the American Way."[83] Coyne's observations concur with Slavoj Žižek's take on the movie's "upbeat final message: what a great country ours must be, when a couple of ordinary guys like you and me can bring down the president, the mightiest man on Earth!"[84] Although Pakula's 1970s thriller, of course, was released a few years after Bernal's novel, they operate within this older Capraesque tradition of state perfectibility that is often absent in Latin American renditions of the genre.

Bernal is worlds away from offering such a perfectible narrative about the Mexican state and its national identity. In subverting the sites of secrecy by exposing the prosaic precarity that surrounds and permeates them, Bernal's legacy for the Latin American political thriller can be found in the abandonment of what Michael Taussig calls "the fetishism of the secret": the gesture of taking secrecy at face value that we see in Pakula and other Anglo-American political thrillers.[85] There is another clear contrast here: taking secrets at face value projects an image of a nation-state that would be better for all if only it could be governed by transparent and benevolent politicians. Far from buying into nationalistic exceptionalism, what we learn in *El complot mongol* is that intrigue, secrecy, mystery, opacity, and darkness—the very inner-workings of the nation-state—are nothing but *teatro* and *puro cuento*. And Bernal manages to do that by centering the prominent role of precarity in the genre.

El complot mongol is also inseparable from precarity in that, as Stavans notes, it shows "how the military legacy of the Revolution left a high concentration of well-paid murderers and displaced thugs roaming the humanity-infested streets."[86] Ultimately, as Bourdieu claims, the precarization of the workplace is not a monopoly of private corporations.[87] Semiretired secret agents parade through Latin American political thrillers as expressions of a precarious public sector.

Beyond the financial element, precarity also reveals itself in language, as when Laski defines "international intrigue" by saying that "most questions remain unanswered" in it.[88] An important point gets lost in Silver's translation here. In the original, Laski says that in international intrigue *nunca se tiene una base sólida ni una verdad completa*: "you never get a solid base or a full truth."[89] The original sentence, including the polysemic word *base* (which means both "the basics" and "basis"), offers an ambivalent reading: you can never grasp the *solid basics* of international politics, because (lost in translation) it can be hard to grasp for amateurs like García. But the impossibility of treading on a *solid basis* amounts to walking on volatile ground, which can never support us. In short, precarity dissolves secrecy (political intrigue) and space (the solid ground).

Treading on a ground that is not solid, of course, resonates with Bauman's understanding of precarity as *Liquid Modernity*. But it could also be read through the relationship that Judith Butler establishes between precarity and state arbitrariness, as precarious populations often turn to "the state for protection" when "the state is precisely that from which they require protection." The paradox, in Butler's notion of "precarious lives," is that the state goes against its own Hobbesian goal: safeguarding all of its citizens from the war of all against all. When describing "precarious populations," however, Butler is mainly thinking within and about the US context. Butler's understanding of "populations [that] are differentially exposed" to precarity could be read in relation to African Americans, Asian Americans, Latinxs, LGBTQIA+ communities, and other racialized and gendered minorities in the country.[90] By contrast, *El complot mongol* exposes us to a state arbitrariness that can turn against anyone, regardless of identity, a ground that can become quicksand even for the conspirators themselves.

More literally, there are no "basics" to grasp when it comes to understanding international intrigue in the novel, simply because there is no international intrigue at all. As Laski admits, "from the beginning, we said they were only rumors."[91] Here rumors could be read as the opposite of "basis" in the sense of foundations, *solid truths*. Bernal seems to be pulling our leg: there was no false advertisement, and we arrive at the end knowing that this could all be smoke and mirrors. By refusing to give us the chance to pry behind closed doors, he seems to concur with Taussig's maxim that "there is no such thing as a secret."[92] Taking secrecy seriously (or rather failing to recognize its precarity) constitutes a pointless endeavor, which actually runs the risk of masking the workings of power even further.

SPACE AND INFRAPOLITICS

As mentioned at the beginning of this chapter, both exteriority and interiority have three layers in thrillers that point to the contours of the state and the nation but also, and perhaps more importantly, the political. I discuss this third layer in these last sections. For Beaudry, García is placed "outside the established boundaries of nation and state" and his condition of being a *pícaro* puts him "at odds with the political order, as the reader finds in [his] recurring oaths."[93] But Bernal locates García more broadly at the edges of the political itself, beyond the Mexican state.

Bernal is not original in this: he follows what is essentially a genre convention. Somehow this seems paradoxical if we expect political thrillers to be mainly about politics and politicians. But it is worth connecting this political threshold with Rubin's definition of the thriller-umbrella as "a double world, at once poetic and prosaic, mysterious and mundane."[94] As I comment in the introduction, following Rubin, the genre's twofold dimension is deeply connected to the action of thrilling, when the poetic world pierces into the prosaic one. Some of the Anglo-American political thrillers that I mention in this chapter represent this disruption in quite literal terms by imagining foreign Communist invasions at the core of the nation-state. But the genre, in the United States and beyond, features a far more compelling, deeper type of invasion that has to do with different understandings of the political itself.

It is in this sense that Paul Cobley visualizes the threshold that separates the thriller's two dimensions in terms of opposed topographies of secrecy: the depths and the surface. For him, thrillers feature "the intrusion of a hidden, coexistent world upon another, surface world," which "is often couched in terms of public sphere disrupting the domestic world."[95] In the case of *El complot mongol*, as we have seen, Bernal imagines this threshold, rather than being between depths and surfaces, in terms of interiority and exteriority, even if other Latin American renditions (as shown in the following chapters) do reproduce Cobley's twofold layers.

What Cobley calls "the domestic world," however, is best described by Alberto Moreiras as "infrapolitical life," the dimension of life that resists hyper-politicization. In this context, the thriller's threshold divides not only the mundane from the extraordinary and the public from the private but, more importantly, what is political from what is not. It is interesting that Moreiras imagines infrapolitics in terms of a key ingredient in thrillers: space. According to him, infrapolitics is a "region," a site of "exception to political existence." The very prefix *infra-* (the Latin preposition "below") connotes a space that points to depths. Following Martin Heidegger and Diogenes Laertius, Moreiras sees an instance of this space in the Ephesian Temple of Artemis, "to which Heraclitus could withdraw with the kids." It was a last refuge where life could become tangible, by escaping and sheltering from "the state of surveillance."[96] As Moreiras notes elsewhere, the genre that foregrounds infrapolitics the most is precisely the political thriller.[97] He focuses on literary examples, but we may add that film and TV renditions of the genre also reproduce the conflict between infrapolitical life and politics. Political thrillers are keen on accentuating the threshold that marks "the absolute difference between Life and Politics"[98] by using the grammar of secrecy's prepositions "outside" and "inside" or "above" and "under."

In this context, critics have tended to misread Bernal's novel as apolitical: Sánchez, for example, sees García in terms of exteriority to the nation, as he "acts without Mexico being his ulterior motive." This leads Sánchez to claim that the political is subject to the personal in the novel, as García "follows the conspiracy through to its final consequences only to avenge the death of Martita." But is that the only goal that García achieves at the end of the novel? Sánchez goes on to describe García's lack of interest in politics as an analogy of Mexican politicians, who "supposedly have the good of the nation as their ultimate objective, but nevertheless pursue personal interests and financial profits."[99] Similarly, Braham sees García as a character who remains in a sort of equidistant position, not siding with either of the two Cold War blocs.[100] In what follows, I would like to offer a radically different reading of García, which positions him far from being an apolitical, materialistic antihero. After all, he acts neither for a financial reward nor entirely out of personal revenge.

Furthermore, García does intervene in the political, in ways that have strong connections with what Moreiras calls "infrapolitical action" elsewhere: an intervention "that is not directly political . . . but will result in political effects."[101] Here Bernal does something very innovative. The novel tells us how García, after finding out that Martita has been murdered, kills the plotters: the military men who hired him to impede the very same magnicide that they themselves hatched as a smoke screen for a military coup. The military's alleged goal is to end decades of PRI one-party rule in postrevolutionary Mexico. This is why killing them should not be read merely as García's personal revenge: after all, it is inseparable from "political effects," as it halts the impending coup.

If Rubin is right to say that thrillers in general feature an invasion in which the extraordinary world thrills its ordinary counterpart through "a murder, a monster, a vital secret, [or] supernatural forces,"[102] the political thriller in particular translates the invading force as the political and the invaded space as infrapolitical life. To put it differently, the political is the monster, often personified by a metonymy of the political: the state. Because it is a monster, the efficacy of the political is obviously distorted and hyperbolic, so that key genre ingredients such as paranoia and suspense can work.[103]

This is what García faces when he stops the coup. Whereas the small Chinatown and the fictional international intrigue initially seem to cite the extraordinary world that thrills its prosaic counterpart (life in Mexico City under postrevolutionary PRI rule), the actual invader—the thrilling agent of the novel—is the Mexican militarized state. This monster reappears, however spectrally and subtly, in Latin American political thrillers, including but not limited to the Mexican context, as I explore in the following chapters.

García's infrapolitical action responds to the invasion of his life by agents of the militarized state, who, as he eventually discovers, have been spying on him. This is why he suspects them and thus avenges Martita's death. Bernal, however, further complicates the contours of the political when the plot twist at the end of the novel is revealed. The last stepping stone in the invasion of García's life appears to be political (perpetrated by the state) but, crucially, it is not: the *pistolero* believes it was the military that killed Martita, but it was her husband Liu who did so, under the false pretense that she was involved in an affair with García.

Braham reads Martita's murder as a product of "the senseless postrevolutionary 'spy' game."[104] But what Moreiras says about other Mexican thrillers also holds true for *El complot mongol*: "it does not matter" that these thrillers are "a radical presentation . . . of politics as brute force in postrevolutionary Mexico."[105] The stakes of the text have to be found elsewhere. Ultimately, Martita's murder has little to do with what Braham calls the "game," as it is not really related to the Mexican postrevolution or even to Cold War espionage, for that matter: after all, neither the spies nor the plotters really murdered Martita.

The state as the monster, however, remains unaltered in García's perception of the source of the invasion of his life, as he does not learn about Liu's responsibility until after he has avenged Martita. Hence the novel juxtaposes the restitution of the personal with an intervention in the political: while satisfying his individual desire for revenge, García also ends up stopping the real conspiracy—not the magnicide, but the coup. This, of course, is also part of the novel's parodic dimension, as the bumbling sleuth ends up solving the crime (halting the coup) by accident. In any case, the fact that the victim who triggers infrapolitical action is a female character makes us turn now to gender.

GENRE, GENDER, AND INFRAFEMINISMS

It is no secret that political thrillers tend to be notoriously homosocial.[106] During the twentieth century, most productions in Hollywood, at least, would cast male actors for the main characters of the story, as "the hero . . . nearly always fits the prototype of the male, white American," in the words of Pablo Castrillo and Pablo Echart.[107] Perhaps because women were traditionally excluded not only from party politics but broadly speaking from the "political" in the sense of "having to do with power relationships," in Carol Hanisch's terms,[108] female characters have traditionally been left out of political strife in the genre. Whenever they are more centrally included, it is through the two different but related tropes mentioned above: the femme fatale and the damsel in distress.

For Castrillo and Echart, this slowly starts to change in the 2000s, with political thrillers like Sydney Pollack's *The Interpreter* (2005), which puts a female character on center stage. Silvia Broome (played by Nicole Kidman) is far from being a "hero," however, and seems closer to the damsel in distress: she is saved at the end of the story by UN agent Tobin Keller (played by Sean Penn). In chapter 4 I explore *Matar a todos* (2007), a Uruguayan rendition of the genre, released only two years later, whose main character, a female lawyer, seems to be more clearly a female hero.

Returning to Bernal, *El complot mongol* was published in 1969, the same year in which Hanisch was writing her well-cited paper "The Personal Is Political," which has become a powerful feminist slogan throughout the globe. As suggested earlier, Bernal leaves not only García but, significantly, Martita at the ambivalent edges of the political until the end of the novel. The genre's horizon of expectations tells us that, because she is a foreigner (and on top of that a scheming woman, a femme fatale), she has to be involved in foreign sedition. Here Bernal is subverting "the convention of the treacherous girlfriend," which Palmer traces back to Dashiell Hammett's *Maltese Falcon*: "the girl [typically] works for the enemy" in thrillers.[109] Martita, nonetheless, never truly betrays García—nor is she really working for any foreign conspirers.

In this context, *El complot mongol* raises an important question: while Martita's murder can be identified as gender violence and the outcome of masculine brutality, can it be fully described as "political" like a magnicide or a coup? This is especially problematic when we (and Garcia) learn at the end of the novel that the murder was not really motivated by party politics or international affairs. Although the reception of infrapolitics has experienced "hostilities" with feminism, in Gabriela Méndez Cota's terms, it is worth noting here that the two are not necessarily at odds. Méndez Cota coins the term "infrafeminism" to propose the possible intersections between them: "asking today about the who of infrapolitics should not be exhausted in re-problematizing the masculinity of philosophy." Instead, it should "envision, in the grammar of the question, a fissure that also allows us to get out of the demand articulated by some contemporary feminisms to convert all life in politics."[110] We could read this demand as an exacerbation of the slogan coined in Hanisch's paper.

Méndez Cota develops her notion of infrafeminism within the Mexican context in particular but also more broadly in conversation with the North American context. Nevertheless, her work resonates with Alexandra Kohan, in an Argentine context not necessarily linked to infrapolitics but with strong echoes of their views of some contemporary feminisms. Kohan claims that "if everything is political, then nothing is."[111] Both Méndez Cota and Kohan are accentuating that at present some feminisms have contributed to hyper-politicization, neglecting the threshold that divides life from the political.

To be sure, Hanisch's text had a distinct purpose: to counter "the criticism of women getting together in consciousness-raising groups to discuss their own oppression as . . . 'personal therapy'—and certainly 'not political,'" as she reflects in a new introduction (published in 2006) to her original piece. In the 1960s, Hanisch says, "both men and women . . . belittled" women "for trying to bring our so-called 'personal problems' into the public arena—especially 'all those body issues' like sex, appearance, and abortion."[112] More than half a century later, the resistance to including or preserving, say, abortion in the political agenda is evidently present in Latin America and beyond. In the 2010s context in which Méndez Cota and Kohan were writing, however, it would be hard to deny that these issues have been considered part of the political for decades (even for those who reject them), with a growing history of feminist movements that constantly bring them back to the fore—however successfully or ephemerally.

What is at stake in Martita's infrapolitical murder is that it emphasizes the existence of a remainder, located on the outskirts of the political. Such emphasis precedes any political viewpoint, as Moreiras claims, to favor what is "always already beforehand an ethical perspective," a reaction against "the suspension of ethics" that any murder (political or not) involves.[113] It is in these terms that John Kraniauskas defines García's quest for justice as an "ethical turn," common to "most thrillers."[114] Through Martita, García certainly intervenes in the political. Far from understanding it as an apolitical cynical tale, then, *El complot mongol* should be read more as an infrapolitical thriller, whose hero personifies what Moreiras calls an "ethical stance,"[115] or, more recently, the "savage moralism" he ascribes to Marlowe:[116] godless ethics, an anarchic, visceral impulse against the thanatotic hyper-politicization of life that the political thriller is so keen to constantly bring back.

INFRAPOLITICS AND HYPER-POLITICIZATION

For some critics, the investigative or "crusading" reporter is one of the most common heroes in European and American political thrillers. As such, reporters inherit, blend, and update the figures of the sleuth and the secret agent of the detective and spy thrillers.[117] For others, such as Castrillo and Echart, more important than the hero's profession is being "always in a position of inferiority with regards to knowledge."[118] What these heroes may often have in common, I might add, is their condition of being civilians within a hyper-politicized context of political and military warfare. As a civilian who remains at the limits of the political, the genre hero is often the recipient and embodiment of the infrapolitical stance against specific types of politics, as I explain later.

Along with journalists, human rights lawyers often occupy this heroic position in the Latin American political thriller. Even though García is far from being either, Bernal's hit man still personifies this ethical stance. This is because he eventually sides with one of the conflicting forces at stake in a genre in which "there is ethics on the one hand and a desire for power on the other," as Moreiras notes.[119] Here Moreiras is following Immanuel Kant's opposed pairs: the "moral politician" and the "political moralist." According to Kant, the latter begins where the former ends: the moral politician "understands the principles of statesmanship [that] do not conflict with morals." Political moralists, by contrast, lack "such a system of ethics," and their politics are constantly interfering with morals.[120] Simply put, the moral politician stands for ethics; the political moralist represents power for power's sake.

Kant uses these two discrete categories to throw light on "the disagreement between morals and politics." To illustrate, he turns to the Roman myths of Terminus and Jupiter. Whereas Terminus is the god of boundary markers, Jupiter is the king of the gods, the personification of absolute power. Kant notes that "the Terminus of morals does not yield to Jupiter," whom he equates instead with "the false advocates of the mighty of the earth."[121] In this context, Terminus could be read as the infrapolitical threshold of Jupiter, who, in turn, personifies hyper-politicization, a force that is constantly aiming to invade, pierce, or (for the purposes of the discussion of the genre studied here) thrill life.

Multiple examples of this threshold between what is political and what is not can be found in the thriller tradition, even before the emergence of the political thriller. For instance, Hitchcock's *The Man Who Knew Too Much* (1934) presents the main character with a dilemma: keeping silent over a magnicide with international consequences to protect his kidnapped daughter or reporting it to the authorities to avoid the murder of other people who have no family ties with him. While they expose to what extent politics and life are, in fact, interwoven, political thrillers at the same time insist on emphasizing that a dividing line separates the political and what is not political, the region or spatial remainder that power cannot fully colonize: infrapolitical life.

García becomes ethical—or, rather, savagely moral—precisely because of his distancing from the unethical postrevolutionary politics, the plotters' acritical desire for power for power's sake. In García's own words, the "revolution" that "wears white gloves" is the one that (he thinks) has caused "one death too many."[122] Braham locates this ethical dimension in García's "painful conversion from a mercenary serving all masters, to a man with a conscience,"[123] which reminds us of Lamb's trajectory in *The Purple Land* (discussed in chapter 1). Moreiras comments on García's restitutive final actions: "love, in a thriller, is never simply a pathological affect, but always already an ethical allegory of the moral law."[124] Unlike Sánchez's contention, then, the hit man's vengeful killings of the statesmen are far from being a mere product of selfish love for Martita. Instead, they should be read as an ethical reaction against power for power's sake, an infrapolitical intervention in the political, the return of the bureaucratically repressed savage moralism of the revolution.

It is worth remembering that 1969 is not only the year of the publication of *El complot mongol* and the writing of "The Personal Is Political." It is also the release date of one of the most critically acclaimed political thriller films in the genre's history, *Z*, Costa-Gavras's filmic reelaboration of a real magnicide, the assassination of the Greek politician Grigoris Lambrakis.[125] Bernal and Costa-Gavras share quite a few things. After all, the genealogy of Latin American political thrillers inaugurated by *El complot mongol* features what for Derry is Costa-Gavras's main subtext, as seen in *Z* or even in later thrillers, such as *The Confession* (1970) and *État de siège* (1972): "governments . . . engag[ing] in conspiracies in order to propagate their own power."[126] Nevertheless, the ways in which both Costa-Gavras and Bernal arrive at this conclusion could not differ more.

To begin with, because "all films are political," according to Costa-Gavras, "There is politics in everything, and in all movies. And we can analyze all films politically."[127] Other important filmmakers such as Wim Wenders have reproduced Costa-Gavras's idea, adding not only that "every film is political" but that "most political of all are those that pretend not to be: 'entertainment' movies . . . because they dismiss the possibility of change . . . they are a continual advertisement for things as they are." Somewhat contradicting his own words, Wenders excludes his neo-noir film *The American Friend* (1977), which, he claims, is "entertainment and it's exciting. But it doesn't affirm the status quo."[128] Wenders does not discuss the political thriller per se, but it is evident that as a type of "entertainment movie" the genre's position would be problematic: it sometimes upholds the status quo even when it aims to produce criticism of political events.

Both filmmakers are ultimately rehashing an older idea here, which George Orwell applied to literature in 1946: "no book is genuinely free from political bias. The opinion that art should have nothing to do with politics is itself a political attitude."[129] Even though part of what these maxims affirm is true, they approach literature and film through a normative lens that updates Plato's demand for *poiesis* (what we now understand as "fiction") to forcefully remain within the boundaries of the polis or else face the risk of being banned from it. The political thriller problematizes these hasty maxims by offering what Moreiras elsewhere calls "infrapolitical distance."[130] Put differently, political thrillers portray stories in which characters stride away from the polis (understood here in its dual meaning of the city and the political) and hyper-politicization of art and life. In fact, they very much actively resist it, even those thrillers that are clearly influenced by Costa-Gavras.

In short, García works as an infrapolitical character: he embodies a space without which the political is invisible. If the political had no edges, then the constitutive aspects of both the political and the personal would be lost. There would be no such thing as life or politics. Costa-Gavras's normative denial echoes a phrase pronounced at the beginning of *Distinto amanecer*, describing Mexico as "a country in which politics sweeps everything along." Perhaps what Costa-Gavras and anyone who parrots that everything (life, the personal, films, novels) is political are missing is that they end up participating in and enhancing this oppressive sweeping (however involuntarily).

After all, the seamless "identification of life and politics," as Moreiras says, "is not just an offense against life" but also "against politics, since it devalues it and reduces it, brings it down to size."[131] Bernal places García in the interstitial region of infrapolitics, inviting us not to think "against politics" but, more precisely, against political moralism. This region is not necessarily or entirely "outside of politics," but rather aligned with its contours.[132] Or at least, in the vein of Piglia's idea that serves as an epigraph for this chapter, it invites us to "conspire against conspiracies."[133]

The legacies of *El complot mongol* for the Latin American political thriller are multiple. Simpson already identified one in the late 1980s: the novel spawned "spy thrillers" in Mexican literature, such as Carlos Fuentes's *La cabeza de la hidra* (1978) and its film adaptation: *Complot petróleo* (1981) by Paul Leduc.[134] Beyond literature, García's savagely moral heroism influenced characters featured in more recent film and TV political thrillers, such as the journalist Verónica and the secret state investigator Andrés in Carlos Bolado's *Colosio* (2013) and the Tijuana municipal police officer Federico Benítez in Hiromi Kamata and Natalia Beristain's Netflix show *Historia de un crimen* (2019). All update García's ethical stance, now transplanted to portray an infrapolitical resistance against the cover-up of a real magnicide that was deeply connected to issues of continuity of power in Mexico: the assassination of PRI candidate Luis Donaldo Colosio in 1994.

Similarly, Bernal's treatment of the *dedazo* as a symptom of precarious succession is central not only to these thrillers about Colosio but also to Alfredo Gurrola's Mexican film *La sucesión* (1980), which imagines a fictional dictator from an unnamed Latin American country struggling to find an heir. Equally, the *dedazo* is an underlying anxiety in Gabriel Ripstein's Amazon Prime Video series *Un extraño enemigo* (2018), which rereads the 1968 Tlatelolco massacre, highlighting the precarious continuity of power between the *sexenios* of Gustavo Díaz Ordaz (1964–1970) and Luis Echeverría (1970–1976).

In turn, *El complot mongol* imported and laid down the foundations so that magnicide and coups would become narrative themes in Latin America. As mentioned in the introduction, they occur in the main plotlines that Derry sees for the political thriller in general. Returning to literature, we can mention Mario Vargas Llosa's forays into the political thriller in novels such as *La fiesta del chivo* (2000) and the more recent *Tiempos recios* (2019) that are rife with magnicides and coups in the Central American theater of the Cold War. We could also mention Marisol Ceh Moo's *X-Teya, u puksi'ik'al koolel* (*Teya, Heart of a Woman*, 2008), the first novel written in Yucatec and published in a bilingual edition that offers the Spanish translation: a political thriller about the assassination of a Communist politician, set in the late 1970s.

Beyond Mexico, and back on the silver screen, Bernal's legacy can be seen in Helvio Soto's *Il pleut sur Santiago* (1975), which offers a reenactment of Augusto Pinochet's 1973 coup against Salvador Allende. The invasion of the political into the personal is allegorized in the bombing of La Moneda by the military. Soto's portrayal of the attack on the presidential palace emphasizes the bullets thrilling the intimacy of the politicians inside the window, resulting in Allende's death. Decades later, Miguel Littín would re-create the coup, centering on the ousted president's perspective in *Allende en su laberinto* (2014).

In Argentina, Juan José Jusid's *Asesinato en el senado de la nación* (1984) depicts the failed attempt to assassinate progressive senator Lisandro de la Torre in 1935. Quique Aguilar's cult movie *Nada por perder* (2001) essentially includes all the motifs that are present in Bernal's novel: the hero as a swindler who ethically intervenes against the monster, personified here by a corrupt senator turned into an unscrupulous presidential candidate, and a plan to assassinate him for personal and political reasons. Similarly, Rebeca Chávez's *Ciudad en rojo* (2009), one of the few political thrillers made in Cuba, pictures the days preceding the overthrow of Fulgencio Batista. The film follows a group of young male and female students who take part in the Cuban Revolution from the streets of Santiago de Cuba (far from the bearded men of Sierra Maestra), ending in the death of virtually everyone at the end of the story. Finally, a very recent political thriller film portrays a magnicide in ways quite similar to Bernal (through precarity and deceptions): Gory Patiño and Luis Reneo's *Pseudo* (2020) foregrounds a fake plot to assassinate the Bolivian president that conceals more prosaic conspiracies.

To be sure, I do not intend to suggest that Bernal directly influenced these authors and filmmakers. In fact, his novel was a delayed cult classic, with its circulation and reception often confined within the borders of Mexico. If anything, it is most likely that other Latin Americans who forayed into the political thriller did so directly following American and European models instead. But Bernal still should be credited with initiating the appropriation of these themes that clearly became increasingly common in Latin American popular culture.

This chapter examines *El complot mongol* as the first literary political thriller in Latin America. Chapter 3 turns to the first cinematic expressions of the genre in 1970s and 1980s political films from Mexico to Argentina (including Peru), building on a trait already present in Bernal's novel: the issue of the infrapolitical in the genre, now tied to tensions between innocence and presumed guilt. Bernal's explicit influence also reappears in the last two chapters of the book. Chapter 4 discusses thrillers in which García's savage heroism and picaresque nature are reproduced in human rights lawyers and journalists who investigate state-sponsored crimes against humanity perpetrated by Southern Cone dictatorships. I center on how the figure of the *pícaro* helps us to read these genre heroes in terms of their inability to speak up to power. Chapter 5 examines how the *pícaro*'s nature, evident in García, morphs into something new: the *pícaro* in other Southern Cone political thrillers is incarnated in villainous characters, always informed by precarious secrecy.

CHAPTER THREE

Picturing the Slaughter

MASSACRES, INNOCENCE, AND THE POLITICAL

POLITICAL THRILLERS HAVE A SOFT SPOT FOR INNOCENCE. The last part of chapter 2 examines *El complot mongol*'s dénouement, with the political and ethical implications of Martita's murder. Her death is perhaps the only one that causes the *pistolero* García real grief. As John Kraniauskas notes, "death takes on a political dimension" in Bernal's novel.[1] This is especially true for Martita's gratuitous death, which is not intrinsically caused by politics but results in a "political dimension." Even though she is not murdered in retaliation for political involvement, her death becomes political because it triggers García to stop the coup. In this context, her death speaks to a problematization of innocence in regard to the political, which would become all-pervasive in Latin America beyond Bernal. This is especially true for the series of films examined in this chapter, which depict mass murders of civilians in Argentina, Mexico, and Peru.

I read the following films in terms of a judicial and cultural category proposed by human rights scholar Inés González Bombal: the "hyper-victim." Bombal uses the word to describe a peculiar kind of casualty of state-sponsored dictatorial violence in Argentina: the children, teenagers, pregnant women, and elderly people who were kidnapped, tortured, forcibly disappeared, and murdered during the 1976–1983 dictatorship.[2] In other words, these civilians were socially perceived in terms of absolute defenselessness. The hyper-victim became a binding figure of consensus in postdictatorial times (especially in the 1980s), legitimizing human rights movements across the political spectrum. The inadmissible crimes against hyper-victims exposed the Argentine dictatorship's cruelty beyond any political agenda. It showed that the junta's political rationale, with its frequent invocations of the dictatorship's "war against subversion," did not suffice to explain the state's treatment of its people.

Bombal, however, laments that the popularization of the idea of hyper-victims resulted in downplaying the political identity of many casualties of the dictatorship: guerrillas, left-wing Peronist or Communist activists, union leaders, and others.[3] Innocence, then, is perceived to be inversely proportional to political involvement: after all, a child or a baby could hardly be held responsible for "subversion" or armed struggle. Transplanted to a different context, Martita, in *El complot mongol,* is also a hyper-victim. Building on Bombal, historian Sandra Raggio examines the cinematic representation of hyper-victims. She traces it to 1980s political dramas portraying Argentina's last dictatorship. Raggio notes that these films emphasize the military's radical evil in the treatment of hyper-victims, whose innocence was always self-evident. It was one thing for Argentine postdictatorial society to watch explicit scenes of the military punishing guerrillas (who were overwhelmingly politicized adult males), but a very different thing to see the misappropriation of children kidnapped from their disappeared mothers or the torture of unarmed adolescents, whose sole political involvement was to have demonstrated for cheaper student bus tickets, as portrayed in *La historia oficial* and *La noche de los lápices*, respectively.[4]

Raggio notes that the aim of representing hyper-victims in mainstream culture was to emphasize the comprehensive scope of dictatorial brutality against society as a whole. But this also came with the same negative by-product that Bombal sees in the narrative of human rights movements: obscuring the "political belonging" of many desaparecidos, especially those linked to the armed struggle. The overrepresentation of hyper-victims sanitizes and oversimplifies historical conflicts by depoliticizing the desaparecidos: "innocence . . . became synonymous with apoliticism."[5] At the same time, the opposite is also true: presumption of guilt arises from and is lumped together with the victim's involvement in politics. From the dictatorship's perspective, ideology did not really matter that much: guerrillas or not, massacred people were equalized by state-sponsored violence.

Postdictatorial Argentine political thrillers partially follow this trend that Raggio traces in political dramas. Rafael Filipelli's *Hay unos tipos abajo* (1985), for instance, is about a depoliticized middle-class man who becomes paranoid about being surveilled by the dictatorship.[6] Perhaps the 1980s predilection for hyper-victims explains why Argentine political thrillers depicting guerrillas only started appearing more prominently in the 2010s. The decline of Argentine New Cinema films (and their general pretense of not being involved in explicit politics) along with the three decades of postdictatorship brought a historical distance that restored the political identity of the desaparecidos. This can be seen in Filipelli's own *Secuestro y muerte* (2010), in Benjamín Ávila's *Infancia clandestina* (2012), and in Diego Corsini's *Pasaje de vida* (2015), all of which include main characters belonging to the left-wing Peronist urban guerrilla Montoneros. Ávila's film, however, has the distinctive feature of combining the figure of the politicized character with the hyper-victim in the story's protagonist: Juan, a child whose parents are Montoneros and are brutally killed at the end of the film.[7] I return to those films about guerrillas in chapter 4.

The four political thrillers examined in this chapter, however, complicate such tensions between the hyper-victims' innocence and the political by focusing on the figure of the civilian as a victim. Political scientist Benjamin Valentino notes that the vast majority of casualties of political violence throughout the twentieth century, across the globe, were civilians. In addition, he claims that "political violence against civilians most often occurs in the context of armed conflicts involving military organizations."[8] The civilian as a victim echoes what sociologists Gabriel Gatti and María Martínez have called *el ciudadano-víctima*: unlike the traditional understanding of victimhood, which implied a loss of citizenship, they argue that the citizen-victim emerges as the product of discourses concerning state-sponsored terrorism.[9] All of this could partially explain why the civilian is such a central character in the genre's history in Latin America, a region that was largely militarized throughout the twentieth century.

In the thrillers examined here, however, the massacred civilians are not necessarily innocent hyper-victims from the onset. Instead, they are presumed to be guilty by their executioners, regardless of their gender, age, political inclination, or degree of involvement in the armed struggle. In other words, these films portray presumption of guilt as something that goes beyond discrete sociopolitical and ideological identities: all the casualties of political violence are turned into defenseless hyper-victims irrespective of their origin.

In deemphasizing the political ideas of the victims of massacres, these films are not suggesting that it is not possible to be politicized and also innocent or that rebelling against the dictatorial state was not legitimate. They are instead arguing that being politicized is not really at stake or at least that politicization and political ideas do not fully explain state-sponsored violence. The blending of innocents and civilians in these thrillers also tells us something else. According to the genre's horizon of expectations, innocence is based on the extent to which a civilian casualty is positioned inside or outside of the political. Hence innocence brings to the fore the contours of the political. Innocence underlines that the political has boundaries. The foregrounding of the narratives of civilian casualties in these thrillers can be explained in similar ways: civilians accentuate the existence of something outside of the political, which is circumscribed in these thrillers by the strife that pits members of the military against each other or against guerrillas.

As such, this cluster of films often equates the hyper-politicization of the state with hyper-politicization of activism (though not always and not to the same degree, as I detail later). For some of these films, they are essentially the same, turning the political into a Schmittian world of friends and enemies. Chapter 4 examines different clusters that I call "guerrilla thrillers" and "human rights thrillers." In these films the hyper-politicization of guerrillas and political activism more broadly is treated in a more differentiated way. They avoid the dichotomy that equates the two sides of political violence, which in Argentina is often called the "theory of the two demons."

This chapter explores how these thrillers engage with other oppositions, such as interiority and exteriority, darkness and light, and the affective invasion of the personal by the political, which pierces through life from the outside to the inside. "Invasion," after all, is etymologically linked to both violence and interiority.[10] Through the genre's grammar of secrecy and its preposition of space, I argue that these political thrillers picture slaughters through these oppositions not because they aim to depoliticize historical events, their witnesses, or their main actors. They do so because they want to highlight the destructive effects of the hyper-politicization of life, especially (though not exclusively) at the hands of unethical states.

MASSACRES AND THE POLITICAL THRILLER

In this chapter I examine four political thrillers that deal with mass killings: Jorge Cedrón's *Operación masacre* (Argentina, 1973), Felipe Cazals's *Canoa* (Mexico, 1976), Jorge Fons's *Rojo amanecer* (Mexico, 1989), and Francisco Lombardi's *La boca del lobo* (Peru, 1988).[11] The first two were produced and released in the 1970s, before the last Argentine dictatorship and the concept of hyper-victim it produced in the 1980s. The last two were made at the end of that decade, but in different national contexts (Mexico and Peru).

It is important to stress that these contexts should not be too easily conflated. Set in 1956, *Operación masacre* was produced in secret and circulated only in clandestine circles at the end of the 1966–1973 dictatorship and was commercially released during democratic times, in September 1973. Argentina was then in the middle of a series of intermittent dictatorships: there were only three brief democratic periods from 1955 until 1983 that amount to less than ten years: 1958–March 1962, October 1963–1966, and 1973–1976. To make things worse, the last of them, defined by Juan Domingo Perón's last administration, was still rife with state-sponsored violence as well as urban and rural guerrilla warfare, serving as a prelude to the even crueler 1976–1983 dictatorship.

Both *Canoa* and *Rojo amanecer* are set in 1968 in Mexico, but they were shot in different historical moments. *Canoa* was filmed in the mid-1970s, when Mexicans were experiencing blatant disillusionment with the post-revolutionary one-party democratic order (as we have seen in *El complot mongol*), which triggered the emergence of politicized student movements and guerrilla warfare. Between the *sexenios* of PRI presidents Gustavo Díaz Ordaz (1964–1970) and Luis Echeverría (1970–1976), the Mexican population endured political authoritarianism and massive killings, such as the Tlatelolco massacre (1968) and the Halconazo (1971). *Rojo amanecer* was filmed and premiered much later, in the late 1980s, at a time of relative softening of censorship but still under PRI rule.

Peru, in turn, experimented with a mix of left-leaning (Juan Velasco Alvarado, 1968–1975) and right-leaning (Francisco Morales Bermúdez, 1975–1980) dictatorships. As Beasley-Murray reminds us, the country's "experience of authoritarianism differs from that of Southern Cone countries" and its "post-dictatorship has been anomalous."[12] The military in Argentina, Uruguay, Brazil, and Bolivia, after having defeated guerrillas through genocidal practices, would gradually transition to democracy in the early 1980s. Peru's case is somewhat out of phase when compared to these other countries: it was defined by the emergence of its own Maoist guerrilla group, Sendero Luminoso. Therefore, Peruvian democratic administrations through the 1980s still featured state-sponsored violence against their own population. Set in 1983, at the beginning of the country's dirty war, *La boca del lobo* was released in 1988, at the peak of the conflict during Alan García's first tenure (1985–1990).

Adding nuance to the distinctions between political filmmaking in Mexico and the Southern Cone in the 1970s, Sánchez Prado notes that filmmakers under dictatorial regimes were typically opposed to and outside of the state, while their Mexican counterparts such as Cazals paradoxically criticized the state that enabled and even funded *Canoa*.[13] Lombardi worked against and outside of the state in democratic Peru but was not persecuted as much as his Southern Cone colleagues, although his film was not well received by the military. Censorship, then, had an uneven degree of intensity in each of these national contexts. Whereas in Mexico it was "semi-soft," involving "review . . . and pressure on filmmakers," in the dictatorial Southern Cone it included "outright bans or persecution," in Sánchez-Prado's words.[14] To a large extent, the military had a say in the different degrees of censorship in *Canoa*, *Rojo amanecer*, and *La boca del lobo*, making the portrayal of the respective national armies a crucial element in the fate of the films. Most critics believe that *Canoa* was possible only because it absolved and to an extent ended up extolling the military.[15]

By contrast, *Rojo amanecer* had to exclude the film's final scene (among others), with footage that explicitly depicted the army in the streets after Tlatelolco.[16] *La boca del lobo* is the only one of the four films that put the military on center stage, subtly criticizing its brutality toward Indigenous communities. As Jorge Valdez Morgan mentions, Lombardi managed to do so because "it is not clear" in the film whether the perpetrators "are members of the army or the police, as their outfits and means of transportation are the same."[17] It was this ambiguity that enabled the film's "eventual acceptance by the state," as Sarah Barrow claims.[18] Even though military leaders still attempted to censor the film and managed to change its title, they did not try to ban it altogether.[19]

The mass-killing shown in *Operación masacre* is perpetrated not by the military but by the police within a military dictatorship. Gloria Zarco sees the 1973–1976 democratic Peronist interlude (when Cedrón's film was released) as a brief "truce" in terms of censorship.[20] But the filmmaker still had to tone down what could have come across as a positive portrayal of the armed struggle: although Perón had previously toyed with Montoneros to gain support for his return to power in 1973, the guerrillas were no longer accepted by the time his third tenure started.[21]

With these caveats in mind, it is still possible to place all these films under the same umbrella. They share many elements, while each introduces a unique variant in the treatment of innocence and the political, interiority and exteriority, darkness and light. Despite the films' divergent national peculiarities, they all represent periods of political turmoil associated in one way or another with domestic reverberations of the Cold War. The massacres portrayed in these thrillers (except for *Operación masacre*) share a democratic context, however precarious this might be. In addition, by portraying massacres of innocent civilians, all these films aim to denounce the state for committing these crimes or, in the case of *Canoa*, for fueling them. Moreover, all the real massacres portrayed in the films had survivors who brought the stories to light.

All these thrillers were shot in secret due to the aforementioned concerns over censorship, with the exception of *Canoa*, which still had to negotiate how to provide a criticism of the state within the boundaries of what was possible. Finally, in one way or another, they were all received as unprecedented, seminal works that influenced future productions, creating a watershed in the representation of the political within their corresponding national contexts.[22]

According to Thomas Schatz, film genres experience a natural "life span." He applies art historian Henri Focillon's four stages to genres: experimentation, classicism, refinement, and baroque.[23] When experimentations are successful (and are reproduced in subsequent films), tentative ingredients eventually crystallize in recognizable, stable conventions at the classicist stage. It is important to note that Schatz establishes this classification with Hollywood productions in mind. These stages, however, can be still traced in the case of film genres exported to other national contexts. In these terms, we can say that these four films are among the first local examples of the genre in their own respective countries. As such, they are all part of the experimental stage of the Latin American political thriller, featuring formal and thematic explorations of genre conventions.

Perhaps because the genre was not yet so easily identifiable as it is today, most critics did not read these films as political thrillers. Instead, they viewed them as documentaries, as "political cinema," or in similar broad categories. As I show later, these films experiment with and establish genre conventions in complex ways: they either embed documentary footage and style or use suspense to talk about key political events, becoming at least a local foray or—better—an appropriation, an *acriollamiento* of the genre.

OPERACIÓN MASACRE (1973)

From Nonfiction to Experimenting with the Political Thriller

The tension between innocence and the political in Latin American political films starts before the 1980s when the concept of hyper-victim appears in Argentine public discourse. It is already at stake in Jorge Cedrón's *Operación masacre*, an adaptation of Rodolfo Walsh's 1957 book. With Raymundo Gleyzer's *Los traidores* (released clandestinely only a few weeks afterward), it was one of the first films that turned to fiction to narrate recent political events within the circle of Third Cinema and Argentine *cine militante*, which were predominantly focused on documentaries.[24]

For Daniel Link, Walsh's book "destabilizes literary genres."[25] Similarly, the adaptation (co-written by Cedrón and Walsh himself) turns film history in Latin America upside down by becoming one of the foundational political thrillers in the region. The process that Cedrón and Walsh followed to turn the book into a film is not as straightforward as the more common adaptation of literary fiction for the silver screen. To begin with, Walsh published his original work first as a series of journalistic articles and then as an *avant la lettre* nonfiction novel.[26] This poses formal challenges that speak to the conventions of political thrillers: how should a nonfiction text that talks about a historical and political event be represented on-screen?

Much like *Los traidores*, some of the first scenes of *Operación masacre* engage with an important convention of the political thriller: embedding historical found footage into the narrative. Whereas these films are perhaps the first to do so in Latin American renditions of the genre, it had been done in 1960s political thrillers set in the region, such as R. G. Springsteen's *Operation Eichmann* (1961) and Alfred Hitchcock's *Topaz* (1969), which, respectively, include historical found footage of the Shoah and cameo appearances by Fidel Castro and Che Guevara. In turn, Cedrón embeds footage that takes us back to the mid-1950s, the period in which Walsh's book was published.

In fact, *Operación masacre* and *Los traidores* both start with different footage from the very same event: a state-sponsored political massacre at the hands of the military, the 1955 bombing of Plaza de Mayo. As the voice-over narration reminds us, the bombing was aimed at innocent civilians who were demonstrating in support of reelected president Juan Perón. The massacre, which caused hundreds of casualties, is widely understood as a prelude for the 1955–1958 dictatorship that would oust Perón three months later.

The footage of the bombing in *Los traidores* provides background to the rise and fall of Peronist union leader Roberto Barrera (a fictional composite of real *sindicalistas* such as Timoteo Vandor, José Ignacio Rucci, and Lorenzo Miguel).[27] Barrera pretends he has been kidnapped to obtain political gain, much like the fanciful conspiracies we see in Mexican political thrillers such as *La sombra del caudillo* and *El complot mongol*. *Los traidores* follows Barrera's life from the mid-1950s until his assassination in the 1970s.

By contrast, in *Operación masacre*, the 1955 bombings mirror and introduce the story of another mass killing. Set one year after the coup, Cedrón's film depicts the secret execution of twelve men at the hands of the police, which took place in the dumping ground of José León Suárez, on the outskirts of Buenos Aires, in 1956. The execution happened in the context of a failed Peronist countercoup against the dictatorship. The thwarted rebellion was led by Juan José Valle, an army general loyal to Perón, who was seeking to restore Peronismo and its 1949 constitution (among other demands), all of which had been made illegal by the dictatorship. Led by then president General Pedro Eugenio Aramburu and vice president Admiral Isaac Rojas, the dictatorship quickly defeated the countercoup, publicly executing Valle and another fifteen rebellious military men.

Like the other films examined here, *Operación masacre* was mostly not read as a political thriller.[28] Scholarly critics tended to use vaguer definitions such as "political film that blends fiction with documentary."[29] Victoria García, for instance, considers it an outright "cinematographic documentary," despite the fact that most of the film features a dramatized narrative with characters and dialogue. García admits that the film reproduces an "array of genre films" but never details which genres.[30]

In spite of this, in addition to including historical found footage, Cedrón starts, punctuates, and closes the film with original ingredients that point to the political thriller's cachet of authenticity. The film fits comfortably into Derry's definition of the genre: it reveals the "essential conspiratorial nature of governments and their crimes against their people."[31] But unlike, say, Costa-Gavras's *Z* (1969), which premiered only four years earlier, and Julio Bracho's *La sombra del caudillo* (1960), Cedrón does so without focusing on the main political actors—Valle, Aramburu, and Rojas. In reconstructing the event, the film (much like the book) does not pay attention to the way the countercoup was plotted and how it was averted. By contrast, *Operación masacre* foregrounds the separate mass-killing of these twelve working-class men. In other words, it stresses the secret murders of civilians, not the public execution of military men.

If *Operación masacre* could be associated with any Costa-Gavras political thriller, it is *The Confession* (1970), the story of a public servant who is tortured, imprisoned, and condemned for treason in Communist Czechoslovakia, even though he always remained loyal to his government. Like Costa-Gavras, Cedrón foregrounds how the state imposes upon innocent civilians a presumption of guilt that would not come unstuck, regardless of the casualties' actual political inclinations.

The irrelevance of political identity in Cedrón's film stems from the fact that some of the victims of Operación Masacre were Peronist activists—but, crucially, not all. To be sure, many of the soon-to-be-executed men would enthusiastically have welcomed a successful Peronist countercoup. Strictly speaking, however, not all of them were actively participating in it, at least not in the same way that Valle and his colleagues did. Being civilians, the executed men are in a different, much more marginal position in regard to the political than the military men involved in the coup.

Much like the fanciful coup that we see in *El complot mongol*, the real extrajudicial secret execution of these men at the hands of the police in 1956 was also a botched job, as more than half of the victims managed to escape. Some eventually disclosed their testimony to Walsh, who brought it to light in his writing. It is in this context that Link mentions Walsh's "fascination with using genres from popular culture."[32] His nonfiction novel is informed by structures taken from genre fiction, especially the detective thriller, which has a special relation with secrecy (as I discuss in the introduction, following Piglia).[33] Unlike the book, however, the film (grounded in anti-imperialist filmmaking) has a more complex relationship with Hollywood conventions. For instance, it does not feature Walsh as the story's narrator or turn him into a journalist-hero who extracts secrets (the state-sponsored clandestine massacre and its cover-up) from the depths.

Instead, the film's narrator is Julio Troxler, one of the actual surviving victims of the 1956 massacre. Through a voice-over, Troxler situates the event in the broader context of the Peronist resistance. But to complicate things even further, he also plays two other prominent roles in the film: he portrays himself in the narrative reconstruction of the events and opens the film by speaking directly to the camera, as if he is going to play the role of an interviewee or commentator in a documentary about the massacre.

Despite this radical difference, the emphases of the book and the film are aligned: they are both concerned with the way these men were executed, which makes us think of the tension between innocence and the political. Even though these twelve men were not hyper-victims (they were all adult males), the film shows us very clearly how the state puts them in a similar position of defenselessness, regardless of their political involvement. Walsh himself had an ambivalent relation with the Peronist armed struggle during the 1970s, when the film was being made. As Silvana Flores says, he was always less interested in "extolling violence and death as instruments" for revolutionary purposes than in exposing how state-sponsored political crimes against humanity always target innocent civilians first.[34]

For Victoria García, Jorge Locane, and Silvia Schwarzböck, Walsh's emphasis on the victims of the massacre beyond their political affiliation is more explicit in the book. In contrast, Cedrón's film brings a more Peronist perspective than in the original story.[35] Locane explains this difference by reminding us that the situation was different by the time the film was produced than it had been in 1956, as Montoneros had executed Aramburu in 1970 in response to Operación Masacre.[36] This is also evident in the way the film puts Troxler literally on center stage. The book instead emphasizes another important survivor: Carlos Livraga, who, unlike Troxler, was not a Peronist activist and was not even aware of the countercoup.

Livraga is central in the book. Walsh starts with a line that cites him, which would resonate for decades in Argentine culture: *Hay un fusilado que vive* (There is an executed man who lives),[37] someone who is ready to reveal the covert operation. The original sentence is left untranslated in the English edition of Walsh's book to reflect the unsettling oddness of such a situation: executed people obviously do not often survive. It is Livraga's testimony that triggers the book. Even though he is not as important in the film, the line that alludes to him is central to the political thriller. Livraga serves as a specter that would eventually haunt many Latin American renditions of the genre. In this sense, the line in Walsh's 1957 book foretells Costa-Gavras's canonical political thriller *Z*, a Greek tag in graffiti that literally means "he lives." It alludes to Greek politician Grigoris Lambrakis (assassinated by the Far Right six months before John F. Kennedy's magnicide) and his posthumous, spectral legacy, while *un fusilado que vive* highlights the potentially transformative testimony of a surviving working-class man without any specific political affiliation.

Livraga went into exile in Los Angeles in the mid-1960s (where he still lives, in his nineties, as I write this book). Unlike Troxler, he was not residing in Argentina in the early 1970s. To a certain extent, then, García, Locane, and Schwarzböck are right to say that the film is interested in representing state-sponsored violence against a specific political identity: the Peronist resistance during Perón's exile, which started in 1955 and ended in 1973, the year *Operación masacre* premiered.[38] But it is also true that what is at stake in both the novel and the film is the detention of the soon-to-be-executed men before martial law was enacted. This exposes the dictatorship's brutality and is fundamental to understanding the tension with innocence at play, beyond Peronism.

The book's whole argumentative arc makes that point.[39] But the film still speaks to this more subtly, through soundscape and image, showing a clear continuity with the original story. It is in this sense that Anabella Castro Avelleyra notes that the film pictures the events immediately preceding the massacre by juxtaposing medium shots of a clock in the background with the sound of the radio announcement of martial law.[40] The contrast between image and sound highlights a contradiction: the detention of the twelve men happened before midnight, while martial law was supposed to be valid only after midnight. Therefore, their execution was not lawful, as Walsh never stopped repeating until he himself became a desaparecido in 1977.

From Interiority to Exteriority

I turn now to important scenes that the filmmakers chose to include in translating nonfiction to fiction. They all emphasize the casualties' innocence beyond their political identity. Some may seem to portray something trivial, even commonplace: the moments before and after the forced entry of a house. Unlike what we typically see in many police, crime, or detective thrillers, however, the scene is actually showing us that the police are not detaining but actually kidnapping workers. These scenes are different because they showcase the political as the source of the crime and the state as the murderer, not as the incarnation of the law. This type of scene would be reproduced in many Argentine political thrillers dealing with the later 1976–1983 dictatorship as the starting point of forced disappearance, from Marco Bechis's *Garage Olimpo* (1999) and Israel Adrián Caetano's *Crónica de una fuga* (2006) to Javier Torre's *El almuerzo* (2015). It would even influence political dramas such as *La noche de los lápices* (1986) and, in an allegorical scene that depicts children playing cops and robbers, *La historia oficial* (1985). Transplanted to different contexts, the Mexican and Peruvian thrillers examined later in the chapter also feature similar scenes.

Before the forced entry into the house, Cedrón and Walsh picture the soon-to-be executed men gathered inside, playing the card game *truco* and listening to a boxing match on the radio. Most of them, as Troxler reminds us, were unarmed. The critics seem not to have noticed that both the card game and the fight clearly speak to the imaginary of the political thriller. Much as the close-up shot of a chess game alludes to the political strife between generals in *La sombra del caudillo* (1960), here *truco* and boxing point to intrigue, uncertainty about which of the two factions will eventually win out: the Peronist resistance or the anti-Peronist dictatorship. As García eloquently puts it, even though the film is set in the 1950s, it also talks in a veiled manner about 1970s guerrilla warfare.[41] It is in this context that *truco* and boxing also inform the scene, with a double entendre involving politics and sports, a common convention of political thrillers. One of the men, in casual conversation, asks Pilar (the owner of the house) who she thinks is going to win the boxing match. "Everyone loses," she replies, a commonplace of the depoliticized middle class in regard to the 1970s guerrilla warfare against the militarized state.

Some of the men (those who were explicitly involved with politics) are shown as waiting for the official announcement of the countercoup to be made on the radio. As Troxler tells us, if Valle was successful, they were planning to go to Plaza de Mayo to demand Perón's return from exile. In this sense, the voice we hear coming from the radio (a precarious artifact that functions only at times) works as an aural cachet of authenticity, typical of the genre.

The police forcibly enter the house looking for General Raúl Tanco, Valle's second in charge in the countercoup. Most of the men genuinely do not know who Tanco is, but they are all nonetheless kidnapped and taken to prison—including Giunta, one of the neighbors who happened to be arriving at his house across the street. This scene, in addition to being a realistic depiction of factual events, shows the trope of the thrilling invasion of the personal by the political. The fact that the police kidnap all the men (those who know about Tanco and those who do not) lessens the importance of their political ideas. The police's forced entry in *Operación masacre* works as a metonymy for the invasion of the monster, typical of the political thriller: power for power's sake thrilling infrapolitical life—which is here represented by men listening to a boxing match, playing *truco*, and even hoping (with uneven degrees of involvement) for a better political future, encapsulated in the fall of the dictatorship.

The trespass of external agents pierces through the domestic space of the house, pointing to two clearly demarcated poles of the grammar of secrecy's prepositions of space—inside and outside—and their respective topographies: interiority and exteriority. But it does so with a subversion: whereas secrecy is typically stored indoors, there is no secret plot inside the house, only some men cheering for it to happen. If anything, secrecy is confined to exteriority: the clandestine massacre, which happens in a dumping ground, of all places. This takes us to another prominent scene, the one that opens the film. Before the found footage of the 1955 bombing and Troxler's first appearance, we see the dumping ground through a long shot. The distance between the camera and the landscape mimics the precarious secrecy of the cover-up: the long shot turns the bodies of the *fusilados* into shapes that are indistinguishable from the waste. The garbage at once camouflages and exposes the casualties. The camera immediately zooms in on the bodies. An amber light tinges the horizon, signaling the arrival of dawn after the massacre—committed, as we see later on, in the darkness of night—and hellish brimstone colors.

We are in front of a paradigmatic site of precarious secrecy, which many political thrillers would later reproduce. The garbage dump is, first of all, an obviously public space: the final destination of society's waste. It is also charged with exteriority, located in the outdoors, where no walls or roofs can contain the state secret. This landscape could best be described with a Spanish word that defies translation: *la intemperie*, an open space that connotes instances of secrecy and precarity such as isolation, abandonment, and neglect, all of which are the result of political will. But *intemperie* also implies the defenselessness that permeates the working-class men that the state hyper-victimizes, snatching away the possibility of a trial or any recourse to the law.

We would have to hark back to *La sombra del caudillo*, whose dénouement also deals with a massacre, to see a previous instance of *la intemperie*. The scene pictures the secret magnicide of General Aguilar as part of a broader massacre of military rebels that took place out in the open, on the roads of Huitzilac, a small town located about seventy kilometers south of Mexico City. Both Huitzilac and the garbage dump of José León Suárez are sites of precarious secrecy, in which clandestine murder supersedes official executions.

The dumping ground's exteriority is also geographical: it is literally placed on the margins of the polis, the periphery of Buenos Aires. The site is seemingly far away from society and politics, where dictatorial power chooses to execute its victims secretly. Here corpses would decompose and blend seamlessly with the garbage or emerge spectrally, injured and moribund, to reveal the state's precarious secret. No wonder Cedrón and Walsh chose to open the film there.

The scenes depicting the forced entry and the dumping ground point to secrecy, space, and precarity, telling us that the film connects with the genre in a unique way. It innovates not only through Troxler's threefold role but also by subverting the typical prepositions of space "inside" and "outside." Latin American political thrillers would later reproduce similar sites by foregrounding the way dictatorial power places secrecy in the most imaginable exteriority, including the Peruvian highlands, the Chilean desert, the Paraguayan woods, and the Argentine Pampas.

Presumption of Guilt and the Infrapolitical

What do we make of hyper-victims and *Operación masacre*? Raggio claims that the privileged inclusion of hyper-victims in postdictatorial political dramas has to do with trans-generational acceptability: the struggle of high-school students, as shown in films like *La noche de los lápices*, sparks a more immediate sense of identification in a broader audience. The idea of hyper-victims goes beyond the dictatorial context and can be acceptable in democratic times, as the students' "struggle is easily understandable and cannot be a matter of objections or controversies." In short, "fighting for the student ticket is more translatable to our current times than fighting for *la patria socialista* or the revolution."[42] Then how should we read the execution of the twelve men in *Operación masacre*, who were neither guerrillas nor teenagers?

One way to read *Operación masacre* today is as a celebration of left-wing Peronismo's resilience—not only the classic 1950s resistance during Perón's exile but also the movement's survival and lingering presence after his death. After all, as Locane and Sebastián Hernaiz observe, *Operación masacre* is an open text because its meanings transcend even Walsh's own forced disappearance.[43] More than half a century separates us from the film's release and almost seventy years from the actual massacre. Once legalized, Peronismo has been in power since 1983, totaling twenty-eight of the forty-two years of Argentine democracy. Whether politicians such as Mauricio Macri and Javier Milei like it or not, it is improbable that Peronismo will go away anytime soon.

Cedrón and Walsh offer Troxler as a collective political hero who embodies Peronist resistance as a whole. His assassination at the hands of the far-right Peronist death squad (the Argentine Anticommunist Alliance) in 1974 (only one year after the film) amplifies Troxler's selfless nature. He was brave enough to appear in the film, knowing all too well the risks he was taking. This type of heroism was not always well received. Ángel Rama, for instance, laments that Cedrón's film does not follow Costa-Gavras's model for the political thriller more closely, which excludes the possibility of a hero.[44] Part of what Rama dislikes about the film has to do with the way it engages with heroism. But *Operación masacre* also subverts the thriller conventions (including those established by Costa-Gavras) by placing a collective hero in a genre rife with individualistic heroes.

Beyond the celebration of Peronismo's legacies, however, *Operación masacre* can also be read today as a political thriller that goes beyond political identities to expose the unethical wielding of power for power's sake. After all, the film's collective hero is not exclusive of Peronismo: it is composed of innocent civilians who gathered one night in the wrong place at the wrong time and were seen as presumably guilty, Peronist or not. The men's innocence is independent of the political: it is located in exteriority, in the *intemperie*. Not because the film tells us that innocence depoliticizes them, but because the *fusilados*' heterogeneous degree of politicization is not sufficient to understand a slaughter perpetrated to assert sheer cruelty toward society as a whole, politicized or not. In short, *Operación masacre* can be read today, beyond its testimonial value, as further from the documentary and closer to the political thriller tradition, which renders visible the extent to which not everything is political.

CANOA (1976)

From Dictatorial Argentina to Democratic(ish) Mexico

As several critics have observed, *Operación masacre* is close to *Los traidores*.[45] Both use fiction, as noted, in a context in which documentaries and avant-garde auteur political dramas were the dominant forms to engage with the political through film. Cedrón and Gleyzer chose genre fiction (still punctuated with documentary footage and a documentary-like style) in the hope of reaching a broader audience than the one that Third Cinema documentaries had reached. These were well-documented, thoroughly researched fiction films, but fiction still. Something similar could be claimed about Felipe Cazals's *Canoa*, which premiered in 1976, only three years after the Argentine films.

For Sánchez Prado, Cazals moves closer to Gleyzer only later, with the low-budget political thriller *Bajo la metralla* (1983), in that both filmmakers work with a "minimalistic guerrilla filmmaking" and "clandestine forms."[46] Following the transnational genre's history in the region, however, the link between the Argentine and Mexican filmmakers could be traced, coincidentally or not, to the 1970s. Despite the different conditions of production, *Canoa*'s form and content are already close to *Los traidores* and perhaps even closer to *Operación masacre*.

As with Cedrón and Gleyzer, most critics noticed *Canoa*'s use of a documentary style. But they did not read this as a strategy to confer authenticity on the retelling of a historical event, in the vein of political thrillers.[47] The film, however, can also be convincingly assimilated into the genre. Cazals reproduces Cedrón's narrative strategy, this time by featuring a professional actor (Salvador Sánchez), who plays a nameless narrator also testifying about a political crime committed against civilians, albeit in a sarcastic tone. The film thus engages formally with the genre's cachet of authenticity.

Through the nameless narrator, *Canoa* subverts genre conventions in innovative ways, even when compared to Cedrón's film. Instead of merely blending the narrative with historical found footage, *Canoa* offers its own documentary-like footage, which was made ad hoc for the film. Swaying between black-and-white and color, the twenty-minute footage introduces us to San Miguel de Canoa, a town located only twelve kilometers from Puebla, at the foot of La Malinche dormant volcano. In addition, as the massacre unfolds mainly at the end of the film, Cazals uses suspense to talk about the political. Furthermore, much in the vein of the genre, the film announces spatial and chronological coordinates, with intertitles such as "16 de septiembre" and "San Miguel Canoa, 1968." Finally, *Canoa* organizes its climax around the invasion of life at the hands of the political.

The film even toys with and subverts the aesthetics of British and American film models, like James B. Harris's *The Bedford Incident* (1965) and Alan J. Pakula's *The Parallax View* (1974). *Canoa* opens with a brief isolated scene, in which two journalists have a phone conversation. One speaks from the crime scene; the other from the newsroom, where he is typing the news about a massacre. We can only see the latter and hear the former. They then essentially disappear from the film. Cazals denies the investigative plotline, led by journalists turned genre heroes. Instead, we follow the victims through a suspenseful plotline that privileges their perspective and irreversible path to a tragic fate.[48] This main narrative is punctuated with abrupt cross-editing, flashbacks, and flash-forwards. The victims are five young co-workers from the Universidad Autónoma de Puebla who decide to go hiking on La Malinche. A storm suddenly halts their outing, and they have to spend the night in Canoa. The town is hostile toward them, so they struggle to find a place to spend the night. They eventually encounter a friendly villager, who decides to host them.

Canoa is ruled by a staunch anti-Communist priest. Charles Ramírez Berg sees him as a conservative and isolationist small-town dictator,[49] yet he is also reminiscent of a villainous archetype central to the genre: the gangster of the noir political thriller. In Latin America, this villainous character is often translated as a thug with a regional reach, a strongman with political influence (informed by the traditional cacique), inaugurated by *La sombra del caudillo*. Helped by his entourage, the priest spreads a false rumor through the town's loudspeakers: the five men, the rumor goes, are actually leftist students who want to raise a black and red flag in the plaza and therefore must be stopped.

As Gema Klope-Santamaria observes, rumors "transmitted by neighbors or passersby" were often the driving force behind spontaneous public executions, which were not an isolated practice in postrevolutionary Mexico: several lynchings "took place from the 1930s to the 1950s." The church often played a central role in these massacres, as Klope-Santamaria goes on to say: "the tolling of church bells often followed" the rumors, thus "allowing neighbors to congregate and possibly participate—either as perpetrators or witnesses—in the lynching."[50] This is precisely what *Canoa* shows us, in that the priest sets the stage for a massacre to happen, as the town's mob trusts him blindly. The townspeople are viscerally affected by the leftist student movements that were developing in Mexico City at the time. The mob heads to the house of the friendly villager and lynches him for protecting and defending the five workers. They then lynch the Poblano outsiders, killing two of them and maiming one of the survivor's fingers. The massacre is not completed only because the army and the ambulances appear to stop the mob and save the day. *Canoa*, then, is the only one of the four films examined here that does not, strictly speaking, feature a state-sponsored massacre. Reading against the grain of critics, however, I hope to show how Cazals still invites us to see the mass killing as state-fueled.

From Exteriority to Interiority

The voice-over actor in *Canoa* is different from the actor we see on-screen, which further enhances the film's cachet of authenticity.[51] He describes Canoa as a liminal site, the last human border before La Malinche. In other words, he subtly announces that we are in another instance of *la intemperie*, where anything can happen and everything and everyone is precarious. In this sense, the thwarted outing to La Malinche reminds us of the genre's roots in the adventure tale, explored in chapter 1: the naïve and disoriented workers embark on a trip to a site of adventure, much like, say, Lamb in *The Purple Land*.

Maxwell and Trumpener's comment on the relation between the Uruguayan Pampas and Lamb is also true for the opposition established between the space and victims here, represented, respectively, by La Malinche/Canoa and the workers. The story's emphasis is not so much on the characters' transformation "but on the space itself as dangerous and transformative."[52] It is the threatening landscape that affects and politicizes the workers: much like Lamb in the Uruguayan civil war, they gradually become less innocent and more aware of the space's oppressive atmosphere.

Like most of the sites of adventure examined in chapter 1, Canoa's threatening landscape is twofold: natural and political. Something about it is inherently destructive. La Malinche, a volcano that has remained dormant for thousands of years, epitomizes the natural landscape, much as El Ajusco does in *La sombra del caudillo*. The improbability of eruptions makes it look like a harmless space. But La Malinche is also known as *la devoradora de hombres* (the man-eater),[53] a site of deceit, from which no escape is possible. All of this is typical in the genre's genealogy. In turn, the town's political landscape is represented by the ultraconservative, far-right Catholic lynch mob and the terrorist priest. Linked to this hellish landscape, the voice-over actor describes Canoa as a site of precarity: *lo que da la tierra no alcanza* (what the land provides is not enough). In addition, Canoa is crowded with illiterate, poor villagers, with little schooling. Like a caudillo, the priest emerges as an arbiter, a strongman who can stand above precarity.

Being part of a threshold, Canoa is marked by interiority and exteriority. Both topographies of secrecy should be understood here geopolitically. The town proper is placed within interiority. It is located inland, in a rural area perceived to be unaltered by the outside world, though, as Sánchez Prado reminds us, it is not that far from Puebla, an urban hub in central Mexico.[54] Exteriority is represented not only by Puebla but by a more spectral presence in the film: Mexico City. The capital was then linked to other countries through the imminent Olympic Games, which would take place a few weeks later, attracting "many prominent international personalities," as David William Foster reminds us.[55] Mexico City was also much more exposed to the two foreign superpowers involved in the Cold War. Although *Canoa* is very focused on an episode of domestic history, the film still features a transnational ingredient typical of thrillers: the workers' presumption of guilt in the form of covert Communist students/insurgents. Here the film is also close to *Los traidores*: both include transnational elements, however subtly, in their national stories.[56]

From the Poblano workers' perspective, the adventure at La Malinche, a tourist destination, points to exteriority. But the story slowly reveals that the volcano and the town are inseparable from interiority. This is particularly true for the host's house. His hazardous shack partially mirrors the town, like a Matryoshka doll: the town obviously contains the shack, but both are equalized as threatening, precarious sites of confinement and death. Canoa is a trap, a prison where the workers are literally thrilled, in the form of a lynching. The precarious shack only differs from the town in that it promises to be a shelter but is not adequate: it is easily pierced by the mob's machetes and axes. The close-up shots of its perforated door are the film's translation of the invasion of life by the political. *Canoa* echoes *Operación masacre* here, too: this scene reminds us of the police's forced entry scene in Cedrón's film. In addition, Cazals also introduces the tension between innocence and the political, through affect and the multitude.

From Innocence and Guilt to Affect and the Multitude

Innocence and presumption of guilt are presented in *Canoa* in terms of being inside or outside political movements. As Sánchez Prado reminds us, the film portrays "being a student" as something that "was in and of itself a form of guilt."[57] In contrast, the five lynched Poblanos were workers, which was then understood to be synonymous with innocence, because workers were not typically involved with the sixty-eight politicized student movements.

Sánchez Prado contextualizes the film within the Luis Echeverria *sexenio* (1970–1976), when Rodolfo Echeverría (the president's brother) was the director of Mexican film institutions that regulated censorship.[58] This *sexenio* featured a "degree of politicization" that was only superficial: it enabled new political liberties while also monopolizing regulation. In addition, Sánchez Prado notes that the choice of telling a story about "the innocence of the lynched men was justified by them being employees, a part of the working class that Echeverrismo wanted to recover for the state."[59] The treatment of innocence is not innocent in this film, which, let us remember, was sponsored through state funds.

Canoa, however, further complicates the tension between innocence and the political: although the workers belong to a depoliticized lower middle class, they are not entirely apolitical either. In fact, before they go on their trip, they engage in brief conversation, showing "a rather ambivalent stance regarding the students' right to demonstrate," as Sánchez Prado notes.[60] Their actual political stance, however, becomes irrelevant once they enter Canoa. As Guadalupe González Bravo observes, the workers "arouse suspicion . . . just because of their age."[61] They are all young, which, of course, is widely associated with being a student. In other words, they are killed not because of anything they say or do but just because of something deeply connected to affect: their looks, the first impressions set up right after their encounter with the villagers.

In the same way that Cedrón highlights how the massacre renders being outside or inside of Peronismo irrelevant, *Canoa* makes being outside or inside the student movements insignificant: in lynching the workers, after all, the mob does not really care about distinguishing between students and workers. Here, too, both the invasion and the massacre have less to do with political ideas than with affect. It is no coincidence that Deleuze and Guattari precisely define affect as a thrilling intensity: moving through space, from exteriority to interiority, affect "transpierce[s] the body like arrows."[62] This is why the mob does not even care to listen to the workers' words that would explain their true reasons for being in the town that night—or their opinion about the student movement, for that matter. By explicitly showing us how presumption of the guilt of the victims and their punishment have already been determined beforehand (viscerally, not ideologically), *Canoa* offers a critique of terror arising from affect rather than from political ideas.

The thrilling invasion of life at the hands of the political in these films is as inseparable from affect and the body as it is from violence and death. We can clearly see this in the close-up of the axe trespassing the door and the many naturalistic shots portraying the brutal treatment of the victims' bodies, including the worker's maimed fingers.

Unlike other Latin American political thrillers, here the militarized state does not play the role of the genre monster. Instead, the political as the monster in *Canoa* is encapsulated in the lynch mob, which we could read through Beasley-Murray's definition of a "bad multitude": "a truly monstrous and corrupt figure of devastation and destruction."[63] Multitudes, structured by affect, are rife with ambivalence.[64] Whereas multitudes are always perceived to be bad in the eyes of constituted power, the constituted power (embodied by the priest) in *Canoa* embraces the bad multitude.

As the workers' political ideas are rendered irrelevant in the lynching, the bad multitude itself also does not really express political ideas about student movements. The mob only secretes pure terror, which Beasley-Murray defines as "affect at fever pitch." Both multitude and affect are defined by contact and encounters between bodies.[65] The scene of the invasion of the shack also depicts the encounter between the lynch mob and its victims, the moment in which negative affect is unleashed, thrusting onto the defenseless, innocent civilians the status of presumed guilt that, again, will not come unstuck. During the encounter, a close-up shows the family of the killed host, focusing on one of the now orphaned children, inconsolably crying and screaming. As the scene reminds us, even when films like *Operación masacre* and *Canoa* foreground the killing of adult males, there are always hyper-victims surrounding them, whether they are on-screen or not. This takes us to the issue of visibility and invisibility and its contiguous opposing topographies of secrecy: darkness and light.

Darkness and Light: From Canoa to Tlatelolco

In addition to exteriority and interiority, the film also makes use of another opposing topography of secrecy: darkness and light. The scene that immediately precedes the lynching is an example. Shot outdoors and at night, it shows the mob marching toward the host's shack. The scene is illuminated almost exclusively by the church's outdoor lighting and, significantly, the lynch mob's torches.[66]

Aesthetically, the contrast between darkness and light points to the chiaroscuro typical of embryonic political thrillers from the 1940s film noir period that the 1970s productions were reflecting. We need only think of the dark parking-lot scenes that show and hide the silhouette of Deep Throat in *All the President's Men*, a film released only a few weeks after *Canoa*. Darkness contains and conceals secrecy, which the hero's investigative efforts typically bring to light.

But darkness and light also point to melodramatic and biblical Manichean imagery of good and evil, preached by the town's priest. As Bible scholar Elizabeth Achtemeier reminds us, "throughout the Old Testament, light is continually associated with God and his word, with salvation, with goodness, with truth," and, perhaps the most important here, "with life."[67] But in this scene it is the torches that carry light, which immediately reminds us of the opposite of life: the Inquisition, which condemned supposed heretics to death according to criteria disturbingly similar to the ones the mob follows in the lynching. Cazals subverts darkness and light, in that light brings damnation, evil, and death. Equally, the lynching in and of itself is based on *chismes* (false rumors), the opposite of truths, much like those that triggered the fictional conspiracy in *El complot mongol*.

The instigator, the lying priest, is portrayed through a combination of darkness and interiority: as the massacre erupts, he remains safe and sound inside the dimly lit church. Darkness is resignified here in political terms, with the grammar of secrecy's prepositions of space "ahead" and "behind," pointing, respectively, to what is visible and invisible. The priest literally operates in the dark, almost invisibly, behind a black veil. This veil has different iterations. Several times we see him as if hiding behind his black soutane or his black suit. But the most prominent black veil is his dark sunglasses, which allow the priest to remain in obscurity throughout the film: we never fully see his face.

Moreover, the priest's darkness is linked to the issue of interiority and exteriority of the state. He is not part of the government, so there is consensus among critics that he exonerates the state. Ramírez Berg, for instance, calls him "a handy scapegoat." He even goes so far as to say that by "appearing to attack the system" *Canoa* "becomes yet another political film promoting the status quo," much like the representation of the state in classical Mexican cinema.[68] Similarly, Sánchez Prado notes that *Canoa* "did not challenge state authority directly";[69] in fact, it presented the state as the hero, the Mexican population's only defense in the face of "rural obscurantism."[70] In this sense, the state, by stopping the massacre, becomes an agent of light of sorts, defeating the darkness associated with the countryside.

This criticism of the film arises from the fact that it tangentially (or "metaphorically," in Juan J. Rojo's terms) talks about larger-scale killing of civilians in Mexico City,[71] this time by the state itself: the Tlatelolco massacre. At the end of *Canoa*, the state captures the multitude and its intensely negative affect only partially and temporarily. Tlatelolco's affective multitude was just around the corner. In fact, the two massacres were separated by only two weeks. The link between them goes beyond chronological proximity: both were extrajudicial executions of civilians who were presumed to be guilty beforehand. But *Canoa*'s relation to the Tlatelolco massacre is problematic: following the opposition between darkness and light, Cazals obscures the role of the state behind Tlatelolco.

As John Mraz points out, the film portrays a "Tlatelolco turned inside out and standing on its head": whereas it was the army that massacred civilians in the Plaza de las Tres Culturas, *Canoa* emphasizes that the army actually saves at least some of the civilians' lives, as noted.[72] In fact, both Mraz and González Bravo even go as far as to claim that it was the very dénouement that made the film possible.[73] Again, the film's treatment of innocence is not innocent.

But it is important to remember that Cazals was treading on eggshells. President Echeverría was the secretary of the interior when the Tlatelolco events happened, during the previous *sexenio* of Díaz Ordaz (1964–1970). Echeverría's legacy was widely associated with the massacre. As Sanchez Prado notes, by stressing that "the lynched men are not students but university employees," *Canoa* absolves not only the state but also its head, Echeverría.[74]

Nonetheless, we can still find examples of the film's criticism of the state. It is not my intention to defend Cazals here. But I would like to add nuance to what seems to me harsh criticism that dwells too much on the film's failure to push the boundaries of censorship. Some critics lose sight of the value of Cazals's political commentary within those boundaries.

The priest, for instance, may well seem separate from the PRI-controlled state, but the film constantly underlines how closely the two are allied. Cazals repeatedly suggests that state and church were not that disconnected after all. As Rebecca Janzen observes, the film "subtly criticizes the state through its representations of the clergy."[75] No wonder an unnamed politician (with Díaz-Ordaz's portrait hanging on the wall) is one of the few to praise the priest. This reminds us of Alec Dawson's definition of the caudillo as an interlocutor "between marginalized people and the state," who thrives in territories where the state is absent.[76] This is what the priest clearly stands for: not as a small-town dictator but as someone who negotiates with and intercedes for the state.

As the narrator puts it, the priest is an *amigo de los meros chingones del gobierno* (friend of the very powerful men from the government). The host villager also emphasizes this by telling the workers before the lynching that there is no point in complaining to the government about the priest, because *traen acuerdo* (they are in agreement). In short, the priest may sanitize the role of the state and its anti-Communist practices and rhetoric, but their seamless relationship is still emphasized.

Similarly, when the army saves the day, one of the military men learns that the Poblanos are university workers. His response is "Always the university!"—an ironic allusion to Tlatelolco, whose main casualties were university students. Much like the mob, the army does not listen to the lynched men or distinguish between university students and workers. Finally, the film sneaks in a subtle close-up of a newspaper (yet another example of the genre's cachet of authenticity) that explicitly mentions the military, highlighting its role in the intervention at the University of Puebla. These scenes, which have gone unnoticed by most critics, show that *Canoa* should not be reduced to its dénouement.

But it is perhaps the moment to turn to another film, the first that used fiction to talk more directly about the Tlatelolco massacre: *Rojo amanecer.*

ROJO AMANECER (1989)

Thriller and Sound between Isolation and Exteriority

Critics have written a great deal about Jorge Fons's *Rojo amanecer,* especially the ways in which it portrays Tlatelolco. Less has been said, however, about how the film's narrative strategies engage with the political thriller, even though the connections between the two are multiple.

At a time when the political thriller was more recognizable, when compared to the 1970s films already examined, most critics still did not read *Rojo amanecer* as part of the genre. Laura Podalsky, for instance, reads it as a film that "deploy[s] the conventions of the melodrama."[77] Foster is one of the few critics who links it with Costa-Gavras's work, especially *Missing.* The similarities between them go beyond the influence of the European filmmaker. Both *Rojo amanecer* and *Missing* were shot in Mexico City in the same decade. Foster reminds us of the uneven conditions of production, reflecting the structural precarity that informs the genre's history in the region: the Mexican state eagerly welcomed the Hollywood multimillion-dollar production in 1981, whereas Fons had to film his independent feature in hiding to dodge censorship only a few years later.[78]

In addition, one of *Rojo amanecer*'s screenwriters was Xavier Robles, who had previously written Cazals's political thriller *Bajo la metralla* in 1983. Even the film's title cites the genre's history in Mexico and beyond: *Rojo amanecer* reminds us of Julio Bracho's *Distinto amanecer* (1943), also set in the country's capital. In both films the dawn is related to the ending. The dawn closes the plot of Bracho's film, set in Mexico's urban nocturnal underworld, rife with corruption and political crime. Fons, by contrast, portrays the historically significant dawn of October 3, 1968 (the morning after the Tlatelolco massacre), as a transition from darkness to light, from interiority to exteriority, from image to sound, leading to the film's climax.

On the other hand, *Rojo amanecer*'s title reminds us of John Milius's homonymous *Red Dawn*, an American political thriller released in 1984, only five years earlier. The "red" in Milius's title refers to a fictional Communist invasion of the United States that happens overnight. China, the Soviet Union, and Latin American countries (especially but not only Cuba) attack the United States in the dystopian context of a World War III. Fons subverts the strong associations of the color red with the Eastern bloc to resignify it in terms of bloodshed sponsored by a capitalist state.

Rojo amanecer is connected to the history of censorship that prevented the Mexican political thriller from burgeoning earlier. The Mexican Secretaría de Gobernación, in charge of surveilling film productions, has a key term for this: *enlatamiento*. When a film is *enlatado* (literally, "canned"), it partakes in what Salvador Velazco calls "a bureaucratic limbo": the period in which a film's release is not strictly speaking banned but put on hold for an indeterminate period, awaiting official approval.[79] Robles and co-scriptwriter Guadalupe Ortega Vargas note that the film was *enlatado* for months, even claiming that the state released another political thriller first, which had been *enlatado* for more than three decades: *La sombra del caudillo*.[80]

Finally, much like *Operación masacre, Canoa Rojo amanecer* pictures a slaughter by means of innocence and the political, with a peculiar emphasis on the transitions between exteriority and interiority, visibility and invisibility. Fons also foregrounds the lethal invasion of the personal at the hands of the political. The film depicts the fictional execution of almost an entire family, perpetrated by a state-sponsored paramilitary death squad that critics identified with the "Batallón Olimpia" in the context of the Tlatelolco massacre. The grammar of secrecy's prepositions of space inside and outside are prominent. The film is almost entirely set in a public housing apartment building called Chihuahua, located right in front of Tlatelolco.

Critics took note of the prominent role that space plays in the film. Samuel Steinberg, for instance, reads *Rojo amanecer* in terms of "teichoscopy,"[81] an ancient Greek literary trope in which the audience views everything from the walls to observe multiple synchronous events. Fernando Celin mentions *huis clos* (behind closed doors): the claustrophobic atmosphere that defines the film's portrayal of interiority. Belmonte Grey comments on its counterpart, the *fuera de campo* (off-screen): everything the camera excludes, unleashing our imagination about the unseen horror.[82] Using prepositions of space, these techniques point to interiority and exteriority.

Like all the political thrillers examined in this chapter, *Rojo amanecer* portrays a political event through a type of fiction deeply entrenched in the documentary tradition of its country. As most critics note, the film owes a lot to Leobardo López Arretche's documentary *El grito* (1968).[83] Whereas *Canoa*'s relation to the massacre was only tangential and metaphorical, *Rojo amanecer* was the first film to turn to fiction to portray Tlatelolco more centrally, albeit in a well-documented way, as Cedrón's film did with *Operación masacre.*

To construct this aura of historicity dear to the genre, the plot of *Rojo amanecer* thoroughly parallels the chronology of Tlatelolco. If, as Alberto Moreiras claims, the "ostensible topics" of thrillers "are always and precisely concerned with nothing other than time and history,"[84] Fons turns that genre convention into a central theme. The plot unfolds over a specific day, from the morning of October 2 until the next day's red dawn. The film opens with a close-up shot of an alarm clock. The camera quickly goes to the family's grandfather waking up, looking at the clock, which tells him (and us) that it is 6:40 a.m. Shots of the clock and its noises punctuate the film in what Steinberg sees as a spectral "aural punctum."[85] Right after the clock's first appearance, the camera offers a rare glimpse at the outside of the apartment, visually anchoring the story in a specific place, with an ephemeral long-shot of Tlatelolco, where the massacre will occur only a few hours later.

The film, then, brings us back to interiority and temporality, moving from space to time, now with a close-up of a paper calendar hanging on a wall. As the grandfather tears off the page of the previous date (October 1), we are left, again, in isolation with time. The calendar marks the ominous ephemerides, the last day in the life of most of the family members and several students. The character's gaze and the treatment of image are fundamental to read the film. But sound, as I elaborate later, is just as important.

I explore in chapters 4 and 5 how screens (especially TVs) are overwhelmingly present in Latin American political thrillers. They provide a great shortcut to represent a historical event without having to deal with the high costs of visual reenactments. As Velazco notes, "a realistic depiction" of Tlatelolco, "with soldiers and tanks . . . thousands of extras for street demonstrations, ambulances, helicopters . . . would have required a high budget."[86] To compensate for this, *Rojo amanecer* opens with TV historical footage. Jorge Majfud sees the inclusion of the TV news in the film as a trite gesture on the part of the filmmakers, but he misses the point that the film does so with an innovative twist, by eliding its image and focusing instead on its audio.[87] We never get to see the screen: the camera only shows us the family members' faces and the sofa where everyone is sitting. The grandfather and his grandchildren watch the latest news on the preparations for the Olympic Games and the Soviet invasion of Czechoslovakia. The news is quickly interrupted by ads from the time, establishing the genre's cachet of authenticity.

In this sense, the screen works as an unseen "electronic window," a metaphorical display that points to geopolitical exteriority, the world beyond the domestic space of the Chihuahua apartment. This scene announces the visual strategy that permeates most of the film: just as we never see the TV, we are denied the portrayal of the massacre outside the apartment's actual windows. As such, both the literal and metaphoric windows fail to "broadcast" history. The film confines our gaze to interiority and limits exteriority to the film's spectral soundscape. This may give us the first impression that exteriority is essentially canceled in the film, with only scenes at the beginning and at the end explicitly portraying it. But, by emphasizing interiority, everything in the film screams "outside." Exteriority's tacit reverberation can certainly be heard in the background, with noises of bullets being shot, students yelling, people crying, glass shattering, tanks moving, sirens wailing: the echoes of an imminent massacre.

Film, after all, is much more than sight. *Rojo amanecer* in this way foreshadows what Deborah Martin calls the "immersive, tactile aesthetics, which emphasizes sound over the visual," in Lucrecia Martel's filmmaking over the first quarter of the twenty-first century.[88] The notion of "tactile aesthetics" stems from Martel's own ideas on sound being more real than image in film. Martel describes images as "an optical illusion," while sound is more tangible, made of "waves [that] touch the viewer."[89] Of course, one could make the counterargument that light waves also do so and, conversely, that sound is often altered in film. But sound, "the tactile and three-dimensional component of cinema,"[90] is perhaps even more affective than image, as it has the virulent capacity to impact our body beyond the main sensory organ in charge of receiving its waves: our ears.

From head to toe, sound thrills us. This is perhaps why Derry made sure to mention it in his definition of the political thriller.[91] But whereas he talks about a "rhythmic soundtrack" (a central ingredient of American renditions of the genre), *Rojo amanecer*, like many Latin American political thrillers, features soundscapes that eloquently supplement what images cannot give us for different reasons—precarity, censorship, irrepresentability.

Foster reminds us that the real massacre occurs in "a highly visible place," not only because it is located in *la intemperie* (the openness of a plaza, of all places), for all to see, but also because it happens "in full view of TV cameras, photographers' cameras, and the residents of the high-rise buildings in the neighborhood." Despite this high visibility, Foster tells us, the state essentially kept secret the magnitude of its role in the massacre by never truly providing an accurate, transparent accounting of casualties.[92] In this sense, Tlatelolco is but one of the many precarious secrets in Latin American history: everyone knows about the degree of the state's involvement, but the state keeps it a secret as if no one knows.

The Poblano workers in *Canoa* are depicted as if they were imprisoned in the villager host's shack, awaiting their death sentence, with no possibility of escaping the lynch mob. Fons allegorizes "the protesters . . . cornered in the plaza," as Foster notes, in the same way: "the families are cornered in their apartments" with "no chance of escaping the power of the state or of countering its decision to exercise violence."[93] The family's isolation in the apartment mirrors the isolation faced by the victims of the outdoor massacre in the plaza.

Unlike Cazals or Cedrón, Fons places secrecy within both interiority and exteriority. Secrecy is twofold in *Rojo amanecer*. By privileging interiority, Fons seems to render the outdoor massacre invisible. But if the visual links between secrecy and exteriority are elided and recovered only through sound, this is perhaps because the film is trying to point to the precarious secrecy surrounding the massacre. Sound supplements image in relation to irrepresentability: soundscape and visual elision expose the Mexican state's narrative regarding unacknowledged political events. If the state does not represent the massacre (with statistics, documents, and so forth), if it censors any attempt to do so, how could the film explicitly engage with visual representation? As I examine in chapters 4 and 5, Southern Cone political thrillers would later reproduce this crisis of representation by foregrounding sites of precarious secrecy and linking them to forced disappearance. I now turn to the precarity surrounding the film's production and its effects.

Precarity, Censorship, Creativity

Precarity informs Fons's low-budget independent production in multiple ways. Of course, it does so by conditioning the production's formal choices, restricting most of the action to affordable indoor spaces.[94] But it is also present in the themes explored in the plot itself. To begin with, *Rojo amanecer* portrays the characters' lives in terms of social class: a lower middle-class family modestly living in the housing projects.

By privileging the onslaught against this mundane family and a few students, instead of presenting a grandiloquent reenactment of the whole massacre, Fons follows the tradition of the Latin American political thriller, which goes against the glamour of global high stakes. In this sense, precarity (much as in *El complot mongol*) also appears in terms of prosaicism. Foster notes the film's all-pervasive domesticity and "commonness":[95] its characters wake up to an alarm clock, prepare breakfast, and share a meal, while a major political event is about to take place only a few meters away from them.

Precarity also takes on a political meaning, appearing as a state-sponsored invading force. Fons further denies us the chance to connect with exteriority when a state-instigated blackout ends any possibility of communicating with the exterior. As Haddu notes, the blackout and increasingly defective telecommunications between the family members inside and outside of the apartment should be read in terms of isolation.[96] The disconnection can also be linked to precarity. *Rojo amanecer* pictures state-sponsored secret practices, creating precarious conditions to ensure the success of the massacre. Precarity and isolation, linked to secrecy and space, work here against solidarity.

Another instance of precarity's political dimension is linked to censorship. The off-screen technique simultaneously helped the film keep to a low budget and dodge censorship: Fons claimed to his censors that *Rojo amanecer* does not explicitly portray the state in a negative light. Rojo notes the difficulties that filmmakers experienced in Mexico during the twentieth century when they tried to fundraise for films that risked never being released if they did not manage to dodge censorship first.[97] Even though censorship is often solely associated with politics while precarity tends to be linked to economics, *Rojo amanecer* makes it clear that they are actually closer to each other than we think.

Just as Cazals dodged censorship by turning the military into the hero in *Canoa*, Fons did something similar by foisting the massacre onto the Batallón Olimpia, thus exonerating the military. As Rojo reminds us, the film portrays paramilitary snipers, who are not wearing uniforms but are instead depicted in civilian clothes. But the film's release itself is a positive by-product of political precarity: president-elect Carlos Salinas de Gortari's low popularity after the 1988 electoral fraud resulted in the film's eventual premiere to enhance a more benevolent perception of the state.[98]

Ultimately, as Sharryn Kasmir suggests, precarity "is not necessarily, or not always, a negative force." She reminds us of how Michael Hardt and Antonio Negri, for example, note that precarity can potentially have positive outcomes, leaving the door open for "new social arrangements and expectations."[99] Practitioners of the genre translate precarity's more positive dimension very clearly: independent filmmakers (such as the Uruguayans Enrique Buchichio and Esteban Schroeder, whose thrillers are examined in chapter 4) note that precarity can often spawn creativity.[100] It is hard to think of a more suitable example of this in the genre's history than *Rojo amanecer*. This is why Álvaro Vázquez Mantecón and Rojo concur that the filmmakers turned the financial scarcity that conditioned the film into one of its main virtues.[101] Much like sound, precarity enables imagination, which in turn is fed by one of the most important ingredients of political thrillers: suspense.

Suspense and the Political

Beyond its financial and political advantages, the off-screen technique used in the film produces an affective reaction of anxiety in the viewer: the suspense caused by the unseen. Suspense here is connected to invisibility and exteriority. Moreover, suspense is tied to spectrality, the haunting absence of Tlatelolco, evoked through the technique of emphasizing off-screen sights, events, and sounds,[102] which brings inside whatever is happening outside.

Interiority and exteriority, however, are not as separate from each other as it seems. Even though Haddu opposes the order inside the apartment (where the family dines with the fugitive student after the ceasefire) to a "chaos" she locates outside,[103] chaos could hardly be circumscribed to exteriority, as it constantly trespasses the apartment's porous boundaries. The "buildup of suspense" (in Foster's words) intervenes in the precarious threshold between interiority and exteriority. Foster reads this buildup as the narrative strategy that regulates the invasion of the personal at the hands of the political, which he calls "the increasingly violent incursion of public life into private life."[104] Suspense in thrillers, as Martin Rubin reminds us, can be defined as the expectation of the answer to a question posed by the plot.[105] Here suspense protracts the resolution of two central questions.

The first one revolves around whether we will ever see the actual plaza. If we were to go by the genre's horizon of expectations (with constant movement and fast-paced editing), we may think we will. But Fons subverts this convention by making us remain within the boundaries of the Chihuahua apartment until the end of the film. Even in the final scene of the uncensored version, we do not get to see exteriority in its entirety: the camera turns its back on Tlatelolco, focusing instead on the façade of the building and Carlitos, the youngest grandson, who becomes the massacre's only spectral survivor.

The second question has to do with the invasion: how far will it go? As critics have noted, this invasion has several layers.[106] It starts when the two politicized sons introduce information about the political state of affairs over breakfast.[107] It then proceeds to a scaffolded series of three gradually more tangible instances. The first scene takes place when snipers, preparing for the slaughter, access the building's balcony to study high-angle shots. They do so in front of the grandfather and Carlitos, who are staging a battle with toy soldiers. In the second scene, the political, once more portrayed as an invading monster coming from outside, again attacks, now impersonally and from a safe distance. Echoing *Canoa*'s axes and machetes perforating the door of the host villager's shack, *Rojo amanecer* features a close-up of a window pierced (thrilled) by a state-sponsored stray bullet. Both the shack and the Chihuahua apartment work as easily pierceable, precarious refuges. They are spaces that cannot manage to provide the shelter they were designed for.

Foster links this scene to the "scarring of the buildings" associated with Southern Cone dictatorial coups that happened not much later (for example, La Moneda in 1973). In turn, Rojo sees it as the moment in which the family loses its innocence.[108] But the scene can also be read, like Cazals's film, as a visual instantiation of transpiercing affect, now wielded by the state itself. As Beasley-Murray claims, "affect threatens social order"; even more importantly, affect "is never simply exterior to the state."[109] Political affect in *Canoa* is embodied in the bad multitude. In *Rojo amanecer* the same negative intensity against youth and students is now attributed to the state and unleashed against all civilians, regardless of their political ideas, becoming state-sponsored terror.

The third instance of this scaffolded invasion appears in regard to the bodies of the victims: the arrival of the family's older sons (who were at the plaza when the state opened fire) and other wounded, bleeding students. As they heal and mourn in one of the bedrooms, we hear what could be described as another echo of the history of the political thriller. Perhaps I am reading too much into it, but one of the students desperately grieves for his sister, who was left behind in the plaza to face certain death. Her name, coincidentally or not, is Martita, like the hyper-victim of *El complot mongol*.

Whether this is a coincidence or an intertextual gesture, the mention of Martita takes us back to the issue of hyper-victims. This last instance of the scaffolded invasion takes place in the climactic scene where suspense is resolved and the political finally completes its colonization of the personal. The Batallón Olimpia enters the apartment, seeking students in hiding, resulting in the cold-blooded execution of the students and almost the entire family. As several critics have pointed out, this scene is based more on anecdotal evidence and less on widespread documentation.[110] In other words, it is the most fictional scene of the film, the one that escapes the historical event, the testimony, the documentary, to thrill and affect the audience. For Podalsky, affects are always "errant": they always escape, as the state can never capture them permanently, at least not entirely.[111] In this sense, too, fiction in political thrillers works like affect: it always manages to slip away. Through affect and fiction, this final scene blends interiority and exteriority, effectively dissolving the genre's grammar of secrecy.

Rojo amanecer was filmed in the late 1980s, a few years after the successful transnational circulation of *La historia oficial* (winner of the Academy Award for Best Foreign Language Film in 1986) and *La noche de los lápices* (featured in global film festivals, including New York, Toronto, and Moscow), two Argentine political dramas that engage with hyper-victims. This tendency in Latin American political films of the 1980s is perhaps why (unlike *Operación masacre* and *Canoa,* shot in the 1970s) *Rojo amanecer*'s final scene puts hyper-victims on center stage, as the state's attack includes the mother, the grandfather, and the youngest children.

Sánchez Prado sees the invasion portrayed in the film in socioeconomic terms, as a disruption targeted specifically at the middle class.[112] Majfud (who openly expresses his dislike for the film) argues that the family members are overly stereotypical.[113] Steinberg, in turn, observes how the film genderizes politicization by placing characters inside or outside of Mexican political history according to their gender. Whereas the men in the family stand for different historical stages (the grandfather for the revolution; the dad for its institutionalization; the grandchildren for the student movement), the mother is "excluded from this series."[114] In other words, much like Martita in *El complot mongol,* she is placed outside of the political.

Nevertheless, I would like to suggest here that, like Martita, the mother should not be read as an apolitical character. Despite her reservations regarding her children's politicization, "she does not hesitate in receiving and hiding the students in her house," as Vazquez Mantecón notes.[115] The scene underlines, once more, the inextricable ties between secrecy and space. At the same time, *Rojo amanecer* (like many Latin American political thrillers) treats motherhood as an infrapolitical force against power for power's sake. Argentine political dramas and thrillers such as *La historia oficial* and *Infancia clandestina* tangentially echo this by showing the struggle of *madres* and *abuelas* of the Plaza de Mayo against the dictatorship (and also against the guerrillas in the case of Ávila's film).[116] I return to the links between motherhood and infrapolitics in chapter 4.

Aligned with Raggio's reading of *La noche de los lápices,* Steinberg claims that Fons "replaces the potentially militant political desires of the movement's activists with the innocence of the family."[117] For him, innocence also supersedes and sanitizes the political. Like the villager who hosts the hidden Poblano workers in *Canoa,* the members of the family are slaughtered along with the politicized students they hide, not in isolation. Hence *Rojo amanecer* ultimately insists that the students, too, are innocent: their politicization does not automatically criminalize them. The film emphasizes that the family and the students are not guilty of any crimes and are nonetheless punished with death.

As in the other two films examined in this chapter, however, *Rojo amanecer* is also telling us that the state-sponsored death squad (which incarnates power for power's sake in the film) treats them all as presumably guilty, without discerning (without secrecy) between students and family, demonstrators and bystanders, what is political and what is not.[118] Once more, the victims are murdered regardless of their degree of political involvement: from the grandfather (who initially even welcomes the state "giving a scare" to the students) and the father (who works inside the state), to the mother, most of their children (the politicized sons and the daughter), and, last but not least, the politicized students.

Like many Latin American political thrillers, *Rojo amanecer* is about precarious life, made vulnerable in the face of the political.[119] Much like *El complot mongol,* these thrillers expose us to a state arbitrariness that can turn against anyone (even the grandfather, its most fervent apologist), going beyond discrete political identities, gender, and social class. These thrillers portray state-sponsored violence as an erratic force adrift, with no specific target. In short, they all seem to say: the state is a stray bullet. The film offers other forms of infrapolitical forces in opposition to that stray bullet—broadly speaking, the affective enthusiasm produced by the students and in particular the mother's visceral ethics of care. Ultimately, it is these responses and reaffirmations of life that the state-sponsored stray bullet comes to destroy, more than political ideas or beliefs.

LA BOCA DEL LOBO (1988)

Space and Suspense

Francisco Lombardi's *La boca del lobo* tells the story of Vitín, a keen young policeman who asks to be transferred to Chuspi, a remote Andean town, to fight the Maoist guerrilla group Sendero Luminoso. Set in 1983, the film shows us how Vitín ventures into the wolf's mouth (the lion's den): relocating to the highlands at that time essentially meant entering a thrilling site of danger. Vitín is trapped between Sendero Luminoso and the Peruvian police in Chuspi and witnesses their brutality. He ends up abandoning the police at the end of the film out of visceral repugnance, in reaction to state-sponsored violence against Indigenous peoples native to Chuspi. Lombardi blends the genre with a coming-of-age story featuring a young hero who grows up after facing a series of obstacles that led to a transforming situation.

This is perhaps why critics like Ricardo Bedoya have read *La boca del lobo* as an adventure "more than as an overtly political film," which showcases "men in extreme circumstances in a hostile and threatening environment," emphasizing "the repercussions of a violent event upon an individual." Just as Rojo reads the impact of the stray bullet on the family in *Rojo amanecer*, Bedoya sees *La boca del lobo* as a story about the loss of Vitín's innocence.[120] Similarly, Barrow mentions his "naïve enthusiasm" in joining the counterinsurgency.[121] The film, however, can be linked to the political thriller via its genealogy in the adventure tale, which often includes a Bildungsroman plotline connected to the political and space, as shown in chapter 1.

La boca del lobo, then, can be read otherwise. Vitín's transition to adulthood and his increasing infrapolitical awareness are only possible thanks to the affective impact of the highlands. The landscape's threat in Chuspi, after all, is inseparable from a political conflict, well defined in time and space: the state's dirty war against Sendero Luminoso. In addition, Lombardi uses suspense to deal with the political. Reminding us of *Operación masacre*, the film mirrors two different mass killings: the first one is perpetrated by members of Sendero Luminoso, who slaughter Vitín's police detachment, killing his superior in the process.[122] The second is the massacre of Indigenous peoples, superficially presumed to have been guilty of the first attack. Nonetheless, unlike Cedrón, Lombardi does not resort to embedding historical or fictionalized footage of the mass killing that triggers the plot. Visibility is constantly protracted through suspense.

Bedoya himself admits the presence of ingredients in the film that are characteristic of the political thriller, including paranoia, which we could understand here as a strategy to bring in suspense through the character's psychological traits. The suspense lies in wondering if we will ever see the Senderistas. As the story unfolds, the film magnifies suspense, as they always remain invisible, off-screen, "a faceless enemy," in Bedoya's terms.[123] Just as we never see Tlatelolco, we never get to see the guerrillas, only their specter, camouflaged in the highlands.

As Beasley-Murray notes, Sendero "was spectral but no less frighteningly real. Unseen, the insurgents could be anywhere."[124] I return to the genre's uses of spectrality and precarious secrecy in chapter 5, with my close reading of the Paraguayan film *Matar a un muerto*. Here I elaborate on the ways Lombardi harnesses spectrality through suspense. In this regard, *La boca del lobo* relies heavily on the technique of off-screen sights: The film exploits Sendero's present absence, which almost seems tailor-made for the genre's conventions.

Noël Carroll defines suspense as a way of ethically ensuring the audience's involvement in the story, typical of thrillers.[125] Carroll argues that "the audience is provided, often aggressively, with a stake in one of the alternatives by having its moral sensibility drawn to prefer one of the uncertain outcomes."[126] Through suspense, Lombardi makes us position ourselves in front of Sendero's absence.

Suspense also takes on a political meaning when we remember that the guerrillas' invisibility is also tied to a crisis of representation. Sendero's visual irrepresentability, according to Valdez Morgan, is due to the fact that "it was still almost impossible to sketch a plausible Senderista character" when the script was written; "therefore it was decided not to represent them."[127] According to Beasley-Murray, "enigma was part of Sendero's strategy: its militants worked hard to maintain their invisibility, mysteriousness, and unrepresentability."[128] The film mimics Sendero's deliberate opacity by showing us only the virulent consequences of their acts, their traces.

But Sendero has another function in the film that speaks to the tension examined throughout this chapter about innocence and the political. As Beasley-Murray notes, Sendero was perceived in the 1980s and early 1990s as "a repository of barbaric affect and feared as a highland counter-state."[129] This is why the guerrillas in *La boca del lobo* function as the pole of presumed guilt: anyone who could be remotely tied to them is immediately sentenced. Conversely, anyone who was opposed to or dissociated from them was considered to be innocent.

Interiority and Indigeneity

Much as in the Mexican thrillers, exteriority and interiority are defined in *La boca del lobo* in geopolitical terms: while the highlands point to the inside of the country, the exteriority can be found on the Peruvian coast. Each has long-standing connotations that are variants of the South American literary and political dichotomy of civilization and barbarism. Closer to the Spanish metropolis through its maritime ties, the coast has traditionally been linked to modernity and wealthier, whiter colonial settlers. The Andean inland areas, by contrast, have often been perceived as more backward and with a poorer, more Indigenous population.[130] The police and the Indigenous peoples in the film are metonymies of the coast and the highlands, respectively: the state comes from outside, with the whiter police taking the post in Chuspi.

As Valdez Morgan notes, the police "work as a means of communication between the film and its audience," which is more likely located on the coast.[131] Put differently, the state becomes a bridge between interiority and exteriority. Much as in the Mexican political thrillers, interiority is imagined as a prison. Bedoya describes Chuspi as "isolated by the violence of Sendero."[132] Indeed, everyone in the film is somehow land-locked, even the Senderistas, circumscribed to their mandated invisibility. In turn, the coastal police are confined to their rigid hierarchy and oppressive tasks, whereas the Indigenous peoples are caught between Sendero's violence and the police's surveilling.

In this context, the Quechua speakers from Chuspi serve as another important spectral absence. We barely see or hear from them in most of the film,[133] but they constantly have the potential to be lumped together with the Senderistas, whose origins were also marked by the interiority of the highlands. For most of the police, the Indigenous characters are constantly suspected of collaborating with the Maoists, but the film's portrayal of Indigenous characters sways between innocence, victimhood, and presumed guilt.

The Indigenous peoples' shifting states take us to the end of the film, with its portrayal of the second mass killing, informed by a real event that took place in 1983 in Soccos. Chuspi is located in the Áncash region (north of Lima), while Soccos is an Andean region near Ayacucho, which used to be Sendero's stronghold. The Soccos massacre involved the murders of more than thirty Indigenous civilians of different genders and ages, regardless of their actual involvement with Sendero.[134] The police detachment, however, never managed to prove any real involvement.

La boca del lobo foregrounds hyper-victims: the massacre's casualties include women, children, and the elderly. Much like other Latin American political films made in the 1980s, such as *La historia oficial, La noche de los lápices,* and *Rojo amanecer, La boca del lobo* shows an attempt to incorporate other identities in a genre that is intensely homosocial. As a case of masculine brutality, the real and the fictionalized massacres are best described by what Rita Segato calls "pedagogies of cruelty": the normalization of violence through repetition, isolation, and desensitization.[135] The massacre, part of one of the film's climactic scenes, is scaffolded much as in *Rojo amanecer,* with three previous instances of the invasion of the personal by the political. These scenes work as the normalizing repetition, the pedagogy that renders cruelty possible.

In the first instance, Lieutenant Roca (Vitín's new superior) kills an Indigenous farmer's calf. After shooting the animal, Roca says *ningún terruco va a comer mejor que nosotros* (no terrorist will eat better than us). The second instance involves Kike (Vitín's best friend), who trespasses on the small convenience store of Julia, an Indigenous girl. After invading her store, Kike rapes Julia: a paradigmatic example of the state's invasion of life. In the third scene Kike and other police trying to scrounge some food and drinks intrude on a private engagement party in a house. The Indigenous peoples respond by not letting them in. In retaliation, Kike goes back to his detachment to tell Roca that the party is rife with Senderistas. Once more, it is *chismes* and affective resentment, rather than political ideas, that trigger political violence.

Initially, these instances of the scaffolded invasion seem gratuitous, but they work as stepping stones for the masculine cruelty to come. In the second and third instances, the state fails to complete its thrilling of interiority. The camera reproduces this by remaining outside the door for most of the two scenes. We do not see the rape, just Julia's violated body, as we see the party always from outside the house.

The culmination of the invasion of the personal takes place when the detachment forcibly enters the house (where the party is still going on), seeking incriminatory evidence. But, as Vitín tells Roca, there is no secret plot to be found. Again, secrecy is not located within interiority. Regardless of this, Roca still decides to kidnap the Indigenous people and finally orders his detachment to execute them. Vitín, the infrapolitical character in the story, who does not yield to the state's power for power's sake, is the only policeman who refuses to shoot.

The execution happens outdoors, near a precipice, with the Andean mountains in the background. The film thus pictures the massacre in a paradoxical landscape that features an exteriority land-locked by the mountain range, far away from the polis (the coast). Rubin compares suspense to labyrinths.[136] Chuspi, a remote site of suspense and claustrophobic openness, could be defined as a labyrinthine *intemperie*, where the state perpetrates its secret massacre against defenseless civilians. In turn, the Andean highlands work as another site of precarious secrecy, as the police dispose of the corpses by throwing them over the precipice, without ever burying them. Precipices, ultimately, are defined by an empty depth. They are filled with air, not land; they constitute the opposite of solidity. The corpses thus remain suspended on the cliff's rocks, neither totally falling to the bottom nor totally remaining on top.

In her reading of the film, Barrow cites the declaration of Alejandro Toledo (who, she reminds us, was "Peru's first President of Andean descent") at the 2003 Comisión de la Verdad y la Reconciliación. Toledo claims that "three of every four victims" of the dirty war "were peasants whose mother tongue was Quechua," emphasizing the Indigenous identity of most of the casualties.[137] The film, however, shows us that the Indigenous peoples are killed under the pretext of being connected to Sendero, not because of their ethnicity per se. Once more, presumed guilt is conflated with politicization. They are executed not because they are Indigenous but because they are deemed to be politicized Indigenous people.

The massacre of Indigenous peoples in Peru in the 1980s and 1990s and elsewhere was often associated with and promoted ethnic cleansing that resulted in economic benefits for the perpetrators, such as the appropriation of the deceased's lands. As in the other thrillers examined here, however, politicization of the victim is merely an irrelevant excuse to showcase the wielding of power for power's sake. The film seems to be asking who is the wolf/lion: Sendero or the Peruvian state?

Much like the corpses, the Soccos massacre itself never really reached the depths, since María Cárdenas, one of the Indigenous women, survived to bring it to light.[138] Much like fiction and affects, secrets always escape to reach exteriority. Even though *La boca del lobo* does not dramatize the disclosure of this secret, the film was only possible thanks to it. Although the police buried the corpses after the Soccos massacre, Lombardi deliberately chose not to. Perhaps this is because precarious secrets are never fully buried, never totally concealed in the depths. Instead, they remain in a shallow space, visibly hanging like strange fruit from a tree.

FINAL THOUGHTS

At first glance, these four films work with three analogous opposing categories that stand for innocence and presumed guilt. On the one hand, non-Peronists, workers, and Indigenous peoples are deemed to be innocent because of their alleged apoliticism. On the other, Peronists, students, and Senderistas are presumed to be guilty because of their politicization. These political thrillers subvert these oppositions, however, turning them into false dichotomies. Ultimately, innocence and presumed guilt cannot be fully equated with apoliticism and politicization. The state (or the lynch mob in *Canoa*) renders politicization irrelevant and innocence inconceivable for anyone. To sum up, all these political thrillers are about crimes against humanity, whose casualties tend to be civilians, regardless of their actual political inclinations, ideas, or actions.

Octavio Paz, writing about Tlatelolco in 1970, emphasizes how "the massacre . . . shows that the past which we thought was buried is still alive and has burst out among us."[139] Much like the genealogy of the genre explored in chapter 1 and in *El complot mongol,* discussed in chapter 2, the past is not past in any of these thrillers. This is perhaps even truer now, as the state brutality against popular dissent in Argentina, the violence against students in Mexico, and the cruelty against Indigenous peoples in Peru are all still topical today, decades after these films were released.

Returning to Bobbio's twofold understanding of conspiracies—*arcana dominationis* and *arcana seditionis*—sedition always works as a "natural by-product" of secrecy's spatial dimension. As such, it can either take place "in the corridors of the imperial palace" or be "prepared in rugged and inaccessible places." In both types of *arcana* that point to interiority and exteriority, visibility is denied: conspiracies take place "away from the sight of the inhabitants of the palace, just as the prince acts as much as possible away from the sight of the people."[140] Even when these massacres are plotted in the dark in these Latin American political thrillers, their execution becomes clearly visible to the state and the citizenry through sites of precarious secrecy, despite their remoteness from "the palace": a dumping ground, a hazardous shack, a public square, the highlands.

The state's secrets occur in front of any veil and outside of any box that could contain it. Even though the plotting of these massacres is intended to be hidden from the population, these films depict their executions in a scenic, even iconic landscape, which is best described as *la intemperie*, partaking in the visual spectacularization of politics that is typical of the political thriller. The recurrent elements in these films show their common genre. Although these works were read as political films or documentaries, they can also be read as political thrillers, isolated cases of a broader genre tradition that flourished a few years later, as shown in the last two chapters of this book.

CHAPTER FOUR

Resisting and Investigating Genocide

GUERRILLA THRILLERS AND HUMAN RIGHTS THRILLERS

Mariana: Você está se comportando de uma forma passional e isso não tem nada a ver com política. (You are behaving in a visceral way and this has nothing to do with politics)
Miguel: Tem sim, Mariana. (Yes, it does, Mariana)

PRA FRENTE, BRASIL (1982) BY ROBERTO FARIAS

LATIN AMERICAN PRACTITIONERS OF POLITICAL thrillers often confront a narrative and ethical challenge: depicting serious issues within a popular genre that must also entertain its audience. As explored in previous chapters, these authors and filmmakers portray the political with themes such as conspiracies and massacres, ensuring that their treatment is different than in a nonfiction novel or a documentary film. The grounding for the films examined in this chapter is secrecy's ties with genocide, specifically in Southern Cone political thrillers. One of their most visible characteristics is the way they echo issues like torture and forced disappearance beyond explicitly portraying them by means of central genre elements, such as suspense, vulnerability, and uncertainty. Through these and other conventions, they contribute to the extensive cultural production in response to the trauma induced by authoritarian experiences, while also taking part in a five-decade-long discussion that involves history, memory, and postmemory.

Most of these thrillers focus on the resistance against Operation Condor. Here "resistance" should be understood both as physical violence and as nonviolent activist movements: through guerrilla confrontation and human rights investigations. Each of these film clusters typically points to two different periods: the "guerrilla thrillers" tend to be set in the 1960s and the 1970s (usually during dictatorial rule), while the "human rights thrillers" are often set in the postdictatorial period from the 1980s onward.

In this context, it could be said that these two clusters are direct inheritors of Costa-Gavras's twofold legacy of "Latin American" political thrillers, outlined in chapter 1: *État de siège* (1972), set in Uruguay but filmed in Chile, and *Missing* (1982), set in Chile but filmed in Mexico. *État de siège* explicitly privileges the armed struggle's point of view through the lens of Uruguayan Tupamaros, as they kidnap and assassinate an American official working in Montevideo in 1970. *Missing*, by contrast, tells the story of a conservative father's search for his son, an American journalist who became a desaparecido at the onset of Pinochet's dictatorship. The emphasis here is not on armed struggle but on forced disappearance from the perspective of civilians and their surviving family members. The desaparecidos in these films may or may not have been involved in the armed struggle—and most of them are not. *Missing* provides the perfect blend of the history of desaparecidos in the region and a genre convention: detective-like investigations that aim but fail to speak up to power. In other words, forced disappearance is absorbed by political thrillers as a seemingly tailor-made theme: it elicits the investigative storyline through a sense of suspense that essentially never ends.

As Diego Brodersen notes, the main contribution of Argentine and (more modestly) Uruguayan political thrillers is the representation of dictatorial rule.[1] This could also be said of other countries in the region (like Brazil, Chile, and Paraguay) and even outside of the Southern Cone (in Bolivia and Peru). Both clusters are the most innovative Latin American contributions to the genre. Even though they stem from Costa-Gavras's films, they gradually build a unique tradition in which left-wing guerrillas are not stereotypical villains and human rights investigations have dignity but not earnest heroism.

In one way or another, they all reproduce the invasion of the political into infrapolitical life, which can be literal (for instance, in the many forced entry scenes) as the first stage of forced disappearance, inaugurated by Cedrón's *Operación masacre*. But this invasion can also be read more symbolically: as the brutal dictatorial past's piercing through the postdictatorial present. Most of these films were made after the dictatorships ended. As a response to that invasion, these films could be read as infrapolitical counterforces, featuring the impulse to ethically rectify the traumatic past either by a reassessment of the guerrillas or by portraying characters in torment attempting to expose crimes against humanity.

This chapter offers a panoramic overview of each of these clusters, followed by three close readings of understudied films that represent them. The guerrilla thriller example is Toni Venturi's *Cabra-cega* (2004) from Brazil. The two examples of human rights thrillers are from Uruguay: Esteban Schroeder's *Matar a todos* (2007) and Enrique Buchichio's *Zanahoria* (2014). Although interpretations of these clusters have often engaged with memory and post-memory studies, here I take the approach I have been using throughout this book, emphasizing the genre's grammar of secrecy and its prepositions of space. Added to the mix are a series of common genre ingredients closely linked to secrecy and space: triangles, screens, and specters.

I put my close readings in dialogue with Jacques Derrida's take on secrecy. As Charles Barbour claims, this conversation between film and philosophy can be risky: "we cannot really telegraph what Derrida has to say without missing too much."[2] But it would be riskier, or rather poorer, to disregard him. For Derrida, to begin with, "the secret is not reducible to the private,"[3] which resonates with Taussig's public secrets, echoed throughout this book in my reformulation of precarious secrecy. This could be read as a paradigmatic illustration of forced disappearance, unacknowledged truths that were essentially well-known secrets (in Spanish, *secretos a voces*). As these thrillers portray forced disappearances were secrets showcased out in the open, state-sponsored political crimes never fully admitted by most of their perpetrators but available for everyone to see as a deterrent against dissent, activism, or any other type of political activity opposing the dictatorial state.

I also build on Andreas Huyssen in relation to what he describes as "a turning toward the past" (from the 1980s onward) that "stands in stark contrast to the privileging of the future so characteristic of earlier decades of twentieth-century modernity," such as utopian projects that always looked forward. Huyssen explains this shift based on the political and aesthetic problems discussed here: the universalization of the Shoah as a transnational instance of genocide and the representation of memory through screens, such as the "'self-musealization' by video recorder" and genres that are adjacent to the political thriller, such as "the increase of historical documentaries."[4] Huyssen informs my discussion of the seamless continuity between past and present in these thrillers, the past (1960s–1990s) that is not past (from the 1990s onward).

Derrida wonders, "[W]hat should democracy do with the possibility of the secret?"[5] Perhaps this is how we should read these thrillers. They are cultural devices, often fostered by Latin American democratic states through autarchic institutions such as the Brazilian Agência Nacional do Cinema (ANCINE) and the Argentine Instituto Nacional de Cine y Artes Audiovisuales (INCAA) that try to snatch secrecy from the (post)dictatorial states, to inspect and expose it, working as privileged witnesses of fragile democratization processes filled with precarity.

THE GUERRILLA THRILLERS: RECKONING WITH THE PAST

The first production of the guerrilla thrillers cluster is materially connected with *État de siège*. Pablo de la Barra, Costa-Gavras's assistant director of the film in Chile, is one of the first Latin American filmmakers to make a political thriller of his own: *Queridos compañeros* (1979).[6] The film is informed by the director's brother's experience with the Movimiento de Izquierda Revolucionaria (MIR), a leftist urban guerrilla movement in Chile right before Allende came to power. Set in 1967, during the tenure of Eduardo Frei Montalva (1964–1970), the film follows MIR guerrillas through operations such as planning heists and seizing plots of land from Patagonia. Like many of the films in this cluster, *Queridos compañeros* stresses the intergenerational family conflicts between the guerrillas and their parents, who are often portrayed as alienated from the armed struggle. It also questions the support (or lack thereof) from the working and middle classes, another common theme in the guerrilla thrillers.

In the Southern Cone context, the film is exceptional: it is perhaps the only one that portrays guerrillas operating during democratic times. De la Barra started shooting during Allende's administration and maintained a supportive yet critically distant relationship with the government even after Augusto Pinochet's 1973 coup, which crucially interrupted the film's production and caused its premiere to be postponed for six years. As Iván Pinto and Luis Horta note, the film's treatment of the political thriller à la Costa-Gavras was contaminated to a certain extent by a voice-over that organizes the portrayed historical events and at the same time removes the suspense.[7] Apart from this important film, however, the guerrilla thriller cluster is not so strong in Chilean cinema—yet it appears on TV.[8] A very recent exception is Juan Ignacio Sabatini's *Matar a Pinochet* (2020), which portrays a failed assassination attempt by the Manuel Rodríguez Patriotic Front (a guerrilla group founded in 1983 to resist the dictatorship).

This cluster is especially strong in Brazil, foregrounding urban and rural guerrilla movements such as the Maoist Ação Libertadora Nacional (ALN), the Vanguarda Popular Revolucionária, and the Movimento Revolucionário 8 de Outubro (MR8, named after the date of Che Guevara's capture in Bolivia). The cluster is so prominent there that it began during the dictatorial period itself, with Roberto Farias's *Pra frente, Brasil* (1982) and Oswaldo Caldeira's *O bom burguês* (1983), the country's first films to explicitly portray the dictatorship. It is worth noting here that the Brazilian dictatorship was going through its last stages at the time: it passed the Amnesty Law in 1979, which pardoned political crimes perpetrated under dictatorial rule (by both sides of the conflict) and welcomed exiles back to the country.[9]

The guerrillas in these thrillers are still a more marginal element of the plot and are not identified with any of their real counterparts. *O bom burguês*, for instance, retells the story of a banker loosely based on Jorge Medeiros, a real person who transferred funds from the Bank of Brazil to guerrillas. Blending political, crime, and heist thrillers, the film follows his activities as he escapes from the country, avoiding being captured by the police. *Pra frente, Brasil* is a much more complex film, emphasizing the comprehensive scope of forced disappearance as a dictatorial measure that affected society as a whole, which brings it closer to the human rights cluster. Set in 1970 (one of the bloodiest years of the Brazilian dictatorship),[10] the film makes use of Hitchcock's "mistaken identity" trope: Jofre, a depoliticized middle-class man, is mistaken for a guerrilla who carpooled with him and forcibly disappeared at the end of the story, after enduring illegal imprisonment and torture. His narrative is yet another instance of precarious secrecy, as the military literally has no secrets to extract from him. Thus, *Pra frente, Brasil* allows for greater audience identification with the victim than if he had been one of the guerrillas, who were perceived (and still are) as more polarizing and controversial.

The film does include a prominent guerrilla narrative. Miguel, Jofre's brother, has no choice but to join his ex-girlfriend Mariana (who is involved with the armed struggle) in order to find Jofre because the police deny all support. The transnational ties of the Southern Cone guerrillas are subtly underscored through the genre's cachet of authenticity: in the carpooling scene that opens the film, a voice on the car radio delivers the news of the execution of General Aramburu at the hands of the Argentine urban guerrilla Montoneros, in retaliation for Operación Masacre and Operativo Traslado (the kidnapping and disappearance of Eva Perón's corpse).

Much like other films from this cluster, *Pra frente, Brasil* offers what Laura Podalsky calls "affective reckoning" with the dictatorial past. She links this reckoning to later Brazilian "mainstream political thrillers" about the guerrillas in the 1990s that "function as affectively engaged interrogations that encourage us to reconsider our knowledge about the dictatorial past in Brazil . . . and its relationship to the present."[11] Farias's film, somewhere between independent productions and the more mainstream thrillers of the 1990s, clearly uses political affect to mobilize our gut feeling, forcing us to reckon with the past. This is evident in the dialogue cited in the epigraph to this chapter. Miguel refuses to agree with Mariana, who believes that the political can be separated from "passional" behavior (affect). The film sides with Miguel's affective understanding of the political as a legitimate reason to join the guerrillas.

The guerrilla thrillers gradually became more explicit after the transition to democracy in the 1990s, with the advent of the mainstream political thrillers studied by Podalsky. Bruno Barreto, a Brazilian filmmaker based in Los Angeles, premiered the Brazilian-American coproduction *O que é isso, companheiro?* (1997), which was released in the United States a year later as *Four Days in September*. The film tells the story of the kidnapping of Charles Elbrick (the American ambassador to Brazil during the late 1960s) by the ALN and MR8, which was a model for the Tupamaros' operation with Dan Mitrione. Much like De la Barra's film, Barreto's film brings to the fore reflections on the extent to which Brazilians backed the armed struggle. It also explores ethical hesitations in the guerrillas as well as in the American characters. At the same time, it foregrounds explicit scenes of torture, including methods that were native to the Brazilian history of slavery, such as the *pau de arara* (literally, "macaw's perch"), as instances of power literally thrilling the guerrillas' skin.

In turn, Beto Brant's *Ação entre amigos* (1998) is set in the postdictatorial present, deeply haunted by a past that is not past. Brant pictures a group of four former guerrillas who ambush and avenge their torturer, an *ação* (action, the common Portuguese word for both a military and a guerrilla operation). The *ação* unleashes a series of negative affective reactions in the friends, while it brings a restitutive form of justice in the form of vigilantism. We also see this dénouement in Gonzalo Justiniano's *Amnesia* (Chile, 1994) and Juan José Campanella's *El secreto de sus ojos* (Argentina, 2009), films that fit more clearly within the human rights thrillers cluster.[12]

It is worth noting here that the guerrilla thriller cluster is still very active in Brazil. We need only think of the thrilleresque biopics of Carlos Lamarca and Carlos Marighella—the two most important guerrilla leaders in the country—in Sérgio Rezende's *Lamarca* (1994) and Wagner Moura's *Marighella* (2019), respectively. Both use tropes that are typical of Hollywood political thrillers (especially chase scenes: both Lamarca and Marighella are constantly on the run before the state finally catches them to execute them). What distinguishes these biopics centered on their main character is that they emphasize the individual over the impersonal historical process. "Purer" political thrillers are always keen to emphasize that individuals ultimately are pawns, cogs in rudimentary wheels.[13]

Lamarca shows significant links to the Latin American political thriller. The film tells the story of a former captain of the Brazilian military who goes rogue and becomes a guerrilla. This picaresque character is perhaps what led Luiz Zanin Oricchio to call the biopic "a bit Quixotic."[14] To be sure, the film follows the documented life story of the guerrilla, but not without accentuating some of the thriller's aesthetic conventions. For instance, Rezende chooses to set most of the film in the *sertão*, an immense outdoor space located in the rural hinterlands of northeastern Brazil. Lamarca is portrayed in this Brazilian translation of the *intemperie*, doing what many picaresque and thriller characters do: trying to escape to survive and, of course, failing to do so. His endurance is both individual and political because it personifies the survival of the armed struggle he leads. Much as in the adventure tales examined in chapter 1, the hostile political and natural landscape—here the arid *sertão* and the military dictatorship—ends up thrilling the victim's body, in this case, to death.

Argentine guerrilla thrillers appear much later, in the 2010s. They privilege the urban guerrilla Montoneros (Catholic left-wing Peronists) over their rural counterpart (the Guevarista Ejército Revolucionario del Pueblo). Rafael Filipelli's *Secuestro y muerte* (2010), for instance, almost aseptically recreates the Montoneros' execution of Aramburu in 1970. Benjamín Ávila's *Infancia clandestina* (2012) foregrounds the Montonero counteroffensive in the late 1970s, after the organization had been annihilated by the Argentine military dictatorship (1976–1983). It does so, however, from the point of view of a child, the son of two guerrillas who were exiled in Cuba and returned to Argentina. They take part in the counteroffensive, which ends in a calamitous, deadly defeat. This peculiar perspective is what led critic Gonzalo Aguilar to argue that—rather than being about politics—Ávila's film "is about the passions that politics unleash and that precede it" (i.e., about affect).[15] The innovative aspect of *Infancia clandestina* is to bring in the child's perspective by means of what Rita De Grandis calls "the innocent eye," typical of political dramas from the 2000s but up to that point excluded from the adult-centric universe of the thriller.[16]

Diego Corsini's *Pasaje de vida* (2015) shares Ávila's perspective (both directors are children of Montoneros), instead featuring an adult son who grew up in Spain, raised by his exiled father. The film's narrative arc follows the son in the present as he gains political awareness of his parents' guerrilla past through his dad's flashbacks. As Diego Brodersen observes, Corsini's film rehashes several commonplaces already rehearsed by other political thrillers and dramas about the dictatorship.[17] A significant ingredient perhaps worth noting in passing in both Ávila and Corsini is the problem of motherhood in the face of resisting dictatorial genocide: in *Pasaje de vida* and *Infancia clandestina*—but also in *Ação entre amigos*—motherhood is represented as an infrapolitical threshold that female characters must cross once they become guerrillas. These thrillers frequently showcase debates about the hyper-politicization of the armed struggle, which often involves privileging the engagement with political violence over the more traditional role of raising children. All these thrillers problematize and do not necessarily condemn or endorse this issue.

Another significant source of the guerrilla thrillers is Mexico, which was not part of Operation Condor but still experienced guerrilla warfare during its dirty-war period in the early 1970s. Felipe Cazals contributed to the genre with *Bajo la metralla* (1983), set in Mexico City during that period. As Sánchez Prado reminds us, the film draws heavily from low-budget B movies and was filmed at Estudios Churubusco, which also served as the production site for another significant political thriller: Costa-Gavras's *Missing*.[18] *Bajo la metralla* moves away from *Canoa*'s avant-gardist aesthetics, resulting in a more mainstream film that is closer to an action thriller.

Beyond the Southern Cone and Operation Condor, there is the Peruvian case. Palito Ortega Matute's films, especially *El rincón de los inocentes* (2005) and his posthumous film *La casa rosada* (2018), are political thrillers that retell the dirty war in Sendero Luminoso's stronghold: Ayacucho. His films do not elide Sendero to the same extent as Lombardi's *La boca del lobo*, but they are still told from the point of view of civilians caught in the cross fire, not guerrillas. *El rincón de los inocentes* deals with the story of a grieving father whose young son was killed by the military and the unintended consequences of Sendero's involvement in his quest for justice. *La casa rosada*, instead, uses Hitchcock's "mistaken identity" trope to portray a real story (much like *Pra frente, Brasil*), in this case, a university professor mistaken for a Senderista.[19]

Alternatively, Sendero was portrayed through neighboring genres. For instance, Eduardo Mendoza de Echave's *La hora final* (2017) depicts the capture of Abimael Guzmán (the guerrilla leader) through conventions typical of the police thriller more than the political thriller: the police involved in the operation could well have been involved in capturing a counterfeiter, for that matter. Similarly, Uruguayan-Peruvian Alejandro Legaspi's *La última noticia* (2015), a film that oscillates between political drama and political thriller, also focuses on civilians caught in the cross fire, putting center stage the figure of the genre hero: journalists. Still, there are no main characters playing the role of the guerrillas. Much as in most of these Peruvian forays into the genre, the focus is on denouncing the escalation of violence by the Maoists, the Sinchis (a counterinsurgent unit), and the militarized state more broadly.[20]

This first cluster has a strong testimonial component, chronicling the ways in which armed struggle unfolded in Latin America. In addition, returning to Podalsky's "affective reckoning," these films often side with the guerrillas in democratic times (with the evident exception of the Peruvian case).[21] Some do so through an acritical romantic glorification of their activities. This cluster thus brings genre cinema together with the legacies of Third Cinema, in which many left-wing directors found a way to combine their more militant approach to filmmaking with a more mainstream way of expressing themselves. This was not an easy task. Parts of the audience were often estranged by the armed struggle both during and after the dictatorship, as I examine in my reading of *Cabra-cega*.

CABRA-CEGA (2004)

Blindness and Space

Blindness is a common theme in examining the dictatorial past in Southern Cone genre fiction.[22] This is the case with Toni Venturi's *Cabra-cega* (Blind Goat). The title refers to an ancient game: blind man's bluff. Once played by aristocratic adults in palaces, it has since become exclusively a children's game, found in many cultures. Like secrets, it is inseparable from space, either when played outdoors or in its parlor version. The rules are simple: a blindfolded person must catch others without the aid of sight.

The Brazilian version, as in many other cultures, is animalized.[23] The blindfolded person, referred to as the *cabra* (goat), must chase opponents by following the sound of their voices, as they pronounce the word *gulosa,* which means both "gluttonous" and "greedy," a call-and-response mechanism similar to "Marco" and "Polo" in English-speaking countries. It is worth noting that *cabra* implies stubbornness in Portuguese, much as "mule" does in English. Venturi suggests we understand guerrillas in these terms: as an ambitious, mulish generation who was unable to see what they were facing. The film is dedicated to the "many Brazilians, blind goats, who tried to go through darkness to take heaven by storm," as stated in the closing credits.

Tânia Sarmento-Pantoja understands Venturi's choice of narrating from the perspective of the guerrillas as a way of conveying that "resistance does not end in armed confrontation but in its representation." She cites Federico Lorenz's notion of "dignity in defeat" as a guiding principle to portray Latin American guerrillas: "the defeated becomes a moral victor, a paradigmatic hero," like "university students, intellectuals, artists, activists, . . . who adopted a posture of resistance" against the dictatorship.[24] In other words, a defeat in politics becomes a victory in aesthetics: history may well be written by victors, but cultural narratives belong to those who lost.

The political intrigue is set in 1971, during the bloodiest period of the Brazilian dictatorship (1964–1985), much like *Pra frente, Brasil.* These years are commonly referred to in the country as the Anos de Chumbo, a translation of the international term "Years of Lead" that describes the intensified political turmoil between the Left and the Right during the Cold War. This period coincided with the tenure of Emílio Garrastazu Médici (1969–1974), the former head of the secret police. Garrastazu exacerbated the genocidal practices of his predecessor, Artur da Costa e Silva, who died in office (1967–1969). The film opens by engaging with this context, including the typical strategy of recovering history through the genre's cachet of authenticity by embedding black-and-white historical found footage, which, in this case, depicts students and strikers demonstrating against the dictatorial regime.

The historical and the political also appear by means of flashbacks that are blurred in the memory of Tiago, the leading character. The flashbacks display shootouts between the military and guerrillas. They are filmed in sepia to distinguish his epic memories as a guerrilla from what his life has become: a prosaic confinement. After being badly injured in a police shooting, Tiago has sought refuge in the apartment of Pedro, a daddy's boy who has inherited the place and sympathizes enough with the armed struggle to hide him. However, Pedro's political sympathies are portrayed as too moderate: he never fully gets involved with the guerrillas.

Exteriority and interiority are once more at play here: the memories of the shootings that took place in the streets work as ephemeral parentheses that take Tiago (and the audience) outside of Pedro's apartment. Venturi claims that outdoor chase scenes are rare in Brazilian cinema. This can be explained in terms of precarity, as "the technical requirements involved expose the scarcity that our productions always faced, from the lack of gear to specialized staff," as Solange Toccolini Zorzo notes.[25] The fact that most of the film was shot indoors can also be understood along these lines: precarity informs the plot and production, as in *Rojo amanecer.*

Because of this, the ties between space and secrecy could not be more explicit: the setting provides a claustrophobic feel ("asphyxiating,"[26] in Sarmento-Pantoja and Pinheiro's term) that functions as a continuation of prison and torture through other means. Tiago's physical confinement highlights the secretive networks (for some, of solidarity; for others, of complicity) that a part of the Brazilian middle class created with those involved in the armed struggle.

As in many of the films examined here and in chapter 5, the plot is structured around a triangle. This might be taken from classic political thrillers, especially those of the 1940s film noir period, which typically featured triangles, often including the melodrama aspect of the story, such as *Gilda* and Carol Reed's *The Third Man* (1949), where a mysterious third-party serves as a disruptive political element. In the Latin American context, the case of Argentine-Chilean Ariel Dorfman's play *Death and the Maiden,* adapted as a political-psychological thriller by Roman Polanski in 1994, also sets a precedent. The film features a triangle of characters who serve as allegories of different social agents in the transition to democracy of an unnamed South American country that shows many resemblances with Chile. This is the type of triangle that Southern Cone political thrillers explore the most.

In the case of *Cabra-cega,* we have a heteronormative love triangle. A motherly nurse and leftist activist named Rosa (alluding to a quintessential personality in the leftist imaginary: Rosa Luxemburg) visits Tiago daily to heal his wounds. Rosa, the hero's only contact with the outside world, becomes his lover. The film seems to examine the tensions between the characters according to the degree of political commitment of each side of the triangle: on the one hand, those who effectively intervene in the historical and the political (Tiago and Rosa); on the other, the one who merely contemplates it from a safe distance (Pedro).

More importantly, Tiago's location, known only to his closest colleagues in the guerrilla group (whose name we never know), is an embodiment of precarious secrecy in and of itself. The first time we see him, he is lying in bed, cutting Garrastazu Médici's portrait out of a newspaper while looking at an image of precarity: the bedroom ceiling that is falling apart, an apartment that is about to collapse. The unstable building mirrors Tiago's secret: he is unable to keep his whereabouts to himself. His presence overflows his confinement. I return to this later.

Cabra-cega is set in São Paulo, a metropolis whose population of 8 million at the time had already surpassed the population of New York City in the 1970s. São Paulo's anonymity, however, does not preclude the same precarious secrecy that can be found in political thrillers set in small towns. In fact, throughout the film, the building serves as a small town. Exteriority, which stands for state-sponsored politics, "threatens to invade the impenetrable apartment," as Zorzo notes: "the phone calls, the bell rings, the eavesdropper neighbor knocking at the door" and, I might add, the soundscape of police cruisers' sirens.[27] Everything prowls and menaces to disclose Tiago's whereabouts, thrilling the apartment windows. Venturi, like Fons, uses sound and visuals off-screen to heighten the suspense typical of thrillers, in the circumscribed margins that a precarious budget allowed. All these threatening agents seem to know about Tiago's secret. The gossip surrounding the apartment works in favor of effectively surveilling Tiago, who obsessively crawls around in the apartment to avoid being seen. By hiding, he is blindfolding his opponents in the game of blind man's bluff: those who might be looking for him to kill him.

Whereas other thrillers display humor, irony, or cynicism, this commitment to the armed struggle sometimes makes *Cabra-cega* a much more earnest and militant rendition of the past than most guerrilla thrillers. The dictatorial experience is treated with a solemnity that often hinders identification with the characters. We also see this in *Lamarca* and *Marighella,* which focus on glorifying the heroism of the leaders, who are also explicitly mentioned in Venturi's films: The tedium of isolation causes Tiago to spend many hours watching TV, another iteration of the centrality of screens in Latin American political thrillers. Here the screen broadcasts the news of Lamarca's execution, which later sparks a conversation between Tiago and Pedro. As Pedro reminds the audience (and at the same time teaches younger generations), Lamarca is the latest in a list of leaders successively killed in a matter of months in 1969 and 1970, including Carlos Marighella, Aderval Alves Coqueiro, and Comandante Toledo. Che Guevara himself—whose portrait we see in the background of the scene—was executed in 1967. As Sarmento-Pantoja notes, the guerrilla fighter's death is represented as "a heroic sacrifice, a death for a just cause."[28] So this dialogue should be read not only as pedagogical or mournful but also as an emphasis on the heroism of the guerrillas, specifically Tiago.

Space and Paranoia

Beyond this earnest tone, the film's most interesting aspect is Pedro's ambivalence, which is maintained until the end of the story. The political engagement with the guerrilla is personified, following a gradual level of triangular intensification: Pedro the petty bourgeois sympathizer, Rosa the working-class activist, and Tiago the armed fighter. These layers are problematized in Pedro's character. Precisely because of his apparent lack of commitment, he is constantly suspected of being a traitor: the most dangerous of the three. Tiago wonders why Pedro, who does not even know how to hold a gun, is helping him. Pedro's ambivalence insinuates that he perhaps might be the most committed, although of course not to the guerrillas but to dictatorial power. The film plays with this ambivalence by juxtaposing Pedro's reluctance to fully participate in the guerrilla movement with his visible support for the cause by hiding Tiago.

Sarmento-Pantojo and Pinheiro highlight the film's engagement with a typical ingredient of thrillers: paranoia. They focus on the ways in which Venturi sketches Tiago's personality, as the mystery of Pedro's real intentions toward him creates an atmosphere of paranoia.[29] At first, Pedro seems to be the third person in the triangle, the one who introduces the political element. He smokes marijuana, which could catch the attention of neighbors and eventually the police. From Tiago's perspective, it almost seems that Pedro is doing it intentionally. Hence we are constantly expecting Pedro to turn Tiago in. In one scene Tiago even sees through the window that Pedro is talking to the police. But the film's dénouement absolves Pedro (who has always remained loyal to Tiago) by showing that another guerrilla tipped off the police.

In this light Tiago himself could be read as the third person, the destabilizing side of the triangle: not because he brings in the political in the sense that he embodies armed struggle but because he constantly jeopardizes the triangle's safety. At the beginning of his confinement, he never lets his guard slip, but everything starts to change as the days in isolation go by. Tiago suddenly starts opening the curtains that once hid him, willingly letting the political invade him, thrill his life, from exteriority to interiority.

The critics seem not to have noticed that the blindness alluded to in the title is not limited to the heroic guerrillas. Tiago is not the only *cabra-cega*: his opponents from the military look for him blindly. As he starts to open the curtains to see others through the windows, letting others overtly spy on him in the process, he also does so to be seen. Put simply, he removes the blindfold of his pursuers. As comparative literature scholar Jack Halberstam notes, "for the paranoid . . . the only thing worse than being watched is not being watched."[30] In this sense, Tiago could be read not necessarily as a hero but as a narcissist who sees himself and his heroism as more important than the collective causes he fights for. His tedious confinement serves in the film to reproduce a cliché of the guerrilla fighter as a man of action, somebody who cannot wait to get into combat again. He starts by seeing his female neighbor through the spyhole without being seen but becomes increasingly visible until he ends up accepting a dinner invitation from her.

Equally, he "opens the curtains" to Rosa, in the sense that he gets more and more involved with her. The most prominent instance of this is when she blindfolds him and takes him to the building's rooftop to eat *macarronada* (spaghetti with tomato sauce), a typical Italian-Brazilian working-class dish. In her reading of the scene, Zorzo describes this as a climax: "Tiago leaves darkness, from enclosure to clarity."[31] Here the secret of his whereabouts is temporarily disclosed, following the two typical prepositions of the grammar of secrecy: "inside" and "under." Tiago is concealed behind Pedro's walls, but he is also underneath. He goes "underground" by engaging in the armed struggle: his political activities are no longer legal. In going upstairs, Tiago and his secret emerge from interiority to the outdoors, ascending from the "depths" of the apartment to the surface of the terrace. The scene is especially impressive, as it is one of the few filmed outdoors. The police sirens coming from the streets swiftly truncate the scene (which is romantic in the multiple meanings of the term: marked by affection and an idealized atmosphere), announcing the end of the film, in which the dictatorial state finally manages to thrill Pedro's apartment.

To conclude my reading of *Cabra-cega,* I reread this scene by focusing on the São Paulo skyline as backdrop, which gives an ephemeral sense of escape, freedom, and release. A reading against the grain of this scene could suggest an irony: on the rooftop Rosa and Tiago have *tomado os céus por asalto* (taken heaven by storm). *Céu,* after all, means both "heaven" and "sky." This thriller that seems to celebrate Latin American guerrillas features an underlying critique of the armed struggle, much like several films in this cluster. The irony is that the most revolutionary and liberating thing Rosa and Tiago manage to do—the closest to heaven/the sky they ever get—is to share a prosaic working-class meal on a rooftop. The view from there shows São Paulo's financial power, an emblem of everything the armed struggle fought against. By doing something that is liberating only at a surface level (both literally and metaphorically), they actually jeopardize the whole operation. In other words, they turn their secret into a precarious endeavor. After all, anyone could recognize Tiago, whose face is supposed to be on every wall of the city, as the state is blindly looking for him. In short, the terrace works as yet another *intemperie*: another site of precarious secrecy, hiding as much as it exposes a defenseless subject.

For Sarmento-Pantoja, "*Cabra-cega* can be seen as anachronistic in relation to the treatment" of Brazilian guerrillas, as its glorification was considered outdated. She adds the nuance that Venturi's relation with the armed struggle could be read in terms of the past not being past, emphasizing that the film "is related to its time of production: times of discredited utopias but also of chewing over the past."[32] In defense of the guerrilla thrillers, Oricchio reminds us that "when the guerrillas started no one was really sure about their outcome."[33] He compares the fate of Brazilian and Cuban guerrillas: if the Brazilians had triumphed as the Cubans did, the current reception of these films would differ notably.

Despite the rooftop scene, the film's romanticization of Tiago detracts from rather than enriches the conversation about the past. What gets lost in this romanticization is not merely the obsolescence of utopias but the fact that Southern Cone dictatorships often operated by focusing more on arbitrary actions than on the targeting of political ideas. This is where blindness becomes important: after all, it can signify more than acting without fear of consequences. As the portrayal of Tiago suggests, blindness can also mean being unaware of your surroundings—a flaw that, to be sure, goes beyond Brazilian borders and the guerrilla movement itself. By contrast, the human rights thriller cluster opens our eyes to the state's arbitrariness beyond the armed struggle.

THE HUMAN RIGHTS THRILLERS: GENOCIDE AND REPRESENTATION

The human rights cluster was much more prolific in Argentina and Uruguay than in Brazil or Chile, but it was also present outside of the Southern Cone, in countries affected by Operation Condor, such as Peru and Bolivia. According to Alberto Moreiras, thrillers are "an ethical aesthetization of politics," where the gradual disclosure of secrecy is inseparable from treatment of politics rooted in an "ethical stance."[34] Whereas guerrillas personify this ethical stance in the previous cluster, here ethics is embodied by human rights lawyers, journalists, victims of forced disappearance themselves, or their surviving family.

Leger Grindon, in a study about film genre and clusters, examines the trajectory of films that "have moved from the margins of the genre eventually to emerge as key prototypes."[35] This is perhaps the way in which the human rights thrillers cluster originated: with a political "melodrama." Luis Puenzo's *La historia oficial* (1985), in the words of Alberto Elena, is a story that privileges a domestic setting with family members as its main characters.[36] Nevertheless, through these melodramatic ingredients, Puenzo still heavily engages with the investigative armature and suspense of the political thriller. This is perhaps why Charles Derry considers the film to be part of the genre, one of the few non-American examples in his study. Puenzo blends historical processes with the genre strategy of detective-like investigations: the film follows the journey of Alicia, the adoptive mother of a child, who is unaware that her daughter was appropriated from the family of a desaparecida. The film explores how Alicia gains political awareness of the struggles of the families of the desaparecidos. As Derry reminds us, Alicia's narrative arc implicitly cites Ed Horman's in *Missing*[37]—or, we could add, Richard Lamb's. Unlike Horman and Lamb, Alicia is obviously not a foreigner, but her obliviousness to the state-sponsored political crimes almost makes her one.

Puenzo's foundational political drama almost immediately spawned two important 1980s human rights political thrillers: Carlos Lemos's Swedish-Argentine co-production *Los dueños del silencio* (1987) and Santiago Carlos Oves's *Revancha de un amigo* (1987). But his influence goes beyond the 1980s: even though this cluster waned in Argentina until the late 1990s, it then reappeared in Marco Bechis's *Garage Olimpo* (1999) and was further refined in the twenty-first century by Israel Adrián Caetano's *Crónica de una fuga* (2006), Juan José Campanella's *El secreto de sus ojos* (2009), Santiago Mitre's *Argentina, 1985* (2022), and Daniela Goggi's *El rapto* (2023).

Even though Argentina has the strongest and most prolific tradition of political thrillers in the region, human rights thrillers went beyond Argentine borders, as is evident in Mexican Carlos Bolado's thriller *Olvidados* (2013) from Bolivia, Michel Gómez's *La pena máxima* (2022) from Peru, and Esteban Schroeder's *Matar a todos* (2007) and Enrique Buchichio's *Zanahoria* (2014), both from Uruguay. As noted earlier, my close readings in this chapter engage with these last two understudied films.

Thomas Schatz divides Hollywood film genres into four stages: experimentation, classicism, refinement, and baroque. Although his taxonomy is not always fully translatable in a Latin American context, it still helps to describe some historical trends. Chapter 3 examines what I see as political thrillers that fit in the experimental stage in the 1970s and 1980s. They foreground civilians caught in the cross fire between the police, the military, the paramilitary, and the guerrillas through a heavy use of formal experimentation, such as embedding or creating documentary footage. For Schatz, the classicist stage takes place when genre "conventions reach their 'equilibrium' and are mutually understood by artist and audience." In turn, refinement happens when "certain formal and stylistic details embellish the form."[38] Early examples of this human rights cluster, such as Adolfo Aristarain's *Tiempo de revancha* (1981, filmed toward the end of the Argentine dictatorship) and Gonzalo Justiniano's *Amnesia* (1994, filmed in Chile right after Pinochet's downfall), could be considered somewhere between the first and the second stage.

As Constanza Burucúa observes, Aristarain introduces "the political thriller as [a] suitable genre to represent (state) violence."[39] As such, these classicist films no longer involve experimentation as their forerunners did, but their extensive use of allegory distinguishes them from more recent renditions, which portray the political and the historical in much more realistic, explicit terms, making use of the genre's cachet of authenticity.[40] Political thrillers such as Miguel Littín's *Allende en su laberinto* (2014), *Argentina, 1985* (2022), and *El rapto* (2023) fall more clearly in the refinement stages: they were filmed in very identifiably political landscapes, such as palace-like buildings (La Moneda, La Casa Rosada, the Argentine National Congress), and spotlight iconic politicians such as Salvador Allende, Jorge Rafael Videla, and Raúl Alfonsín, with actors resembling them.

Unlike guerrilla thrillers, this cluster emphasizes not so much (or at least not always) explicit representations of political crimes from the past but the evocation of their spectral regurgitation in the postdictatorial present. The crisis of representation that hovers over the region's cultural production is tangible here: whereas we often witness forceful entries and torture scenes, we rarely witness the act of killing itself, as we do in *Operación masacre, Canoa,* and *Rojo amanecer,* to name some of the political thrillers examined in the previous chapter. Killing remains off-screen: unlike iconic massacres, genocide eschews representation for two reasons: the incommensurable scale of industrial murder, which makes the act of mass killing nonrepresentable, and the peculiar history of forced disappearance in the Southern Cone, which adds another layer to the impossibility of depicting mass murder. After all, the military regimes never fully acknowledged forced disappearances: the complete number of victims and the locations of their corpses were never admitted. The absence of aesthetic representation mimics the absence of political representation. As such, most of these thrillers go beyond explicit instances of state-sponsored violence to show its continuation in other spheres of life and beyond the dictatorial context.

Moreover, investigations in these thrillers do not follow a conventional whodunit pattern: everyone knows who the perpetrators are. Instead, investigations are more invested in dismantling the cover-ups. In fact, investigation itself is quite often irrelevant, becoming a pretext for the exploration of the effects that these crimes against humanity have in a present that fails to be clearly demarcated as present. An evanescent present looks more and more like a never-ending past, mainly due to this lack of military acknowledgment but also, in most contexts, because of the failure of many democratic administrations to bring justice for the victims.

This cluster emphasizes the prominence of authoritarianism in democratic times and, more broadly, updates the idea that the region is still caged in a past that is not past. These films do so in multiple ways. One example is through double storylines, where the present is told in parallel with the past, typically through flashbacks, as in *Amnesia* and *El secreto de sus ojos*. The origin of this narrative strategy to represent the dictatorship with a double storyline, however, should be found outside of the political thriller. It was perhaps inaugurated by and problematized in Lita Stantic's *Un muro de silencio* (1993), a political drama in which the dictatorial past and the postdictatorial present are portrayed in complex ways, evoking the issue of the crisis of representation caused by the figure of the desaparecido. Another possibility is directly foregrounding the past, leaving the audience to establish the seamless connections with the present, as in *El rapto*. Or, inversely, representation may be limited to a postdictatorial democratic present (which may or may not coincide with the audience's world) that is constantly evoking the past, as in the Uruguayan thrillers analyzed in this chapter.

MATAR A TODOS (2007)

From Language to Genre

In 1977 the *New York Times* published an editorial that included a quotation by the de facto governor of the province of Buenos Aires, Ibérico

Manuel Saint-Jean: "First, we kill all the subversives; then, their collaborators; later, their sympathizers; afterward, those who remain indifferent; and finally, the undecided."[41] The statement, deemed to be plausible, described the genocidal practices at play in the country. It was a precarious secret: information known even in New York City that the Argentine state did not acknowledge. The quotation was attributed to a member of the dictatorial state, which gave it an eerie sense of legitimacy, tainted with unabashed brutality. A few weeks later, however, the newspaper published an apology and a statement by Saint-Jean, who denied having uttered those words, much as Videla and other members of the junta brushed aside (then and later) any accusations of a systematic plan of forced disappearance in the country.[42]

Regardless of its actual authorship and veracity, a modified excerpt of this quotation—"to kill them all" (without the direct object "subversives")—entered the vocabulary of Argentine Spanish as a belligerent colloquialism blithely used in daily language ever since. The expression eventually became popular in other countries of the region and was transplanted to other contexts. *(Hay que) matarlos a todos* ([You gotta] kill them all) now implies eliminating an imagined enemy, not necessarily a political one. Throughout the past few decades, the expression has even been used as part of a racist slur against Bolivian and Paraguayan minorities in Buenos Aires (often racialized through Indigeneity) in the context of football fan chants.[43]

The expression fits well in author and translator Marguerite Feitlowitz's *A Lexicon of Terror*, a study of the impact of the Argentine dictatorship on language: "expressions originating with torturers in the camps [that] have become part of current slang." This vocabulary is "so familiar that even if one doesn't agree" it still "gets internalized" and appears in different contexts, such as a football stadium.[44] Feitlowitz's examination can be transplanted to a regional setting that includes the filmic representation of dictatorial experiences beyond Argentine borders. The title of Esteban Schroeder's political thriller *Matar a todos* (2007), for example, signals the linguistic normalization of this expression, cinematically exploring genocidal practices, now transplanted to the Uruguayan and Chilean postdictatorial contexts.

Set mainly in Montevideo during 1993, only eight years after the downfall of the Uruguayan dictatorship (1973–1985), *Matar a todos* is based on *99% asesinado* (2004), a novel by Pablo Vierci, who also participated in writing the script. It was the first Uruguayan film to engage with the dictatorial legacy through fiction. As in many other Latin American countries, the documentary was the preferred genre to take part in that conversation.[45] The film features Julia Gudari, an archetypical hero of the Latin American political thriller: a human rights lawyer.

Unlike the guerrilla thrillers already examined, Julia is depicted resisting postdictatorial power through one of the typical narrative strategies of the genre, especially in the Southern Cone: a detective-like investigation of crimes against humanity perpetrated by a dictatorial state. These investigations are expected to lead to an ethical suture of society's wounds, but they typically fail to do so: in this context, these films reproduce what I call elsewhere the "poetics of failure" so prominent in postdictatorial Southern Cone literary detective stories.[46]

In addition to *Missing*, the more explicit model for *Matar a todos* could be *Hanna K* (1983), another political thriller directed by Costa-Gavras. Shot in Israel, *Hanna K* foregrounds a female American lawyer who defends in court a Palestinian accused of terrorism. Hanna is echoed in *Matar a todos* by Julia Gudari, a female lawyer who navigates an authoritarian environment, always shadowed by powerful men who apply pressure to keep her from investigating state-sponsored crimes. Paradoxically, despite their female heroes, both films enhance the political thriller's homosocial universe: *Matar a todos* constantly highlights Julia's isolation in the face of the male-dominated cast.

Julia seeks to reveal a transnational secret that involves both Chile and Uruguay. Following a series of inquiries in both countries, she investigates the whereabouts of Eugenio Berríos, who, as the film reminds us, was an important chemist during Pinochet's regime and a former director of the Dirección de Inteligencia Nacional (DINA), the secret police founded shortly after the 1973 coup.

After the publication of the Rettig National Commission for Truth and Reconciliation Report in 1991 (only one year after Pinochet's downfall), the Chilean state started to investigate Berríos. This caused him to flee and hide in Uruguay. Julia's investigation reaches a dead end when the Uruguayan government leaks false documentation to the press, stating that Berríos escaped to Italy. The secret is revealed at the end of the film, when the final credits (a typical paratextual ingredient of the genre) expose the state's mendacious narrative by explaining that Berríos never went to Italy: he was found dead in 1995 near Montevideo. His whereabouts are a well-known secret unacknowledged by the state (much like the practices of Videla, Pinochet, and Ibérico Saint-Jean): an instantiation of precarious secrecy.

Such secrets, which should be cast away or isolated underground, eventually find a way to return to the surface in *Matar a todos*. The disclosure of secrecy, however, does not change the course of history: Julia never manages either to find Berríos or to demonstrate the state's connivance in his hideout and possibly his death. As Slavoj Žižek claims in an article published in 2008 (one year after the film's premiere), "today, in our cynical era," speaking up to power "no longer works . . . since everyone is publicly saying all the time that the emperor is naked (that Western democracies are torturing terrorist suspects, that wars are fought for profit) and nothing happens": everything "goes on functioning as if the emperor has his clothes on."[47] Here Žižek is obviously referencing Hans Christian Andersen's story "The Emperor's New Clothes" (1837).[48]

A less-known fact is that Andersen's story is a rewriting of a Spanish medieval cautionary tale, included in Don Juan Manuel's *Tales of Count Lucanor* (1335). This story is linked to the tradition of the Spanish picaresque, central to the political thriller. In this tale three *pícaros* claim to have fabricated a suit for the king that is visible only to those who are legitimate sons. This element is entirely absent in Andersen's version, where being unable to see the suit implied unfitness for the emperor's office.[49] Andersen's modern retelling focuses on meritocracy in the workplace.[50] The Spanish medieval tale instead emphasizes issues of nobility's lineage and adultery.

In both texts, everyone eventually realizes that the swindlers were only pretending to weave: there is no actual suit. Nonetheless, everyone in the story maintains this precarious secret in a tacit agreement. Revealing it could have dire consequences. In Andersen, it could mean contradicting the emperor and potentially losing a position in his office. But the stakes are higher in Don Juan Manuel because it entails exposing the king, who, unable to see the suit, already suspects that he himself is illegitimate. In short, disclosing precarious secrecy brings to the fore the problem of continuity of power. This is a central theme in Latin American political thrillers, as we see in the examples examined in chapter 2 with the Mexican *sexenios* but also here in *Matar a todos* with the prolongation of dictatorial power in democratic times.

Žižek describes this type of secret as "pretended ignorance."[51] In Andersen, this secret is shared by the emperor and all his subjects. The story ends with the emperor deliberately deciding to continue with his procession, despite the whole town having publicly acknowledged that he is naked, after a truth-telling "innocent" child says it out loud.[52]

At this point, there is another significant difference between the stories: Don Juan Manuel excludes one character from such pretended ignorance. He is immune to secrecy because he already considers himself and is perceived by others as an outcast: the *palafrenero, que non avía que pudiesse perder* (a Black boy, who held the king's horse and had nothing to lose).[53] The *palafrenero* foreshadows and is intricately connected to Bakhtin's understanding of the *pícaro* as a precarious servant, "who goes from one master to the other." Because he is also a *pícaro*, the *palafrenero* is attuned to what Bakhtin sees as the object on which *pícaros* focus their powers of observation: "the underside and the falseness of every situation." The function of the *pícaro*, after all, "consists in externalizing things."[54] This is why it is the *palafrenero* who warns the king about his invisible suit. Due to his race, the boy is presumed to be outside medieval European society, his legitimacy not an issue. Žižek follows Andersen, explicitly describing the boy in terms of innocence.[55] But Don Juan Manuel tells us the exact opposite: because he is presumed guilty—or, rather, because he is outside of the polis (as an infrapolitical character)—he can point at the naked king. In the human rights thrillers the picaresque *palafrenero* deeply informs the hero, a truth-telling outcast, who is a human rights female lawyer in the case of *Matar a todos.*

From Genre to Allegory

Berríos himself is a triggering anecdote, barely appearing in Schroeder's film. He functions as a pretext for the exploration of postdictatorial memory and masculine domination through the seamless criminal ties between equally male-dominated institutions: the military, the legislative branch of government, the secret police, and the official police, all of which are condensed and dramatized in Julia's family.

Writing about the aesthetics of contemporary Argentine cinema, Joanna Page claims that "if allegory was indispensable to artistic production under the censorship of the military regime, it has also been extensively used as a representational tool in the post-dictatorship era."[56] This is especially true in Argentine political thrillers that feature different kinds of resistance against the dictatorship during the 1980s, including those filmed during the regime's downfall. We need only think of classic films such as *La historia oficial,* with an intense use of allegorical parables that can be explained through the lingering censorship and the lurking presence of the military, which was reluctant to return to the barracks and frequently invaded democratic life during Alfonsín's precarious tenure (1983–1989).[57]

Allegory is still central in Schroeder's film, set in the early 1990s but produced more than ten years later, in the mid-2000s. The impact of postdictatorial censorship was still at play. As Fiorella Gargaglione Turk notes, the film "replaces the proper names of the military men involved and omits any explicit reference to then president Lacalle Herrera's administration."[58] Most characters personify political or historical forces: Julia embodies, at the same time, human rights movements and survivors of state-sponsored violence. Her dying father (a retired general) stands for the agonizing dictatorship (1973–1985) that once tortured her in the 1970s. In turn, her eight-year-old son incarnates the new order, for which the past must be left behind: the Uruguayan democracy.

One of the many examples of this allegorical structure can be found early in the film. Julia's sleepless son, the troubled democracy, leaves his bedroom at night and interrupts her while she watches footage about Berríos and the use of sarin nerve gas in Nazi Germany. Concerned, she turns the TV off and puts him back to bed, postponing the unveiling of past secrets to the future. Of course, these scenes are not just about parental protection from the nightmare of history. They could also be read as the impossibility of discussing the past—even in democratic times. Here the idea that the past is not past reappears once more.

In the first scene that features Julia's father, he and his grandson are playing with a radio-controlled airplane. As the old man holds the joystick, the plane crashes into a bush in the backyard patio of his house. The child-like setting stands for a political event only legible and visible for adults, a secret selectively hidden from children: as Gargaglione Turk observes, the plane crash evokes the death flights practiced during the dictatorship.[59] A form of extrajudicial execution that was performed on both sides of the Río de la Plata (more frequently in Buenos Aires than in Montevideo, although it existed there, too). Death flights involved dropping desaparecidos (who were typically alive and often drugged) from an aircraft into the water.[60]

An allegorical hermeneutics is constantly in motion. The military later intimidates Julia by sending a general (her father's friend) to pick up her son from school without prior notice. In other words, we witness the dictatorship bringing democracy to a home it owns: the general holds a key to Julia's house. The grandfather shows that he can threaten his own grandson's life: in other words, the military institution is capable of jeopardizing a young democracy. Finally, Julia's brother (played by César Troncoso, a recurrent actor in Argentine and Uruguayan political thrillers) is a captain who protects their father's legacy.[61] A new generation of the military ensures that the dictatorship's crimes go unpunished and continues the masculine lineage of domination.

A last but still important allegorical scene can be traced to the use of screens. *Matar a todos* opens with historical found footage. Echoing *Hamlet*'s portrayal of court politics through a play within a play, political thrillers' inclusion of screens within screens foregrounds a mirror game. If, as Jameson contends, "video" is "postmodernism's most distinctive new medium,"[62] screens are the material, tangible objects that are constantly rendering this medium possible in political thrillers by broadcasting and replaying history through found footage.

In *Matar a todos* this materializes with a close-up of a TV broadcasting footage from the 1992 attack on the Israeli embassy in Buenos Aires, whose investigation remains controversial even now, more than three decades later. Daniel Burman's *Iosi, el espía arrepentido* (2022–2023), a political thriller series made for Amazon Prime Video, recovered the footage. This unsolved political crime with transnational ramifications highlights the prominence of impunity in the Southern Cone. It cites the unsolved genocidal crimes in Uruguay and the region as a whole. As Carolina Rocha notes, Schroeder's film, being an Argentine, Chilean, and Uruguayan co-production, "brings to the fore the transnational dimension of the politics of amnesia (and memory) in the Southern Cone in the early 1990s." As she reminds us, the Southern Cone states "collaborated not only during Operation Condor, but also over the first years of the re-democratization period."[63] This connivance, which exposes how the past is not past, is what is at stake in the film.

Gender and Space

One of the innovative aspects about Schroeder's film is that it subverts the genre's conventions while also engaging with a broader discussion on gender and power through the grammar of secrecy's prepositions of space and its ties to gender conflicts.

An instance of this subversion is a series of scenes shot in an indoor swimming pool, enhancing, first and foremost, the topographies of depths and interiority. Most of the critics have lost sight of these scenes, which deserve further attention. In passing, Rocha treats them as digressions, in which "[Julia] is seen swimming in a pool as if cleansing herself from the trauma of the repression."[64] Another possible reading would point to a second allusion to the death flights, as the desaparecidos end up sinking underwater. In any case, the pool scenes are far more central and polysemic: they show Julia helplessly diving, alone, for sunken secrets. As such, these scenes can be read through the genre's grammar of secrecy.

In the first scene, we see her descending into the depths without encountering informants from whom to extract secrets. Instead, the space highlights a woman's loneliness in a masculine world. From an underwater angle, the medium shot centers on her body. We see her for a few seconds, hesitantly standing on the pool's edge. The camera quickly goes above the surface, with a close-up of her eyes, looking into the water, still unconfidently. She finally decides to go into the pool but does not dive. Instead, she plunges vertically: she jumps with her feet first, as the camera switches perspective again to underwater: we see her swimming away without reaching the other edge, as we soon lose her trace in a vanishing point.

All this changes in the brief but eloquent second pool scene. Again Julia can be seen from underwater. This time the point of view is located at the opposite edge, toward which Julia swims. The camera swiftly moves above water again, with an overhead shot. We see her panting at the surface. The final frame shows the ripples caused by her body, an image of *aguas revueltas* (troubled waters), literally and again allegorically evoking the political turmoil caused by her disruptive investigation.

Unlike most of the films examined in chapters 4 and 5, *Matar a todos* does not display a triangle of characters. But the pool scenes, significantly, are triangular: there are three of them. At the end of the film, the progression toward the surface is complete: in the third pool scene the camera shoots everything from above, never going underwater, finishing with an overhead shot from which we once more see *aguas revueltas*.

The portrayal of space in these three scenes seems to be screaming that there is no possibility of diving/digging for too long or else we will drown. The tension of Julia's body, in contact or in proximity with the water, sways between the prepositions of space "under" and "above," depths and surface, within the interiority of the indoor pool. This tension seamlessly reflects the conflicts she experiences with the case: truth seems to be hidden in the abyssal profundity of a world ruled by men, sworn in secrecy to maintain masculine brutality unaltered. As the camera's trajectory follows from underwater to above water, secrecy seems to leave the depths—but, as Žižek warned us, nothing really changes, because speaking up to power is not possible.

Interspersed with these instances of isolation, the film also contains encounters in which the spatiality of secrecy and gender conflict is also prominent. Most of these meetings take place between Julia and men, usually producing a negative and oppressive affect. Almost all the meetings are filmed in public, on the surface level of the street. In one of them, Julia meets a policeman who has seen Berríos, but he refuses to speak, reproducing a trait that is typical of Southern Cone literary detective stories: what I call elsewhere the state's symbolic muteness.[65] The policeman acknowledges the military involvement in the cover-up but does not dare to testify against it. Essentially, he does not want to breach what Rita Segato calls the *mandato de masculinidad* (masculine imperative): a "command between peers or masculine confreres that demands a proof of belonging to the group."[66] His question to Julia says it all: "Do you think I can't see that you are alone in this?" Julia, the lonely swimmer diving into thrilling homosocial waters, repeats these frustrating meetings when she confronts her dad, her brother, her boss (a judge), and a Chilean lawyer who works in the Ministry of Defense.

All these encounters share what Barbour (writing about Derrida) calls "the state's monopoly on secrecy."[67] In other words, it is a fantasy that only the state can keep secrets underground. This mirage claims that state secrets are firm, not precarious. That monopoly, of course, implies that civil society has no secrets of its own. For Derrida, "if a right to the secret is not maintained, we are in a totalitarian space."[68] Set in democratic times, *Matar a todos* portrays a society in which secrets are not rights but privileges, laying out the seamless continuity of dictatorial practices after the military's return to the barracks.

Sebastián Carassai addresses the social perception of dictatorial sovereignty in Argentina, which resonates with the monopoly on secrecy: "The state, to exist efficiently, requires that its citizens suppose it to have an unlimited . . . even secret knowledge." Carassai defines it as "a civil superstition,"[69] which bestows an omniscient dimension on the state. This is what is at stake in the film, whose powerful male characters (metonymies of the state: the military, the law) are portrayed as fully aware of Julia's agenda. They are implausibly privileged in spying on her moves: keepers of the state's secrets and invaders of society's private ones.

But, as Judith Butler points out, "there is nothing of life that is not precarious—except, of course, in fantasy, and in military fantasies in particular."[70] Even though the military men in the film believe in their fantasy and manage to maintain it as part of the democratic state's narrative, Julia's investigation shows us that their monopoly on secrecy is starting to crumble. Despite the lack of acknowledgment of their connivance with Berríos and the Chilean military men and, more broadly, their participation in forced disappearances during the Uruguayan dictatorship, Julia (and the audience) knows they are guilty. She might need to be able to prove it, but the secret has long been leaked, its monopoly clearly thrilled by the negative affect of each encounter we see.

Language and Politics

Perhaps the most meaningful of these negative encounters is Julia's experience with her father. When she asks him about Berríos, he responds *dejame en paz* (leave me alone/in peace). In this context, Southern Cone political thrillers offer a panoramic and diachronic portrayal of how empty signifiers like "peace" or "freedom" can be ascribed, in Ernesto Laclau's terms, to multiple, often contradictory and "temporary signifieds," which ultimately "are the result of a political competition."[71] Political thrillers show how these meanings are ephemeral: they change across different countries—as well as within them.

It is hard not to hear Latin American dictators themselves in the voice of Julia's father, pressuring postdictatorial societies to stop meddling with them, to let them die (or keep secretly operating) "in peace." The father's voice echoes the cynical meaning that the use of the word *paz* had during the dictatorship. As Feitlowitz notes, "tranquility did not equal peace," which was understood as "the continuation of war by other means."[72] In *Matar a todos,* "peace" entails the absence of conflict and dissent to ensure that the dictatorial legacy and impunity prevail.

When the father accuses Julia of always getting into trouble (*siempre metiéndote en problemas*), the reflexive verb *meterse* explicitly cites a dictatorial leitmotif: *no te metas* (do not get involved), common in both Uruguay and Argentina. *Meterse* (literally "to put oneself somewhere") lacks the adverbial complement it requires—it does not specify where one would put oneself. But it presupposes a where: this elided space, in daily language, was tacitly occupied by *problemas* (troubles: politics). Getting involved in politics, troubling the waters, presupposes an affront to "peace." As Feitlowitz claims, "peace" could be "destroyed by independent thought; an individual quietly thinking was likely committing an act of war."[73] When Julia asks her father what kind of trouble he is talking about, he replies "the same as always." In this sentence, language exposes the crack of a precarious secret: the acknowledgment that, even after the dictatorship was over, the problems of the past "always" remained, oblivious to the course of history.

In this conversation Julia's father mentions Alejandro, her Argentine ex-partner, the only man who actually encourages her to keep digging/diving. The father describes him bluntly with another prominent dictatorial expression, *subversivo* (subversive), which is key to understanding the political backdrop of these political thrillers and their transnational ties. In the prologue of the *Nunca más* (1984) report that laid the groundwork for the subsequent trial of the military juntas in Argentina in 1985, the novelist Ernesto Sabato defines "subversive" as an "epithet" that "itself came to be used with a vast and vague range of meaning." A "semantic delirium," whose polysemy can be understood as another empty signifier, *subversivo* could mean not only "Marxist-Leninist, traitors to the fatherland, materialists and atheists" but also "enemies of Western, Christian values," to name a few. This semantic laxity implied that "anyone was at risk—from those who were proposing a social revolution, to aware adolescents who merely went out to the shanty towns to help the people living there."[74] It is unclear whether Alejandro is a former Uruguayan Tupamaro, an Argentine Montonero, or simply a civilian involved in politics, because the signifier *subversivo* could entail all these different meanings.

After the dictatorship, *subversivo* often metamorphoses into *populista* (populist). Although the term has been used in Spanish at least ever since the 1920s, there is enough documentation to detect a semantic displacement in this signifier from a technical to a pejorative meaning in the late 1990s and early 2000s.[75] Such displacement could be linked to a reaction against the democratization processes experienced in certain parts of Latin America (but also in Spain) after long dictatorial periods. In the Southern Cone, in particular, *populista* became a camouflaged version of *subversivo*, a new popular slur to stigmatize and lump together with progressive politics, because it denoted those who challenged a series of right-wing dogmas. In Argentina and Uruguay these dogmas were tied to denying the possibility of carrying out trials against the military and more state intervention in health, education, and wealth distribution.

As political scientist Gerardo Aboy Carlés points out, "the so-called neo-populism" of the postdictatorship period "should not be equated to the classic Latin American populisms, like Yrigoyenismo, Varguismo, Cardenismo, or Peronismo . . . because of the very way in which all these political identities were structured." Aboy Carlés is here thinking not only of the Pink Tide but also more specifically about 1990s right-wing administrations (Carlos Saúl Menem, Alberto Fujimori, Fernando Collor de Melo) that implemented policies often seen as right-wing populism in the region. For Aboy Carlés, the only element that these postdictatorial and predictatorial populist experiences share is "personalist features."[76] But beyond the multiple nuances and contradictions surrounding the political concept itself, *populista* has come to be a very popular insult (a possible addition to Feitlowitz's lexicon) from the 2000s until our days, especially as a reaction to the Pink Tide.[77]

In the late 2010s, after female presidencies linked to the Pink Tide (Michele de Bachelet, Cristina Fernández de Kirchner, Dilma Roussef) but even more after the impact caused by the fourth-wave grassroots feminist movement such as Ni Una Menos (Not One [Woman] Less), a new empty signifier occupies this derogatory space: the term *ideología de género* "denounces" the so-called indoctrination of "gender ideology" and its undermining of the "traditional family."[78] Of course, ascribing causality between the movement and its reaction would amount to blaming feminism for its denigrations. As Segato points out, these alt-right responses may have to do more with a growing generalized economic disenfranchisement.[79] But in any case, the *ideología de género* is perceived as a way of understanding politics that aspire to defy the status quo, as *subversivo* and *populista* once were, with very different and often contradictory agendas.

To put it briefly, these three derogatory signifiers are essentially straw men. As a strong female character, fighting to redefine what a democratic state should be and diving into a patriarchal society that resists past examination of the dictatorship's legacy, Julia embodies them.

In this context, her failed attempt to speak up to power echoes the failures of the other important female character of the film: a Chilean madwoman who witnessed Berríos's political crimes in the 1970s. Julia interviews her in Santiago. The encounter is still tainted with negative affect, in which the grammar of secrecy is explicitly featured through the preposition of space "under."

The woman tells Julia about the literary gatherings that used to take place in her house, where the basements were used for torture.[80] She commodifies the past, leasing her knowledge about the state secrets. Her knowledge does not seem to be superficial in the sense that it is tied to the witnessed truth of torture, hidden underground. Nevertheless, due to her madness, no one "buys" her secrets about the past, which therefore become shallow, untrustworthy, volatile—in a word, precarious. Once again, extracting secrets is portrayed as a futile task.

The father's last words to Julia from his hospital deathbed sound like both a dictatorial death rattle and a prophetic warning from constituted power: "Your strength is worthless if you don't have power." This stertorous maxim sums up the *palafrenera*'s failure to denounce the king's new clothes. Moreover, from the perspective of the 2020s, his words also resonate in the downfall of many progressive administrations throughout Latin America. Their intention to produce structural change in most cases led to the strengthening of autocratic regimes, veiled coups d'état, deepening economic instability, the return of rampant crises of representation, and the emergence of an alt-right that would agree with Julia's father.

ZANAHORIA (2014)

Space and Secrecy

Zanahoria: detrás de la verdad explicitly problematizes the grammar of secrecy of classic American political thrillers. In Enrique Buchichio's film, truth is not located "under" or "behind" a veil through which characters and spectators cannot see. Prepositions of space work here in the opposite way: it is the characters that are placed "behind the truth." The ambivalent subtitle announces this problematization. For one thing, *detrás de* can be translated "in pursuit of," which alludes to the genre's investigative dimension: the film tells the story of two journalists from a newsroom invested in unveiling a secret provided by a mysterious source that could potentially affect the upcoming elections.

As Edwin Culp notes, all of this immediately cites *All the President's Men*.[81] Nevertheless, *detrás de* can also be translated with one of the central prepositions of space of the grammar of secrecy: "behind." Whereas a state secret is hidden underground in a parking lot in Pakula's thriller, here secrecy is actually visible on the streets. The film's subtitle offers a countertopology of secrecy: instead of depths, we get surface. The Uruguayan journalists are always a few steps behind the truth, however, in the sense that they are always delayed in the process of exposing a secret that is paradoxically visible to all.

The film's title also has several meanings. To begin with, *Zanahoria* (carrot) is a common insult in the Río de la Plata culture to imply lack of intelligence and lack of vivacity. This describes the story's main characters quite well, as we find out by the end of the film. *Zanahoria* explicitly cites a cover-up ("Operation Carrot") that allegedly took place during the downfall of the Uruguayan dictatorship (1973–1985). The operation involved the exhumation of the bodies of desaparecidos, conducted by the military regime in 1984, "in order to destroy them or make them disappear permanently,"[82] as determined by the forensic anthropologist José López Mazz in 2011. The operation was named after the position in which most bodies were initially buried: vertically (like carrots growing underground), to hinder their eventual discovery.

What is at stake in this cover-up is the very existence of a state secret: a military regime desperately seeks to erase its traces, knowing that a democratic government will soon take control of the state. Eliminating a body completely is the ultimate way of duplicating and culminating forced disappearance: corpses concealed underground leave open the possibility of a report of the crime, while missing bodies ensure the perpetrators' impunity. The permanence of disappearance guarantees that the repressive methods of the military against the detainees' bodies remain obscure, concealing if and how they were treated, tortured, killed, and disposed of.

At the same time, *Zanahoria* also evokes a broader connotation: the carrot-and-stick metaphor. It is a blending of reward and punishment that linguists call a "conative effect" (an action that induces a desired behavioral response from an interlocutor). The carrot-and-stick metaphor is often used to explain sociopolitical phenomena. A cart driver holds the carrot in front of a donkey or mule's bridle, just close enough to keep the animal moving forward (tantalized by the smell and sight) but still out of reach. The closeness of the dangling carrot constitutes a deceiving promise for the animal (which does not know that it will never get the chance to bite the carrot) and thus serves the driver's interest without reward.

Buchichio plays with this metaphor through the fictional retelling of a report written by Alfredo García, a senior journalist of the leftist weekly newspaper *Voces* (where the real report was originally published), and Jorge Lauro, one of his younger staff members. The film is an account of their fruitless attempt to reveal classified information. Much like a donkey or mule, they are always a few steps behind the truth, serving someone else's purpose.

The cart driver holding the film's carrot is Walter Morales, an enigmatic character who contacts Alfredo and Jorge, claiming to be a former secret agent. At their first meeting Walter claims he wants to offer them classified information, tangible evidence of the dictatorial crimes against humanity: footage of torture, the location of corpses, and, finally, the details of "Operation Zanahoria." Like most of the film, the meeting scene is shot at night, creating an obvious aura of enigma, the chiaroscuro of film noir.

Despite its mysterious atmosphere, *Zanahoria* subverts the genre's horizon of expectations. The meetings between Woodward and Deep Throat (whose face we never see clearly) in *All the President's Men* are always filmed in an underground parking lot, through medium to long shots. The camera keeps its distance from the informant, who is always seen from the journalist's point of view. The camera shows us Woodward going downstairs to meet him: a rewriting of the Christian *descensus ad inferos*, a harrowing but triumphant descent to hell.

In *Zanahoria*, we soon find out, hell is on the streets. The encounters between the journalists and their informant initially reproduce this opacity. In fact, the first meeting plays with the spatiality announced in the film's subtitle ("behind the truth"): Walter, promising knowledge, sits in the back seat of the car, behind the journalists, who remain temporarily ahead of the truth. But, unlike what happens in Pakula's film, things quickly become complicated. In exchange for money, Walter drip-feeds believable hints to the journalists. At first, we see him only partially, through the reflection in the rearview mirror. When asked about the physical location of the footage and documents, he says they are in a safe space, on VHS tapes and floppy disks.

In their second encounter Walter reveals that his secrets are *en el fondo de casa*. This is again an ambivalent use of the genre's grammar of secrecy: the word *fondo* can mean "backyard" but also "basement," evoking the two typical prepositions of space (behind and under) and their respective topographies (interiority and depth). After these first meetings, Walter's face (even his whole body) starts to be clearly and distinctively visible, in front of any other character and above ground. Much like the camera work in the pool scenes of *Matar a todos*, secrecy leaves interiority and the depths. The fourth encounter even happens in broad daylight, out in the open.

One of the last meetings (significantly, shot now from the informant's perspective) takes place outside a parking lot whose sign acts as a backdrop, reading *Estacionamiento/Parking* (in Spanish and English), another reference to the classic scene in Pakula's film. Streetlamps illuminate the face of Walter, who seems to be a Latin American translation of Deep Throat. Here almost everything is surface.

But why is Walter, a former intelligence officer, helping a bunch of leftist journalists anyway? He claims that he wants the modernization of the military, but is it all a smoke screen? These questions trigger the presence of "paranoid fiction" in the plot, a notion coined by literary theorist Leo Bersani, further developed and made popular by Piglia in the Hispanic literary field. According to Piglia, this narrative strategy features in all contemporary literature. Paranoid fiction is exacerbated in detective stories and, I may add, in political thrillers, which are also infested with unreliable testimonies that obfuscate the disclosure of secrets. For Piglia, paranoid fiction presupposes a "paranoid consciousness . . . a hermeneutical delirium," which "considers that everything obeys a hidden cause, a sort of encrypted message that is 'addressed to me.'"[83] Alfredo and Jorge fall prey to this fiction for most of the film. They feel they are being chased and watched and that solid secrets will soon be revealed to them.

Paranoia references a central trope of the genre: high stakes. *Zanahoria* plays with the genre's horizon of expectations, in that revealing secrets often leads to high stakes, but no one is really spying on the journalists in the film. They are merely fantasizing and filling in the gaps left by Walter's fictionally curated testimony. What Piglia sees as the transition from not knowing to knowing in the detective thriller is constantly deferred here. In turn, state secrets remain elusive and precarious.[84]

After fruitless encounters, they realize that Walter's hints, like the carrot-and-stick metaphor, are only indeterminately postponing the materialization of truth. By the end of the film, the journalists have become aware that their informant has no secrets to unveil—or, if he does, he will not disclose them. They practically dismantle a car in a parking lot, trying to find the VHS tapes and the floppy disks that Walter claims to have hidden there. But deep down there is nothing to be found. Much as in *Matar a todos*, the emergence of underground secrets does not change the course of history: the *palafreneros* here are once more impotent.

This scene in the film subverts other classic thrillers. The most explicit one is William Friedkin's police thriller *The French Connection* (1971). In particular, I am thinking of the scene, also set in a garage, in which New York City police officer Popeye Doyle and his sidekicks dismantle the car of their person of interest. They tear it apart, piece by piece, looking for drugs. The scene is a typical example of how suspense works in classic thrillers: after a long wait and apparent dead ends, the police eventually find the drugs in the least expected place inside the car, emerging successfully from the challenge.

Similarly, Buchichio's scene implicitly cites Fritz Lang's *The Ministry of Fear* (1944), where we see Scotland Yard digging up the ground for a cake, which contains a microfilm that is evidence of an act of Nazi espionage. Ultimately, the officers manage to extract the secret, materializing the high stakes and resolving suspense.

By contrast, *Zanahoria* offers us the opposite: heroism, high stakes, and suspense do not find a straightforward resolution. The encounters were mere transactions in exchange not for knowledge but only for the superficial appearance of it. The journalists were always behind the truth (*detrás de la verdad*). Buchichio plays with the precarious threshold that the prepositions of space try but fail to separate: the "above" and "outside" of Montevideo streets subvert the "under" and the "inside" of Pakula's Washington underground parking lots. Surface beats depth; exteriority trumps interiority.

Secrecy and Precarity

Walter, then, should be read not so much as a Latin American transparent translation of a Deep Throat figure but as his problematization. Walter reminds us of Bernal's García, as he, too, is contaminated by the Hispanic *pícaro* who has no morals (hence Walter's ironic last name: Morales) and scams others for survival.[85] Whereas the *pícaro* often informs the figure of the hero in political thrillers, *Zanahoria* offers an innovative variation on this convention, as Walter instantiates how the *pícaro* can also inform the figure of the villain instead. Because Walter is an unethical *pícaro*, his secret is an exhibition of precarity. He sells *pescado podrido* (literally, rotten fish), a Río de la Plata idiom meaning commodified "false information," not that different from the fake news we have become familiar with in recent years.

Walter's precarious secrets also remind us of Derrida's discussion of Søren Kierkegaard's exegesis of biblical secrets—particularly, Yahweh's undisclosed secrets. Unlike Kierkegaard, Derrida argues that the secrecy surrounding God's command for Abraham to sacrifice Isaac does "not have the sense of something to hide." Instead, "it is a secret without content . . . without any secret other than the very request for secrecy."[86] Similarly, Walter's secrets are contentless: they do not seem to entail any hidden political message or intention. Despite their lack of content, his secrets are temporarily effective because they are plausible: Walter knows well the lexicon of the secret police and the military modus operandi. But unlike Deep Throat's, his secrets do not seek to change the course of history, only to maintain business as usual.

Walter, however, is not even deceiving the journalists to secure the impunity of the dictatorship. He tries to sell a secret because his commodity is in demand: as Huyssen points out, "the past is selling better than the future."[87]

Or, as Kraniauskas puts it in discussing the Mexican context, "now it is money that has imposed itself as *nomos*—replacing the public square—once the space of possible political transformation."[88] Reduced to and motivated solely by exchange value, Walter's secrets are precarious because they do not contain any solid truths about Uruguay's past: they are merely a response to and the ultimate expression of economic precarity.

But precarity, once more, overflows economics, contaminating the political. Much like other Southern Cone political thrillers, *Zanahoria* imagines and dramatizes the political and the historical through triangles. Like secrets, these triangles are precarious, susceptible to destabilization, and often initiated by the apparition of the unstable third side (the third person mentioned in my discussion of *Cabra-cega*). The prominence of the third person has been studied in depth by linguists as well as literary and political theorists—throughout the past decades—from Émile Benveniste, Emmanuel Lévinas, and Maurice Blanchot to Roberto Esposito and Alberto Moreiras. The discussion is especially productive in terms of the impersonal dimension of the third person.[89] As Moreiras notes, paraphrasing Lévinas, "the third is a problem" because "its manifestation as absence breaks proximity" and this "perturbed proximity . . . is the typical place of the political."[90] In this context, Walter's triangular disruption mimics Deep Throat in *All the President's Men*'s. He disturbs the journalists' dialogical community while simultaneously perpetrating a hyper-political invasion in their infrapolitical lives, similar to the ones discussed in chapter 3.

This is made clear in the narrative of Jorge, the younger journalist: his father was killed during the dictatorship, but as part of a common felony that was completely unrelated to the genocide. In addition, unlike Alfredo, Jorge has not experienced the dictatorship. Knowing all of this too well, Walter pierces through the boundary that reaffirms "the absolute difference between life and politics,"[91] in Moreiras's terms. He does so by capitalizing on Jorge's personal grief. The father's murderers were never caught, so Walter cynically compares Jorge's situation with that of the child of a desaparecido. Later on, when Jorge no longer believes in any of Walter's *pescado podrido*, Walter promises he will obtain information from the secret services to clarify the situation in which his father was killed. In short, Walter trades in history and spectrality.

History and Specters

In Uruguay, as Buchichio himself notes, Walter is easily identified as a *tira* (cop, often with a negative or distrustful connotation).[92] That is, he stands for many men who, after being used as workers by dictatorships, had no steady income, either becoming unemployed or being hired by organized crime. Drug dealers as well as intelligence agencies and police gangs were and still are tolerated (sometimes even fueled) by democratic states, revealing the seamless power of masculine brutality in Latin America and beyond.

Like Bernal's García in *El complot mongol,* Walter evokes Bobbio's *sottogoverno* (subgovernment), an invisible power "constituted and organized not only to fight against public power but also to obtain unlawful benefits" from it.[93] This is why Walter's prepositions of space point to interiority and depths, behind and underneath us: the backyard and the basement of power (*el fondo*).

But even if he might not necessarily be connected with the dictatorship, Walter's intentions are not entirely disconnected from it either. Rosalba Oxandarat states in her review of the film that "the story of a minor scam . . . puts on center stage the problem of the major scam":[94] the absence of a trial against the Uruguayan military juntas. The minor scam is only possible thanks to greater scam. Although Walter's goal is not to secure impunity for the dictatorship, this impunity enables someone like him to exist and operate in the world, trading in the spectral secrets of the past. What is fascinating about the real person who inspired Walter, according to Buchichio, is that he used to scam for small amounts, a sign of precarity and lower stakes: an inversely proportional reflection of the major scam mentioned by Oxandarat.[95]

As Idelber Avelar claims, "the erasure of the past as past is the cornerstone of all commodification, even when the past becomes yet another commodity for sale in the present."[96] In this sense, the specters of the dictatorship and Buchichio's tale of picaresque precarity are not as disjointed as Walter's intentions may initially suggest. The political aspect of his secrecy, however, is visible not in content but in form, displaying what Derrida calls a "request for secrecy," which is the condition for the perpetuation of Walter's deceit. Until the journalists hear from colleagues at other newspapers that they went through the same experience, the swindler's fictional narrative can be sustained for the journalists and the audience.

In terms of the political thriller, all of this takes us to the film's use of suspense. According to Lars Ole Sauerberg's classic definition, two basic factors are involved in suspense: concealment and protraction. In other words, suspense can be produced when a camera or a plot hides something from the audience or when the answer to an expected outcome is postponed.[97] In leaving us with nothing at the end of the story, Buchichio innovatively uses suspense as a tool to talk about how military secrecy imposes a prolongation of dictatorial torture by other means in democratic times: there is no way to truly know what happened to the desaparecidos' bodies as long as the military keeps withholding the information.

Zanahoria portrays the past as a force invading the present, which is echoed in the film's frustrating use of suspense. Walter's "rotten fish" (or "rotten meat," as it is sometimes also called) about the desaparecidos reverberates in their "rotten flesh," still reeking because the location of many of their bodies remains unknown to this day. This is why the transition from unknowing to knowing never takes place. The unveiling of the dictatorship's secrets, like Walter's, ultimately follows the same stick-and-carrot logic: they "never arrived and are still waited upon," as Oxandarat notes.[98]

One of López Mazz's conclusions based on his forensic work is that securing the dictatorship's secrecy in democratic times was the very premise of "Operation Carrot," as understood by the controversial report by the Comisión para la Paz (2000–2003), under Jorge Batlle's right-wing administration. According to López Mazz, that report states that "evidence from military figures . . . suggested that all of the missing bodies had been exhumed . . . then burned and the ashes thrown into the Bay of Montevideo." He believes, however, that this evidence was more *pescado podrido*, "false information [that] also sought to continue concealment of the bodies and discourage any further search activity being demanded by relatives."[99] To put it differently, for López Mazz, Operation Carrot itself (at least in the terms disclosed by the military) was a bluff to dissuade victims' families from looking for their desaparecidos.

Regardless of the nature of Walter's intentions (financial or political), his smoke screen imitates the military's falsification of history. As Avelar claims in his analysis of Piglia's postdictatorial novels, "if in the exactitude of representation, appropriated by the State, our narrations have become archival citation in the bureaucratic machine, the only course is to invent false and apocryphal stories."[100] This is precisely what Walter does, although his goal, of course, is not to create fictions to help us cope with falsehood but to perpetuate and profit from it.

According to Culp, Latin American space is defined by lack: "a landscape without bodies." In turn, *Zanahoria*'s "use of contiguity, analogy, repetition, deceit and falsehood" is a response to a time "when the image is incapable to denounce."[101] In other words, when speaking up to power, crying out loud that the king is naked does not seem to change the course of history. Denouncing remains ineffective in the film because the alleged space where the bodies were buried and exhumed remains unknown.

The failure to locate the site serves as a metonymy for the extraction of truth that is part of political thrillers' horizon of expectations: in *Zanahoria* there is nothing to extract/exhume and nowhere to do it. As Culp notes, "the only way to recuperate [the bodies], would be to excavate it all, to remove the entire surface of the ground."[102] Unveiling the state secret becomes an impossible archaeological task: it would mean effacing the entirety of the common ground we walk on. Much like *Matar a todos* and the Paraguayan *Matar a un muerto* (examined in chapter 5), Buchichio's film should be read as a story about the impossibility of unearthing. This is perhaps the key subversion of one of the genre's main conventions: the extraction of secrets.

Genre and History

Zanahoria engages with genocide and forced disappearance not by directly portraying scenes of torture, secret burials, or exhumations but through the spectrality they leave behind. The film opens with a close-up of a TV screen broadcasting the poll results for the 2004 Uruguayan general elections—another example of the embedding of historical found footage into the main narrative. On a certain level, as Buchichio admits, the embedding of historical found footage also works as a shortcut to deal with precarious budgets.[103] Reenacting a past election is a privilege that only Hollywood political thrillers can comfortably afford.

This inclusion of screens could also be read as a time and storytelling machine—synthesizing, framing, and organizing the historical narrative for the audience. Derrida links spectrality, spatiality, and politics precisely to the media and mediums, in that the "news, the press, tele-communications, techno-tele-discursivity, . . . that which in general assures and determines the *spacing* of public space, the very possibility of the *res publica* and the phenomenality of the political . . . is neither living nor dead, present nor absent: it spectralizes."[104] Compared to previous forms of capturing the ephemeral nature of history (such as painting, literature, and photography), the phantasmagorical footage spectralizes even more because it is efficient (due to its recording possibilities) and intense (because of the way cameras can capture motion pictures).

Using historical found footage in film is not a new trend and did not start with the political thriller. As Jaimie Baron writes, "filmmakers and other media practitioners have been drawing on preexisting audiovisual documents for over a century." Baron traces this use of preexisting footage to documentaries since the 1920s, but its use in fiction has become increasingly productive since the late twentieth century. The presence of screens is integral to the genre, with its roots traceable as far back as *The Manchurian Candidate* (1962), where the TV works almost like a character that mediates in the plot. What might be new, says Baron, is that "as home video and digital photography collections as well as online digital video and photography archives have grown, the reuse of such documents in films has also expanded."[105] This is true for the footage that we see, but even more so for the footage we do not see—for instance, Walter's VHS tapes, which may not even exist.

Baron defines this growing visual repository as "the archive affect": the "desire for the presence of history," which "is always accompanied by our recognition of its absence."[106] In this context, she links the "archive affect" to nostalgia. Latin American political thrillers often (though not always, as we have seen in the guerrilla thrillers) shun this nostalgia because the past they portray is often not likely to be missed. Perhaps one of the main points of the use of these screens in political thrillers has to do with what Haddu terms a "visual palimpsest,"[107] where different layers of the past become indistinguishable from the present. Because the past is not past, there is no room for nostalgia. In *Zanahoria* the palimpsest resonates in the literal underground soil layers that point to the metaphorical tensions between the depths and the surface of secrecy.

Zanahoria and similar thrillers thus use screens because this increasing amount of footage constitutes "ever larger chunks of the social and political perception of the world," in Huyssen's terms.[108] Political thrillers engage in a kind of symbolic teleportation, where the TV news of any given Tuesday evening, which otherwise would be susceptible to being swallowed by the following newscast, reappears (like a specter) in the "afterlife" of the events and people who were originally involved in them.

As such, Buchichio overlaps another triangle, this time chronological layers, key years in recent Uruguayan history that inform each other: 1984, 2004, and 2014. These dates punctuate a historical arc. The year 1984 evokes the twilight of the dictatorship (1973–1985), encapsulated in "Operación Zanahoria." It also alludes to the subsequent resumption of a democratic bipartisan order that would see two decades of administrations led by the Colorado and Blanco parties (from 1984 to 2004), which made sure to keep the military's crimes against humanity under wraps. After all, it was the Partido Colorado itself that created the conditions for the self-coup in the early 1970s that led to the dictatorship. Perhaps the most blatant image of this resumption was the Expiry Law, an amnesty for the military signed in 1986 by both mainstream parties.

The film is set in 2004, when the progressive Frente Amplio (Broad Front, led by Tabaré Vázquez) was elected, which interrupted the bipartisan order. The emergence of this new third party (constituting yet another triangle) brought hope of justice for the victims of the genocide to some (and threats to others). Equally, 2004 stands for the anxieties and fears that constituted a disruption in Uruguayan democracy, as the incipient Frente government would include former Tupamaros, the left-wing urban guerrilla movement (active before and during the dictatorship) that features in *État de siège*.[109]

Zanahoria was released a decade after the 2004 election, in 2014, during the campaign for Vázquez's second term at the end of José Mujica's administration (2010–2015). By 2014 the three consecutive Frente governments had managed to put behind bars the dictators Gregorio Álvarez and Juan María Bordaberry (as well as his chancellor Juan Carlos Blanco Estradé and Colonel Luis Maurente). Until then, they were the only ones who served time in prison due to their involvement with forced disappearance.[110] Nevertheless, whereas Uruguay put Bordaberry and Maurente on trial, they were quickly put under house arrest, where they died a few years later. It was Italy, not Uruguay, that prosecuted Blanco Estradé, as some of the desaparecidos were Italian Uruguayans. By 2014 the Frente had managed to promulgate a law that superseded the amnesty but was not capable of annulling it.[111] In this context, *Zanahoria* displays the journalists' failed attempt as an echo of this major truncated endeavor: the impossibility of restoring the ethics breached by genocide.

FINAL THOUGHTS

Following Michel de Certeau's idea that "an event is not what we can see or know about it but what it becomes,"[112] *Zanahoria* plays on these triangular milestones (1984, 2004, and 2014) that punctuate Uruguayan recent history. In Benveniste's terms, the film juxtaposes the *énoncé* (the past, what is said) and the *énonciation* (the present, the act of saying).[113] Both inform each other, as the film engages with precarious secrets not only during dictatorship but also under democracy, much like *Matar a todos*. By contrast, *Cabra-cega*, like many guerrilla thrillers, foregrounds only events from the dictatorial past, which nonetheless still speak to the democratic present.

In spite of Žižek's claim that everyone fails to speak up to power in our times, contemporary American political thrillers keep maintaining the illusion that this is still possible. We need only think of Doug Liman's *Fair Game* (2010), which ends with a blend of fictional reenactment, historical found footage, and closing credits that reaffirm this illusion. The film tells the story of Valerie Plame, a former covert CIA agent whose identity was publicly exposed by an officer from the George W. Bush administration. The secret was leaked in retaliation against Plame's husband, a diplomat who had challenged the government's accusations that Iraq had weapons of mass destruction. The film's closure visually translates this by depicting Plame testifying about her case before a congressional committee, literally speaking up to power, which led to convicting Dick Cheney's chief of staff for the leak. Similar arguments could be made about other recent political thrillers, such as *Rendition* (2007), *State of Play* (2009), and *The Post* (2017), whose dénouements continue to heroize the role of journalists in leaks, as agents who successfully speak up to power and manage to expose the powerful in ways that are not that different from, say, a classic, now remote in time: *All the President's Men*.

By contrast, Latin American political thrillers challenge the confidence we see in these American models, which all too often pose the idea that stable representation can be restored, that criminals eventually get their comeuppance, that heroism is still a valid approach to portray political and historical events, and that revealing secrets can have an effective impact in the world. In short, the films discussed in this chapter take the point of view of the resistance against genocide, embodied either in the guerrillas or in the often-defeated human rights lawyers or journalists. Instead, chapter 5 explores political thrillers told from the perspective of characters precisely like *Zanahoria*'s Morales, which subvert the genre figure of the villain in innovative ways.

CHAPTER FIVE

Screening Oppression

PARAMILITARY, ACCOMPLICES, AND UNEMPLOYED THUGS IN ACTION

Esa es la trampa: el presente no existe.

GASPAR GALAZ, CHILEAN ASTRONOMER INTERVIEWED IN PATRICIO GUZMÁN'S *NOSTALGIA DE LA LUZ* (2010)

IT TAKES TWO TO TANGO; IT TAKES MORE THAN ONE ruthless military junta to orchestrate a genocide. Or so Latin American political thrillers insist on telling us. This chapter examines three political thrillers from Argentina, Paraguay, and Chile: Benjamín Naishtat's *Rojo* (2018), Hugo Giménez's *Matar a un muerto* (2019), and Andrés Wood's *Araña* (2019). These films are recent instantiations of a long-standing genealogy in Southern Cone genre cinema (particularly within the Argentine context) that can be traced back to the early 1970s. They explore the extent to which the militarized state was the sole agent behind the dictatorships' crimes against humanity.

As such, they raise questions that are often posed by political and historiographical accounts of Southern Cone dictatorial regimes.[1] Yet these questions are also central to the genre itself, evoking the whodunit, typical of the detective thriller and some political thrillers. It could be argued that the genre problematizes the whodunit by comprehensively implicating society itself as an accomplice in Operation Condor. These thrillers complicate the Kantian notion of radical evil by enhancing the role that civil society has played in indirectly enabling or directly participating in the emergence of the different coups throughout the region in the 1960s and the 1970s as well as its involvement during and after the dictatorships.

The films examined here, however, engage with these questions against the grain. Unlike the human rights thrillers examined in chapter 4, they do not offer investigative plots filled with characters who try but fail to solve the whodunit and restore justice at the end. By contrast, these thrillers privilege stories from the perpetrators' side of the genocide, without necessarily empathizing or aligning with it. Significantly, none of these thrillers reenact historical events from the military's perspective. Instead, they offer us the perspective of agents who share different degrees of connivance with the military.

Unlike some critics' interpretations, the thrillers examined in this chapter fit in a broader and complex genealogy that goes beyond Costa-Gavras's influence.[2] Instead, some of these films update what Elena Goity and David Oubiña call the Argentine *thriller parapolicial* or *policial post-Proceso,* the "paramilitary thriller" of the 1980s as Burucúa would translate it.[3] As Goity and Oubiña observe, this type of political thriller does not feature "the dialectic between knowing and not knowing" typical of the human rights cluster.[4] The emphasis is not so much on investigating a political crime (in this case, various instances of Operation Condor) but on screening the ways in which oppression operates in civil society, without presenting a hero to rectify it. As a film review of one of these paramilitary thrillers eloquently puts it, these stories are "told from the point of view of the enemy."[5] Heroes are either absent or reduced to impotent avengers.[6]

Instead of following Costa-Gavras, most of these films could be best described as Southern Cone translations of a tradition (within the political thriller) inaugurated by Fred Zinnemann's *The Day of the Jackal* (1973). The plot privileges the narrative exploration of the villain more than the vicissitudes of the hero or the victim. In Zinnemann's film radical evil is embodied by the titular Jackal, a cold-hearted hit man hired to assassinate Charles de Gaulle after participating in the assassination of Rafael Trujillo. The magnicide attempt is sponsored by a far-right paramilitary organization.

Following the example set by Zinnemann's film, the political thrillers analyzed here explore the Far Right's ties with Operation Condor—before and after seizing state power—and its impact on civil society in the national contexts of Southern Cone countries. As such, they emphasize the "civic" side in the phrase "civic-military dictatorship,"[7] a term that originated in Argentine political and intellectual debates in the late 2000s and was later transplanted to other Southern Cone countries, remaining controversial to this day.[8] The phrase aims to expand the understanding of the role played by civilian institutions (corporations, the church, and, more broadly, nonmilitarized sectors of society as a whole) in legitimizing and upholding dictatorial rule.

This important genealogy of political thrillers starts in Argentina. Unlike Goity, Oubiña, and Burucúa, however, I trace their origin back long before the postdictatorial paramilitary thriller, to Raymundo Gleyzer's *Los traidores*

(1973), a film that tells the story from the point of view of an ethically and politically ambiguous union leader, as noted in chapter 3. This tradition also has an important forerunner in Brazil, with Argentine director Héctor Babenco's film *Lúcio Flávio: o passageiro da agonia* (1977), a crime thriller that portrays an outlaw whose sinister ties with the Brazilian dictatorship's death squads are shown only tangentially to avoid censorship.[9] In postdictatorial films, ambiguity—the key ingredient to portray the civilian's complicity with the military—is sometimes incarnated in a strongman, a male villain who often has ties with or directly belongs to the paramilitary. The figure of the paramilitary villain has deep roots beyond postdictatorial Argentina. We can already see him in the Mexican priest in *Canoa*, for example. In addition, we could trace a lineage that connects these Southern Cone postdictatorial villainous figures with the film noir far-right gangsters of the postwar thrillers set in Argentina and Brazil, examined in chapter 1. The link that connects them perhaps can be found in the caudillo-like *matón* (thug) that we see in classic Argentine political dramas, such as Fernando Ayala's *El jefe* (1958) and Leopoldo Torre Nilsson's *Fin de fiesta* (1960). This typical villain, however, is problematized in political thrillers, often portrayed as a rudimentary cog in the precarious wheel of constituted power.

Juan Carlos Desanzo's *En retirada* (1984) is another foundational film of this genealogy. Portraying Buenos Aires as a labyrinthine city, in the more conventional tradition of the thriller, Desanzo puts on center stage a hit man, El Oso (played by Rodolfo Ranni), who becomes unemployed after the dictatorship ends, much like Walter Morales in *Zanahoria*. While Argentina is voting for its first democratic president after seven years of dictatorial rule, we see El Oso reproducing the cruel practices he once imposed on political prisoners (such as kidnapping, rape, torture, and blackmail), now inflicted on his personal relations. Desanzo imbues El Oso with the *pícaro*'s survival skills in an environment in which his life is at risk. El Oso's precarious position enhances his sense of ambiguity—after all, he is chased by both sides of the conflict—not only by the father of a desaparecido who recognized him but also by his own former paramilitary colleagues and employers, who are aligned in lying low as part of a tactical retreat. Once he becomes a liability to the dictatorial agents, he is killed by friendly fire at the film's conclusion.

En retirada and the films it influenced pay attention to the financial dimension in the way oppression was precariously funded during the region's dictatorships. As such, they yet again underscore precarity's key role in the genre. At the same time, despite the "retreat" suggested in the title, Desanzo's film inaugurates another instance of "the past is not past" that is far from being in retreat: the seamless continuities of the past shift in these thrillers from the victim's perspective to show how the murderers and their accomplices keep operating in democratic times. These thrillers spotlight "the sensation . . . that the democratic transition is not a qualitative change but a simple transfer of power," in the words of Goity and Oubiña.[10] In Burucúa's terms, they convey the overarching idea that the past serves as "the driving force that sets the narrative in motion."[11] In other words, the past is not past, not even for the perpetrators.

Elena reads *En retirada* as a film that "begins, in some way, to represent the acts of state terrorism on the screen."[12] While this was true in the mid-1980s, Desanzo's film exceeded its conditions of production. Unlike Elena and Burucúa's understanding of the paramilitary thriller as a "transitional sub-genre" that declined in the mid-1980s,[13] Desanzo's innovative point of view, in particular, is still visible in later productions, such as Martin Donovan's English-Argentine co-production *Apartment Zero* (1988). Echoes of *En retirada* can be found more recently (admittedly, after the publication of Burucúa's work), gaining renewed meanings in Argentina and beyond, in Pablo Trapero's *El clan* (2015), Daniela Goggi's *El rapto* (2023), and Andrés Wood's *Araña* (2019), one of the films examined in detail in this chapter.[14]

These films showcase "unemployed labor" (*mano de obra desocupada*), which, as Elena notes, was the common way of describing the idle thugs and hit men after the downfall of the dictatorship that we see in *En retirada*.[15] Much like El Oso, these characters appear in films kidnapping, arbitrarily torturing, illegally imprisoning, and executing their victims well into the 1980s. The more recent iterations of this cluster, such as Trapero and Goggi's films, emphasize the inability or slowness of the Argentine state and its civil society to surmount the authoritarian armature that had shaped the country in the previous decades.

Beyond Argentina, the point of view of the perpetrators and their accomplices is represented in the greedy Uruguayan bankers who profit from the dictatorship's monetary policies in Federico Veiroj's *Así habló el cambista* (2019) and the Swiss bankers in Andreas Fontana's Swiss-Argentine co-production *Azor* (2021). This point of view is also central to the political thrillers discussed in detail in this chapter. In addition to portraying the paramilitary ties that sustained the dictatorships and their legacies, these films also emphasize the complicity of different social classes: *Rojo* and *Matar a un muerto* foreground the middle and working classes, personified by an Argentine male lawyer and two Paraguayan gravediggers who handle the bodies of the desaparecidos, respectively. Whereas *Rojo* aims to depict the social conditions that led to the 1976 coup, *Matar a un muerto* privileges the peak of Alfredo Stroessner's dictatorship. In turn, *Araña* underscores the paramilitary's role in shaping Chilean society to facilitate August Pinochet's rise to power. In underscoring the civic involvement in oppression, these films explore one of the dictatorships' most dramatic outcomes: the impossibility of solidarity.

ROJO (2018)

Space between Literature and Film

Set in 1975, Benjamín Naishtat's *Rojo* is one of the few Argentine postdictatorial thrillers to foreground not the dictatorial years themselves but the period that immediately preceded and set the stage for the 1976 coup. This predictatorial period was also the focus of Andrés Wood's *Araña* (2019) in Chile and Rafael Russo's *El año de la furia* (2020) in Uruguay. Both are set in 1972: a year before the coup in those countries. Naishtat explores the social complicity that produced the conditions for the coup's wide acceptance in Argentina.

Rojo bridges present and past not only through the representation of 1970s politics but also by means of the aesthetics of those years, which are not only filmic but also literary. This is especially evident in the film's topology of secrecy. The opening credits in red announce a vague setting: "an Argentine province." We later hear the characters referring to the fictional town as "Granada," which could be read as an allusion to Córdoba, as both places are named after Spanish neighboring provinces. Much like Córdoba, Granada seems to be located hundreds of kilometers from Buenos Aires.

In this sense, Granada reminds us of two fictional small towns of late 1960s and early 1970s Argentine literature. The first is Coronel Vallejos, in which Manuel Puig sets his novels *La traición de Rita Hayworth* (1968) and *Boquitas pintadas* (1969) to mimic his hometown, General Villegas. The second one is Colonia Vela (an allusion to a town called María Ignacia), where Osvaldo Soriano sets *No habrá más penas ni olvido* (1978) and *Cuarteles de invierno* (1980) to dramatize the historical and political events of the early 1970s, especially the confrontation between right-wing and left-wing Peronists.

Much like them, Granada is a *pueblo chico, infierno grande* (small town, large hell, as the Spanish proverb says), where secrets are precarious because gossip spreads quickly. Granada is defined as a space with no room for secrecy: villagers, controlled by their neighbors' omniscient gaze, lack the typical anonymity of a more urban setting. The hustle and bustle of city life typical of the thriller is here pitted against the perceived "peace" of the small town, where surveillance can be all the more effective due to the close-knit community. In this context, *Rojo* transplants the genre from its typical urban environment into another literary space par excellence of Argentine cultural tradition: the gates of the barbaric desert. The Argentine Pampas are pitted against *civilización*. Such an iconic dichotomy hovers over most of Argentine literature, from Echeverría, Sarmiento, Borges, and Jorge Barón Biza to Samanta Schweblin.

Going back to cinema, *Rojo* reminds us of early classic political thrillers. I am thinking of 1950s films set in little towns, such as Lewis Allen's *Suddenly* (1954) and Don Siegel's *Invasion of the Body Snatchers* (1956). The settings of these American models are places where nothing usually happens "suddenly" until everything does: hence the title of Allen's film and the name of the fictional town in which it is set. Thrilling situations would not normally be conceivable in Suddenly or Granada, where daily routine seems to trump surprise. When they do finally happen, they further enhance the thrilling effect, the invasion of the political. In addition, because all these literary and cinematic towns are fictional composites, they could be any town.

Rojo opens with a master shot and a long take of a house façade, distinctively decorated with exposed red brick. The town's apparent calmness can be heard in the birds' tweets and the absence of traffic, as people quietly leave the house through the front door. Most of them are wearing something red (scarves, jackets), and they are all carrying furniture or household appliances—a TV, a mirror, and so forth. Everything makes us think that we are witnessing a prosaic and innocent act: someone seems to be moving out. We soon discover, however, that this is a sinister scene typical of thrillers: the house, previously owned by desaparecidos, is now abandoned. Their neighbors are ransacking their belongings. The appropriation of desaparecidos' houses, clothes, and offspring is one of the many systematic state-sponsored practices before (1974–1976) and during the Argentine dictatorship (1976–1983) that political thrillers well before and after *Rojo* foreground. For instance, the main point of *La historia oficial* is the investigation of a case of child appropriation. The climax of *Azor* is the unveiling of appropriated assets, ready to be sold to a Swiss banker.

After this opening scene, *Rojo* moves on to a failed suicide attempt. Dieguito, *el hippie*, has just come back to Granada from Buenos Aires. Visibly irate, he picks a fight in a restaurant with Claudio, a local lawyer. After dinner, he confronts Claudio and his wife, who are driving back home. He pierces through their car by throwing projectiles at them. Dieguito finally manages to escape. Claudio chases him, only to witness him shooting himself. Wheezing and agonized, Dieguito does not die. Claudio drives him to the desert, under the cover of night. An impressive master shot triggers the plot, establishing its precarious secret. The car, filmed from behind, faces the Pampas at dawn. The scene eschews representation, as Claudio drags Dieguito's body off-screen, leaving him there to become yet another desaparecido, engulfed by and conflated with the barbaric desert of the Pampas.

The film then jumps forward three months, with a scene in which Claudio and his wife host a tea gathering for their friends. The scene is reminiscent of Marcelo Piñeyro's coming-of-age political drama *Kamchatka* (2002), set in 1976. Both films feature children "toying with history," as Jordana Blejmar puts it.[16] Significantly, they do so through war strategy board games, with diametrically opposed connotations.

In Piñeyro's film, son and father play TEG (Táctica y Estrategia de Guerra), an Argentine version of the French board game La Conquête du Monde (known in the United States as Risk).[17] The scene takes place in a provincial town, also far from Buenos Aires. But here the father, also a lawyer, is a soon-to-be desaparecido. Therefore, the TEG board game (which, as Blejmar reminds us, was published in 1976, the year of the coup) mirrors the father's strategy of constantly switching homes with his family to hide from the lurking military.[18] The critics read this as a tribute to different types of resistance: by the middle class, by children, or by civil society against economic and political crises.[19] In one of the matches, the father is losing for the first time, defending himself successfully but keeping only the Kamchatka Peninsula. The final scenes recover this moment and explain the film's title: a new Numantia, "Kamchatka is the place for resisting," the son's voice-over says. He stares at his parents before they leave, never to see him again.

By contrast, in Naishtat's *Rojo*, the ones who toy with history are the children of the complicit middle class. Paulita, Claudio's daughter, is playing an American war game called 1914: Diplomacy with a friend. When the friend says, "I annex Poland and reject the invasion," she responds, "You can't reject it. You signed the treaties." The dispute echoes the battles that took place in Silesia—a theater of war during World War I. The scene is brief but significant, because it hints at the personality of Claudio, a lawyer who, unlike the father in *Kamchatka* (or most of the thriller heroes examined in the previous chapter), personifies not the dictatorship's victims but its accomplices.

Played by Darío Grandinetti (who played Julia's ex-boyfriend in *Matar a todos*), Claudio is "the only one who knows the rules" of the game, in his wife's words. Accordingly, he is in charge of resolving the territorial dispute. By stating that "there's nothing to do," he obediently accepts the law of domination. By showing that there is no room for resistance, the scene highlights the complicity with the imminent dictatorial coup, which, like a thrilling invasion, can no longer be stopped.

In this context, *Rojo* was loosely inspired by Sebastián Carassai's *Los años setenta de la gente común*, a sociohistorical examination of the 1970s from the perspective of the "silent majority": portions of the Argentine population who were not involved in politics during a hyper-politicized time.[20] To conduct his study, Carassai played 1970s TV and magazine ads for his interviewees, "the common people," to explore what memories they triggered. Naishtat embeds one of these ads in his film, following the genre's convention of providing a cachet of authenticity and literally screening oppression. The ad features two men: one is chewing a candy; the other one (off-screen) insistently asks him to share it. After a few seconds, the chewer shoots the beggar. Carassai examines this and other ads to show the normalization of explicit violence in Argentine TV: according to him, they created the conditions for legitimized state-sponsored violence.

The ad in *Rojo* precedes a scene that foregrounds the state's presence. A federal auditor exchanges gifts with American cowboys, who are visiting the town to perform in rodeo shows. The visitors are given a mate gourd, while the auditor receives a whip, a metonymy of oppression and slavery but also of American involvement in Operation Condor. The cowboys (played by American actors) reappear later on another screen: Claudio's TV. In this scene we hear but never see the ad. Instead, an over-the-shoulder shot (normally reserved for dialogue between characters) humanizes the TV, which "speaks" to Claudio and to us: "The American cowboys embellish our province with their majestic presence. . . . We Argentines are made the right way and not the other way around" (*Los argentinos estamos hechos al derecho y no al revés*). This real found footage tangentially cites a maxim that became popular in the country in 1979. After an inspection by the Inter-American Commission on Human Rights, the dictatorship spread a slogan: *los argentinos somos derechos y humanos* (we Argentines are straight/right and humane), an obviously perverse play on words. Being *al revés* is tantamount to being left, the opposite of being right—in its political (*la derecha*) and legal (*el derecho*) sense. This is embodied in the film by Claudio, the complicit lawyer.

Aesthetics and Language

Claudio's secret becomes more and more precarious when the father of Paulita's friend tells him that his brother-in-law (Dieguito) has become a desaparecido. The father hires Detective Sinclair (played by Chilean actor Alfredo Castro), a Latin American translation of the detective show character Lieutenant Columbo. Much like him, Sinclair became famous thanks to a TV show (through a screen). Sinclair comes from the Santiago Police service: "one of the best of the world," as he describes it.[21] As such, he resignifies the ways in which detectives are placed at the outskirts of the state in political thrillers. Whereas a character like Bernal's García would start by working inside and finish by going against the state, Naishtat's Sinclair, a private eye, works outside of but closely aligned with the state, conniving in its genocidal practices. Sinclair eventually figures out Claudio's involvement in Dieguito's death, because everyone in Granada (small-town gossip) saw or heard about the restaurant quarrel.

Significantly, under Sinclair's questioning, Claudio reverts to the overexposed empty signifier *paz* (examined in chapter 4): "this quiet place is full of people who want to work and live in peace." Here *paz* entails living apolitically—shirking political conflict, like Granada's superficially "peaceful" streets, where empty houses are nonetheless looted. Sinclair chooses not to prosecute his own client, strengthening not peace but war, because "the important thing is that we are fighting a greater evil here": the left-wing guerrillas. Sinclair reinforces Claudio's connivance between law and crime, highlighting the civil side of the dictatorship.

At the same time, the inclusion of a Chilean detective in this Argentine film echoes a broader complicity, highlighting the transnational ties between the neighboring countries via their engagement with Operation Condor. Naishtat toys with a genre convention. Detectives in the classical political thriller play the role of genre heroes and Communist agents are usually typecast as foreign villains, but here the detectives incarnate that villainous threat, while Dieguito (suspected of being left-wing) is the victim. In addition, as in many of these types of political thrillers focused on the side of oppression, there are no heroes, going against Palmer's idea that "thrillers need a hero."[22]

It is no coincidence that Víctor Jara's lyric "El derecho a vivir en paz" reappears at the end of the movie. After slowly zooming in, the camera offers a close-up of Paulita's teacher, who is reading a nationalistic speech with a red curtain visible behind her. She praises the greatness and heterogeneity of the Argentine land: "we are the ordinary people," she says, citing *la gente común* of Carassai's essay, "the ones who go to work every day full of joy. . . . Don't let politics ruin our lives. They can't take away our right to live in peace." Everyone applauds her, as Dieguito's brother-in-law whispers a small-town rumor in Claudio's ear: the declaration of the coup is imminent. The grammar of secrecy's preposition of place "behind" is once more prominent: *vivir en paz* is inseparable from turning one's back on red-blooded politics figuratively but also literally, as the teacher does.

Film critic Gustavo Noriega loses sight of these nuances when he claims that the film misunderstands Carassai's book. For Noriega, political violence fatally attracts Naishtat's characters but repels Carassai's interviewees. The main difference, he argues, is the treatment of the middle class: "the characters in *Rojo* are mean, violent, mediocre, superficial, and, in the worst cases, they foresee the worst methods of the dictatorship."[23] While Noriega may have a point in that *Rojo* lacks rounder characters, the film goes beyond a criticism of the middle-class's violent impulse beneath the veneer of a rhetoric of peace. Instead, *Rojo* complicates the boundaries of the political. In this case, Dieguito's death could serve as an example. It is important to emphasize that Claudio does not execute Dieguito. Claudio is not as "mean" as he seems. Dieguito's demise (at least initially) is unrelated to genocide or any explicit type of state-sponsored violence, for that matter. Like *El complot mongol*, the film features a death that is not political but becomes political, in this case because of the historical context.

In this sense, *Rojo* mirrors a classic Argentine thriller whose political implications were evidently toned down due to censorship: Adolfo Aristarain's *Últimos días de la víctima* (1982), an adaptation of José Pablo Feinmann's novel. The film premiered during the prelude of the dictatorship's downfall, as announced in its title (*The Last Days of the Victim*), as Burucúa brilliantly observes.[24] It follows hit man Raúl Mendizabal and his isolated common murders, which go unnoticed and blend into systematic forced disappearances. To a certain extent, Mendizabal foreshadows El Oso in *En retirada* (Feinmann was the scriptwriter for both films): both *sicarios* work for an outgoing dictatorial state that ends up annihilating them during the transition to democracy.[25]

Informed by Desanzo and Aristarain's ambivalent and complicit characters, Naishtat (born in 1986) reimagines the dawn of the dictatorship in 1975 through a postmemory lens. He does so by portraying a crime (filmed, significantly, at the crack of dawn) that is exempt from prosecution because many other people like Dieguito were being disappeared and killed. *Rojo*, then, poses infrapolitical questions, similar to the ones addressed by other Latin American renditions of the genre. These questions challenge the precarious contours of the political: for example, where does politicization end and where does it start? Or, perhaps more importantly, the film inquires into what makes a crime (or a citizen) political. Equally, it could be read as a metacinematic question about the genre itself: what makes a thriller political? What are the blurred boundaries that separate it from neighboring genres, such as crime thrillers or period dramas?

Naishtat never answers these questions, but perhaps another common element in this film and in political thrillers is the treatment of space, which we can read through the grammar of secrecy. Although the film's treatment of space has been seen as parodic,[26] it also goes beyond parody. The Pampas, as an epitome of the prepositions of space "outside" and "above," conceal and expose the film's conspiracy, out in the open and on the surface: the cover-up of Dieguito's politically ambiguous death in the desert. The Pampas, in this sense, are another site of precarious secrecy, another instance of *la intemperie*: a landscape that cannot fully contain political secrets. In this case, secrecy

(Dieguito's corpse), flimsily stored in this landscape, echoes the aesthetic representation of forced disappearance as a precarious secret, as discussed in chapter 4. Finally, the Pampas work as Naishtat's translation of the labyrinthine setting of the thriller in the form of a Borgesian paradoxical labyrinth: not a complex walled structure but the flat, endless surface of the desert.[27]

At the same time, *Rojo* evokes another desert: the Atacama in Patricio Guzmán's documentary *Nostalgia de la luz* (2010), a site of precarious secrecy and forced disappearance but also of astronomical observation. Guzmán went to Atacama to film mothers who were looking for the remains of their disappeared children, clandestinely buried under the desert by Pinochet's dictatorship. Both films emphasize the idea that the openness of the desert constitutes an unrivaled power to kill and hide but also to be found and eventually exposed.

Beyond space, the ties between the thriller and the documentary are also about time. It is not a coincidence that Guzmán introduces this landscape by literally stating, "I am under the impression that the desert reveals a secret to us." Whereas we may commonly understand astronomy as a discipline that deals with the remote past (the origins of the universe, the solar system, and so forth), the documentary shows that it can also shed light on the more recent past, especially Operation Condor. Interspersed with the shots of Guzmán meeting the mothers of the disappeared are interviews with Chilean astronomers. One of them, Gaspar Galaz, notes the idea quoted in this chapter's epigraph: "that's the trick, the present doesn't exist." Because of the fraction of a second that light takes to travel and to be processed by us, events that we may perceive to be happening now are actually happening in the past. Galaz gives the example of the eight minutes it takes for sunlight to reach the earth. Saying that the present is permanently absorbed by the past is another way of saying that the past is never past, that we are always inhabiting it. The Atacama Desert exposes the contradictions of Chilean society: it neglects and forgets recent history but reveres the more remote past through astronomical exploration.[28] *Rojo* exposes similar contradictions in the Argentine context, where apologists for the crimes against humanity have constantly pushed for forgetfulness and impunity over the past decades.

As Noriega notes, *Rojo*'s title is extremely polysemic.[29] Almost all the scenes throughout the whole film have an element of red. Most obviously, red symbolizes the bloodshed of the 1970s. But it also echoes communism: the Spanish word *rojo*—although it is a disused variant of the more common derogatory term *zurdo* (leftie)—still evokes left-wing politics in Argentina.[30] The color appears explicitly when Claudio inspects the vacant house with walls painted with blood, for instance, while the camera shows us the reddening sunlight reflected through the window. Different chromatic variations of red punctuate the plot: Claudio's crimson sunglasses and scarlet vest and Sinclair's ruby tie (both worn for most of the film); the bright red taillamp of Claudio's car, which carries Dieguito to his death (vividly contrasting with the darker colors of the night in the desert); and even Paulita's burgundy pantyhose, to name a few.

Red also features in subtler ways. Crimson is famous in Argentine history for being the color of one of the most prominent political phenomena of the nineteenth century: the red insignia of caudillo Juan Manuel de Rosas's Federal Party. One of the scenes in the film depicts an art exhibit with paintings of gaucho soldiers, dressed in their crimson military uniform of the 1830s–1850s. A strong personalist leader, Rosas has often been considered a forerunner of Perón, whose disruptive death in 1974 spectrally appears at the center of the period portrayed in *Rojo*.[31]

The most powerful scene with red, however, occurs in Mar del Plata. Claudio and his family temporarily hide from Sinclair there, because the lawyer fears the detective will prosecute him. The frame itself suddenly is filtered in red. Nearby beachgoers are looking at an eclipsed sun through their viewers, a filter that protects them from seeing the reddening sun as it is. Claudio, who does not have a viewer, seems confused. A disembodied voice warns him: "Don't look. It'll be over soon"—a disclaimer for the approaching coup. The eclipse works as a reddening fever: it must pass sooner or later. Despite its fleeting nature, the impact of the eclipse will be felt to this day.

An example of this can be found in the 2018 Toronto International Film Festival question-and-answer session. Naishtat commented there that what troubles him about Argentine politics is not so much (or not solely) the past as past but its reapparitions in the present. Argentina, unlike most South American countries, successfully convicted most of its military junta involved in crimes against humanity—after many comings and goings throughout the last decades. In spite of this, although members of the military have returned to their barracks, the Argentine police have inherited a residue of dictatorial authoritarianism and masculine brutality. This is evident in the alarming number of cases of forced disappearance during democratic times and the genealogy of political thrillers outlined at the beginning of this chapter.[32]

We need only think of a case that took place while *Rojo* was being shot, as Naishtat reminds us. In August 2017 a young activist named Santiago Maldonado went missing in Patagonia after being evicted and chased by the police during a demonstration. Maldonado had joined the Mapuche Indigenous community to protest against the Italian Benetton Group's appropriation of their land. The gendarmerie repressed the demonstration. As a consequence, Maldonado's whereabouts were unknown for two months, until he was found dead. At the time, this caused national and international concern about Mauricio Macri's administration and its alleged involvement, if not in Maldonado's disappearance at least in its cover-up. Macri's administration was eventually absolved of any responsibility in Maldonado's death.

Beyond this specific case, however, the seamless prolongation of authoritarian practices in democratic times is one of the main underlying anxieties of the Argentine political thriller. This anxiety about the vestiges of dictatorial rule is well founded if we think of other cases of forced disappearance during democratic times before and after 2017, during the administrations of Néstor Kirchner (2003–2007) and Alberto Fernández (2019–2023).[33] *Rojo* is part of this genealogy of films that remind us of a series of postdictatorial crimes against humanity for the past four decades, from *En retirada* onward. Perhaps Naishtat invites us to do precisely the opposite of the disembodied normative voice's advice to Claudio during the eclipse: we should keep staring at the past, without succumbing to the threat of blindness, so that we can actually look at the present with clearer eyes.

MATAR A UN MUERTO (2019)

Space and Language

Paraguayan films dealing with the country's dictatorial past have been scarce when compared with the prolific production of neighboring Argentina, Brazil, Chile, and even Uruguay.[34] This asymmetry is especially significant if we remember that Alfredo Stroessner's dictatorship was the longest in twentieth-century Latin America, lasting from 1954 to 1989. The very longevity of the regime, known as El Stronato, could be precisely the reason for this meager film tradition. This lack of productions gradually started to change over the last decade, especially after the administration of the ousted president Fernando Lugo (2008–2012) opened the public conversation about Stroessner's crimes against humanity.[35] Hugo Giménez's first fictional film, *Matar a un muerto*, is an example of this modest but growing tradition.

This tradition starts with isolated political thrillers that were set in Paraguay but were made by foreign production companies, such as the British films *The Honorary Consul* (1983) and *One Man's War* (1991), as mentioned in chapter 1. Perhaps inspired by other Southern Cone national cinemas, Paraguayan productions began dealing with the country's traumatic past through documentaries and allegorical dramas.[36] Giménez, by contrast, chose to make a political thriller, after having directed documentaries—much like other filmmakers who forayed into the genre before him. He followed the example of Jeremías Espínola's medium-length film *La cárcel de barrio* (2016), a less sophisticated rendition of the genre when compared to Giménez's work.

Matar a un muerto sounds like a cryptic tongue twister: *Killing the Dead,* as it was translated to English, works as both a pleonasm and an oxymoron, exploring how it is possible to kill someone who is already dead. Giménez's film privileges the tension between the prepositions of space "under" and "outside," placing secrecy underneath the Paraguayan woods—another site of precarious secrecy, another *intemperie*.

The film is set in one of the harshest years under Stroessner's rule: 1978. By the late 1970s, the dictatorship had dismantled most of the resistance through forced disappearances and illegal executions, as Tereza Dulci Spyer and Manuella Sampaio da Silva remind us.[37] The story centers on Pastor and Dionisio, two gravediggers in charge of burying the corpses of Paraguayan desaparecidos. The bodies arrive floating on a river, as a sinister South American translation of the ancient Greek myth of the Styx, which separated the living from the underworld. At their campground the gravediggers perform clandestine burials in common graves, interring both the corpses and the precarious state secret of forced disappearances.

Giménez problematizes the genre's conventions even further, however, by combining national and international models that go beyond political thrillers. At a national level, Giménez draws heavily on a film that paved the way for Paraguayan cinema in the twenty-first century, according to Júlia González de Canales Carcereny: Paz Encina's *Hamaca paraguaya* (2006), the first national production in almost three decades.[38] The influence of this auteur film is a clear example of how the Latin American political thriller goes beyond genre formulas, through what Laura Podalsky calls an "authorial vehicle."[39] In turn, at an international level, *Matar a un muerto* cites canonical authors and filmmakers: Shakespeare, Lang, and Hitchcock.

English drama scholar Lori M. Culwell understands the role of gravediggers in *Hamlet* as a way of introducing a popular perspective to give more legibility to the play. According to her, the clownish characters' mundane language connects with an audience that might feel alienated by the sophisticated Danish court. "By using recognizable references from contemporary times" and oral tradition, the gravediggers "make the audience understand the theme being played out by the court-dominated characters in the play."[40] *Hamlet*'s grave themes (existence and mortality) are toned down through colloquialisms and references intelligible to the audience, who, like the gravediggers, do not necessarily belong to the court.

Similarly, Giménez's gravediggers speak for most of the film in the audience's language: Guarani. The film blends *Hamlet*'s treatment of "oral tradition" with *Hamaca paraguaya*'s use of Guarani's orally transmitted culture. *Matar a un muerto* is one of the later instantiations of what Alejo Margariños calls "the globalized refoundation of Guarani cinema" in relation to Encina's film.[41] These productions, which received national and international acclaim, were entirely or almost entirely shot in the Indigenous language. For González de Canales Carcereny, what explains Encina's success is precisely the conjunction of glocal elements: a narrative offered for transnational audiences within an almost Costumbrist landscape.[42] All of this is also true for Giménez's film: its language, space, colloquialisms, localisms, and Shakespearean references are central to understanding his take on the political thriller.

It is worth remembering that Guarani is one of the few Indigenous languages that rivals Spanish as the most widely spoken language in a Latin American country. As linguist Guilherme von Streber Lee notes, however, "Guarani faces a deep condition of diglossia": Spanish holds more prestige, especially in education and the media.[43] This is why Guarani constantly brings a daily-life effect in *Matar a un muerto*: when Pastor and Dionisio are not burying bodies, they drink *terere* (cold yerba mate tea) and eat Paraguayan peaches, while always chatting in Guarani—a national translation of the prosaicism typical of Latin American political thrillers.

American political thrillers tend to portray "images of national monuments like the Lincoln Memorial, political institutions such as the Capitol, intelligence and security agencies (Langley, the Pentagon),"[44] the spatial incarnation of what Ian Scott calls "the mythology at the heart of American democracy."[45] In contrast, *Matar a un muerto* privileges the *intemperie*, where Pastor and Dionisio connect with the audience in terms of spatiality—like *Hamlet*'s gravediggers, they are outside and far from the "court" (monuments, institutions, and intelligence agencies).

Whereas the film places secrecy underground, politics is both tacit and remote: located on the other side of the river (whence the corpses come), a central landscape in the region's film production.[46] For Rubin, "the modern city is the primary (though not exclusive) locale of most types of thrillers,"[47] while Giménez's genre subversion also features in his choice of the story's rural setting. Here he follows Encina, partaking in the "new kind of Latin American regionalism" that Jens Andermann sees in *Hamaca paraguaya*, which "turned towards landscape as a harbinger of singularity."[48] In using this rural landscape, *Matar a un muerto* brings in the same infrapolitical distance we saw in the films examined in chapter 3.

Despite the slowness of life in the woods and the absence of an investigative plot, Giménez manages to create an atmosphere tainted with a sense of political intrigue, foregrounding the point of view of those who work for the perpetrators. This is what led Diego Brodersen to describe the film as a "narrative game of confinement in the outdoors that toys with suspense."[49] Emancipated from the thrillers' vertiginous streets and its detectives camouflaged as journalists or lawyers, the film partakes in the genre in an innovative way. This is clearer if we think of its ties with film classics. For instance, Giménez borrows expressionist elements of Lang's *Man Hunt* (1941), whose plot starts in the German forest, featuring scavenging dogs trained to trace human corpses and a foreigner condemned to death: an amateur English spy in Nazi Germany who survives his sentence. He becomes a hero, and the plot quickly abandons the German forest for London. The Paraguayan film (entirely shot in the woods), instead, features a survivor who never ceases to be a victim.

At the same time, *Matar a un muerto*'s treatment of the Paraguayan woods reminds us of Hitchcock's *The 39 Steps* (1935) and *North by Northwest* (1959), where accidental spies are entrapped in equally outdoor spaces: the Scottish Highlands and an American labyrinthine cornfield, respectively. These spaces work as "an unlimited prison," containing both "confinement and infinitude," as Pascal Bonitzer notes.[50] The Paraguayan woods, despite their openness, reproduce a similar sense of paradoxical claustrophobia, confusion, and entrapment. Giménez follows what Morris Dickstein describes as Hitchcock's reaction "against the confined frame and shadowy locations of the film noir . . . to create a sense of terror in broad daylight and in public spaces."[51] Giménez imports these tensions between interiority and exteriority into the Paraguayan context.

In this sense, the political is subtle in *Matar a un muerto*, almost inaudible or invisible, as it cannot be automatically deduced from the wilderness. Thanks to the film's soundscape, we get a sense of the living ecosystem and its superficial serenity: the sonic backdrop consists of birds tweeting, thunder announcing the subtropical downpours, mosquitoes buzzing, the melody of river crickets chirping, and the wind swirling in leaves and branches. The hints of the political are made visible, once more, through the grammar of secrecy: every time the gravediggers report to their superiors, they are forced to identify themselves with a deictic that points to their campground—a *kokue* (a Guarani word for a small farm). The *kokue* is a precarious headquarters, located amid the natural landscape, within the boundaries of the woods. It is a farm (a plot of domesticated land), but it is also a *campo*: a "labor or death camp," a minefield, the hyper-politicization of nature, riddled with bodies buried underground, above which Pastor and Dionisio speak Guarani and play football.

Politics and Football

Amid the tense calm, a drunk Pastor sings old love songs in Guarani to distract himself from his oppressive task, reminding us again of Shakespeare's jester who sings in the midst of death, to Hamlet's astonishment. Pastor is different from his Danish counterpart in that he does not sing to cast off mortality (understood in an abstract way) but to chase away his remorse for the mortality of others: for his involvement in genocide. Pastor and Dionisio are not jesters. We could read them, instead, as characters who experience the hyper-politicization of life in their bodies. This becomes evident in the parallelisms between politics and another topic that makes the court readable for the audience, a topic overlooked by most of the film's critics: football.

It is June 1978: the Football World Cup is taking place in Argentina. Isolated in the Paraguayan woods, the gravediggers' only way of connecting with the rest of society is a small defective radio, through which precarity again takes center stage. This seclusion enhances the sense of paradoxical claustrophobia that underlines the genre's grammar of secrecy: the precarious secret of forced disappearances oppresses the gravediggers to such an extent that they seem trapped even though they are outside (not confined to close quarters). Dionisio, anxious to follow what goes on in the real outside world (the World Cup), uses the radio to ask his superiors for some news. They reply that "Brazil has beaten Peru a few days ago. . . . Argentina . . . is getting there too. They all say that both are in the group of death." Coined by journalists eight years earlier, during the 1970 World Cup matches held in Mexico, the Spanish term *grupo de la muerte* alludes to a competitive group tournament, where most teams are strong but not all of them will be able to qualify for the play-offs, hence the link between death and defeat.

The philosopher Jean Baudrillard showed concern over three decades ago about the growing influence of hyper-politicization on other spheres of life, including, of course, sports.[52] Building on his work, political scientist Tamir Bar-On pointed out in the late 1990s that football, an "essential staple of the national and regional imagination" in Latin American countries, had become a paradigmatic example of this invasion of politics outside of the political. "Football acts as the great societal equalizer" in a region of widespread inequalities, in that players from uneven backgrounds blend together in their teams. Something similar happens in the film at a national level: with the metaphorical uses of football, Giménez equalizes Paraguay with its more renowned neighbors, the "established football powers like Argentina and Brazil."[53] As the only Latin American national teams that won the World Cup (along with Uruguay), they hold more symbolic capital in the region.

Paraguay, by contrast, only qualified for the tournament eight out of twenty-two times, which testifies to the economic disparity between nation-states in the region.

For Baudrillard, "sport can be . . . a parade of prestige or of violence."[54] This is precisely what is at stake in a later scene of the film. While playing kick-about with Dionisio, Pastor impersonates and identifies himself with Argentine striker "Matador Kempes," mimicking a football commentator. This is a disruptive scene, one of the few in which Pastor speaks Spanish, the language of the media. It is reminiscent of a scene from *One Man's War*, where members of the military (a higher link in the chain of state oppression) invade a kick-about involving children of the disappeared.

As Pastor scores, the scene immediately evokes the porous boundaries that divide football and politics: Kempes scored twice in the final match, giving the World Cup to the local team. Of course, the nickname *matador* (killer, as in high-scorer) reminds us that Argentina's sports victory would have not been possible without true killing—the genocide—in the same way that the Stronato's victims would not have been possible without people like Pastor. A mere gravedigger from a poorer neighbor country, Pastor momentarily transcends his subaltern position in society and through football (the great equalizer) becomes the famous Argentine hero, citing, at the same time, Baudrillard's parade of prestige and violence.

In this context, *Matar a un muerto* is part of an extensive tradition of Latin American cultural production that explores the ever-blurrier boundaries between football, politics, and violence.[55] Football tends to be depicted as affecting politics and vice versa. The sport is especially central to the political thriller and appears prominently in several films. For instance, we see TVs broadcasting footage of Pelé's legendary national team in the 1970 World Cup in Brazilian thrillers such as *O que é isso, companheiro?* and *Pra frente, Brasil,* named for a song sponsored by the dictatorship to represent the country in Mexico. The 1978 World Cup also plays an important role in the recent Peruvian political thriller *La pena máxima* (2022). Written by Santiago Roncagliolo, Michel Gómez's film is ambivalently titled to allude to both penalties in football and capital punishment in politics. In addition, *La pena máxima* features footage of Jorge Rafael Videla introducing the World Cup and is structured around Peru's matches, including the very controversial one with the local team, Argentina.[56]

In particular, Kempes's disruptive appearance in *Matar a un muerto* reminds us of the Argentine political thriller *Hay unos tipos abajo* (1985), directed by Rafael Filipelli. Julio, a journalist who is paranoid about being surveilled by a *grupo de tareas* (death squad), is shown in that film obsessively watching the 1978 World Cup on TV. The footage once again cites the genre's cachet of authenticity. Filipelli, however, brings in the final match aurally: Julio hears it on a radio. The scene is significant because Julio leaves Buenos Aires for good after Argentina's victory.[57] In a way, football-related triumph brings political defeat through Julio's exile and Pastor's oppressive task.

Matar a un muerto displays this and several other connections between Paraguay and Argentina. Premiered in the Museo de Arte Latinoamericano de Buenos Aires (MALBA) in late 2019, months before its release in Paraguayan cinemas, the film is marked by the tensions between the two countries. They hark back to the bloodiest interstate war in Latin America's history (1864–1870), involving a disastrous defeat of Paraguay at the hands of the Triple Alliance of Argentina, Brazil, and Uruguay—the established football powers.[58] As Bar-On notes, Latin American dictatorships "have traditionally used football as part of their strategy to strengthen nationalist loyalties."[59] Giménez mirrors this political use of football against dictatorial politics to symbolize Stroessner and Videla's underlying collaboration.

Furthermore, Dionisio and Pastor's clandestine burials in the woods echo those of the Escuela Superior de Mecánica de la Armada (ESMA), an Argentine navy facility that became the deadliest illegal secret detention center for desaparecidos. ESMA is located only two miles away from River Plate's soccer stadium in Buenos Aires, where the final match (which Pastor acts out and Julio listens to) is taking place. As Bar-On reminds us, the 1978 World Cup is infamous for the controversial relationship with the Argentine dictatorship and the way it influenced the national team's victory, "a short-term measure used to win international favor, quick profits, and achieve an aura of modernization for both domestic and international audiences," especially in the eyes of international human rights organizations.[60] This policy, too, could be read as another instance of the surrounding precarity in the region: prolonging the dictatorship's legitimacy was an ephemeral achievement prior to its final downfall a few years later (in 1983).

For Bar-On, football "tended to reinforce narrow nationalistic, authoritarian, class-based, and gender specific notions of identity and culture." In this sense, *Matar a un muerto* is the only political thriller examined in this chapter that does not feature any female characters. The Kempes scene takes the genre's homosocial landscape to the extreme, through football, exacerbating traits typically associated with masculinity such as virility and physical strength. Not coincidentally, "Paraguay as late as 1979 specifically banned women from playing football," as Bar-On reminds us.[61] Besides football, Giménez uses the grammar of secrecy to explore political specters.

Language and Specters

Like the journalist-detectives Alfredo and Jorge in *Zanahoria,* the senior Pastor and the inexperienced Dionisio stand for different generations. The issue of seniority is exhibited when Pastor commands Dionisio to "dig deeper." Here the grammar of secrecy points to a twofold topology: on the one hand, literally digging deep down to hide the corpses better. On the other hand, Pastor's command implies that Dionisio must go deeper metaphorically into the depths of his own consciousness to find the courage to compensate for both his inexperience and his remorse.

Giménez's film, however, goes beyond duality, featuring a homosocial triangle—much like Buchichio. Reminding us of *Zanahoria*'s Walter (the swindler informant who deceives the journalists), here again a third party disrupts the two male characters, who were already divided by a generational gap. This evokes a Christian representation of triangles, linked to the doctrine of the Trinity—the father and the son (Pastor and Dionisio), confronted by an unholy spirit or specter: a scavenging dog. This is another intertextual tribute to Encina: like *Hamaca paraguaya, Matar a un muerto* starts with voice-overs, interrupted by background barks that punctuate the film, constituting its main soundscape. Along with the off-screen dog that will not stop barking, Encina's film features the conversations of an old couple, Cándida and Ramón. The dog initially constitutes the third side of the triangle in both stories. In turn, Giménez's thriller opens with a black screen and a voice-over in Guarani: *Jagüa ñarõ pe'a. Huguy tyakû'are ou,* which can be roughly translated "It was a hunting dog. It is drawn by the smell of blood." We soon learn that Pastor is speaking about his dog "Negro," which has abandoned him. Nevertheless, the gravedigger quickly notes that it "never truly left."

Again, Giménez blends *Hamaca paraguaya* with *Hamlet,* where "everything begins by the apparition of a specter. More precisely by the waiting for this apparition," as Derrida notes in his reading of the Shakespearean play. This specter "is at once impatient, anxious, and fascinated, [it] will end up coming."[62] But unlike the spirit of Hamlet's father, who actually appears at the end of the tragedy, the dogs in both Paraguayan films never really show up. The spectral barks forebode the animal's imminent return, but it never quite materializes.

Matar a un muerto can be read following the "spectropoetics" that Derrida sees in *Hamlet.* To begin with, the choice of a dog as a disturbing animal is not innocent. After all, as Carolina Rocha reminds us, "barking dogs . . . were used to torture and kill political dissenters" in Southern Cone dictatorships.[63] But spectrality should not be assigned only to the dog: as Brodersen notes, the gravediggers themselves "go through the day like automatons or, even worse, specters."[64] In short, specters incarnate secrecy in the Paraguayan woods. In a scene where Pastor hears his dog Negro close by, the bark sounds more like the roar of a lion, a personification of masculine virility in the wilderness. Here the grammar of secrecy's prepositions of space is central, as the bark emerges from inside a black cave. We cannot see Negro, an ambivalent ghost, dwelling between Pastor's trauma and hallucination. The camera shows only a black hole that separates the cave from Pastor, who observes and listens. Negro's bark remains in the dark and in the interiority of the cave but is still audible.

Without ever passing through it, the camera approaches the abyssal entrance in a slow close-up. The cave opening is like an opaque mirror: the barks are an echo of Pastor's own secrets and terrors. After all, as Dulci Spyer and Sampaio de Silva note, the dog is dangerous precisely because it has the ability to unearth corpses, exposing its master's handiwork.[65] But the camera quickly changes the scenery, foreshadowing the anticlimactic gesture that will take place again at the end of the film. The barks, tied to the topographies of secrecy of interiority and darkness, vanish into precarious secrecy. We do not hear about the dog again in the film. In its stead, another specter comes to replace it.

As the narrative unfolds in *Matar a un muerto*, we see the gravediggers lifting corpses that "arrive" on the shore, which they call "packages," a signifier that Feitlowitz identifies as part of her lexicon.[66] The corpses' reification is obvious, but even more eloquent is the way Pastor refers to them in the Guarani impersonal third person plural. Worried about the rain, he confesses that he hates to be cold like *che umi ohuague* (those that arrive). The depersonalization takes place through the ellipsis introduced by the demonstrative pronoun *umi* (those ones).

Feitlowitz notes that a typical strategy of the Argentine dictatorship was to neutralize the executioners' (and, more broadly, civil society's) remorse about desaparecidos by "depersonalizing the enemy." The military officer Emilio Massera, for instance, used to equate desaparecidos with a machine. As Feitlowitz asks, "Who after all could possibly feel any sympathy for a machine?"[67] Something similar could be said about these "arriving packages": Pastor and Dionisio do not refer to them as "prisoners" or even "people." Through language, packages arrive naturally and impersonally, almost like the subtropical downpour or the wind swirling through leaves and branches, merging with the woodlands. As political scientist Pilar Calveiro notes in her discussion of concentration camps in the Argentine dictatorship, this euphemistic use of language has a twofold goal: "the dehumanization of the victims, but also the relieving aim of absolving actions that otherwise society's moral code would punish the most."[68] The gravediggers, immersed in a dictatorial lexicon that flows transnationally from Argentina to Paraguay, distance themselves from their oppressive task and their contribution to the industrial production of death.

But everything changes when one of the arriving packages turns out to be a living man. Encina's influence reappears here: a human dethrones the dog as the third side of the triangle, to become the embodiment of the film's precarious secret. In *Hamaca paraguaya,* this third person is Cándida and Ramón's spectral son, Maximiliano, who is stuck in the Chaco war, perhaps dead in combat, perhaps still alive. The barks in the film stand for Maximiliano, because he left the dog with his parents before joining the war. In *Matar a un muerto* the third person is a moribund man with a foreign accent. The gravediggers call him *kurepi,* a Guarani derogatory term to refer to Argentines. A compound word, stemming from *kure* (swine) and *pire* (skin), *kurepi* alludes to the type of shoes used by the Argentine army during the War of the Triple Alliance. But here the *kurepi,* much like Kempes, is used to highlight the transnational nature of the "death group," the renewed dictatorial alliance between Paraguay and Argentina.

Under the 1970s dictatorial regimes in the Southern Cone, citizens like the *kurepi* often disappeared in neighboring countries, where they were residing (or hiding). According to Judith Rolón, the director of the Paraguayan Commission of Truth and Justice, the report *Anive Haguá Oiko* (So That It Never Happens Again) estimates that, of the 12,000 victims of human rights violations by El Stronato, "130 were disappeared in Argentina during Operation Condor,"[69] including Stroessner's most important opponent, Agustín Goiburú. Similarly, there were Argentines who disappeared in Paraguay as well as Uruguayans, Chileans, and Brazilians who disappeared in Argentina and vice versa. The *kurepi* is yet another symbolization of Operation Condor's transnational ties.

Politics and Space

Pastor and Dionisio represent a paradox: they are constantly in touch with genocide, but the way they intervene in it is exempt from explicit violence. Strictly speaking, they are neither executioners nor torturers, only gravediggers. In this sense, Giménez subverts the political thriller tradition inaugurated by *The Day of the Jackal.* Pastor and Dionisio, two simple peasants, are not villainous hit men, like the Jackal in Zinnemann's film. They are not personifications of Stroessner's rule either. They are common men trapped by oppression, which makes them do things that they would not do otherwise. As Giménez himself defines them, they are "the last link of a chain,"[70] structured by a division of labor that ultimately removes the influence of any political doctrines.

Their encounter with the *kurepi*, however, puts them in a conundrum, as Dulci Spyer and Sampaio da Silva mention: they must decide if they will also become murderers.[71] Perhaps this is the most important element that brings the film closer to the more conventional political thriller, fitting Erik Lundegaard's definition of the genre as a narrative that features ordinary men trapped by politics, often placing them in the position of victims.[72] Here, however, the trapped men are simultaneously "perpetrators and victims, direct witnesses and final performers of institutionalized terror," as Brodersen notes.[73] If it were not for the *kurepi*, they would still be caught up in their job's prosaic aspects, alienated from its political workings. Much as Walter does for the journalists in *Zanahoria*, the *kurepi* works as a destabilizing dimension in the third side of the triangle, a force that further strengthens the hyperpoliticization of life in the gravediggers' own bodies.

In this context, the gravediggers instantiate Derrida's magical sequence that goes from the highest spheres of state power to the lowest minions who carry out their mandates. The magic of state sovereignty—the decision of who lives and dies—becomes a business managed by specters and gravediggers. Magic, says Derrida, "always busies with ghosts . . . it becomes a business" that "attracts the undertakers, those who deal with cadavers but so as to steal them, to make the departed disappear."[74] Whereas burials are a conventional way of making any body "disappear" from the visible spectrum, here the desaparecidos' bodies, effaced by the state's sinister magic, endure a second disappearance that would not be possible without the lowly undertakers. Their position responds once more to the surrounding precarity in which they are immersed, not only as disposable labor but also spatially, in that they work with the lowest part of the world, the underground.

The gravediggers, however, do not become murderers. They never have the courage to give the *kurepi* the *coup de grâce*. Instead, they keep him as a prisoner in Negro's doghouse, one of the many instances in which an Argentine prisoner replaces the space left by an animal. Pastor later pressures Dionisio to finally execute their living package, but he cannot bring himself to do it. When Dionisio is about to shoot him, the *kurepi* suffers an epileptic seizure. As his body shakes, we hear him panting loudly, his respiration sounding distinctly like a bark. In fact, the constant fear of the dog itself is one of the reasons why the gravediggers cannot execute the *kurepi*: attracted by the fresh smell of the *kurepi*'s blood, the animal might attack them at any moment. In short, the *kurepi* and the dog are one and the same.

The title *Matar a un muerto* evokes images of Argentina not just because of the *kurepi* but also because it references *Operación masacre*. The *kurepi* is already "a dead man" before dying, because he has already lost his selfhood and his space in society after becoming a desaparecido. He is a specter, as defined by Derrida, not only because he is a "lifeless body" but because he is "a life without personal life or individual property."[75] Derrida in *Aporias* discusses the impossibility of talking about one's death, deconstructing the notion of "death as a threshold": "In crossing a border ... one exchanges deaths; one no longer speaks the same death where one no longer speaks the same language."[76] In surviving in the river as a package, the *kurepi*, a foreigner who barely speaks in the film and does not seem to understand Guarani, crosses multiple borders: geographical, linguistic, and ontological. In this sense, Giménez ultimately reexamines Walsh's question: how can somebody who was executed be alive?

As in *Operación masacre*, there is an Argentine *fusilado que vive* in *Matar a un muerto*: somebody whose survival menaces the dictatorial order in the same way the intimidating scavenging dog threatens the gravediggers. The living body of a desaparecido signifies the potential destabilization of the state's precarious secret, which, in Brodersen's words, is "that which should remain outside of scope for the whole society, although its existence was a well-known secret."[77] The Paraguayan woodland, like the garbage dump in *Operación masacre*, the soil in *Zanahoria*, the swimming pool in *Matar a todos*, and the Pampas in *Rojo*, is yet another site of precarious secrecy, another *intemperie*.

Alongside the common thread between these spaces lies in an interesting paradox: secrets are buried/sunk underneath them, despite (or rather because of) their openness. Secrets in Latin American political thrillers are hidden not in enclosed spaces but in some of the most open and exterior spaces imaginable. Bodies are concealed and exhibited at the same time, sufficiently untraceable to hinder their finding but with a tangible absence that serves as a deterrent to anyone who wants to become involved in politics. Thus, forced disappearance is performed in a visible space, constituting a truth that everyone knows but no one dares to disclose.

Derrida defines "the secret that we *speak of* but are unable to *say*" in terms of a paradox: "the best-shared thing in the world ... the sharing of what is not shared."[78] The well-known secret of forced disappearance, after all, was talked about publicly. The *kurepi* is someone who is dead but still must be killed, a specter, an undead, a *muerto viviente* (living dead). He is charged with what Calveiro calls "the torment of an end and a beginning": prisoners, once they were desaparecidos, were already *muertos que caminan*, "walking deads."[79] For Derrida, the menace of making visible the edges that separate life from death arises precisely "where the identity or indivisibility of a line ... is compromised," where "the possible identification of an intangible edge—the crossing of the line—becomes a problem." Derrida links this "problem" to the idea of an aporia, which happens to be central to *Matar a un muerto*: the impossibility of trespassing on mortality, the ultimate "non-passage."[80] For Derrida, this aporia is essential to the definition of specters, dwellers between both poles: "one does not know if [the specter] is living or if it is dead." The specter is "some 'thing' that remains difficult to name."[81] Perhaps this is why the gravediggers always address their specter with the word *kurepi*, instead of calling him by his proper name, Mario.

Space and Specters

Feitlowitz notes the centrality of *traslado* (transfer, move) in her lexicon of terror that resonates with the genre's grammar of secrecy: "to take prisoners away to be killed."[82] The euphemistic movement of the desaparecidos' bodies (such as the *kurepi*'s) follows a twofold process—first from an extrajudiciary prison to a clandestine death and then to an untraceable secret site located out in the open, exposing the strong ties between space and secrecy in the workings of genocide that Latin American political thrillers emphasize. As he floats toward a common grave, the *kurepi*'s *traslado* is thwarted: he survives the execution.

His story resonates with an Argentine survivor who reported in *Nunca más* a fear of "that particular death which is dying without disappearing or disappearing without dying. A death in which the person dying had no part whatsoever . . . as though dying meant being already dead, or like never dying at all."[83] The *kurepi* occupies this aporetic space, in that his location is an impossible and unnamable locus between life and death. The Paraguayan woods work as a sinister limbo, in Giménez's own words.[84] This transnational limbo stands for what victims of state-sponsored violence endured in Paraguay, Argentina, and beyond.

The *kurepi*'s potential breach of the state secret occurs because, despite being animalized, he is treated in a more or less humane way by the gravediggers, who keep him alive. After temporarily suspending precarity by fixing the defective radio, the *kurepi* shares a glass of *caña* (sugarcane spirit) with those who otherwise would have illegally buried his living body underground. But precarity is quickly restored when a military technician shows up unannounced at the *kokue*, presuming that the radio is still not working properly. The *kurepi* hides. The gravediggers never even think of turning him in, since that would only underline their own vulnerability within the chain of oppression. The technician speaks Spanish, bringing in the language of state power (the soundscape of the court), temporarily putting the prosaic dialogues in Guarani on hold.

Once more, the film conflates football and politics, through the technician's comment on the World Cup: "They say it is rigged, but we still love it." Of course, he is not really (or not only) talking about football. He reminds us of *El Conde Lucanor*'s cautionary tale (examined in chapter 4), the technician and the gravediggers know that the king is naked but still choose to pretend he is not. Everybody carries on as if the clothes were real. Nevertheless, *Matar a un muerto* and the other films examined in this chapter provide no place for a *palafrenero* to tell the king that he is naked. This is because there is no room for a detective-like character trying to speak up to power. What Pablo Debussy says about *Últimos días de la víctima* applies to most of these thrillers: they all operate under the "noir certainty that the new order of evil has triumphed, and that justice no longer exists."[85] Instead we are confronted with a society left alone, without anyone even trying to speak up to power, because everybody seems to know all too well how power works: it is inextricably linked to criminality.

Here the technician provides a discussion on ideology and habit that is closely linked to *El Conde Lucanor*. His statement about football, to begin with, speaks to Slavoj Žižek's rewriting of Karl Marx's dictum about ideology: far from ignoring the way football and politics are rigged, they "know very well what they are doing, but still, they are doing it."[86] In turn, this takes us to Louis Althusser's understanding of the "ideology of ideology." He cites seventeenth-century philosopher Blaise Pascal, who comments on the hypocrisy of Christian believers: "Pascal says more or less: 'Kneel down, move your lips in prayer, and *you will believe*.'" Althusser updates this: ideology is actually structured not by ideas but by "material practices," governed by equally "material rituals," corporeal habits, such as kneeling down or moving our lips.[87] The habit practiced by the technician and the gravediggers in *Matar a un muerto* is to "kneel down," to bow to the World Cup/Southern Cone dictatorships, as if their laws were not rigged. Secrets themselves become spectral in this context, existing and not existing at the same time. Argentina, no matter what, wins the cup/kills and terrorizes its citizens (like Paraguay), but a pretense that this does not happen in the end seems to be essential to continuing with business as usual.

In other words, as Jon Beasley-Murray puts it in his own critique of ideology and hegemony through habit, "when we are already 'enlightened' without our enlightenment altering our behavior," as is the case of the technician and the gravediggers, "then. . . . Ideology is no longer at issue." This is at the core of the political thriller, which, as I insist throughout this book, is less about political ideas than about affect. That is why the technician and the gravediggers are "social actors [who] are [not] persuaded . . . by ideology; rather, they are indifferent."[88] Giménez makes this clear by using football as a metaphor for politics and its enjoyment as a powerful habit that sustains it.

The looming disaster gets diluted in the gravediggers' silence, and nothing really occurs at the end of the story. The anticlimactic dénouement subverts our horizon of expectations: we anticipate that something will happen with the gravediggers' secret of keeping an enemy of the state alive—but nothing does. Much as in other Latin American political thrillers, secrets, because they are precarious, ultimately do not "work": disclosing secrets does not amount to exposing the high stakes at play. The technician leaves soon after. The suspenseful but anticlimactic scene is contrasted with the subsequent storm that throws everything into turmoil. The camera stops for a few seconds above a triangle of graves ravaged by thunder and lightning. The geometrical figure, to be sure, is not innocent: it materializes the three specters (Pastor, Dionisio, and the *kurepi*) trapped in the Paraguayan wilderness. As Dulci Spyer and Sampaio da Silva note, the three are once more equalized by their lack of freedom, paradoxically confined to the outdoors.[89]

It is not a coincidence that Dionisio's last words are "It's cold, Pastor. As you said, the cold came," indirectly alluding to a previous conversation in which Pastor expressed his distaste for the corpses' cold skin. As soon as Dionisio says this, the *kurepi*, the revenant (the one who eventually returns, like the ghost of Hamlet's father), comes back to them, this time not involuntarily through the river but by actively traversing the rainfall. We see him emerging from a focal point, his body like an apparition in the scene, located in between Pastor and Dionisio. The spectrality of the gravediggers and their prisoner comes full circle—or closes the triangle. By the end of the film, the three have become full specters: three undead people who have nowhere to escape.

Dulci Spyer and Sampaio da Silva conclude that what is at stake in *Matar a un muerto* is the allegorical task of unearthing memories from the Paraguayan dictatorship.[90] I suggest, instead, that the film does not engage in an extracting task. After all, the camera does not fully conceal secrets that could be unburied later. Corpses are not solidly covered underneath the woods. Depths, otherwise an efficient topography of secrecy, cannot fully conceal the secret of forced disappearance here. This is clear in the final scene, where we witness the three graves that stand for the three specters. Significantly, the graves are not underground tombs. Instead, they are burial mounds. Their relief works as the perfect metaphor for the precarious secrecy of forced disappearance, hiding but exposing corpses at the same time. Like *Zanahoria, Matar a un muerto* exposes the true impossibility of unearthing, but it does so without featuring an investigative plot. The final scene frames them sheltering from the thunderstorm, under the wobbling tent of the *kokue*. In all these different iterations of unsteadiness we can sense the fragile chain of command, the volatile mechanisms of power at work, the precarious secrets of a dictatorship.

Specters and Politics

Like most Latin American political thrillers, *Matar a un muerto*'s recreation of the past is inseparable from the present. According to Giménez, his film aims to fill a gap in Paraguay's public discussion about its recent history, which (like the overall national film production) is scarcer than in other countries of the region: in Paraguay, he says, "we haven't managed to introduce the discussion about the thirty-five years of dictatorship [that] permeated our social fabric."[91] Despite the efforts of the Commission of Truth and Justice, there were "no more than five prosecuted cases."[92] All these efforts were thwarted when Lugo's administration, which was starting to open the discussion, ended abruptly in a controversial impeachment.[93] For Giménez, the consequence of this collective silence and state of impunity is that the dictatorship "incubated its children, who, today, thirty years after the regime's downfall, are again in charge of the Paraguayan government."[94] The filmmaker elliptically evokes here the administration of Mario Abdo Benítez (2018–2023), the son of Stroessner's private secretary, who belongs to the same Partido Colorado that put the dictator in power in the first place.

Perhaps these inheritors of the dictatorial power can be understood as another specter that haunts Latin America, as democratically elected far-right administrations return throughout the region, from Bolsonaro to Milei, including Nayib Bukele. Ultimately, specters are not necessarily partisan. For instance, the specter that haunts the journalists in *Zanahoria* is linked to the dictatorship but also to the 1970s leftist guerrilla movements: it is precisely out of a fear of the Tupamaros' return that Walter, the picaresque informant, transiently succeeds in his sale of false information.

Derrida examines the French signifier *revenant* as the thing that comes back from the dead and the thing that comes from the past to be projected into the future. Both connotations define the specter that haunts these political thrillers: the threatening prospect of pasts that imagined alternative futures, from either the Left or the Right. As Derrida says, more than belonging to the past, "the specter is the future, it is always to come."[95] After all, the threat of a specter is effective not because of its past origin but because it can still materialize in a future that, as we have seen repeatedly in Latin America (and beyond), constantly defies the limits of predictability.

ARAÑA (2019)

Space and History

A seemingly affluent grandmother asks the coach on a soccer field when her grandson and his friends can leave the bench and join the team. Faced with refusal, she unilaterally encourages the kids to enter the field. The coach (who is also the referee) seems distracted but at the same time too focused on the match, insistently telling the first-choice players to keep their game to the center of the field. He does not impede the grandmother's disruption, becoming an impotent arbiter who is controlled by external, more powerful forces, located at the edges of the field. Perhaps this is what is at stake in *Araña*, the latest film made by Andrés Wood, who rose to international fame for his political drama *Machuca* (2004): a parable of a democratic state too worried about "sticking to the center," while at the same time being coerced by authoritarian agents whose authority is defined by class, who always remain outside of and above the rules of the game.

Immediately after this opening scene, the camera takes us to the streets, where poorer kids are also playing football. *Araña*'s setting is the more urban, conventional landscape of political thrillers. The narrative is set in present-day Santiago, a universe filled with signs. The camera draws our attention to Chile's old and new minorities: Indigenous and Asian peoples but also Haitians, who migrated massively to the city after the 2010 earthquake.[96] Santiago is decorated with women's soccer ads and graffiti with the Pablo Neruda quotation *Aunque tú no lo creas ganaremos* (Even though you don't believe it, we will win), the last two verses of his poem "Ode to the Simple Man."[97] These signs are thoroughly scrutinized from the wandering perspective of a middle-aged man driving his car. Gerardo, we will soon learn, is a sinister ex-member of Patria y Libertad (the Fatherland and Liberty Nationalist Front), a paramilitary far-right terrorist group that contributed to the 1973 coup, of which Eugenio Berríos (as in *Matar a todos*) was a member.

After hiding for a few years on the other side of the Andes, secretly working in Argentine Patagonia, Gerardo is finally back in Chile. Santiago, exuding democratization and multiculturalism, is like a nightmare to the fascist newcomer. From his point of view, the utopia of a criollo, settler, conservative, Spanish-speaking, and misogynist Chile seems to be extinct on the surface of the city streets. This could give us a first impression that the film distinguishes present and past in ways that other thrillers do not. Nonetheless, of all these political thrillers, *Araña* interweaves different periods of history in a most explicit way.

Wood had already shown an interest in depicting members of Patria y Libertad in *Machuca*, highlighting the ties between the middle class and the Chilean Far Right with a similar tone, though in a much more minor role. In the political drama the far-right activists are confined to the past. By contrast, in *Araña* they are still very much with us. As film critic Pablo Vázquez Pérez notes, unlike *Machuca* (circumscribed to the 1970s), *Araña* features two plotlines, constantly juxtaposing the past and the present.[98] The film opens with a petty crime, which triggers the plot and acts as a pretext to explore other elided political crimes, located in the past. The violence of the past appears in this scene of the present, when Gerardo chases and brutally runs over a pickpocket, squashing him against a wall and instantaneously killing him. This scene innovatively portrays vigilantism, blending a twofold anxiety from the past and the present about punishment as a means of social restoration.

On the one hand, this anxiety stems from the survivors of state-sponsored torture and family members of desaparecidos, because the Chilean state failed to sentence members of the military who committed crimes against humanity during its dictatorship (1973–1990). As is well known, Augusto Pinochet died in 2006, before any court could ever convict him. Manuel Contreras, the head of Pinochet's secret police, was convicted in 1993 and received a lenient punishment of only eight years. As in most parts of the Southern Cone, there was never a proper collective trial of the junta in Chile. This anxiety is well explored in other thrillers, but this scene also offers a comment on the perception of an increase in petty crime in the last few decades of democracy in the region.[99] The scene foregrounds nostalgia for the martial order (which ended after the military's retreat), which allegedly kept crime under control: the act of vigilantism funnels a reactionary demand for the return of the militarized state to control petty crime.

What complicates things is that Gerardo himself is a criminal who benefits from that lack of punishment: he is a runaway murderer who never gets convicted for his crimes, like Pinochet and Berríos. But in killing an indigent thief, he brings out a thirst for class revenge. A crowd forms to applaud and photograph him, filming the scene with smartphones while the police arrest him. At the end of the film, Gerardo still manages to avoid punishment by being declared mad. As in *Matar a todos*, madness plays an important role, once more delegitimizing the disclosure of dictatorial secrets and this time becoming a shield that protects the perpetrators and their accomplices.

Screens appear in this film, again, as narrative windows that send us to the same concrete time-space as in the other works examined in chapter 4: the 1970s. Updating the genre's cachet of authenticity, these recent political thrillers make it clear that phone and computer screens are the chronotope of our times. Unlike TVs, these screens are not merely passive objects onto which we project our vision. Ever since their development, they have constituted yet another intersection of time and space—and a productive one at that—in this century's filmic representation. Screens constitute another space where secrets are produced, stored, concealed, shared, leaked, monetized, commodified, and sold.

Like Bakhtin's classic chronotopes (the carnival, the road, the castle, the market), screens become "spatial and temporal indicators . . . fused into one carefully thought-out, concrete whole," in which "time . . . thickens, takes on flesh, becomes artistically visible" and "space becomes charged and responsive to the movements of time, plot and history."[100] After all, as Huyssen suggests, "space and time are fundamental categories of human experience and perception," which, "far from being immutable, . . . are very much subject to historical change."[101] In a way, this prominence of the past (the new broadcasting the old) can be read in line with Huyssen's interpretation of the memory turn: as a response to anxieties about these spatial-temporal shifts in the ever-vanishing present. In this context, *Araña* inverts this through Gerardo's point of view on current life in Santiago: the old scrutinizing the new, haunting and cornering it to the point of death, much as he does to the thief.

Gender and Politics

Like *Matar a todos*, *Araña* features a female protagonist: Inés, the upper-middle-class businesswoman who tries to interfere with her grandchild's match at the beginning of the film. Unlike Julia in *Matar a todos*, Inés is the villain. After Gerardo's brutal act, we can read her chat with her husband, Justo, in a close-up of her smartphone. Through her smartphone screen we see how Inés finds out about the act of vigilantism: Justo sends her a link that takes her (and us) to an online newspaper article entitled "Another Citizen Takes Justice into His Own Hands." As Inés's fingers zoom in on the touchscreen, she recognizes a specter, Gerardo, bringing us into the film's triangle. We soon find out that the three are linked through their secret involvement in Patria y Libertad during the early 1970s. The political is again dramatized in a triad of characters. Unlike the others, this is not a homosocial but a heteronormative love triangle, a common theme in popular fiction and as old as literature, featuring in classic texts such as *Oedipus Rex* by Sophocles. In the following scene, the police conduct a search at Gerardo's house. In his hidden basement they find weapons, bullets, and Patria y Libertad leaflets. On the back of the bedroom door, an old poster shows a young Inés, posing as "Reina Universitaria," the winner of a beauty pageant of sorts. Here, too, secrets are introduced by the grammar of secrecy's conventional prepositions of space "under" (the basement) and "behind" (the door). Whereas the iPhone screen zooms into the present, an image (an element inseparable from screens) serves as the opposing analog window that takes us to the 1970s plotline.

As the image transitions from present to past, the soundtrack plays a love song: *Más, yo quiero más, yo quisiera una tormenta, un diluvio en el desierto* (More, I want more, I would want a storm, a flood in the desert). The lyrics serve as a comment on Inés's personality as well as that of 1970s youths from both the Left and the Right, a driving force in the Chilean desert. After Inés comes the flood: she is an ambitious girl who would become a powerful businesswoman in her adulthood. This scene opens the past narrative, set in 1971 (a few years before the coup). A journalist is interviewing Inés, asking hollow questions, while she holds her beauty crown. The conversation soon turns somber when they ask her about her ideal man. In response, she points at a young Justo, who always does the dishes while she reads Ezra Pound, an obvious reference to fascism. The camera, though, focuses not on Justo but on a young Gerardo, watching. This is the first time that the members of the love triangle meet. From then on, they will become obsessed with each other. Over the course of the film, Inés has intercourse with both, while the two men are fascinated with and frightened by each other.

As in many other political thrillers, the film's title is also polysemic. In a visual and literal sense, *Araña* alludes to Patria y Libertad's logo (a Chilean translation of the Nazi swastika), which resembles a spider. Carlos Aguilar reads the insect in the title in relation to the "a turbulent shared past [that] acts as an enduring cobweb."[102] But "spider" also stands for more interesting things: in one of the few scenes where the word is spoken, Justo is holding a bottle of sparkling wine. He points it at Gerardo as if it were a gun, playfully accusing him of being a Communist. Gerardo constructs an analogy between their group and champagne: "These bubbles are us, putting pressure on the cork . . . which is Allende, our drunk president." Struggling to open the bottle, Justo points at Gerardo's fingers: "And these are the spider's little legs that keep pressuring and pressuring." *Araña* imagines Patria y Libertad's youngsters as an effervescent force that can unleash an outburst (a coup) against a cork, which in turn is equated to the state. Much like the referee at the beginning of the film, the state is imagined as an arbiter that fails to prevent the carbonation from bubbling out. Furthermore, another element related to the bottles looks like a spider: a muselet, the wire cage that contains the cork. Whoever has control of a muselet can enable or impede the release of pressure, spontaneously or deliberately. The muselet, another way of reading the "spider's legs," ultimately can usurp the state.

This scene also links female eroticism, power, and secrecy, all of which hover over the entire film. As Justo seizes the bottle (an obvious phallic object), he finally "ejaculates" in public, letting all the wine's foam explode and fall to the ground. While he pronounces the words "spider's legs," the camera takes a close-up of the legs of Inés, who is wearing a miniskirt, concealing her inner thigh with a pillow. All of this, again, is seen from Gerardo's perspective. A former military man, Gerardo makes the acquaintance of the couple but, unlike them, does not belong to the Chilean elite. At least initially, he occupies the position of the disturbing side of the triangle. An outcast, Gerardo produces and destabilizes the love triangle, the *tercero en discordia* (a Spanish saying that means "three is a crowd"). The following scenes string together the triangle, driven by the tension that magnetizes and divides them. Gerardo, Inés, and Justo are predators who connive against Allende's project of a socialist state. They construct intricate webs within the Chilean elite, injecting their venom into leftist demonstrators by infiltrating and terrorizing their organizations.

From Language to Gender

The signifier "peace" reappears in an ironic and cynical way in *Araña*. Back in the plotline of the present, Gerardo is now on the spot because of the crime he committed, leading Inés to fear that her secret past will become public if he is interrogated. Unveiling her involvement in Patria y Libertad would endanger her reputation. Jean Franco claims that "the restructuring of the economy on a neoliberal principle . . . promoted a business class that is impatient of reminders of the past."[103] It is interesting that in this instance the "impatience" of Inés, a businesswoman, is sparked not by the Left but by friendly fire: Gerardo's spectral return. After a long speech in which she brags about her contributions to Chilean society (working as a chief executive officer, teaching at the Universidad Católica, inaugurating schools for the poor), Inés says that she earned her *derecho de vivir en paz* (right to live quietly/in peace): her privilege not to be prosecuted for her involvement in genocide.

Spoken by a former fascist terrorist, these words have a bleak echo to them, replicating the title of Víctor Jara's popular Chilean protest song—especially because Jara was kidnapped and tortured on the morning of the coup and executed a few days later. Both a Communist propagandistic ode to Ho Chi Minh and a pacifist lyric against the Vietnam War, the song became a hymn of the Latin American Left. Even recently, in late 2019, multiple guitar players sang the song during the demonstrations against increases in Santiago subway fares and the rampant inequality in the country.

The film closes with a scene in which Inés repeats that she wants peace for the country. Patria y Libertad (Fatherland and Freedom), first and foremost, is about being freed from the Left, the freedom to rule the country with business as usual (in "peace"). Much like Schroeder and Naishtat, Wood shows how the empty signifier *paz* is constantly subject to potential usurpation and appropriation, just like the rules of a football match, the cork of a bottle, or the reins of the state.

In reviewing the film, Paula Vázquez Prieto distinguishes the plotline of the past, filled with "violence and terrorism, marked by the eroticism of counterrevolution," and the present-day plotline, "led by the gray tyranny of neoliberalism and the precarious peace of inequality."[104] But, once more, neoliberalism should not be conflated with precarity: in circumscribing precarity to the "peace" of the present, we run the risk of idealizing and romanticizing the past, even its darkest sides. The past is also precarious in *Araña*. After all, the trio is always on the verge of destruction, not only in the 2010s but also in the 1970s. Negative affect is always lurking behind tense calm, as we can see in multiple scenes where the two men (jealously competing for Inés's attention and desire) threaten to shoot at each other. The film shows a great deal of volatility in counterrevolution, which is less solid and unified than it seems.

Another screen takes us again to the past plotline, with the typical footage-within-footage that marks the genre's cachet of authenticity. The scene provides context for a transnational audience who may not be familiar with Chilean history. But it also addresses national spectators, who may be oblivious of the past. A tilted camera shows the iPad touchscreen of Nadia, the psychiatrist who is observing Gerardo's case in the hospital. She is watching a 1970s German documentary about the "spider that is spreading through the whole country": Patria y Libertad. The camera swiftly broadcasts the documentary itself on a full screen.

The real footage is merged with the film's fictional story, in which a young Gerardo equates "fatherland" with a "woman." This definition of an obviously patriarchal concept (*patria,* the land of the father, even though the Spanish language has an antithetical concept of *madre patria,* the motherland) should not be read as an attempt to feminize power. Gerardo equates the fatherland with women because he sees them as vulnerable to rape and therefore needing to be protected by men. The black-and-white documentary suddenly paves the way for its fictionalization in color, which in turn leads to a public sex scene between young Gerardo and Inés—another breach of the rules of the game.

The anthology of dialogues compiled under the title *Woman Critiqued* suggests that heteronormative triads can be described as an "isosceles triangle" made of a "brotherhood" that "allows a woman into their relationship." The cinematic model of this type of triangle is François Truffaut's *Jules et Jim* (1962).[105] However, homosocial triads are not exactly equilateral triangles either. In these thrillers, all triangles are isosceles: there is always a shifting disparate side. Its difference relies not so much on gender distinctions but, as mentioned above, on the threatening irruption of the political element into the relationship. Equally, men in *Araña* do not allow or forbid anything: they do not have a say. It is Inés who, in a way, disrupts the triangle; because of this, she often replaces Gerardo as the disparate side that brings in the political.

Nadia's digital screen takes us to these scenes from the past, working, once more, as a digital entrance gate, a techno-historical threshold, which welcomes us to a different dimension. But screens are made of crystals, which, in turn, are distorted producers of reflection: black mirrors. This is why Nadia is also the target of the screen's spectral reflections: after having seen on her iPad the brutality in which her patient Gerardo was involved, she seems to be the only one who cares that the hospital is protecting a former member of a terrorist organization. The male doctors do not think anything of it and work to keep him there so he can avoid prison. This collusion broadly echoes the connivance of the Chilean elite when facing the rise of the Far Right during Allende's government. More topically, in present democratic times, it resonates in the return of their children, under the leadership of José Antonio Kast, the runner-up in the 2021 elections and staunch supporter of Pinochet's legacy.[106]

SPECTERS AND HISTORY

The eroticism of power and violence trumps, at least ephemerally, Inés's fear about Gerardo's return. As Vázquez Prieto notes, with his spectral "re-apparition, both fear and desire are activated in Inés." Two driving forces coexist in her: the need to keep a "social status unaffected by the buried past" and "the surfacing of a youthful impulse."[107] In this fright mixed with desire we can see yet another spectral regurgitation of the past, making its "appearances" in a present that does not look that dissimilar from it, despite gradual democratization and the multiculturalism of its streets.

The following scene, set in the 1970s, emphasizes Gerardo's spectrality: Patria y Libertad decides to plot the killing of Allende's naval aide. The Left will be saddled with what is essentially a false-flag attack, to put more pressure on ousting the president. Gerardo volunteers for the task, which means that he will become, in Inés's words, *un mártir muerto* (a dead martyr): another pleonastic specter. But Gerardo will not literally die for the cause; he will just pretend to have been killed by leftists and hide for decades in Argentina. This is how he, too, becomes a specter.

In the present plotline in *Araña*, spatiality and secrecy merge in a swimming pool scene, which reminds us of *Matar a todos*. Justo and Inés argue with their son, who is embarrassed by his parents' precarious secrets, slowly starting to be exposed by the press. The disclosure of secrecy is caused by the return of the repressed, in the figure of Gerardo. Again we witness the intergenerational gap between those who were children during the dictatorship (like the director of the film himself, Andrés Wood) and those who had a leading part in it. As Justo tries to pour sparkling wine, his shaky old hand causes most of the liquid to spill out of the glass. Irate, he throws the bottle in the pool, sinking his virility, his lost ability to wield power. He then walks into the pool with all his clothes on to recover the bottle. As he rants to his adult son, with his body partially covered underwater (concealed in the depths), Justo screams that he cannot hear him, another allusion to the generational gap.

Father and son later have a conversation. The pool is a backdrop, with their feet underwater. Justo (the just, the fair one) makes contradictory statements: he sometimes negates all involvement with Patria y Libertad and sometimes offers an apology for the coup, following trite far-right-wing justifications, accusing Allende of wanting to turn Chile into a copy of Cuba. Finally, Justo also relativizes the dictatorship's death toll. His argument is inextricable from the state secret: the names of the murdered citizens were never made public, so the death toll remains immeasurable, unknowable, underwater.[108]

At the end of the film, an old Gerardo escapes the psychiatric facility and joins a series of younger far-right followers. With their help, he attacks a church, where Haitians are singing religious songs in Creole. As he shoots and kills them, he screams, "This is Chile and here we speak 'Chilean.'" In this hate crime that combines racism and linguistic chauvinism we see the juxtaposition of old fascist doctrines of racial superiority and current political anxieties about multiculturalism that have been funneled by the alt-right, in Latin America and beyond.

FINAL THOUGHTS

Araña's closing credits clarify that Patria y Libertad was dissolved after Pinochet took power in 1973. After all, the Chilean dictatorship moved in a different direction within the right-wing political spectrum. Patria y Libertad's planned conspiracies, like most cases of sedition in Latin American political thrillers, became evanescent. The paramilitary organization was nationalistic and even anticapitalistic. By contrast, Pinochet's dictatorship should be understood as a laboratory for the implementation of neoliberalism, an economic doctrine that favors transnational capital while shunning nationalism.[109] Nevertheless, as Carlos Basso Prieto notes in a recent essay, the country is currently experiencing a reappraisal of the paramilitary organization. After the 2019 social outburst in Santiago, Basso Prieto documents how the perpetrators of the arson of the Communist Party headquarters in Chillán and the attacks against memorials for the desaparecidos in different towns in Chilean Patagonia claim the legacy of Patria y Libertad to justify their terrorist acts.[110]

This current instantiation of far-right revisionism takes us back to the issue of the specter and "the past is not past" motif. In one of *Araña*'s scenes a middle-aged Justo toys with history by doing a puzzle with a picture of the Roman Forum, which points to the presence of a past now materialized in ruins. In early detective fiction, puzzles serve as the perfect image for the enigma that the private eye must solve; in Latin American political thrillers, they speak to the ties between present and past. The scene in *Araña* is reminiscent of one we see in *Zanahoria*, where the frustrated journalists also play with the past: throughout the film, they try to do a puzzle with a reproduction of Pablo Picasso's *Guernica*, but they fail and eventually end up smashing it. This outburst can be read as exhaustion caused by the permanence of far-right movements in the region and the impossibility of overcoming them.[111] Like the journalists, Justo feels frustrated and fails to complete the puzzle. This is interesting because it seems to suggest that the impossibility of solving the past is depicted as affecting not just the Left but also the Right, as the specters that haunt them are not that dissimilar. In the case of *Araña*, the specter is located in the return of Gerardo, who, unlike Inés and Justo, does not have so much to lose in terms of social status and is thus less motivated to hide his past secrets.

Outside the realm of these films, right-wing sectors all too often cynically attack human rights movements, questioning the need to keep dredging up the past and insisting on the necessity to move beyond it, often invoking the claim that the Southern Cone dictatorships ended decades ago. These thrillers are a reminder that this is not the case, not even for the Far Right. We need only think of Hernán Chacón Soto, one of the military brigadiers convicted of Víctor Jara's murder. After the Supreme Court ratified his twenty-five-year sentence, Chacón Soto killed himself in 2022 for a crime he had perpetrated in September 1973 as part of the coup. Even the current resistance to replacing Pinochet's 1980 constitution could also be read in this light. On the other side of the Andes, the past seems not to be past for the Far Right either, as evidenced in the statements of Argentina's current vice president, Victoria Villarruel, who felt the need to justify the 1976 coup to attract voters to her successful 2023 campaign. The 2024 jail visits to Alfredo Astiz and other convicted war criminals by members of parliament from Milei's ruling party go in a similar direction. All of this, we should remember, happened in Argentina, where the past is supposed to be at least a bit more past, as the country has prosecuted far more perpetrators involved in genocide than in Chile.

This is the relevance of thrillers like *Rojo, Matar a un muerto,* and *Araña*: far from treating the past as a harmless aesthetic playground (as some period dramas often do), they show its impending political threat right here, right now. They work as the safety warning engraved on the passenger-side mirror of cars in English-speaking countries, reminding us that the reflected objects are closer than they appear. In other words, Latin American political thrillers make it clear that the present, as Galaz says, does not exist: the past is not past—for anyone.

Coda

> *In the best political cinema . . . politics lies beneath and brings up personal questions related to our own identification with the characters. That's where politics touches the deepest and most real part of the human dimension. Politics is located in the reflection of personal history. Otherwise, politics ends up merely becoming ideas that drift away from reality.*
>
> BENJAMÍN ÁVILA, DIRECTOR OF *CLANDESTINE CHILDHOOD*, INTERVIEWED IN *SECRETOS PRECARIOS* (2024)

THROUGHOUT THIS BOOK I HAVE PRIVILEGED THE analysis of the genre's ties with the political over specific party politics. As I hope to have shown, this is because the political thriller goes beyond politics. With this caveat in mind, it is true that most political thrillers examined here could be described as "left-leaning," "progressive," or "liberal," in the American sense of the term. This is not exclusive to the Latin American context. Charles Derry notes that Allen Drury's last literary political thrillers "were not as well received . . . because they made increasingly overt what in *Advise and Consent* was only latent: [Drury's] right-wing viewpoint."[1] Similarly, Michael Coyne mentions that most Hollywood political films, including but not limited to the political thriller, "are liberal in principle," as they want to avoid "alienat[ing] a sizeable portion of the moviegoing public."[2] In other words, because the political thriller is a popular genre, it rarely sides with political standpoints that are not popularly supported.

Nevertheless, most American political thrillers are not as left-leaning as, say, European renditions of the genre, as Derry notes in comparing both traditions: for him, Costa-Gavras's followers in the United States (such as

Alan J. Pakula and Fred Zinnemann) never truly "assayed a wholesale attack on American capitalism or imperialism and were thus assured the more widespread acceptance of middle-class audiences," in line with the idea of the genre's popular nature.[3]

In Latin America, things were slightly different: the Cold War in the region, caught in between two world powers, was not so much about "the ideological and geopolitical conflict" between them. Rather, it had more to do "with the social struggle over the expansion of rights and economic power in societies where national-popular movements (sometimes combined with communism, sometimes against it) posed a prevailing threat" to constituted power, as historian Ernesto Semán acutely observes.[4] As shown in chapter 2, this can be clearly seen in *El complot mongol*, for example, where the international intrigue typically associated with the Cold War is treated as alien to the domestic matters at stake, which seem to be much more relevant.

As discussed throughout this book, the genre emerged and developed in the region in a much more modest, sporadic, belated, and, more importantly, politicized way than in Hollywood. Originating in *clandestinidad*, as an unruly offspring of Third Cinema, and siding with victims of right-wing state-sponsored massacres, human rights organizations, and guerrillas (as discussed in chapters 3, 4, and 5), most Latin American political thrillers are further to the left than their Global North models.

In this context, it would be inconceivable or at least hard to stomach a political thriller that would portray, say, Pinochet or Videla as heroes, because it would go against the popular perspective of most of the audience. More importantly, such a thriller would breach the genre's ethical aspect, in that the characters would not allow for any identification. This is why *Araña*, for instance, tells us about the years before the 1973 coup from the paramilitary's point of view but never sympathizes with them.

But in any case, we do not need to speculate about what right-leaning Latin American political thrillers would look like. We need only think of two recent Brazilian political thrillers filmed during Michel Temer's tenure: Rodrigo Bittencourt's *Real: o plano por trás da história* (2017) and Marcelo Antunez's *Polícia federal: a lei é para todos* (2017). While foregrounding palace-like Brasília buildings, such as O Planalto and the Itamaraty Palace (the headquarters of the Ministry of Foreign Affairs), and including explicit depictions of presidents Itamar Franco, Fernando Henrique Cardoso, and Lula da Silva, these truly unpopular thrillers serve as an apology for the adoption of neoliberal practices in the 1990s and for what would eventually materialize in Da Silva's imprisonment in 2018 as the result of the Car Wash Operation, respectively. Both thrillers were very negatively received, with one reviewer comparing Bittencourt's film to Leni Riefenstahl's Nazi documentary *The Triumph of the Will* (1935).[5]

The negative reception of these Brazilian right-wing political thrillers (and relatively scattered appearances in the rest of the continent to date) can be explained beyond the fact that the political ideas they defend (that the introduction of neoliberalism was entirely positive for Brazilian society and that Lula was the mastermind of the most famous corruption scandal of the last few decades) come from a right-wing viewpoint. Instead, these thrillers help us better understand the Kantian aesthetic political tradition that I apply to examine the genre: as most film reviewers claim, the problem with them is that we never identify with their protagonists. In other words, these thrillers fail to provide affective and ethical depth to their main characters, who never embody the moral politician imagined by Kant, which seems to be a constant in the genre's hero.

This lack of depth speaks to what Benjamín Ávila says in the documentary *Secretos precarios* when he emphasizes that "in the best political cinema . . . politics lies beneath": literally, in the "deepest . . . place of the human dimension." Ávila's words stress the genre's grammar of secrecy, with its topography of space that points to depths. At the same time, they show why infrapolitics and affect theory are highly relevant for analyzing the genre: not only because these lenses have not been "tested against" Latin American genre fiction to the same extent as, say, more classically ideological readings but also because the political thriller, far from being about ideas "that drift away from reality," is first and foremost infrapolitical and affective.[6] This is why the genre "can be enjoyed even by those resistant or indifferent to a specific political thriller's propaganda content," as Derry eloquently puts it.[7]

If and when right-leaning political agendas find stories that align with ethical claims to which the audience can affectively connect, then it might be possible for other types of political thrillers to emerge in Latin America. In fact, this might already be happening, as political thrillers slowly start to move away from the dictatorial period in the Southern Cone and from Tlatelolco in Mexico. The visible monster, as we have seen, was the militarized state and its accomplices: the predominant political faction throughout the twentieth century in most of the region. Moisés Naím's literary political thriller *Dos espías en Caracas* (2018), for instance, critically chronicles Hugo Chávez's Venezuela, with a story that earned a more favorable reception.[8] Naím's work is part of a wave of more recent political thrillers that venture into new unexplored territories in the Latin American context, privileging the reenactment of political events from the 1990s onward, as I discuss in the next section. In film, in particular, I am thinking of Eduardo Guillot Meave's *Caiga quien caiga* (2018), which follows the downfall of Vladimiro Montesinos at the end of Alberto Fujimori's autocratic regime (1990–2000). All these emerging clusters take us to the genre's ties with the present and the future.

THE POLITICAL THRILLER: THE PRESENT AND THE FUTURE

Martin Rubin correctly predicted in 1999 that "as the dollar-dominated, media-saturated global village becomes ever more inclusive and homogenized, it seems likely that the thriller will extend its reach and follow the blanketing flag of post-cold-war, multinational capitalism."[9] During the first quarter of the twenty-first century, the political thriller in particular certainly extended its reach with the prolific Latin American contributions to the genre, as examined throughout this book. In this context, the thriller ended up reinforcing what it was from the onset: a genre defined by transnationality. Even if, as Rubin claims, the thriller's "cultural perspective" for most of the last century has been "essentially (though not exclusively) bourgeois and Western (i.e.: Euro-American)," this point of view is inseparable from the not-so-peripheral Westernized region of Latin America, as I hope to have shown in chapter 1.[10]

Due to lack of space and to maintain a more cohesive focus, I put special emphasis on film in this book. But political thrillers also have recently "invaded" TV series and streaming platforms. The genealogy starts with the British *House of Cards* (1990) but has become especially prolific since the early 2010s, from the American cable TV production *Rubicon* (2010), which feeds on and updates the paranoid atmosphere of 1970s classics, to the European Canal+ miniseries *Carlos* (2010), which follows Venezuelan hit man Ilich Ramírez Sánchez's operations in Europe in the 1970s and 1980s.

In this case, Latin American renditions of the genre have appeared hand in hand with their Global North models. Andrés Wood's *Ecos del desierto*, for instance, was released as early as 2013. Wood puts on center stage a female human rights lawyer, from the Tanquetazo (one of the attempted coups against Allende that took place in June 1973) to the postdictatorial present. Much like *Ecos del desierto*, other recent TV political thrillers such as Carlos Bolado's *Tlatelolco, verano del 68* (2018), Gabriel Ripstein's Amazon Prime Video series *Un extraño enemigo* (2018), and Rodrigo García Barcha's *Santa Evita* (2022) revisit historical events that have already been portrayed in the Latin American political thriller, as this book attests.

What seems to be innovative about recent TV political thrillers, however, is that they introduce new historical contexts tied to democracy and somehow emancipated from events associated with the Cold War. They are set mainly in the 1990s. For instance, the confrontation between guerrillas, drug dealers, and the state in Colombia is shown in Juan José Lozano and Sergio Mejía's *Sabogal* (a technically impressive animated cartoon series released between 2015 and 2017 that features a human rights lawyer) and in Cristian Conti's Netflix series *Distrito salvaje* (2018–2019). The 1994 magnicide of presidential candidate Luis Donaldo Colosio in Mexico is retold in Hiromi Kamata and Natalia Beristain's *Historia de un crimen: Colosio* (2019, also distributed by Netflix). Menemismo and its legacies in Argentina are featured in Daniel Burman's Amazon Prime Video *Iosi, el espía arrepentido* (2022–2023) and Benjamín Ávila's Star+ *Diciembre de 2001* (2023). This recent and innovative corpus leaves the door open for further research into the genre explored here, a cultural form that seems more alive than ever.

SECRECY BEYOND SPACE

Argentina, Chile, Brazil, and Paraguay have distinctive features, overlapping timelines, and unique circumstances. Pinochet's dictatorship was different from, say, Videla's, Garrastazu Médici's, and Stroessner's. More broadly, the Southern Cone has visible differences from the Mexican context. Nonetheless, I hope to have shown throughout this book a common thread in Latin American political thrillers: their treatment of secrets as fundamentally precarious, understanding this concept in a broad, polysemic way.

In chapter 1 the precarious Latin American political and natural landscape thrills the stories of American or European characters who for different reasons are trapped in the region. In chapter 2 secrecy is precarious in relation to the fragile continuity of power in Mexican thrillers, among other issues—such as prosaicism, amateurism, and parody. In chapter 3 precarity takes on the more spatial dimension that is captured in what I call *la intemperie*: the sites of precarious secrecy, defined by political isolation, abandonment, and neglect, where state-sponsored political crimes turn civilians into defenseless hyper-victims, from the José León Suárez garbage dump to the Andean Highlands, including Tlatelolco Square. In chapters 4 and 5 precarious secrecy speaks to issues related to the crisis of representing forced disappearance and its lingering impunity, within similar sites of precarious secrecy: from the Argentine Pampas to the Brazilian *sertão* and the Paraguayan woods, from the swimming pools in Santiago to those in Montevideo. All these different iterations of *la intemperie* show that secrecy, much like the political thriller, must be transnational, despite the national boundaries.

This is perhaps what Moreiras means when he notes that the thriller "cannot find in the national horizon any secret of the world but rather shows that the secret is always beyond the national."[11] Despite the heterogeneous spaces and geographical contexts in which they are placed, the secrets portrayed in these thrillers ultimately are not that dissimilar: they are simultaneously concealed and unconcealed, dead and alive, precarious secrets that are potentially explosive but remain evanescent, much like the past and the present that these films aspire to portray.

In turn, these films' treatment of space, specifically in the form of sites of precarious secrecy, should not be conflated with what Fredric Jameson sees as the "supreme formal feature" of postmodern art in terms of "depthlessness": Andy Warhol's representations of literally superficial shoes, when compared with Vincent Van Gogh's.[12] There is a precarious, minimal degree of depth, for instance, underneath the burial mounds in the Paraguayan woods or underwater in the swimming pools of Montevideo and Santiago or, more evidently, in the precipice of Chuspi.

Equally, the visual palimpsest produced by the cachet of authenticity through the overwhelming presence of screens in these thrillers should not be read in the vein of Laura Podalsky, who (following Jameson) describes the "loss of an in-depth understanding of the past in a postmodern era" in Latin American political thrillers.[13] Instead, much like the detective thriller's poetics of failure that I identify elsewhere,[14] precarious secrecy need not be seen as a negative or defeatist concept. After all, as I hope to have shown, it often enables a sharper portrayal of the political than the solid high-stakes scenarios of the American political thriller ever could.

As Podalsky admits, political thrillers ultimately do not amount to "an unceasing barrage of new visual images."[15] They do not merely constitute an accumulation of layers. By foregrounding sites of precarious secrecy, these thrillers visually translate political crimes beyond the nation: in the interstitial region of infrapolitics, between the depths and the surface, between fact and fiction, always highlighting the porous but extant silhouette of the political, aiming to imagine it otherwise.

Acknowledgments

Much like many political crimes, books are rarely the work of a lone gunman. The idea for writing a history of the Latin American political thriller took shape one night in Seattle, a month or two after I completed my PhD and just weeks before the pandemic was declared. The book emerged almost involuntarily as the result of a series of conversations with friends, colleagues, and mentors. I would like to begin by thanking one of them, Alberto Moreiras, for whom I have immense admiration. Alberto believed in this book from its inception, and for that—and for his fundamental body of work—I will always owe him my deepest gratitude.

Writing a second book, without the benefit of relying on an academic supervisor's steady guidance, was terrifying. Writing about coups and magnicides amid the 2020 surge of bizarre pandemic conspiracy theories lent the experience an uncanny edge. This became eerily tangible with the failed coup attempts in Washington in 2021 and Brasília in 2023 as well as the thwarted plan to assassinate Cristina Fernández de Kirchner in 2022. Under these circumstances, this book, which devotes numerous pages to exploring secrets and politics, was made possible thanks to the help of my "foreign informers"—my colleagues from around the globe—with whom I had the privilege of engaging in extended conversations about film, history, literature, and politics. I would like to thank them here: my PhD supervisor and now friend Jon Beasley-Murray, Rodrigo López Martínez, Alejandro Soifer, Patricio Robles, Santiago Kalinowski, Jimena Néspolo, Diego Brodersen, Mariano Siskind, Francisco Robles, Alberto Viña, Olga Albarrán, Carolina Navarrete, Mariano Paz, Carmen Miranda Barrios, Ramón Victoriano-Martínez, Rodolfo Ortiz, and Deena Bowman.

I am indebted to the Australian National University (ANU), the Association of Iberian and Latin American Studies of Australasia (AILASA), the School of Literature, Language and Linguistics, the Research School of Humanities and the Arts, the Australian National Centre for Latin American Studies (ANCLAS), and the Latin American Studies Association for providing funding and exchange opportunities that helped bring this book to life. I also wish to thank my students at ANU with whom I have had the pleasure of discussing many of these thrillers. My gratitude goes to the many colleagues who invited me to share portions of this book at various venues and stages of its development: Monique Rooney (ANU/Cultures of Screen, Performance and Print [CuSPP] Canberra), Gemma King (ANU), Leslie Barnes (ANU), Elizabeth Hochberg and Francisco Robles (University of Washington), Robert Mason (AILASA), Cristina Fangmann (Universidad de Buenos Aires), and María Bjerg (Universidad de Quilmes).

Several filmmakers directly contributed to this book, either by granting me the privilege of viewing their films from Australia (many of which would have been difficult to access otherwise, as some are independent productions) or by clarifying narrative aspects and details. I thank them here: Benjamín Naishtat, Enrique Buchichio, Benjamín Ávila, Federico Veiroj, Esteban Schroeder, Daniela Goggi, Joel Novoa, Gory Patiño, Claudio Araya, Rafael Russo, Michel Gómez, and Santiago Roncagliolo. Special thanks go to Iván Cherjovsky for his wonderful work on the documentary *Secretos precarios: el thriller político en el Río de la Plata* (2024), which serves as a companion piece to this book and includes interviews with several of these filmmakers.

Earlier versions of material contained here were published as "Specters in the Paraguayan Woods: The Grammar of Secrecy in Hugo Giménez's *Matar a un muerto* (2019)," *Journal of Iberian and Latin American Research* 29, no. 1 (2023): 55–72; and "Villanos espectrales: el thriller político y la extrema derecha," *Boca de Sapo: Revista de Arte, Literatura y Pensamiento* 39 (November 2024): 2–11. I thank Taylor and Francis and Jimena Néspolo for allowing me to reproduce them here.

For reading parts of the manuscript and providing valuable feedback that made my writing more readable, I thank the blind-peer reviewers, as well as Jon Beasley-Murray, Ash Collins, Ailén Cruz, Thomas Nulley-Valdés, Katie Sutton, Rodrigo López Martínez, Ross Swanson, Patricio Robles, Sergi Viciana, Oliver Wilson-Nunn, Ricardo García Martínez, and Marina Bettaglio. For her flexibility and patience with missed deadlines over the years, and for her hard work throughout all phases of the book's editing and publication, I am truly thankful to my editor, Kerry Webb, and the whole University of Texas Press team that worked so professionally on this book's production: Christina Vargas, Anahi Molinas, Austen Schreib, and Robert Kimzey. I especially want to thank Kathy Lewis for her incredibly thorough copyediting.

For guiding me through the fascinating world of diachronic corpora of English, I thank Susy Macqueen and Elena Semino. For the clarifications of some passages in Guarani, I thank Jorge Larovere-Rivarola and Natalia Molas. For allowing me to include parts of their work in the epigraphs, I am honored and deeply grateful to Jerry Palmer, Patricio Guzmán, Renate Sachse, Gaspar Galaz, Benjamín Ávila, and the heirs of Ricardo Piglia and Roberto Farias. For going the extra mile to help rare texts and films reach Canberra, I thank Maria da Glória del Amore, Paola Beretta, Emma Gerts, Neiva Afyia, and Bronywn Krix, the librarians from ANU's Chifley Library. For their affective support throughout the journey, special thanks go to ANU's Spanish program: Catherine Travis, Thomas Nulley-Valdés, Manuel Delicado Cantero, and Óscar Patiño.

Heartfelt thanks to my closest friend, Pablo Zolldan, for being a tireless listener, and my family, especially my Australian parents, Wayne and Jill Stevens; my sisters, Romina Aira and Mirela Tocco and her wife, Diana Rigata, for their companionship from afar; my mother, Isamara Chiodini, for having taught me never to forget; and my father, Alberto Tocco, for having instilled in me his love for cinema. And last but far from least, to my wife, Stacey Stevens, for her loving patience, encouragement, and generosity and for spending a great deal of the lockdown in Canada, watching and discussing countless political thrillers with me at ungodly hours.

Filmography

This filmography presents a selection of films that participate in the history of the political thriller in Latin America. It is not a comprehensive list of every film referenced in this book and does not include TV shows or political dramas.

Die Spinnen (1919–1920), Fritz Lang, dir.
Distinto amanecer (1943), Julio Bracho, dir.
Cornered (1945), Edward Dmytryk, dir.
Notorious (1946), Alfred Hitchcock, dir.
Gilda (1946), Charles Vidor, dir.
We Were Strangers (1949), John Huston, dir.
Crisis (1950), Richard Brooks, dir.
Captain Scarface (1953), Paul Guilfoyle, dir.
Our Man in Havana (1959), Carol Reed, dir.
La sombra del caudillo (1960), Julio Bracho, dir.
Operation Eichmann (1961), R. G. Springsteen, dir.
Topaz (1969), Alfred Hitchcock, dir.
État de siège (1972), Costa-Gavras, dir.
Operación masacre (1973), Jorge Cedrón, dir.
Los traidores (1973), Raymundo Gleyzer, dir.
Il pleut sur Santiago (1975), Helvio Soto, dir.
Canoa (1976), Felipe Cazals, dir.
Queridos compañeros (1979), Pablo de la Barra, dir.
La sucesión (1980), Alfredo Gurrola, dir.
Tiempo de revancha (1981), Adolfo Aristarain, dir.
Últimos días de la víctima (1982), Adolfo Aristarain, dir.
Missing (1982), Costa-Gavras, dir.

Para frente, Brasil (1982), Roberto Farias, dir.
Tensão no Rio (1982), Gustavo Dahl, dir.
The Honorary Consul (1983), John Mackenzie, dir.
Bajo la metralla (1983), Felipe Cazals, dir.
Under Fire (1983), Roger Spottiswoode, dir.
O bom burguês (1983), Oswaldo Caldeira, dir.
Asesinato en el senado de la nación (1984), Juan José Jusid, dir.
En retirada (1984), Juan Carlos Desanzo, dir.
Contar hasta diez (1985), Oscar Barney Finn, dir.
Hay unos tipos abajo (1985), Rafael Filipelli, dir.
Los dueños del silencio (1987), Carlos Lemos, dir.
Revancha de un amigo (1987), Santiago Oves, dir.
La boca del lobo (1988), Francisco Lombardi, dir.
Apartment Zero (1988), Martin Donovan, dir.
Rojo amanecer (1989), Jorge Fons, dir.
Morir en el golfo (1990), Alejandro Pelayo, dir.
Lamarca (1994), Sergio Rezende, dir.
Amnesia (1994), Gonzalo Justiniano, dir.
Death and the Maiden (1994), Roman Polanski, dir.
O que é isso, companheiro? (1997), Bruno Barreto, dir.
Men with Guns (1997), John Sayles, dir.
Ação entre amigos (1998), Beto Brant, dir.
Garage Olimpo (1999), Marco Bechis, dir.
Thirteen Days (2000), Roger Donaldson, dir.
Nada por perder (2001), Quique Aguilar, dir.
Assassination Tango (2002), Robert Duvall, dir.
Conejo en la luna (2004), Jorge Ramírez-Suárez, dir.
Cabra-cega (2004), Toni Venturi, dir.
El rincón de los inocentes (2005), Palito Ortega Matute, dir.
Crónica de una fuga (2006), Israel Adrián Caetano, dir.
Batismo de sangue (2006), Helvécio Ratton, dir.
Matar a todos (2007), Esteban Schroeder, dir.
El secreto de sus ojos (2009), Juan José Campanella, dir.
Negro Buenos Aires (2009), Ramón Térmens, dir.
Ciudad en rojo (2009), Rebeca Chávez, dir.
Borrar de la memoria (2010), Alfredo Gurrola, dir.
Tropa de elite II (2010), José Padilha, dir.
Trópico de sangre (2010), Juan Delancer, dir.
Secuestro y muerte (2010), Rafael Filipelli, dir.
Infancia clandestina (2012), Benjamín Ávila, dir.
Colosio: el asesinato (2012), Carlos Bolado, dir.

No (2012), Pablo Larraín, dir.
A Dark Truth (2012), Damian Lee, dir.
Tlatelolco: verano de 68 (2013), Carlos Bolado, dir.
Esclavo de Dios (2013), Joel Novoa Schneider, dir.
Olvidados (2013), Carlos Bolado, dir.
Zanahoria: detrás de la verdad (2014), Enrique Buchichio, dir.
Allende en su laberinto (2014), Miguel Littín, dir.
La última noticia (2015), Alejandro Legaspi, dir.
El almuerzo (2015), Javier Torre, dir.
Pasaje de vida (2015), Diego Corsini, dir.
El clan (2015), Pablo Trapero, dir.
Koblic (2016), Sebastián Borensztein, dir.
La larga noche de Francisco Sanctis (2016), Francisco Márquez and Andrea Testa, dirs.
La cárcel del barrio (2016), Jeremías Espínola, dirs.
Salt and Fire (2016), Werner Herzog, dir.
La cordillera (2017), Santiago Mitre, dir.
Real: o plano por trás da história (2017), Rodrigo Bittencourt, dir.
Polícia federal: a lei é para todos (2017), Marcelo Antunez, dir.
Cabros de mierda (2017), Gonzalo Justiniano, dir.
La casa rosada (2018), Palito Ortega Matute, dir.
Rojo (2018), Benjamín Naishtat, dir.
Lo peor de los deseos (2018), Claudio Araya, dir.
Caiga quien caiga (2018), Eduardo Guillot Meave, dir.
Matar a un muerto (2019), Hugo Giménez, dir.
Araña (2019), Andrés Wood, dir.
Así habló el cambista (2019), Federico Veiroj, dir.
Marighella (2019), Wagner Moura, dir.
El supremo manuscrito (2019), Jorge Díaz de Bedoya and Michael Kovich, dirs.
El año de la furia (2020), Rafael Russo, dir.
Matar a Pinochet (2020), Juan Ignacio Sabatini, dir.
Pseudo (2020), Gory Patiño and Luis Reneo, dirs.
Azor (2021), Andreas Fontana, dir.
Lima 3.31 (2021), Marcelo Torcida, dir.
Argentina, 1985 (2022), Santiago Mitre, dir.
La lista (2022), Michael J. Hardy, dir.
La pena máxima (2022), Michel Gómez, dir.
1976 (2022), Manuela Martelli, dir.
El rapto (2023), Daniela Goggi, dir.

Notes

INTRODUCTION

1. "Secret," in *The Concise Oxford Dictionary of English Etymology.*
2. Jacques Derrida and Maurizio Ferraris, *A Taste for the Secret,* 58.
3. Gilles Deleuze and Félix Guattari, *A Thousand Plateaus: Capitalism and Schizophrenia,* 286.
4. Georg Simmel, "The Sociology of Secrecy and of Secret Societies," 441.
5. Norberto Bobbio, *Democracia y secreto.*
6. Elias Canetti, *Crowds and Power,* 290.
7. Michael Taussig, *Defacement: Public Secrecy and the Labor of the Negative,* 7.
8. Silvia Federici, *Witches, Witch-Hunting, and Women.*
9. Ricardo Piglia, "Conversaciones en Princeton," 207–210.
10. Ricardo Piglia, "La ficción paranoica," 5. Unless otherwise indicated, all translations are my own.
11. Alberto Moreiras, "Infrapolitics and the Thriller: A Prolegomenon to Every Possible Form of Antimoralist Literary Criticism: On Héctor Aguilar Camín's *La Guerra de Galio* and *Morir en el Golfo,*" 147.
12. This is a leitmotif in Jon Beasley-Murray's *Posthegemony: Political Theory and Latin America.*
13. See Ian Scott, *American Politics in Hollywood Film*; Jerry Palmer, *Thrillers: Genesis and Structure of a Popular Genre*; and Paul Cobley, *The American Thriller: Generic Innovation and Social Change in the 1970s.* These authors treat thrillers as a unified genre, albeit acknowledging its polyphonic breadth.
14. Martin Rubin, *Thrillers,* 4.
15. Charles Derry, *The Suspense Thriller: Films in the Shadow of Alfred Hitchcock,* 63.
16. See Tzvetan Todorov, "The Typology of Detective Fiction."
17. Rubin, *Thrillers,* 4.
18. Janet Staiger, "Hybrid or Inbred: The Purity Hypothesis and Hollywood Genre History," 6 (quotation), 11, 15.

19. Rubin, *Thrillers*, 40.
20. See Thomas O. Beebee, *The Ideology of Genre: A Comparative Study of Generic Instability*, 27–28. Beebee informs Staiger's conclusions through a poststructuralist reading focused more on genre "instability" than on "purity."
21. See Cobley, *The American Thriller*, 27.
22. See Pablo Castrillo and Pablo Echart, "Towards a Narrative Definition of the American Political Thriller Film," 111 (hereafter cited as Castrillo and Echart, "Definition").
23. Rubin, *Thrillers*, 30. See also Derry, *The Suspense Thriller.*
24. Rubin, *Thrillers*, 7; Castrillo and Echart, "Definition," 111.
25. Derry, *The Suspense Thriller*, 103, 114.
26. The boundaries that separate the political thriller from other neighboring genres are not crystal clear for most critics either. Some would even go so far as to claim that there are simply no distinctions between the political thriller and the spy or detective thrillers. But these are oversimplifications. The political thriller should not be conflated with other types of thrillers or with film noir. For political and spy thrillers, see Tony Davies, "The Divided Gaze: Reflections on the Political Thriller," who treats spy literary thrillers such as John Buchan's *Thirty-Nine Steps* (1915) as political thrillers. See also Ernst Mandel, *Delightful Murder: A Social History of the Crime Story*, 62; Deena Bowman, "The Hollywood Political Thriller during the Cold War" (hereafter cited as Bowman, "Cold War Thrillers"), 18; and Cobley, *The American Thriller*, 29, who all trace a lineage between the spy and the political thriller but do not go as far as Davies's conflation of them. For the political and the detective thriller, see Guy Hennebelle and Renée Delforge, "Z Movies or What Hath Costa-Gavras Wrought?," 29, who claim that the genre takes the ingredients of "the American-style detective story and injects into it . . . a political theme" (29). See also Carlos Monsiváis, "Ustedes que jamás han sido asesinados," 8–9; Rubin, *Thrillers*, 181–182; and Todorov, "The Typology of Detective Fiction." Misleading equations between political thrillers and other types fail to account for many novels and films that foreground politicians or, more simply, tell the narrative of civilians who fall victim to state-sponsored crime, for instance, entirely excluding investigators or investigations. For the political thriller and film noir, see Slavoj Žižek, "The Thing That Thinks: The Kantian Background of the *Noir* Subject," 200: Žižek claims that the term "film noir" is "not limited to hard-boiled detective stories" but is rather a "distortion in every genre it is applied to," whether it be detective or political thrillers. I side with the long list of critics who believe film noir is a style (and the period associated with it) more than a genre in its own right. As such, neither detective nor political thrillers should be conflated with noir: both genres may often feature a noir style, but not always. For an outline of this debate, see Mark T. Conard, "Nietzsche and the Meaning and Definition of Noir."
27. Many contradicting genealogies have been suggested for the political thriller. For some, the genre started in the United States in 1962 with John

Frankenheimer's *The Manchurian Candidate*: see Rubin, *Thrillers*, 149; Michael Coyne, *Hollywood Goes to Washington: American Politics on Screen*, 135, 168; Terry Christensen, Elizabeth Haas, and Peter J. Haas, *Projecting Politics: Political Messages in American Film*, 160–161; and Castrillo and Echart, "Definition," 113. For Hennebelle and Delforge, "Z Movies," 29, the genre emerged later in Europe in 1969 with Costa-Gavras's *Z*. The broad consensus is that the genre's emergence can be traced to the 1950s: see Cobley, *The American Thriller*, 119; and Rubin, *Thrillers*. Other critics hark back to earlier times, such as 1940s film noir featuring the gangster motif that incorporated corrupted public officials: Scott, *American Politics*, 100, 103; and Bowman, "Cold War Thrillers." In turn, Derry, *The Suspense Thriller*, 106, refers to early 1930s sound cinema with political dramas, such as Gregory La Cava's *Gabriel over the White House* (1933). Derry admits, however, that the 1950s "seem an appropriate place to begin," because films made then already feature the genre's "growing paranoia."

28. Bowman, "Cold War Thrillers," 312.
29. Castrillo and Echart, "Definition," 114.
30. Mempo Giardinelli, *El género negro: orígenes y evolución de la literatura policial y su influencia en Latinoamérica*, 231.
31. Early cultural works described as political thrillers include Derek Kartun's 1949 journalistic book on Yugoslavia, *Tito's Plot against Europe* (see Konni Zilliacus, "The Cold War in the Balkans," 90); Christopher Mayhew's 1951 TV play about meetings between British and Soviet representatives at the United Nations headquarters, *Those in Favour . . .* (see Kay Dick, "A Political Thriller," 5); Laurence Olivier's 1955 adaptation of William Shakespeare's *Richard III* (see Harry Schein, "A Magnificent Fiasco?," 410); and Otto Preminger's *Exodus* (1960), an epic retelling of the foundation of Israel (see *Time*, December 19, 1960, https://content.time.com/time/subscriber/article/0,33009,873358,00.html). For more on the history of "political thriller" as a term, see Mark Davies, *The Corpus of Historical American English*.
32. Mandel, *Delightful Murder*, 60–65, mentions the political thriller only in passing in a short chapter, while Derry, *The Suspense Thriller*, features an extensive chapter tracing and examining its history. Palmer's *Thrillers* and Cobley's *The American Thriller* (both focused on literature) and Rubin's *Thrillers* (focused on film) do not use the term "political thriller." Instead Cobley and Rubin talk about "paranoid" or "1970s conspiracy thrillers," respectively, to describe what are now commonly referred to as political thriller classics. In turn, Palmer mainly examines detective and spy thrillers and treats them as "the thriller." He seems to be at a loss when discussing a political thriller such as Frederick Forsyth's *The Day of the Jackal* (1971), which does not feature a spy or a detective hero (Palmer, *Thrillers*, 207, 211). Scott, *American Politics*, and Coyne, *Hollywood Goes to Washington*, talk interchangeably of "conspiracy" and "political" thrillers. Critics who have talked more explicitly about the political thriller include Adam Barker, "Cries and Whispers"; Fredric Jameson, "Cognitive

Mapping"; Christensen, Haas, and Haas, *Projecting Politics*; Castrillo and Echart, "Definition"; and Bowman, "Cold War Thrillers."

33. Even Rubin (more transnational than others) covers European thrillers such as Hitchcock's and Lang's only because they were influential for Hollywood productions. A notable exception is Derry's book, which features Costa-Gavras's films set in Latin America as well as an Argentine political drama that I discuss later in this book: Luis Puenzo's *La historia oficial* (1986).
34. Laura Podalsky, *The Politics of Affect and Emotion in Contemporary Latin American Cinema* (hereafter cited as Podalsky, *Affect and Emotion*).
35. Podalsky circumscribes the political thriller to 1990s and 2000s productions, as if they were disjointed from their 1970s and 1980s forerunners. In turn, Elena Goity and David Oubiña, "El policial argentino," and Constanza Burucúa, "Remnants of the Dirty War: On the *Policial*, the Political Thriller and the Paramilitary Thriller," restrict their reading to 1980s Argentine political thrillers. Burucúa traces them to 1970s films that move away from Third Cinema, especially Héctor Olivera's *La Patagonia rebelde* (1974), which I consider to be more of a political drama with a western component. My reading diverges from theirs in that it includes other important 1970s forerunners such as Jorge Cedrón's *Operación masacre* (1973) and Raymundo Gleyzer's *Los traidores* (1973) and obviously goes beyond postdictatorial Argentina.
36. Mainly Rubin (*Thrillers*), but also Palmer (*Thrillers*).
37. See note 32.
38. Castrillo and Echart, "Definition," 109.
39. For more on other types of films about politics, see Scott, *American Politics*, 22.
40. Ana María Amado, *La imagen justa: cine argentino y política, 1980–2007*, 17. See also Ana Laura Lusnich and Pablo Piedras, *Una historia del cine político y social en Argentina: formas, estilos y registros (1969–2009)*, which includes about a hundred and ninety Argentine documentaries, ninety dramas, and only fifteen political thrillers. José Ramón Santillán Buelna, "Un siglo de cine político mexicano," lists only eight political thrillers out of a corpus of fifty-four political films. In turn, Jorge Majfud devotes *Cine político latinoamericano* mainly to documentaries and political dramas, with only two political thrillers, as does Jessica Stites Mor in *Transition Cinema: Political Filmmaking and the Argentine Left since 1968*.
41. The contrast between 1960s–1970s Third Cinema's preference for documentaries over genre films constantly appears in the literature on Latin American political films. See, for instance, Zuzana M. Pick, *The New Latin American Cinema: A Continental Project*, 42; Paul A. Schroeder Rodríguez, *Latin American Cinema: A Comparative History*, 171; and Luis Zanin Oricchio, *Cinema de novo: um balanço crítico da retomada*, 103.
42. Roman Jakobson, "La dominante."
43. Castrillo and Echart, "Definition," 113.
44. For more on subtext and text in political films, see Coyne, *Hollywood Goes to Washington*, 9.

45. For the political in American and French political thrillers, see Castrillo and Echart, "Definition", 113; and Hennebelle and Delforge, "Z Movies," 31, respectively.
46. For the thriller and entertainment, see Rubin, *Thrillers*, 44.
47. Podalsky, *Affect and Emotion*, 62, 171.
48. Barker, "Cries and Whispers," 10, 11.
49. Tocco and Cherjovsky, *Secretos precarios: el thriller político en el Río de la Plata.*
50. Amado, *La imagen justa*, 9.
51. Wendy Brown, "At the Edge," 569.
52. Chantal Mouffe, "Deliberative Democracy or Agonistic Pluralism?," 754.
53. Rubin, *Thrillers*, 17 (emphasis in the original).
54. Moreiras, "Infrapolitics and the Thriller."
55. Jean-Luc Nancy, "Is Everything Political? (A Brief Remark)."
56. Rubin, *Thrillers*, 18.
57. See Ricardo Bedoya, Mario Lucioni, and Jaime Urco, "La industria cinematográfica en Latinoamérica," 219; and Nelson Carro, "Un siglo de cine en América latina," 241.
58. Underground rail transit networks appeared first in Buenos Aires (1913), Mexico City (1969), São Paulo (1974), and Santiago (1975).
59. See Eduardo Viñuela, "Rock in Spanish: A Field of Dispute and Convergence between Spain and Latin America," 200–201; and Arthur Dapieve, *Brock: o rock brasileiro dos anos 80*, 11.
60. See Octavio Islas, "Los primeros años de internet en América latina."
61. See Carla Masmun, "Raymundo Gleyzer y el Grupo Cine de la Base: compromise, activismo y resistencia," 179; and Anabella Castro Avelleyra, "*Operación masacre* de Jorge Cedrón: la recuperación de la historia para hacer historia." Without explicitly labeling films as political thrillers, they talk about the distinct emergence of Raymundo Gleyzer's *Los traidores* and Jorge Cedrón's *Operación masacre* in this context.
62. See Maité Campillo, "¡Los traidólares! ¡Raymundo Gleyzer flor de revuelo!" See also Silvana Flores, "Experiencia de la militancia en el cine político argentino de los setenta," 208. Flores adds the nuance that the censorship of *Los traidores* was briefly lifted during the democratic period of Héctor Cámpora and Juan Domingo Perón's administrations (1973–1976).
63. As explained by his daughter, Lucía Cedrón (*Operación Masacre* [00:00:43]), who was in charge of restoring the film in 2013.
64. Cedrón, *Operación Masacre* (00:00:43).
65. For more on the film's cast, see pro.imdb.com/title/tt0073149/cast.
66. As explained by the director himself, Pablo de la Barra, *Queridos compañeros* (00:02–00:39).
67. Carla Masmun and Denise Mora, "La liberación está en la base," 94.
68. Carlos Monsiváis, "South of the Border, Down Mexico's Way (El cine latinoamericano y Hollywood)," 35; Miriam Haddu, "Political Violence and Fiction in Mexican Film: The Case of Carlos Bolado's *Colosio: el asesinato* (2012)," 457.

69. Podalsky, *Affect and Emotion*, 177. See also Michael Chanan, "Latin American Cinema in the 90s: Representational Space in Recent Latin American Cinema."
70. Carlos Monsiváis, *Aires de familia: cultura y sociedad en América Latina*, 76. After lamenting the absence of a strong thriller tradition in Mexico, Monsiváis would admit that "especially after the 1990s, the thriller has become an essential genre of talented filmmakers, convinced of the incestuous links between politics and crime." These links would emerge in a smoother way, hand in hand with democratization processes in Mexico and beyond. Similarly, in the Argentine context, Burucúa, "Remnants of the Dirty War," 75, notes that "even if the approach initiated by" national political thrillers "was abruptly halted by the military as soon as they took power in 1976, they should still be credited as the clear predecessors of what was going to become the characteristic mode of production promoted by the Alfonsín government after 1983: committed cinema made in line with the industry's criteria."
71. See Miriam Haddu, *Contemporary Mexican Cinema 1989–1999: History, Space, and Identity*, 13; and Gloria Julieta Zarco, "Argentina: cine, censura y dictadura (1969–1983)," 140.
72. See Haddu, "Political Violence and Fiction in Mexican Film."
73. Bowman, "Cold War Thriller," 182.
74. *Brewer's Dictionary of 20th Century Phrase and Fable*, 374.
75. Bowman, "Cold War Thriller," 162; Scott, *American Politics*, 144.
76. Derry, *The Suspense Thriller*, 103; Bowman, "Cold War Thriller," 55–57. As Castrillo and Echart observe in "Definition," 118, American "political thrillers tend to avoid . . . dystopian or fantasy story worlds and instead take as a starting point . . . certain historical events that have left a significant imprint in the history of the U.S."
77. Derry, *The Suspense Thriller*, 127.
78. Fredric Jameson, *Postmodernism, or the Cultural Logic of Late Capitalism* iv, is quoting William Gibson's cyberpunk novel *Mona Lisa Overdrive* (1988).
79. For Barker, "Cries and Whispers," 10, the 1970s were a golden age for American political thrillers because they would recurrently go back to a series of "crushing defeats of counter-cultural ideals—from Vietnam to Watergate" in the nation's political history.
80. Scott, *American Politics* (2011 edition), 119.
81. Marianne Hirsch, "The Generation of Postmemory," 103.
82. Moreiras, "Infrapolitics and the Thriller," 153.
83. Derry, *The Suspense Thriller*, 124.
84. Bowman, "Cold War Thrillers," 180–182.
85. See Masmun and Mora, "La liberación está en la base," 93.
86. For instance, Enrique Buchichio notes in *Secretos precarios* that "precarity and Uruguayan cinema are synonymous" and Benjamin Naishtat claims that "Argentine cinema is the child of precarity."
87. Monsivais, *Aires de familia*, 75–76, and "South of the Border," 39.
88. See Buchichio, Esteban Schroeder, and Ávila's testimonies in *Secretos precarios*.

89. Peter Brooks, *The Melodramatic Imagination: Balzac, Henry James, Melodrama, and the Mode of Excess*, examines depths and surfaces.
90. Palmer (*Thrillers*, 10) and Rubin (*Thrillers*, 202) understand thrillers as a cultural form that is keen on action and movement. We need only think of the overwhelming presence of chase scenes in thrillers.
91. Taussig, *Defacement*, 57.
92. For Rubin, *Thrillers*, 24, "an archetypal thriller" includes "a hero descending into a . . . maze-like world . . . to defeat the villain . . . and finally . . . making his way out . . . into the light of day."
93. Rubin, *Thrillers*, 142, 234.
94. Scott, *American Politics*, 144.
95. Rubin, *Thrillers*, 90.
96. Taussig, *Defacement*, 5.
97. Maribel Casas-Cortés, "Precarious Writings: Reckoning the Absences and Reclaiming the Legacies in the Current Poetics/Politics of Precarity," 510.

CHAPTER 1: THRILLING GRINGOS

1. *Gilda* © 1946, renewed 1973 Columbia Pictures Industries, Inc. All Rights Reserved. Courtesy of Columbia Pictures.
2. Carlos Monsiváis, "Ustedes que jamás han sido asesinados," 11, wonders "why is the thriller not practiced in Latin America?" This perception is still prevalent. The actor Manolo Cardona, who plays the leading role in the Mexican TV thriller *La hermandad*, directed by Carlos Bolado (one of the big names of the genre in the region), made a similar comment in an interview for *El País* ("Los thrillers latinoamericanos se encuentran todavía en pañales"): "Latin American thrillers are still wet behind the ears." In *Secretos precarios*, film critic Diego Brodersen notes that political thrillers, in particular, can only be traced to the last decade or so in the region.
3. See "Thriller" in Davies, *The Corpus of Historical American English*.
4. See "Thriller" in *The Concise Oxford Dictionary of English Etymology*. Book reviews including the word "thriller" appear in magazines such as the *Athenaeum* (issue 3070, August 28, 1886, 285), https://archive.org/details/sim_athenaeum-uk_1886-08-28_3070.
5. See Karen Sands-O'Connor, "The Stratemeyer Chums Have Fun in the Caribbean: America and Empire in Children's Series," 59.
6. Roy Rockwood, *Jack North's Treasure Hunt: Or Daring Adventures in South America*, n.p.
7. Especially Cuba, Puerto Rico, and the Dominican Republic. See "Stratemeyer Chums."
8. Sands-O'Connor, "Stratemeyer Chums," 62.
9. See Patrick Bantlinger, *Rule of Darkness: British Literature and Imperialism, 1830–1914*.

10. Rubin, *Thrillers*, 13–17 (quotation on 14).
11. Rubin, *Thrillers*, 15, 266.
12. Rubin, *Thrillers*, 16.
13. Sands-O'Connor, "Stratemeyer's Chums," 60.
14. Rubin, *Thrillers*, 40.
15. Mikhail Bakhtin, *The Dialogic Imagination: Four Essays*, 390, details the links between the "modern European adventure novel" (explicitly mentioning Daniel Defoe's work) and the Spanish "picaresque novel." The *pícaro*, for him, is close to the adventure novel's hero: both begin their journey "to the depths" (passing through the lower class). As I examine throughout the book, the political thriller also has a strong connection with depths and surfaces.
16. Franco Moretti, *The Way of the World: The Bildungsroman in European Culture*, 4.
17. Claudia Delgado, "Narrativas del hambre y memoria colectiva: un ensayo sobre la picaresca," 156 (hereafter cited as Delgado, "Hambre y memoria").
18. Rubin, *Thrillers*, 7.
19. Rockwood, *Jack North's Treasure Hunt*, n.p.
20. For the adventure novel, see Rubin, *Thrillers*, 266; for the picaresque, see Jens Elze, *Postcolonial Modernity and the Picaresque Novel: Literatures of Precarity*, 13 (hereafter cited as Elze, *Picaresque Novel*).
21. Monsiváis, "Ustedes que jamás han sido asesinados," 11.
22. Roberto Russell and Fabián Calle, "Periferias turbulentas y penetradas: su papel en la expansión de los intereses de seguridad de Estados Unidos en América Latina," 170.
23. Andrés Malamud and Luis Schenoni, "Sobre la creciente irrelevancia de América Latina," 71.
24. Cuba and Panama are so much a part of the political thriller landscape during and after the Cold War that they feature even in parodies of the genre, such as Carol Reed's *Our Man in Havana* (1959), William Richert's *Winter Kills* (1979), and John Boorman's *The Tailor of Panama* (2001). The Cuban Missile Crisis is also central to Roger Donaldson's *Thirteen Days* (2000).
25. Rubin, *Thrillers*, 21.
26. There are many examples in other clusters, as evidenced in the more comprehensive filmography at the end of this book.
27. For the Cold War political thriller and Kennedy, see Jim Hoberman, "When *Dr. No* Met *Dr Strangelove*: Movies of the Cold War and Kennedy Era"; and Coyne, *Hollywood Goes to Washington*. For more on the Cold War and the genre, see Derry, *The Suspense Thriller*, 106–107.
28. During the silent-movie era that saw the emergence of thrillers in general, a prominent filmmaker such as Fritz Lang was already starting to merge the adventure film with the history of the political thriller in Latin America. *The Spiders* (1919–1920), set in Mexico, Peru, and the Falklands, was released in two parts: *The Golden Sea* (1919) and *The Diamond Ship* (1921). This is Lang's oldest preserved work, as his first two films (*Halbblut* and *Master of Love*, both

released in 1919) are lost. Werner Herzog and Carol Reed are other prominent filmmakers who practiced the genre with films set or filmed in the region.

29. Even before the emergence of the imperialistic adventure tale, we can think of Shakespeare's *The Tempest* (1610–1611), set on a Caribbean island, which informed Latin Americanism through Arielismo.
30. See Mercedes Serna, *Crónicas de Indias*, 40, 49, 62.
31. Gabriel García Márquez, "La soledad de América Latina," 126. See also José Manuel Camacho Delgado, "*Cien años de soledad*: entre las crónicas de navegantes y la novela de aventuras," who notes that José Arcadio, the main character of *One Hundred Years of Solitude*, personifies the influence of the adventure tale in García Márquez's work.
32. Serna, *Crónicas de Indias*, 65–66.
33. Martin Green, *Seven Types of Adventure Tale: An Etiology of a Major Genre*, 62 (emphasis in the original).
34. See Serna, *Crónicas de Indias*.
35. Jorge Luis Borges, *Other Inquisitions*, 141, opens his article on Hudson's *The Purple Land* by tracing it to the picaresque novel. Paul Young, "The *Land* That England Lost: W. H. Hudson's *The Purple Land*, Liebig's Extract of Meat Company, and the Romance of the Outlands," 199, calls Lamb the "picaresque antihero" of the British imperialist adventure tale.
36. Ezequiel Martínez Estrada, *El mundo maravilloso de Guillermo Enrique Hudson* (hereafter cited as Martínez Estrada, *Maravilloso*), 7; Fernando Sorrentino, "*Allá lejos y hace tiempo*: anglos nativos pájaros escuerzos," 17.
37. Angélica Mendoza, "Guillermo Enrique Hudson (1841–1922)," 193.
38. Young, "The *Land* That England Lost," 180.
39. Borges, *Other Inquisitions*, 142.
40. Theodore Roosevelt, "An Introductory Note," x.
41. Mendoza, "Guillermo Enrique Hudson (1841–1922)," 193.
42. Young, "The *Land* That England Lost," 180. The use of the word "return" here suggests an adventure tale that is much more geographical than historical, a departure from Walter Scott, whose adventure novels were often displaced from the present in terms of time, not space, set, for example, in medieval Scotland.
43. Borges, *Other Inquisitions*, 143.
44. Richard Maxwell and Katie Trumpener, "The Romance of the Outlands: The *Fin-de-siècle* Adventure Story between History and Geography," 107 (hereafter cited as Maxwell and Trumpener, "Outlands"). It is worth clarifying, however, that Maxwell and Trumpener misread Borges, who had controversially defined *The Purple Land* as the best piece of gaucho literature, not "the quintessential work of Argentine literature" per se, as they claim.
45. Haddu, "Political Violence and Fiction in Mexican Film," 460.
46. Maxwell and Trumpener, "Outlands," 107.
47. Rubin, *Thrillers*, 200.
48. Martínez Estrada, *Maravilloso*, 290. Several critics have parroted accusations against political thrillers for not being politically committed. In Brazil,

Oricchio, *Cinema de Novo: um balanço crítico da retomada*, 110, 114, qualifies Beto Brant's *Ação entre amigos* (1998) as "superficially" and "falsely political" for using genre conventions that would become the norm over the first quarter of the twenty-first century, including blending the dictatorial past with a detective-like trope. Similarly, he dismisses *O que é isso, companheiro?* for treating armed struggle as "an adventure" that lacks "context" and "politics." In Argentina, Gustavo Noriega, "*Rojo*: un film que despolitiza la historia a través de una mirada terriblemente severa sobre la clase media," argues that Naishtat's film "depoliticizes history." Perhaps they are looking for something that the genre is not about and therefore cannot give them.

49. Alberto Moreiras, *Against Abstraction: Notes from an Ex-Latin Americanist*, 203.
50. Hudson, *The Purple Land*, 13, 232.
51. Martínez Estrada, *Maravilloso*, 290.
52. Hudson, *The Purple Land*, 255.
53. Maxwell and Trumpener, "Outlands," 113, even go as far as to claim that "women and birds . . . define the landscape far more than the civil war" in the novel.
54. Borges, *Other Inquisitions*, 143.
55. Hudson, *The Purple Land*, 28.
56. Allan Hepburn, *Intrigue: Espionage and Culture*, xvi.
57. Rubin, *Thrillers*, 7.
58. Rockwood, *Jack North's Treasure Hunt*, n.p.
59. Rubin, *Thrillers*, 22.
60. See "Intrigue" in *The Concise Oxford Dictionary of English Etymology*.
61. Rubin, *Thrillers*, 20.
62. Claude Lévi-Strauss, *Introduction to the Work of Marcel Mauss*, 55, coined the phrase "floating signifier" to describe concepts found in Indigenous civilizations across the South Pacific islands, such as *mana*, which were "susceptible of receiving any meaning at all."
63. Elze, *Picaresque Novel*, 6, 10.
64. Bakhtin, *The Dialogic Imagination*, 124.
65. Elze, *Picaresque Novel*, 13. See also Delgado, "Hambre y memoria," which links the genre to the unprecedented social mobility made possible by the emergence of the European bourgeoisie.
66. Elze, *Picaresque Novel*, 1.
67. Delgado, "Hambre y memoria," 155.
68. Elze, *Picaresque Novel*, 3 (emphasis in the original).
69. William Faulkner, *Requiem for a Nun*, 85.
70. Beasley-Murray, "Citizenship and Rights in the New Republics," video (00:06:39 and 00:06:34).
71. Derry, *The Suspense Thriller*, 120.
72. Derry, *The Suspense Thriller*, 166–167.

CHAPTER 2: BOTCHED JOBS

1. For Palmer, *Thrillers*, 23, conspiracies are "an absolute structural necessity" because they drive "the plot into action." As noted in chapter 1, Coyne and Rubin identify the political thriller with the "conspiracy thriller." Jameson, "Cognitive Mapping," 358, notes an "inexhaustible production of conspiracy plots of the most elaborate kinds" in postmodernist narratives, including but not limited to political thrillers.
2. Palmer, *Thrillers*, 51–66; Rubin, *Thrillers*, 6, 30–35; Derry, *The Suspense Thriller.*
3. For more on this, see the introduction.
4. See Giardinelli, *El género negro*, 245; Paco Ignacio Taibo II, "La (otra) novela policíaca," 38; and Amelia Simpson, *Detective Fiction from Latin America*, 92.
5. See Ilan Stavans, *Antihéroes: México y su novela policial*, 116.
6. Persephone Braham, *Crimes against the State, Crimes against Persons: Detective Fiction in Cuba and Mexico*, 72 (hereafter cited as Braham, *State and Persons*).
7. Moreiras, "Infrapolitics and the Thriller," links it to the thriller-umbrella, but most of the examples he cites are Mexican political thrillers. In turn, Fernando Fabio Sánchez's "M for *Murder*" and Ignacio Sánchez Prado's "Peripheral Noir, Mediation, and Capitalism: Noir Form, Noir Mediascape, Sociological Noir" are the only studies that mention Bernal's debt to the political thriller tradition.
8. See Maricruz Castro Ricalde, "Un *Distinto amanecer* (Julio Bracho 1943) para la nación mexicana" (hereafter cited as Castro Ricalde, "*Distinto amanecer*").
9. Sánchez Prado, *Screening Neoliberalism: Transforming Mexican Cinema, 1988–2012*, 107; Carl J. Mora, *Mexican Cinema: Reflections of a Society*, 105–149.
10. Rubin, *Thrillers*, 12.
11. All these etymologies were consulted in the online edition of *The Concise Oxford Dictionary of English Etymology*. For the etymology of "secrecy," see the introduction.
12. Scott, *American Politics*, 1–2.
13. Palmer, *Thrillers*, 67.
14. Burucúa, "Remnants of the Dirty War," 82. See also John Hill, "The Political Thriller Debate."
15. Rubin, *Thrillers*, 5.
16. Norberto Bobbio, "Democracy and Invisible Government," 48.
17. Sánchez Prado, "Peripheral Noir," 150.
18. Palmer, *Thriller*, 66–67.
19. Carlos Rodríguez Joulia Saint-Cyr, *La novela de intriga: diccionario de autores, obras y personajes*, 34.
20. See Rubin, *Thriller*, 149, who does not literally use Bobbio's terms but essentially makes this claim.
21. Rubin, *Thriller*, 22.
22. Sánchez Prado, "Peripheral Noir," 150.

23. See Braham, *State and Persons*, 70. See also Ilan Stavans, *Antiheroes: Mexico and Its Detective Novel*, 97; and Derek Beaudry, "Democracy against the State in *The Mongolian Conspiracy* by Rafael Bernal," 168.
24. Sánchez, "M for *Murder*," 133.
25. Adolfo Arreola García, "El deceso del 'dedazo' en la sucesión presidencial en México, ¿mito o realidad?"
26. See Luis Leal, "*La sombra del caudillo*: roman à clef."
27. See Sophie Bidault, "Aspectos estéticos en *La sombra del caudillo*"; and Margo Glantz, "La novela de la revolución mexicana y *La sombra del caudillo*." Both discuss the lack of a precise genre definition in the literature about the novel. Monsiváis, *Aires de familia*, 47, does label it a "thrilling historical novel" and "magnificent exception" that goes beyond the other novels on the Mexican revolution. More explicitly, Moreiras, "Infrapolitics and the Thriller," treats Guzmán and Bernal's novels as thrillers but then turns to examine Aguilar Camín's more recent work instead. Apart from this, it is true that the literary representation of the caudillo precedes the political thriller itself, harking back to the foundational political literature produced in Latin America (especially in Argentina) throughout the nineteenth century, such as Domingo Faustino Sarmiento's *Facundo* (1845). For more on this, see Doris Sommer, "Irresistible Romance: The Foundational Fictions of Latin America," 73. As Sommer claims, in Argentina, Mexico, and Brazil, at least, politics and fiction have been closely intertwined ever since their foundational narratives.
28. Walter Benjamin, "The Paris of the Second Empire in Baudelaire," 27.
29. Piglia, "Teoría del complot," 4.
30. Julio Patán, "Conspiracionismo razonable," 65.
31. For excellent readings of these films see Haddu, "Political Violence."
32. Canetti, *Crowds and Power*, 290.
33. Honoré de Balzac, *Catherine de Medici*, 21.
34. Louis-Ferdinand Céline, *Journey to the End of the Night*, 30.
35. Céline, *Journey to the End of the Night*, 30.
36. Michel Foucault, *The Birth of Biopolitics: Lectures at the Collège de France, 1978–1979*, 77.
37. Rafael Bernal, *The Mongolian Conspiracy*, 27.
38. Canetti, *Crowds and Power*, 295–296.
39. Coyne, *Hollywood Goes to Washington*, 168.
40. Coyne, *Hollywood Goes to Washington*, 168.
41. Pierre Bourdieu, "Job Insecurity Is Everywhere Now," 82.
42. Zygmunt Bauman, *Liquid Modernity*, 160.
43. Derrida, *Rogues*, 154.
44. Derrida, *Rogues*, 154.
45. Bourdieu, "Job Insecurity," 84 (emphasis in the original).
46. Bauman, *Liquid Modernity*, 161.
47. Sharryn Kasmir, "Precarity."

48. Constanza Burucúa and Carolina Sitnisky, *The Precarious in the Cinema of the Americas*, 1–2.
49. For a comprehensive study on precarity in Latin America, see Catherine S. Ramírez, Sylvanna M. Falcón, Juan Poblete, Steven C. McKay, and Felicity Amaya Schaeffer, *Precarity and Belonging: Labor, Migration and Noncitizenship*.
50. Kasmir, "Precarity."
51. Ramírez et al., *Precarity and Belonging*, 5.
52. Bauman, *Liquid Modernity*, 161.
53. Simpson, *Detective Fiction from Latin America*, 92.
54. Bobbio, *Democracia y secreto*, 296.
55. Beaudry, "Democracy against the State," 161.
56. For García and Marlowe, see Stavans, *Antiheroes*, 99; and Braham, *State and Persons*, 70, who also sees the trace of Carlos Fuentes's Artemio Cruz in Bernal's hero. For García and Spillane, see Simpson, *Detective Fiction from Latin America*, 192.
57. Stavans, *Antiheroes*, 99.
58. Beaudry, "Democracy against the State," 166; Sánchez Prado, "Peripheral Noir," 149.
59. See Bidault, "Aspectos estéticos en *La sombra del caudillo*," 558.
60. Sánchez Prado, "Peripheral Noir," 151.
61. For Helú, see Braham, *State and Persons*, 68; for Borges and Bioy Casares, see Fabricio Tocco, *Latin American Detectives against Power*, 47–53.
62. Francisco Goldman, "Introduction," 116.
63. Castro Ricalde, "*Distinto Amanecer*," 557.
64. Castro Ricalde, "*Distinto Amanecer*," 557.
65. Rubin, *Thrillers*, 21.
66. Samuel Steinberg, *Photopoetics at Tlatelolco: Afterimages of Mexico, 1968*, 2.
67. Scott, *American Politics*, 8.
68. Scott, *American Politics*, 9. Scott shows how Capra's Washingtonian iconography is still "alive and well" even in the 1990s parodic episode of *The Simpsons* entitled "Mr. Lisa Goes to Washington."
69. Bernal, *The Mongolian Conspiracy*, 59, 102.
70. Bernal, *The Mongolian Conspiracy*, 6, 150.
71. Raymond Chandler, *The Simple Art of Murder*, 23.
72. Bernal, *The Mongolian Conspiracy*, 132.
73. Palmer, *Thrillers*, 7–15.
74. Stavans, *Antihéroes*, 119, mentions that Bernal is a forerunner of Paco Taibo II, in that both explore "prosaic life."
75. Braham, *State and Persons*, 70.
76. Palmer, *Thrillers*, 25, 70.
77. Rubin, *Thrillers*, 133–135.
78. Rubin, *Thrillers*, 134.
79. Palmer, *Thrillers*, 7.
80. Bernal, *The Mongolian Conspiracy*, 102, 152.

81. Bernal, *The Mongolian Conspiracy*, 187.
82. Linda Hutcheon, *A Theory of Parody: The Teachings of Twentieth-Century Art Forms*, 20.
83. Coyne, *Hollywood Goes to Washington*, 10–12 (emphasis in the original), 17, 77.
84. Slavoj Žižek, "Good Manners in the Age of Wikileaks."
85. Taussig, *Defacement*, 7.
86. Stavans, *Antiheroes*, 97.
87. Bourdieu, "Job Insecurity," 82.
88. Bernal, *The Mongolian Conspiracy*, 72.
89. Bernal, *El complot mongol*, 33.
90. Judith Butler, *Frames of War: Precarious Life, Grievable Life*, 26, 28.
91. Bernal, *The Mongolian Conspiracy*, 135.
92. Taussig, *Defacement*, 7.
93. Beaudry, "Democracy against the State," 162.
94. Rubin, *Thrillers*, 22.
95. Cobley, *The American Thriller*, 153.
96. Moreiras, *Infrapolitics: A Handbook*, 97, 185.
97. Moreiras, "Infrapolitics and the Thriller," 151.
98. Moreiras, *Infrapolitics: A Handbook*, 85.
99. Sánchez, "M for *Murder*," 133–134.
100. Braham, *State and Persons*, 71.
101. Alberto Moreiras, *Against Abstraction: Notes from an Ex-Latin Americanist*, 203.
102. Rubin, *Thrillers*, 17.
103. Mabel Moraña, *El monstruo como máquina de guerra*, 70, notes that one of the continuities between modern and medieval monstrosity is distortion, especially in terms of representation of the monster's body.
104. Braham, *State and Persons*, 71.
105. Moreiras, "Infrapolitics and the Thriller," 149.
106. See Burucúa, "Remnants of the Dirty War," 74.
107. Castrillo and Echart, "Definition," 115.
108. Carol Hanisch, "The Personal Is Political," n.p.
109. Palmer, *Thrillers*, 32–33.
110. Gabriela Méndez Cota, "Feminismo, infrapolítica, extinción," 123.
111. Alexandra Kohan, "Feminismo y punitivismo: un debate en movimiento."
112. Hanisch, "The Personal Is Political."
113. Moreiras, "Infrapolitics and the Thriller," 149–150.
114. John Kraniauskas, *Capitalism and Its Discontents: Power and Accumulation in Latin-American Culture*, 141.
115. Moreiras, "Infrapolitics and the Thriller," 154.
116. Moreiras, *Uncanny Rest: For Antiphilosophy*, 76.
117. Derry, *The Suspense Thriller*, 116, traces the genre's "crusading journalist" to Z. Cobley, *The American Thriller*, 128, traces "the creation of folk-hero status for investigative reporters" to Pakula's films that premiered later in the 1970s

(such as *The Parallax View* and *All the President's Men*). Well before all these films, however, *The Bedford Incident* (1965) features an ethical African American journalist, played by Sidney Poitier. Going even further back, Claudia Springer, "Comprehension and Crisis: Report Films and the Third World," 167, talks about a "reporter film" genre with elements from 1930s screwball comedies, including journalists as their heroes.

118. Castrillo and Echart, "Definition," 116.
119. Moreiras, "Infrapolitics and the Thriller," 154.
120. Immanuel Kant, *Perpetual Peace: A Philosophical Essay*, 175.
121. Kant, *Perpetual Peace*, 161, 147, 174.
122. Bernal, *The Mongolian Conspiracy*, 88, 197. In a clear dialogue with Bernal, Héctor Aguilar Camín, *Morir en el golfo*, 98, puts in the mouth of the story's caudillo the idea that violent and senseless deaths are opposed to "fertile and creative deaths."
123. Braham, *State and Persons*, 70.
124. Moreiras, "Infrapolitics and the Thriller," 155.
125. For Derry, *The Suspense Thriller*, 113–114, 123, Costa-Gavras's *Z* "tremendously" influenced "other political thrillers," becoming "one of the most significant developments" in the genre, which unprecedentedly "won the Academy Award for the best editing" even though it was a European production.
126. Derry, *The Suspense Thriller*, 117.
127. Edwy Plenel, "Cinéma et politique: Costa-Gavras ou l'espoir." Although Costa-Gavras attributes this idea to Roland Barthes, Plenel notes that the statement is nowhere to be found in Barthes's work and does not really align with his dismissive attitude toward cinema.
128. Wim Wenders, *The Logic of Images: Essays and Conversations*, 19.
129. George Orwell, "Why I Write."
130. Moreiras, *Infrapolitics: A Handbook*.
131. Moreiras, *Infrapolitics: A Handbook*, 96.
132. Moreiras, "Infrapolitics and the Thriller," 158.
133. Piglia, "Teoría del complot," 4. See also Mempo Giardinelli, "Variations on Postmodernity, or, What Does the Latin American Postboom Mean?," 224, who claims to be paraphrasing Piglia when he notes that Latin American authors "write against politics" (although he does not cite any specific essay).
134. Simpson, *Detective Fiction from Latin America*, 94.

CHAPTER 3: PICTURING THE SLAUGHTER

1. John Kraniauskas, *Capitalism and Its Discontents*, 139–140.
2. Inés González Bombal, "Nunca más: el juicio más allá de los estrados," 206.
3. González Bombal, "Nunca más," 206.
4. Sandra Raggio, "*La noche de los lápices* y los tiempos de la memoria," 4 (hereafter cited as Raggio, "*Lápices*").

5. Raggio, "*Lápices*," 3–4.
6. Francisco Márquez and Andrea Testa in *La larga noche de Francisco Sanctis* (2016) rewrite Filipelli's film in innovative ways, with a depoliticized, anodyne father who is in charge of warning an acquaintance of his imminent illegal detention.
7. Before these films, Elsa Drucaroff explicitly reconstructs the history of the Argentine guerrillas in the novel *El último caso de Rodolfo Walsh* (2010), a political thriller that imagines Walsh's fictional investigation of his daughter's forced disappearance.
8. Valentino, "Why We Kill," 90–91 (quotation on 91).
9. Gabriel Gatti and María Martínez, "El ciudadano-víctima: notas para iniciar un debate," 8.
10. See "Invasion" in *The Oxford Dictionary of Word Origins* (edited by Julia Cresswell) and *The Concise Oxford Dictionary of English Etymology* (edited by T. F. Hoad).
11. I exclude film representations of other important massacres here, such as Héctor Olivera's period drama/western *La Patagonia rebelde* (Argentina, 1974) and Héctor Babenco's prison drama *Carandiru* (Brazil, 2003), because they are not political thrillers. I also leave out two Mexican political thrillers about Tlatelolco: Alfredo Gurrola's *Borrar de la memoria* (2010) and Carlos Bolado's *Tlatelolco: verano de 68* (2013). Carlos Belmonte Grey, "*Rojo amanecer*: el problema de la imagen de Tlatelolco 1968," 301, is right in criticizing both films for sanitizing Tlatelolco with melodrama plots. In addition, Gurrola follows too closely some narrative strategies of *El secreto de sus ojos*, including a past/present double storyline triggered by constant flashbacks and the role of the female body at the center of the narrative.
12. Beasley-Murray, *Posthegemony*, 109.
13. Sánchez Prado, "Felipe Cazals: The Question of the Film Auteur in the Age of Cinematic Crisis," 193. For the relations between Cedrón and Third Cinema, see Victoria García, "Testimonio literario-documental cinematográfico," 2.
14. Sánchez Prado, "Felipe Cazals," 198.
15. See John Mraz, "Mexican Cinema: Of *Churros* and *Charros*," 24; Guadalupe González Bravo, "Los carácteres psicológicos en el cine mexicano: *Canoa*," 134.
16. See Juan J. Rojo, "La memoria como 'espectro' en *Rojo amanecer* de Jorge Fons," 56; and Salvador Velazco, "*Rojo amanecer* y *La ley de Herodes*: cine político de la transición mexicana," 68.
17. Jorge Valdez Morgan, "Cine peruano y violencia: realidad y representación: análisis histórico de *La boca del lobo*," 189.
18. Barrow, "Political Violence," 136.
19. Valdez Morgan, "Cine peruano," 185.
20. Gloria Julieta Zarco, "Argentina: censura y dictadura (1969–1983)," 134–135.
21. Toning down the appraisal of guerrillas was encouraged by Octavio Getino (linked to Third Cinema), who was in charge of the Ente de Calificación

Cinematográfica during Perón's third administration: see Flores, "Experiencias," 208.

22. For *Operación masacre*, see Castro Avelleyra, "*Operación masacre* de Jorge Cedrón," 1. For *Canoa*, see Ignacio M. Sánchez Prado, "Alegorías sin pueblo: el cine echeverrista y la crisis del contrato social de la cultura mexicana," 51; Gustavo Ricardo Martínez Grijalva and Iván Mercado Ortega, "'Canoa' (1975): el cine y la memoria social," 193; and Charles Ramírez Berg, *A Cinema of Solitude: A Critical Study of Mexican Film, 1967–1983*, 187–188. For *Rojo amanecer*, see Miriam Haddu, *Contemporary Mexican Cinema 1989–1999: History, Space, and Identity*, 13. For *La boca del lobo*, see Barrow, "Political Violence," 133.
23. Thomas Schatz, *Hollywood Genres: Formulas, Filmmaking, and the Studio System*, 36–41.
24. Castro Avelleyra, "*Operación masacre* de Jorge Cedrón," 1.
25. Daniel Link, "Rethinking Past Present," 220.
26. It is commonly understood that Walsh foreshadows Truman Capote's *In Cold Blood* (1966), the first nonfiction novel, which inaugurated the genre. See Silvio Ricardo Waisbord, *Watchdog Journalism in South America: News, Accountability, and Democracy*, 30.
27. Carla Masmun, "Raymundo Gleyzer y el Grupo de Cine de la Base," 179.
28. With the exception of Lucía Feuillet, "Identidad y otredad en la literatura policial Argentina: una lectura del marxismo y el delito desde Ernest Mandel," who examines Walsh's nonfiction novel, following Ernest Mandel's underdeveloped early reflections on the political thriller and sometimes conflating it with hard-boiled fiction.
29. Castro Avelleyra, "*Operación masacre* de Jorge Cedrón."
30. García, "Testimonio literario," 3 (quotation), 4.
31. Derry, *The Suspense Thriller*, 103.
32. Link, "Rethinking Past Present," 222.
33. For Walsh and popular genres, see Ángel Rama, "Rodolfo Walsh: la narrativa en el conflicto de las culturas," 296–297. For Piglia, the detective thriller, and secrecy, see the introduction.
34. Flores, "Experiencias," 215.
35. García, "Testimonio literario," 5; Jorge J. Locane, "Avatares de la *fricción* en el corpus *Operación masacre*," 336; Silvia Schwarzböck, "Cómo se llega a ser peronista: sobre *Operación masacre*, de Rodolfo Walsh, y *Operación masacre*, de Jorge Cedrón," 198.
36. Locane, "Avatares," 336.
37. Rodolfo Walsh, *Operation Massacre*, 10.
38. Most of the literature on the film links *Operación masacre* to Peronism: see especially Rita Filomena De Grandis, "La escritura del acontecimiento: implicaciones discursivas"; and García, "Testimonio literario."
39. García, "Testimonio literario," 6.
40. Castro Avelleyra, "*Operación masacre* de Jorge Cedrón," 9.
41. García, "Testimonio literario," 7.

42. Raggio, "*Lápices*," 9.
43. Locane, "Avatares," 329–330; Sebastián Hernaiz, *Rodolfo Walsh no escribió* Operación Masacre *y otros ensayos*, 15.
44. Rama, "Rodolfo Walsh," 300.
45. See De Grandis, "La escritura del acontecimiento," 200; Castro Avelleyra, "*Operación masacre* de Jorge Cedrón," 10; and García, "Testimonio literario," 4.
46. Sánchez Prado, "Felipe Cazals," 206.
47. See Sánchez Prado, "Alegorías," 60, and Martínez Grijalva and Mercado Ortega, "'Canoa' (1975)," 195. They define the film as "halfway" and "swaying between fiction and the documentary," respectively.
48. Except for Martínez Grijalva and Mercado Ortega, "'Canoa' (1975)," 195, most critics either overlook or take for granted the way the film uses suspense.
49. Ramírez Berg, *Cinema of Solitude*, 188.
50. Gema Klope-Santamaria, *In the Vortex of Violence: Lynching, Extralegal Justice, and the State in Post-Revolutionary Mexico*, 2.
51. This is a significant difference between *Canoa* and *Operación masacre*.
52. Maxwell and Trumpener, "Outlands," 113.
53. González Bravo, "Los carácteres," 132.
54. Sánchez Prado, "Alegorías," 62.
55. David William Foster, *Mexico City in Contemporary Mexican Cinema*, 4.
56. See chapter 1 for Gleyzer and transnational cinema.
57. Sánchez Prado, "Alegorías," 61.
58. Mraz, "Mexican Cinema," 24.
59. Sánchez Prado, "Alegorías," 51, 61.
60. Sánchez Prado, "Alegorías," 62.
61. González Bravo, "Los carácteres," 132.
62. Deleuze and Guattari, *A Thousand Plateaus*, 286.
63. Beasley-Murray, *Posthegemony*, 235.
64. See Beasley-Murray, *Posthegemony* (246–247 for multitude and affect and 233 for multitude and ambivalence).
65. Beasley-Murray, *Posthegemony*, 151 (quotation), 247.
66. Alejandro Pelayo's film *Morir en el golfo* (1990) reproduces this torch-lit lynching in the portrayal of a fictional killing of a local mayor at the hands of another bad multitude.
67. Elizabeth R. Achtemeier, "Jesus Christ, the Light of the World: The Biblical Understanding of Light and Darkness," 439.
68. Ramírez Berg, *Cinema of Solitude*, 189.
69. Sánchez Prado, "Felipe Cazals," 198.
70. Sánchez Prado, "Alegorías," 61.
71. Rojo, "Memoria," 50.
72. Mraz, "Mexican Cinema," 24.
73. Mraz, "Mexican Cinema," 24; González Bravo, "Los carácteres," 134.
74. Sánchez Prado, "Alegorías," 61.
75. Rebecca Janzen, *Unholy Trinity: State, Church, and Film in Mexico*, 13.

76. Alexander Dawson, *Latin America since Independence: A History with Primary Sources*, 54.
77. Podalsky, *Affect and Emotion*, 61.
78. Foster, *Mexico City*, 8. See also Rojo, "Memoria," 52, which compares *Rojo amanecer*'s (US) $100,000 budget with John Duigan's *Romero* (1989), a $3M Hollywood biopic about an assassinated Salvadorean archbishop, also filmed in Mexico in the late 1980s. The contrast with *Missing* is even greater, considering Costa-Gavras's $9.5M budget (see William Wolf, "Costa-Gavras Goes to Hollywood," 44).
79. Velazco, "*Rojo amanecer* y *La ley de Herodes*," 67.
80. Belmonte Grey, "*Rojo amanecer*," 296. Much like *Los traidores*, which also started to circulate more broadly from the 1990s onward.
81. Steinberg, *Photopoetics*, 125.
82. Fernando Celin, "La negra noche de Tlatelolco," 7; Belmonte Gray, "*Rojo amanecer*," 297.
83. The best accounts of *El grito* and its links with *Rojo amanecer* can be found in Steinberg, *Photopoetics*; Foster, *Mexico City*; and Velazco, "*Rojo amanecer y La ley de Herodes*."
84. Moreiras, "Infrapolitics and the Thriller," 153.
85. Steinberg, *Photopoetics*, 130.
86. Velazco, "*Rojo amanecer* y *La ley de Herodes*," 70.
87. Jorge Majfud, *Cine político latinoamericano*, 167.
88. Deborah Martin, "Planeta ciénaga: Lucrecia Martel and Contemporary Argentine Women's Filmmaking," 242.
89. Lucrecia Martel, quoted in Jay Beck, "Submerged in Sound: Lucrecia Martel's *La ciénaga*," 1.
90. Beck, "Submerged in Sound," 1.
91. Derry, *The Suspense Thriller*; see the introduction.
92. Foster, *Mexico City*, 3–4.
93. Foster, *Mexico City*, 9.
94. Álvaro Vázquez Mantecón, "No se olvida . . . *Rojo amanecer* [film review]," 142.
95. Foster, *Mexico City*, 9.
96. Haddu, *Contemporary Mexican Cinema*, 16.
97. Rojo, "Memoria," 51.
98. Rojo, "Memoria," 52–53.
99. Kasmir, "Precarity."
100. See the film *Secretos precarios*. It is important to point out that these arguments in favor of precarity are neither new nor exclusive to the political thriller, as they were commonly invoked in discussions about Argentine New Cinema in the 1990s.
101. Vázquez Mantecón, "No se olvida," 142; Rojo, "Memoria," 52.
102. The best accounts of spectrality and Tlatelolco can be found in Rojo, "Memoria"; and Steinberg, *Photopoetics*. I go back to uses of spectrality in the genre in chapter 5 with my close reading of *Matar a un muerto*.

103. Haddu, *Contemporary Mexican Cinema*, 17.
104. Foster, *Mexico City*, 11.
105. Rubin, *Thrillers*, 32.
106. See Vázquez Mantecón, "No se olvida," 142.
107. Foster, *Mexico City*, 11.
108. Rojo, "Memoria," 59.
109. Beasley-Murray, *Posthegemony*, 136, 162.
110. Velazco, "*Rojo Amanecer* y *La ley de Herodes*," 71; Vázquez Mantecón, "No se olvida," 144; Belmonte Gray, "*Rojo amanecer*," 297.
111. Podalsky, *Affect and Emotion*, 70.
112. Sánchez Prado, *Screening Neoliberalism*, 106.
113. Jorge Majfud, *Cine político latinoamericano*, 165.
114. Steinberg, *Photopoetics*, 133.
115. Vázquez Mantecón, "No se olvida," 143.
116. Motherhood as an infrapolitical force is also central to *Conejo en la luna*.
117. Samuel Steinberg, "Re-cinema: Hauntology of 1968," 5.
118. See the introduction, where I discuss the etymological links between secrecy and discernment.
119. See chapter 2 for more on Butler's precarious life and the political thriller.
120. Ricardo Bedoya, "*La Boca del Lobo/The Lion's Den*," 186 (quotation), 187 (hereafter cited as Bedoya, "*Lion's Den*").
121. Barrow, "Political Violence," 138.
122. Bedoya, "*Lion's Den*," 185.
123. Bedoya, "*Lion's Den*," 186.
124. Beasley-Murray, *Posthegemony*, 99.
125. Noël Carroll, "The Paradox of Suspense," 76. For suspense and thrillers, see Rubin, *Thrillers*, 35.
126. Carroll, "Paradox of Suspense," 77.
127. Valdez Morgan, "Cine peruano," 188.
128. Beasley-Murray, *Posthegemony*, 78.
129. Beasley-Murray, *Posthegemony*, 76.
130. See Carolyn Wolfenzon, "'El pishtaco' y el conflicto entre la costa y la sierra en *Lituma en los Andes* y *Madeinusa*"; and Víctor Vich, "El discurso sobre la sierra del Perú: la fantasía del atraso."
131. Valdez Morgan, "Cine peruano," 189.
132. Bedoya, "*Lion's Den*," 185.
133. Valdez Morgan, "Cine peruano," 190.
134. Barrow, "Political Violence," 135.
135. Rita Segato, *La guerra contra las mujeres*, 21.
136. Rubin, *Thrillers*, 32.
137. Barrow, "Political Violence," 147.
138. As reported in testimony number 202918 of the Comisión de la Verdad y la Reconciliación.

139. Octavio Paz, "The Other Mexico," 225.
140. Bobbio, "Democracy and Invisible Government," 48–49.

CHAPTER 4: RESISTING AND INVESTIGATING GENOCIDE

1. Brodersen in *Secretos precarios.*
2. Charles Barbour, *Derrida's Secret: Perjury, Testimony, Oath,* 14–15, 31 (quotation).
3. Jacques Derrida and Maurizio Ferraris, *A Taste for the Secret,* 75.
4. Andreas Huyssen, "Present Pasts: Media, Politics, Amnesia," 21, 23–24.
5. Jacques Derrida and Maurizio Ferraris, *A Taste for the Secret,* 75.
6. See Iván Pinto and Luis Felipe Horta, "Vías no realizadas en el cine político chileno: parodia, extrañamiento y reflexividad."
7. Pinto and Horta, "Vías no realizadas," 139.
8. In series such as Chilevisión's *Amar y morir en Chile* (2012) and the very recent Amazon Prime miniseries *Vencer o morir* (2024).
9. See Ricardo Normanha Ribeiro de Almeida, "As ditaduras militares no cinema argentino e brasileiro: uma análise de *A história oficial* e *Pra frente Brasil,*" 132, 137.
10. De Almeida, "As ditaduras militares," 141.
11. Podalsky, *Affect and Emotion,* 63.
12. Roman Polanski's *Death and the Maiden* (1994) hints at an act of vigilantism, but its dénouement is less visceral: the victim of state-sponsored crimes ultimately chooses not to execute her perpetrator.
13. Another example of a biopic with thrilleresque elements is Dominican Juan Delancer's *Trópico de sangre* (2010), a film that focuses on Minerva Mirabal, a female guerrilla who resisted against Leónidas Trujillo's regime.
14. Oricchio, *Cinema de novo,* 111.
15. Gonzalo Aguilar, "La política y lo político en el cine argentino reciente: *Infancia clandestina* (Benjamín Ávila, 2012) y *El estudiante* (Santiago Mitre, 2011)," 76.
16. Rita Filomena De Grandis, "The Innocent Eye: Children's Perspectives on the Utopias of the Seventies (*O ano em que meus pais saíram de férias, Machuca,* and *Kamchatka*)."
17. Diego Brodersen, "Mirada que privilegia el suspenso," *Página 12,* May 28, 2015.
18. See Sánchez Prado, "Felipe Cazals," on *Bajo la metralla* and its relationship with precarity and the Mexican dirty war.
19. Palito Ortega Matute's work is understudied. For *La casa rosada,* see Carla Daniela Rabelo Rodrigues, "Cinema regional peruano e políticas culturais a diferença: os casos de *La casa rosada e Wiñaypacha,*" who discusses the film in terms of regional filmmaking more than genre fiction.

20. Other important Peruvian political dramas that feature the conflict with Sendero Luminoso include Nilo Pereira's *Ni con dios ni con el diablo* (1989) and Palito Ortega Matute's *Paloma de papel* (2003).
21. Podalsky, *Affect and Emotion*, 66, 68.
22. See Fabricio Tocco, *Latin American Detectives against Power: Individualism, the State and Failure in Crime Fiction*.
23. The animal is a *gallina* (hen) in Spain; a *gallito* (little rooster) in Argentina and Uruguay; a *mosca* (fly) in Italy; and a *Kuh* (cow) in Germany.
24. Tânia Sarmento-Pantoja, "Cinema e literatura: resistência política e representações do herói guerrilheiro em *Pessach, A Travessia* e *Cabra-cega*," n.p.
25. Solange Toccolini Zorzo, "*Cabra-cega*: do roteiro às telas," 107.
26. Tânia Sarmento-Pantoja and Veridiana Valente Pinheiro, "Resistência e paranóia no filme *Cabra-cega*," 360.
27. Zorzo, "*Cabra-cega*," 108.
28. Sarmento-Pantoja, "Cinema e literatura."
29. Sarmento-Pantoja and Pinheiro, "Resistência e paranóia no filme *Cabra-cega*," 361.
30. Jack Halberstam, *Skin Shows: Gothic Horror and the Technology of Monsters*, 120.
31. Zorzo, "*Cabra-cega*," 107.
32. Sarmento-Pantoja, "Cinema e literatura," 23.
33. Oricchio, *Cinema de novo*, 111.
34. Moreiras, "Infrapolitics and the Thriller," 147.
35. Leger Grindon, "Cycles and Clusters: The Shape of Film Genre History," 51.
36. Alberto Elena, "*En retirada*: violencia política y paisaje urbano en la trilogía noir de Juan Carlos Desanzo (1983–1985)," 162.
37. Derry, *The Suspense Thriller*, 147.
38. Schatz, *Hollywood Genres*, 37–38.
39. Burucúa, "Remnants of the Dirty War," 76, writes about Aristarain's trilogy, which also includes *La parte del león* (1978) and *Últimos días de la víctima* (1982). I exclude them from this genealogy because *La parte del león* is more of a heist thriller (with some minor allegorical political issues) and *Últimos días de la víctima* belongs to the type of political thriller examined in chapter 5.
40. For *Tiempo de revancha*, see Burucúa, "Remnants of the Dirty War," and Pablo Debussy, "Implicancias políticas en la trilogía policial de Adolfo Aristarain." Both go beyond the classical allegorical readings of the film, adding important nuances to the way it constitutes a true resistance against the dictatorship. For *Amnesia*, see Ana María López C., "De la figuración a la imagen ausente: memoria en el cine chileno."
41. "Avoiding the Worst in Argentina," *New York Times*, May 25, 1977, https://www.nytimes.com/1977/05/25/archives/avoiding-the-worst-in-argentina.html?smid=url-share.
42. *New York Times*, June 14, 1977, https://www.nytimes.com/1977/06/14/archives/argentina.html.

43. Javier Bundio, "Un estudio antropológico del ritual del aliento y las prácticas discriminatorias de los hinchas argentinos."
44. Marguerite Feitlowitz, *A Lexicon of Terror: Argentina and the Legacies of Torture*, xi, 22.
45. Fiorella Gargaglione Turk, "¿Monstruosos o disciplinados?: la representación de los militares en *Matar a todos* y *Otra historia del mundo*," 40.
46. Tocco, *Latin American Detectives against Power*, 9.
47. Slavoj Žižek, "Ideology II: Competition Is a Sin."
48. Many more political and literary theoreticians reference Andersen. For instance, David A. Miller, *The Novel and the Police*, 195, discusses the idea of a "secrecy that must always be rigorously maintained in the face of a secret that everybody already knows" as a common problem in nineteenth-century fiction, such as Andersen's. Another obvious example is Edgar Allan Poe's "Purloined Letter" (1844).
49. Hans Christian Andersen, "The Emperor's New Clothes," 287.
50. Hollis Robbins, "The Emperor's New Critique," 670.
51. Slavoj Žižek, "Good Manners in the Age of WikiLeaks."
52. Hans Christian Andersen, "The Emperor's New Clothes," 294. Don Juan Manuel's tale ends with the town looking for the swindlers, who have obviously escaped, emphasizing the picaresque style of the story.
53. Juan Manuel, *El Conde Lucanor o libro de los enxiemplos del Conde Lucanor et de patronio*, 182; Juan Manuel, *The Book of Count Lucanor and Patronio*, 132.
54. Bakhtin, *The Dialogic Imagination*, 124, 159, 160.
55. Žižek, "Ideology II."
56. Joanna Page, *Crisis and Capitalism in Contemporary Argentine Cinema*, 182.
57. Although *La historia oficial* is often linked to democratic times, it is worth noting that the filming took place in the last months of the military dictatorship.
58. Gargaglione Turk, "¿Monstruosos o disciplinados?," 37.
59. Gargaglione Turk, "¿Monstruosos o disciplinados?," 38.
60. See "Uruguay: la Fuerza Aérea admitió que hubo vuelos de la Muerte."
61. Troncoso plays central roles in films such as *Infancia clandestina* and *Zanahoria* and TV shows such as *Iosi, el espía arrepentido* and *Diciembre 2001*.
62. Jameson, *Postmodernism*, xv.
63. Carolina Rocha, "National and Transnational Dimensions of Memory in *Matar a todos* and *Paisito*," 21–22.
64. Rocha, "National and Transnational Dimensions of Memory in *Matar a todos* and *Paisito*," 24.
65. For a study of the state's symbolic muteness in postdictatorial Southern Cone detective stories, see Tocco, *Latin American Detectives against Power*. It is not a coincidence that the cover-up operation to protect the Chilean chemist was named "Operación Silencio" by the military.
66. Segato, *La guerra contra las mujeres*, 18.
67. Barbour, *Derrida's Secret*, 27.
68. Derrida and Ferraris, *A Taste for the Secret*, 59.

69. Sebastián Carassai, *Los años setenta de la gente común: la naturalización de la violencia*, 186–187. I use my translation of the Spanish text: even though the original essay was published in English (*The Argentine Silent Majority: Middle Classes, Politics, Violence, and Memory in the Seventies*), the English version omits this paragraph.
70. Butler, *Frames of War*, 25.
71. Ernesto Laclau, *Emancipation(s)*, 35.
72. Feitlowitz, *Lexicon*, 37.
73. Feitlowitz, *Lexicon*, 37.
74. Ernesto Sabato, "Prologue," in *Nunca más: Report of the Argentine National Commission on the Disappeared*.
75. The technical connotation of the adjective *populista* has featured in the *Diccionario de la lengua española* since 1936, as shown by the *Nuevo tesoro lexicográfico de la lengua española*. The derogatory connotation was added only in the 2014 edition, reflecting the popularization of the term as an insult. Dictionaries, however, do not immediately reflect the semantic displacements of a given language. According to the *Corpus diacrónico del español* (*CORDE*) and the *Corpus de referencia del español actual* (*CREA*), the first recorded use harks back to a 1923 article by José Carlos Mariátegui. By contrast, *populista* as an insult is much more recent, straddling the twentieth and twenty-first century.
76. Gerardo Aboy Carlés, "El nuevo debate sobre el populismo y sus raíces en la transición democrática: el caso argentino," 30–31.
77. See Ernesto Semán, *Breve historia del antipopulismo: los intentos por domesticar a la Argentina plebeya, de 1810 a Macri* for a comprehensive history of *populismo* as a political phenomenon, beyond the transformation of the word's meanings.
78. Far-right-wing journalists Agustín Laje and Nicolás Márquez historicize the term in their book *El libro negro de la nueva izquierda: ideología de género o subversión cultural* (2016). Jair Bolsonaro made his attacks against *ideología de género* a big part of his campaign to win the Brazilian federal elections in 2018. So did Javier Milei in 2023.
79. Rita Segato, "La escritura en el cuerpo de las mujeres asesinadas en Ciudad Juárez: territorio, soberanía y crímenes de segundo estado."
80. *Matar a todos* is reminiscent of Piglia's "La loca y el relato del crimen" (1975), which features a beggar whose testimony about a crime remains unreliable due to her schizophrenia. Similarly, many parts of the film also remind us of Bolaño's novel *Estrella distante* (1996), which locates torture in an underground space. Whereas Berríos's death secures the pact of postdictatorial silence, Bolaño pictures Tagle/Wieder as a killer who may have been executed by his own state—with the connivance of a foreign state. See Tocco, *Latin American Detectives against Power*.
81. Edwin Culp, "Landscapes of Disappearance," 20.
82. José López Mazz, "The Concealment of Bodies during the Military Dictatorship in Uruguay (1973–84)," 83.
83. Piglia, "La ficción paranoica," 5.

84. See the introduction on Piglia and secrecy.
85. "Morales" is used ironically to name a criminal in Subcomandante Marcos and Paco Ignacio Taibo II's detective thriller *Los muertos incómodos* (2004). By contrast, Eduardo Sacheri's *La pregunta de sus ojos* (2005) uses the name "Morales" for a character who personifies an ethical stance that is not exempt from vigilantism.
86. Derrida, *Literature in Secret*, 154.
87. Huyssen, "Present Pasts," 29.
88. Kraniauskas, *Capitalism and Its Discontents*, 142.
89. For recent linguistic and literary inflexions of depersonalization in the third impersonal person in Latin American literature, see Fabricio Tocco, "'A language not of this world': Depersonalization and Unintelligibility in Roberto Bolaño's 'The Part about the Crimes.'"
90. Moreiras, *Infrapolítica*, 110.
91. Moreiras, *Infrapolítica*, 16.
92. Buchichio, *Secretos precarios*.
93. Bobbio, *Democracia y secreto*, 296.
94. Rosalba Oxandabarat, "La estafa menor."
95. Buchichio, *Secretos precarios*.
96. Idelber Avelar, *The Untimely Present: Post-dictatorial Latin American Fiction and the Task of Mourning*, 1.
97. Lars Ole Sauerberg, *Secret Agents in Fiction: Ian Fleming, John le Carré, and Len Deighton*.
98. Oxandabarat, "La estafa menor."
99. López Mazz, "Concealment," 91.
100. Idelber Avelar, "Alegorías de lo apócrifo: Ricardo Piglia, duelo y traducción," 209.
101. Culp, "Landscapes of Disappearance," 17–18.
102. Culp, "Landscapes of Disappearance," 21.
103. Buchichio, *Secretos precarios*.
104. Jacques Derrida, *Specters of Marx: The State of the Debt, the Work of Mourning and the New International*, 63 (emphasis in the original).
105. Jaimie Baron, *The Archive Effect: Found Footage and the Audiovisual Experience of History*, 5.
106. Baron, *The Archive Effect*, 13.
107. Haddu, "Political Violence," 462.
108. Huyssen, "Present Pasts," 28.
109. Former president José Mujica and his wife, Lucía Topolansky (Tabaré Vazquez's former vice-president, 2017–2020), are perhaps the most prominent former Tupamaros who abandoned the armed struggle and became democratic politicians after the dictatorship ended.
110. More recently, the Uruguayan state has managed to sentence other prominent figures of the dictatorship to house arrest, such as Tabaré Sartorio, José Felisberto Lemos, and Jorge Gundelzoph.

111. The annulment had been rejected via referendum twice, in 1989 and in 2009.
112. Michel de Certeau, "Pour une nouvelle culture: prendre la parole."
113. See Émile Benveniste, "L'appareil formel de l'énonciation."

CHAPTER 5: SCREENING OPPRESSION

1. See Pilar Calveiro, *Poder y desaparición: los campos de concentración en Argentina,* which includes comprehensive literature on the subject matter.
2. See, for example, Alci Rengifo, "Benjamin Naishtat's *Rojo* and a Region's Cinematic Reckoning," who links *Rojo* to Costa-Gavras.
3. Goity and Oubiña, "El policial argentino," 228; Burucúa, "Remnants of the Dirty War," 74.
4. Goity and Oubiña, "El policial argentino," 212.
5. Elena, "*En retirada,*" 168.
6. Goity and Oubiña, "El policial argentino," 217.
7. For a thorough discussion of the debate about this term, see Ana Soledad Montero, "Dictadura cívico-militar: ¿qué hay en el nombre? El debate sobre la participación civil en la última Dictadura argentina y sus ecos en el presente."
8. For Uruguay, see Magdalena Schelotto, "La dictadura cívico-militar uruguaya (1973–1985): la construcción de la noción de víctima y la figura del exiliado en el Uruguay post-dictatorial." For Brazil, see Demian Bezerra de Melo, "Ditadura 'civil-militar'?: controvérsias historiográficas sobre o processo político brasileiro no pós-1964 e os desafios do tempo presente."
9. See Lisandro Nogueira, "*Lúcio Flávio: o passageiro da agonia,* de Hector Babenco."
10. Goity and Oubiña, "El policial argentino," 226.
11. Burucúa, "Remnants of the Dirty War," 88.
12. Elena, "*En retirada,*" 167.
13. Burucúa, "Remnants of the Dirty War," 102.
14. For *Apartment Zero,* see Carlos Gamerro, "El terror argentino," who offers a brilliant reading of Donovan's film beyond the political thriller in connection with Argentine gothic narratives and the psychological thriller—a genre that is also combined with the political thriller in Roman Polanski's *Death and the Maiden* (1994). For *El Clan,* see Elios Mendieta Rodríguez, "Emplazamientos del terror tras la dictadura argentina: la importancia del espacio en la película *El Clan* (2015), de Pablo Trapero." Critical readings of *El rapto* are still forthcoming, as the film is very recent, but I refer you to director Daniela Goggi's interventions in *Secretos precarios.*
15. Elena, "*En retirada,*" 167.
16. Jordana Blejmar, "Dictatorship Toys: Play and State Terror in Argentina," 139.
17. See Keith Veronese, "The Origins and Evolution of the Strategy Board Game RISK."
18. Blejmar, "Dictatorship Toys," 139.

19. See De Grandis, "The Innocent Eye," 247; Deborah Martin, "The Child in Post-dictatorship Southern Cone Film," 143; and María José Punte, "Más allá del vano de la puerta: infancia y dictadura en tres películas argentinas," 182.
20. See Noriega, "*Rojo*."
21. This resonates with Roberto Bolaño's investigator Abel Romero in *Estrella distante*, 127, a detective story that revolves around Pinochet's dictatorship. Romero ironically offers a similar hyperbole.
22. Palmer, *Thrillers*, 80.
23. Noriega, "*Rojo*."
24. Burucúa, "Remnants of the Dirty War," 78.
25. Elena, "*En retirada*," 168.
26. David Parkinson, "*Rojo* Review"; Brodersen, "El silencio como estilo de vida."
27. See Borges's "Death and the Compass" and "The Two Kings and the Two Labyrinths." Both short stories are also key to understanding Desanzo and Aristarain's thrillers written by Feinmann.
28. The Chilean desert is a central setting in *Amnesia* (1994), a political thriller that also plays with openness as a claustrophobic space, foregrounding an outdoor labor camp during Pinochet's dictatorship. Significantly, a prisoner in the film yells, "Here we are all imprisoned," including, of course, the regime's guards.
29. Noriega, "*Rojo*."
30. Federico Plager, *Diccionario integral del español de la Argentina*, 1593.
31. See Amelia Royo, "Rosas y Perón, representaciones convergentes en el sistema literario argentino."
32. See Adriana Meyer, *Desaparecer en democracia: cuatro décadas de desapariciones forzadas en Argentina*, who lists more than two hundred cases.
33. I am alluding to Julio López, a desaparecido during the dictatorship and again, for a second time, during Kirchner's democratic government, after testifying in a trial against dictatorship criminal Miguel Etchecolatz. As of 2025, López remains desaparecido. In another case of police brutality, twenty-two-year-old Facundo Astudillo Castro's body disappeared for more than three months, after he was last seen in contact with the police in early 2020.
34. See Nuno Abreu, Alfredo Suppia, and Marcius Freire, *Golpe de vista: cinema e ditadura militar na América do Sul*; and Tereza Maria Dulci Spyer and Manuella Sampaio da Silva, "Desenterrando memórias: a ditadura paraguaia em *Matar a un muerto*."
35. Dulci Spyer and Sampaio da Silva, "Desenterrando memorias," 107.
36. For instance, Miguel Agüero's *Entrevista a un clandestino* (2006) and Galia Giménez Guimpelevich's *El invierno de Gunter* (2007). For a comprehensive list, see Dulci Spyer and Sampaio da Silva, "Desenterrando memorias," and María Esther Zaracho Robertti, "Cultura y Stronismo: memorias de la dictadura en una década del audiovisual paraguayo (2006–2016)."
37. Dulci Spyer and Sampaio da Silva, "Desenterrando memorias," 111–112.

38. Júlia González de Canales Carcereny, "*Hamaca paraguaya*: poesía fílmica glocal," 83. Encina's film is the first national production after Guillermo Vera's *Cerro Corá* (1978), a propaganda film in favor of Stroessner.
39. Podalsky, *Affect and Emotion*, 177.
40. Lori M. Culwell, "The Role of the Clown in Shakespeare's Theatre."
41. Alejo Margariños, *La cámara sin ley:* Hamaca paraguaya *y la refundación globalizada del cine guaraní*, 34.
42. González de Canales Carcereny, "*Hamaca paraguaya*."
43. Guilherme von Streber Lee, "Paraguay and the Complexities of a Bilingual Nation: The Contradiction of the Guarani Language as a National Symbol and Its Condition of Diglossia," 108, 113 (quotation).
44. Castrillo and Echart, "Definition," 119.
45. Scott, *American Politics*, 24.
46. As we can see in the portrayal of the river from Catrano Catrani's *Alto Paraná* (1958) to Luis Zorraquín's *Guaraní* (2016).
47. Rubin, *Thrillers*, 14.
48. Jens Andermann, "The Politics of Landscape," 145.
49. Diego Brodersen, "Juego de encierros al aire libre."
50. Pascal Bonitzer, "Partial Vision: Film and the Labyrinth," 63.
51. Morris Dickstein, "Beyond Good and Evil: The Morality of Thrillers," 68.
52. Jean Baudrillard, *The Transparency of Evil: Essays on Extreme Phenomena*, 8.
53. Tamir Bar-On, "The Ambiguities of Football, Politics, Culture, and Social Transformation in Latin America," 16, 18.
54. Baudrillard, *The Transparency of Evil*, 77.
55. For the ties between Latin American football and culture, see Bar-On, "Ambiguities." See also Pablo Alabarces, *Historia mínima del fútbol en América Latina*; Maurice Biriotti del Burgo, "Don't Stop the Carnival: Football in the Societies of Latin America"; Joseph Arbena, *Sport and Society in Latin America*; and Wood, "Playing by the Book."
56. See Alabarces, *Historia mínima*, 234–237. Another important political thriller that foregrounds football is *El secreto de sus ojos*, although the focus is not so much on 1970s World Cups but on local Argentine football.
57. See Ana Laura Lusnich, "Resistencia política y ficción cinematográfica: Argentina 1976–1989," 106.
58. By the 1970s more than 200,000 Paraguayans were living in Argentina, the destination that most Paraguayans still seek today for migration and exile. See María Antonia Sánchez and Luis Roniger, "El destierro paraguayo: aspectos transnacionales y generacionales," 141.
59. Bar-On, "Ambiguities," 20.
60. Bar-On, "Ambiguities," 20.
61. Bar-On, "Ambiguities," 17–18.
62. Derrida, *Specters*, 2.
63. Rocha, "National and Transnational Dimensions of Memory," 24. Dogs play minor but similar roles in *Matar a todos* and *Araña*, also as evocations of torture.

64. Brodersen, "Juego de encierros."
65. Quoted in Dulci Spyer and Sampaio da Silva, "Desenterrando memorias," 116.
66. Feitlowitz, *Lexicon*, 30.
67. Feitlowitz, *Lexicon*, 30.
68. Calveiro, *Poder y desaparición*, 42.
69. Quoted in Martín Cortés, "Paraguay tuvo la dictadura más larga y silenciosa de América Latina" (hereafter cited as Cortés, "Larga y silenciosa").
70. Dulci Spyer and Sampaio da Silva, "Desenterrando memorias," 117.
71. Dulci Spyer and Sampaio da Silva, "Desenterrando memorias," 105.
72. Erik Lundegaard, "The Manchurian Movie," *Today.com*, April 18, 2005.
73. Brodersen, "Juego encierros."
74. Derrida, *Specters*, 51
75. Derrida, *Specters*, 51.
76. Derrida, *Aporias*, 24.
77. Brodersen, "Juego de encierros."
78. Derrida and Ferraris, *A Taste for the Secret*, 58 (emphasis in the original).
79. Calveiro, *Poder y desaparición*, 61–62.
80. Derrida, *Aporias*, 11–12.
81. Derrida, *Specters*, 5.
82. Feitlowitz, *Lexicon*, 61.
83. *Nunca más*, 167.
84. Quoted in Dulci Spyer and Sampaio da Silva, "Desenterrando memorias," 117.
85. Debussy, "Implicancias políticas," 22.
86. Žižek, *The Sublime Object of Ideology*, 29.
87. Louis Althusser, *On the Reproduction of Capitalism: Ideology and Ideological State Apparatuses*, 186 (emphasis in the original), 260.
88. Beasley-Murray, *Posthegemony*, 176.
89. Dulci Spyer and Sampaio da Silva, "Desenterrando memorias," 114.
90. Dulci Spyer and Sampaio da Silva, "Desenterrando memorias," 116.
91. Giménez, "Palabras del director," n.p.
92. Cortés, "Larga y silenciosa."
93. Dulci Spyer and Sampaio da Silva, "Desenterrando memorias," 107.
94. Giménez, "Palabras del director."
95. Derrida, *Specters*, 48.
96. According to the Chilean Instituto Nacional de Estadísticas (https://www.ine.cl), around 180,000 Haitians have migrated to Chile during the last decade.
97. Pablo Neruda, "Oda al hombre simple," in *Odas elementales*, 142 (my translation). A published English translation can also be found in Pablo Neruda, *All the Odes: A Billingual Edition*.
98. Pablo Vázquez Pérez, "*Araña* (Andrés Wood)," *Cinemaldito*, November 23, 2019.
99. See Marcelo Bergman, *More Money, More Crime: Prosperity and Rising Crime in Latin America*; and Chris Valdés, "The Changing Demographic Landscape of

Chile: Crime and Recent Immigration Patterns," who challenges this perception, claiming that the media overrepresent violent crime.

100. Bakhtin, *The Dialogic Imagination*, 84.
101. Huyssen, "Present Pasts," 34.
102. Carlos Aguilar, "Chile's Oscar Entry Is a Cautionary Tale on How the Far-Right Politics of the Past Still Affects the Present."
103. Jean Franco, "Preface," to Nelly Richard, *Cultural Residues: Chile in Transition*, viii.
104. Paula Vázquez Prieto, "Llega *Araña* de Andrés Wood."
105. *Woman Critiqued: Translated Essays on Japanese Women's Writing*, 228.
106. Juan Carlos Ramírez Figueroa, "Pinochet's Ghost Still Haunts," 19.
107. Vázquez Prieto, "Llega *Araña* de Andrés Wood."
108. In one of the final scenes of the past plotline, after killing Allende's aide, Gerardo throws his rifle into a stream, aiming to sink the hidden truth.
109. See Verónica Valdivia Ortiz De Zárate, "Estatismo y neoliberalismo: un contrapunto militar, Chile 1973–1979"; Naomi Klein, *The Shock Doctrine: The Rise of Disaster Capitalism*; and David Harvey, *A Brief History of Neoliberalism*.
110. Carlos Basso Prieto, *ChileNazi: Un siglo de xenofobia y totalitarismo*.
111. Picasso's *Guernica* (a visual staple of many Latin American political thrillers and dramas, much like Che Guevara posters) appears in *Un muro de silencio*, *Pra frente, Brasil*, and *Cabra-cega*, as a canvas on Pedro's wall, a passive ornament: history and politics become an aesthetic object to be contemplated.

CODA

1. Derry, *The Suspense Thriller*, 109.
2. Coyne, *Hollywood Goes to Washington*, 13.
3. Derry, *The Suspense Thriller*, 123.
4. Ernesto Semán, *Breve historia del antipopulismo*, 144.
5. See Wallace Andrioli Guedes, "O filme *Reparação* e o debate sobre a luta armada como veículo para o antipetismo no cinema brasileiro contemporâneo"; Gustavo Pereira, "*Real—o plano por trás da história*"; and Marcelo Forlani, "*Real—o plano por trás da história*: crítica."
6. Benjamín Ávila in *Secretos precarios*.
7. Derry, *The Suspense Thriller*, 173.
8. See Argenis Monroy Hernández, "Moisés Naím, *Dos espías en Caracas*: reseña."
9. Rubin, *Thrillers*, 266.
10. Rubin, *Thrillers*, 265.
11. Moreiras, "Infrapolitics and the Thriller," 172.
12. Jameson, *Postmodernism*, 9.
13. Podalsky, *Affect and Emotion*, 59.
14. See Tocco, *Latin American Detectives against Power*.
15. Podalsky, *Affect and Emotion*, 59.

Bibliography

Aboy Carlés, Gerardo. "El nuevo debate sobre el populismo y sus raíces en la transición democrática: el caso argentino." *Colombia Internacional* 82 (2014): 23–50.

Abreu, Nuno, Alfredo Suppia, and Marcius Freire. *Golpe de vista: cinema e ditadura militar na América do Sul*. São Paulo: Alameda, 2018.

Achtemeier, Elizabeth R. "Jesus Christ, the Light of the World: The Biblical Understanding of Light and Darkness." *Interpretation* 17, no. 4 (1963): 439–449.

Aguilar, Carlos. "Chile's Oscar Entry Is a Cautionary Tale on How the Far-Right Politics of the Past Still Affects the Present." *Remezcla*, May 12, 2019. https://remezcla.com/features/film/review-arana-spider-andres-wood-chile.

Aguilar, Gonzalo. "La política y lo político en el cine argentino reciente: *Infancia clandestina* (Benjamín Ávila, 2012) y *El estudiante* (Santiago Mitre, 2011)." In *Cine argentino contemporáneo: visiones y discursos*, edited by Bernhard Chappuzeau and Christian von Tschilschke, 67–81. Madrid: Iberoamericana Vervuert, 2016.

Aguilar Camín, Héctor. *Morir en el golfo*. Mexico City: Planeta, 2007.

Alabarces, Pablo. *Historia mínima del fútbol en América Latina*. Mexico City: El Colegio de México AC, 2018.

Althusser, Louis. *On the Reproduction of Capitalism: Ideology and Ideological State Apparatuses*. Translated by G. M. Goshharian. New York: Verso, 2014.

Amado, Ana María. *La imagen justa: cine argentino y política, 1980–2007*. Buenos Aires: Colihue, 2009.

Andermann, Jens. "The Politics of Landscape." In *A Companion to Latin American Cinema*, edited by Maria M. Delgado, Stephen M. Hart, and Randal Johnson, 133–149. Hoboken, NJ: Wiley-Blackwell, 2017.

Andersen, Hans Christian. "The Emperor's New Clothes." In *Andersen's Fairy Tales*, 287–294. New York: Dutton, 1899.

Arbena, Joseph. *Sport and Society in Latin America*. Westport, CT: Greenwood Press, 1988.

Arreola García, Adolfo. "El deceso del 'dedazo' en la sucesión presidencial en México, ¿mito o realidad?" *Vinculando* 9, no. 2 (2011): n.p.

Avelar, Idelber. "Alegorías de lo apócrifo: Ricardo Piglia, duelo y traducción." In *Ricardo Piglia: valoración multiple*, edited by Jorge Fornet, 209–233. Havana: Casa de las Américas, 2000.

Avelar, Idelber. *The Untimely Present: Post-dictatorial Latin American Fiction and the Task of Mourning*. Durham, NC: Duke University Press, 1999.

Bakhtin, Mikhail. *The Dialogic Imagination: Four Essays*. Edited by Michael Holquist. Translated by Michael Holquist and Caryl Emerson. Austin: University of Texas Press, 1981.

Balzac, Honoré de. *Catherine de Medici*. Translated by Katherine Prescott Wormeley. Project Gutenberg, 2010.

Bantlinger, Patrick. *Rule of Darkness: British Literature and Imperialism, 1830–1914*. Ithaca, NY: Cornell University Press, 1988.

Barbour, Charles. *Derrida's Secret: Perjury, Testimony, Oath*. Edinburgh: Edinburgh University Press, 2017.

Barker, Adam. "Cries and Whispers." *Sight and Sound* 1, no. 10 (February 1992): 10–12.

Baron, Jaimie. *The Archive Effect: Found Footage and the Audiovisual Experience of History*. New York: Routledge, 2014.

Bar-On, Tamir. "The Ambiguities of Football, Politics, Culture, and Social Transformation in Latin America." *Sociological Research Online* 2, no. 4 (1997): 15–31.

Barrow, Sarah. "Political Violence, Cinematic Representation, and Peruvian National Identity: *La boca del lobo* (Francisco Lombardi, 1988) and *La vida es una sola* (Marianne Eyde, 1993)." In *Political Violence and the Construction of National Identity in Latin America*, edited by Will Fowler and Peter Lambert, 131–148. New York: Palgrave Macmillan, 2006.

Basso Prieto, Carlos. *ChileNazi: Un siglo de xenofobia y totalitarismo*. Santiago de Chile: Penguin Random House, 2020.

Baudrillard, Jean. *The Transparency of Evil: Essays on Extreme Phenomena*. Translated by James Benedict. New York: Verso Books, 1990.

Bauman, Zygmunt. *Liquid Modernity*. Cambridge: Polity, 2000.

Beasley-Murray, Jon. "Citizenship and Rights in the New Republics." UBC Latin American Studies, September 19, 2017. Video. https://www.youtube.com/watch?v=uEbxvtf7dM4&list=PLFjDuS6mZI_lgiq7IhOIJh4HOAiinVIUj&index=7.

Beasley-Murray, Jon. *Posthegemony: Political Theory and Latin America*. Minneapolis: University of Minnesota Press, 2010.

Beasley-Murray, Jon. "Zorro and Hollywood's Latin Unconscious." Paper presented at the II LALISA Conference "Peripheral Mappings: Social and Cultural Geographies from the Underside of Modernity," Eugene, Oregon, April 2017, provided by the author.

Beaudry, Derek. "Democracy against the State in *The Mongolian Conspiracy* by Rafael Bernal." *New Centennial Review* 20, no. 2 (Fall 2020): 155–176.

Beck, Jay. "Submerged in Sound: Lucrecia Martel's *La ciénaga*." *Cine-Files* 8 (2015): 1–8.

Bedoya, Ricardo. "*La Boca del Lobo/The Lion's Den*." In *The Cinema of Latin America*, edited by Alberto Elena and Marina Díaz López, 185–191. London: Wallflower Press, 2003.

Bedoya, Ricardo, Mario Lucioni, and Jaime Urco. "La industria cinematográfica en Latinoamérica." *Lienzo* 16 (1995): 219–242.

Beebee, Thomas O. *The Ideology of Genre: A Comparative Study of Generic Instability*. University Park: Pennsylvania State University Press, 1994.

Belmonte Grey, Carlos. "*Rojo amanecer*: el problema de la imagen de Tlatelolco 1968." *Fotocinema: Revista Científica de Cine y Fotografía* 18 (2019): 291–306.

Benjamin, Walter. "The Paris of the Second Empire in Baudelaire." In *Selected Writings: Volume 4, 1938–1940*, edited by Howard Eiland and Michael W. Jennings, translated by Harry Zohn, 3–92. Cambridge, MA: Harvard University Press, 2003.

Benveniste, Émile. "L'appareil formel de l'énonciation." *Langages 17: L'énonciation* (March 1970): 12–18.

Bergman, Marcelo. *More Money, More Crime: Prosperity and Rising Crime in Latin America*. Oxford: Oxford University Press, 2018.

Bernal, Rafael. *El complot mongol* (1969). 8th ed. Mexico City: J. Mortiz, 1994.

Bernal, Rafael. *The Mongolian Conspiracy*. Translated by Katherine Silver. New York: New Directions Books, 2013.

Bidault, Sophie L. "Aspectos estéticos en *La sombra del caudillo*." *Neophilologus* 73, no. 4 (1989): 548–559.

Biriotti del Burgo, Maurice. "Don't Stop the Carnival: Football in the Societies of Latin America." In *Giving the Game Away: Football, Politics and Culture on Five Continents*, edited by Stephen Wagg, 52–71. Leicester, UK: Leicester University Press, 1995.

Blejmar, Jordana. "Dictatorship Toys: Play and State Terror in Argentina." In *Témoigner par l'image*, edited by Paul Bernard-Nourard and Luba Jurgenson, 125–143. Paris: Pétra, 2013.

Bobbio, Norberto. *Democracia y secreto*. Translated by Ariella Aureli and José Fernández Santillán. Mexico City: Fondo de Cultura Económica, 2013.

Bobbio, Norberto. "Democracy and Invisible Government." *Telos* 52 (June 20, 1982): 41–55. DOI: 10.3817/0682052041.

Bolaño, Roberto. *Estrella distante*. Barcelona: Anagrama, 1996.

Bonitzer, Pascal. "Partial Vision: Film and the Labyrinth." Translated by Fabrice Ziolowski. *Wide Angle* 4, no. 4 (1982): 55–63.

Borges, Jorge Luis. "Death and the Compass." In *Collected Fictions*, translated by Andrew Hurley, 147–156. London: Penguin Books, 1998.

Borges, Jorge Luis. *Other Inquisitions*. Translated by Ruth L. C. Simms. Austin: University of Texas Press, 1964.

Borges, Jorge Luis. "The Two Kings and the Two Labyrinths." In *Collected Fictions*, translated by Andrew Hurley, 263–264. London: Penguin Books, 1998.

Bourdieu, Pierre. "Job Insecurity Is Everywhere Now." In *Acts of Resistance: Against the New Myths of Our Time*, translated by Richard Nice, 81–87. Cambridge: Polity Press, 1998.

Bowman, Deena. "The Hollywood Political Thriller during the Cold War, 1945–1962." PhD diss., University of Exeter, UK, 2014.

Braham, Persephone. *Crimes against the State, Crimes against Persons: Detective Fiction in Cuba and Mexico*. Minneapolis: University of Minnesota Press, 2004.

Brewer's Dictionary of 20th Century Phrase and Fable. Boston: Houghton Mifflin, 1992.

Brodersen, Diego. "El silencio como estilo de vida." *Página 12*, October 26, 2018. https://www.pagina12.com.ar/151031-el-silencio-como-estilo-de-vida.

Brodersen, Diego. "Juego de encierros al aire libre." *Página 12*, September 19, 2019. https://www.pagina12.com.ar/216579-juego-de-encierros-al-aire-libre.

Brodersen, Diego. "Mirada que privilegia el suspenso." *Página 12*, May 28, 2015. https://www.pagina12.com.ar/diario/suplementos/espectaculos/5-35648-2015-05-28.html.

Brooks, Peter. *The Melodramatic Imagination: Balzac, Henry James, Melodrama, and the Mode of Excess*. New Haven, CT: Yale University Press, 1995.

Brown, Wendy. "At the Edge." *Political Theory* 30, no. 4 (2002): 556–576.

Bundio, Javier. "Un estudio antropológico del ritual del aliento y las prácticas discriminatorias de los hinchas argentinos." In Proceedings of the *XI Congreso Argentino de Antropología Social*, Rosario, 23–26 July 2014, 2–20. Acta Académica. https://www.aacademica.org/000-081/257.

Burucúa, Constanza. "Remnants of the Dirty War: On the *Policial*, the Political Thriller and the Paramilitary Thriller." In *Confronting the "Dirty War" in Argentine Cinema, 1983–1993: Memory and Gender in Historical Representations*, 72–109. Martlesham, UK: Boydell and Brewer, 2009.

Burucúa, Constanza, and Carolina Sitnisky. *The Precarious in the Cinemas of the Americas*. London: Palgrave Macmillan, 2018.

Butler, Judith. *Frames of War: Precarious Life, Grievable Life*. New York: Verso, 2009.

Butler, Judith. *Precarious Life: The Powers of Mourning and Violence*. New York: Verso, 2004.

Calveiro, Pilar. *Poder y desaparición: los campos de concentración en Argentina*. Buenos Aires: Colihue, 1998.

Camacho Delgado, José Manuel. "*Cien años de soledad*: entre las crónicas de navegantes y la novela de aventuras." *Cuadernos Hispanoamericanos* 803 (May 2017): 37–49.

Campillo, Maité. "'Los traidólares' ¡Raymundo Gleyzer flor de revuelo!" LaHaine.org, March 26, 2017. https://www.lahaine.org/mundo.php/llos-traidolaresr-iraymundo-gleyzer-flor.

Canetti, Elias. *Crowds and Power*. Translated by Carol Stewart. New York: Continuum, 1962.

Carassai, Sebastián. *The Argentine Silent Majority: Middle Classes, Politics, Violence, and Memory in the Seventies*. Durham, NC: Duke University Press, 2014.

Carassai, Sebastián. *Los años setenta de la gente común: la naturalización de la violencia*. Buenos Aires: Siglo XXI, 2013.

Cardona, Manolo. "Los thrillers latinoamericanos se encuentran todavía en pañales." Interviewed by Elena Reina. *El País*, July 8, 2017. https://www.elpais.com/cultura/2017/07/06/television/1499293278_386820.html.

Carro, Nelson. "Un siglo de cine en América Latina." *Política y Cultura* 8 (1997): 241–246.

Carroll, Noël. "The Paradox of Suspense." In *Suspense*, 71–91. New York: Routledge, 2013.

Casas-Cortés, Maribel. "Precarious Writings: Reckoning the Absences and Reclaiming the Legacies in the Current Poetics/Politics of Precarity." *Current Anthropology* 62, no. 5 (October 2021): 510–538.

Castrillo, Pablo, and Pablo Echart. "Towards a Narrative Definition of the American Political Thriller Film." *Communication & Society* 28, no. 4 (2015): 109–123.

Castro Avelleyra, Anabella. "*Operación masacre* de Jorge Cedrón: la recuperación de la historia para hacer historia." In Conference Proceeding, *III Congreso Internacional de la Asociación Argentina de Estudios de Cine y Audiovisual*, n.p. Córdoba, Argentina: 2012.

Castro Ricalde, Maricruz. "Un *Distinto amanecer* (Julio Bracho 1943) para la nación mexicana." *Revista de Estudios Hispánicos* 51, no. 3 (2017): 543–569. DOI: 10.1353/rvs.2017.0056.

Celin, Fernando. "La negra noche de Tlatelolco." *El semanario*, November 11, 1990.

Céline, Louis-Ferdinand. *Journey to the End of the Night*. Translated by Ralph Manheim. New York: New Directions Books, 2006.

Chanan, Michael. "Latin American Cinema in the 90s: Representational Space in Recent Latin American Cinema." *Visual Culture in Latin America* 9, no. 1 (1998): n.p. DOI: 10.61490/eial.v9i1.1097.

Chandler, Raymond. *The Simple Art of Murder*. New York: Knopf Doubleday, 2002.

Christensen, Terry, Elizabeth Haas, and Peter J. Haas. *Projecting Politics: Political Messages in American Film*. New York: Routledge, 2005.

Cobley, Paul. *The American Thriller: Generic Innovation and Social Change in the 1970s*. London: Palgrave Macmillan, 2000.

Conard, Mark T. "Nietzsche and the Meaning and Definition of Noir." In *The Philosophy of Film Noir*, edited by Mark T. Conard, 7–22. Lexington: University Press of Kentucky, 2006.

The Concise Oxford Dictionary of English Etymology. Edited by T. F. Hoad. Oxford: Oxford University Press, 2003. DOI: 10.1093/acref/97801928309OI82.001.0001.

Cortés, Martín. "Paraguay tuvo la dictadura más larga y silenciosa de América Latina." *Infojus: Agencia Nacional de Noticias Jurídicas*, March 23, 2014. http://www.infojusnoticias.gov.ar/entrevistas/paraguay-tuvo-la-dictadura-mas-larga-y-silenciosa-de-america-%20latina-82.html.

Coyne, Michael. *Hollywood Goes to Washington: American Politics on Screen*. London: Reaktion Books, 2008.

Culp, Edwin. "Landscapes of Disappearance." *Performance Research: A Journal of the Performing Arts* 24, no. 7 (2020): 16–22. DOI: 10.1080/13528165.2019.1717860.

Culwell, Lori M. "The Role of the Clown in Shakespeare's Theatre." *Early Modern Literary Studies: Shakespeare*. 2005. https://www.shaksper.net/documents/library-of-essays/60-role-of-the-clown?category_access=1.

Dapieve, Arthur. *Brock: o rock brasileiro dos anos 80*. São Paulo: Editora 34, 1995.

Davies, Mark. *The Corpus of Historical American English* (*COHA*). 2010. https://www.english-corpora.org/coha.

Davies, Tony. "The Divided Gaze: Reflections on the Political Thriller." In *Gender, Genre & Narrative Pleasure*, 118–135. New York: Routledge, 2012.

Dawson, Alexander. *Latin America since Independence: A History with Primary Sources*. New York: Routledge, 2013.

De Almeida, Ricardo Normanha Ribeiro. "As ditaduras militares no cinema argentino e brasileiro: uma análise de *A história oficial* e *Pra frente Brasil*." *Baleia na Rede: Revista Online do Grupo Pesquisa em Cinema e Literatura* 1, no. 6 (2020): 128–145.

Debussy, Pablo. "Implicancias políticas en la trilogía policial de Adolfo Aristarain." *Secuencias* 56 (2023): 9–27.

De Certeau, Michel. "Pour une nouvelle culture: prendre la parole." *Études* 329 (June–July 1968): 628–635.

De Grandis, Rita Filomena. "The Innocent Eye: Children's Perspectives on the Utopias of the Seventies (*O ano em que meus pais saíram de férias*, *Machuca*, and *Kamchatka*)." In *The Utopian Impulse in Latin America*, edited by Kim Beauchesne and Alessandra Santos, 235–258. New York: Palgrave MacMillan, 2011.

De Grandis, Rita Filomena. "La escritura del acontecimiento: implicaciones discursivas." *Nuevo Texto Crítico* 6, no. 2 (1993): 187–204.

Deleuze, Gilles, and Félix Guattari. *A Thousand Plateaus: Capitalism and Schizophrenia*. Translated and foreword by Brian Masumi. Minneapolis: University of Minnesota Press, 1987.

Delgado, Claudia. "Narrativas del hambre y memoria colectiva: un ensayo sobre la picaresca." In *Precariedad, exclusión y marginalidad: una historia conceptual de la pobreza*, edited by Nuria Sánchez Madrid and Juan Manuel Forte Monge, 153–171. Zaragoza: Prensas de la Universidad de Zaragoza, 2022.

Derrida, Jacques. *Aporias*. Translated by Thomas Dutoit. Stanford, CA: Stanford University Press, 1993.

Derrida, Jacques. *The Gift of Death & Literature in Secret*. Translated by David Wills. Chicago: University of Chicago Press, 2008.

Derrida, Jacques. *Rogues: Two Essays on Reason*. Translated by Pascale-Anne Brault and Michael Naas. Stanford, CA: Stanford University Press, 2005.

Derrida, Jacques. *Specters of Marx: The State of the Debt, the Work of Mourning and the New International*. Translated by Peggy Kamuf. New York: Routledge, 1994.

Derrida, Jacques, and Maurizio Ferraris. *A Taste for the Secret*. Edited and translated by Giacomo Donis and David Webb. Cambridge: Polity, 2001.

Derry, Charles. *The Suspense Thriller: Films in the Shadow of Alfred Hitchcock*. Jefferson, NC: McFarland, 1998.

Dick, Kay. "A Political Thriller." *Radio Times* 131, no. 1699 (June 1956): 5.

Dickstein, Morris. "Beyond Good and Evil: The Morality of Thrillers." *American Film* 6. no. 9 (July 1981): 49–52, 67–69.

Drucaroff, Elsa. *El último caso de Rodolfo Walsh*. Buenos Aires: Interzona, 2010.

Dulci Spyer, Tereza Maria, and Manuella Sampaio da Silva. "Desenterrando memórias: a ditadura paraguaia em *Matar a un muerto*." *Revista Eletrônica Trilhas da História: Dossiê: História Social do Paraguai* 21 (2021): 103–120.

Elena, Alberto. "*En retirada*: violencia política y paisaje urbano en la trilogía noir de Juan Carlos Desanzo (1983–1985)." In *Diseño de nuevas geografías en la novela y el cine negros de Argentina y Chile*, edited by Sabine Schmitz, Annegret Thiem, and Daniel A. Verdú Schumann, 161–174. Madrid: Iberoamericana, 2014.

Elze, Jens. *Postcolonial Modernity and the Picaresque Novel: Literatures of Precarity*. New York City: Springer, 2017.

Faulkner, William. *Requiem for a Nun*. London: Chatto & Windus, 1953.

Federici, Silvia. *Witches, Witch-Hunting, and Women*. New York: PM Press, 2018.

Feitlowitz, Marguerite. *A Lexicon of Terror: Argentina and the Legacies of Torture*. New York: Oxford University Press, 1998.

Feuillet, Lucía. "Identidad y otredad en la literatura policial Argentina: una lectura del marxismo y el delito desde Ernest Mandel." *RECIAL: Revista del Centro de Investigaciones de la Facultad de Filosofía y Humanidades, Letras* 8, no. 11 (2017): n.p.

Flores, Silvana. "Experiencias de la militancia en el cine politico argentino de los setenta." In *Una historia del cine político y social en Argentina: formas, estilos y registros, 1969–2009*, edited by Ana Laura Lusnich and Pablo Piedras, 205–224. Buenos Aires: Nueva Librería, 2011.

Forlani, Marcelo. "*Real—o plano por trás da história*: crítica." *Omelete*, May 30, 2017. https://www.omelete.com.br/filmes/criticas/real-o-plano-por-tras-da-historia-critica.

Foster, David William. *Mexico City in Contemporary Mexican Cinema*. Austin: University of Texas Press, 2002.

Foucault, Michel. *The Birth of Biopolitics: Lectures at the Collège de France, 1978–1979*. Translated by Graham Burchell. New York City: Springer, 2008.

Gamerro, Carlos. "El terror argentino." *Amerika: Mémoires, Identités, Territoires* 26 (2023): n.p. DOI: 10.4000/amerika.17240.

García, Victoria. "Testimonio literario-documental cinematográfico: acerca de la transposición al cine de *Operación masacre* (1973)." In Conference Proceeding: *VIII Congreso Internacional Orbis Tertius de Teoría y Crítica Literaria*, n.p. La Plata, 2013.

García Márquez, Gabriel. "La soledad de América Latina." *Nueva Sociedad* 64 (January–February 1983): 126–128.

Gargaglione Turk, Fiorella. "¿Monstruosos o disciplinados?: la representación de los militares en *Matar a todos* y *Otra historia del mundo*." *Encuentros Uruguayos* 14, no. 2 (2021): 32–48.

Gatti, Gabriel, and María Martínez. "El ciudadano-víctima: notas para iniciar un debate." *Revista de Estudios Sociales* 59 (2017): 8–13.

Giardinelli, Mempo. *El género negro: orígenes y evolución de la literatura policial y su influencia en Latinoamérica*. Buenos Aires: Capital Intelectual, 2013.

Giardinelli, Mempo. "Variations on Postmodernity, or, What Does the Latin American Postboom Mean?" Translated by Daniel Joseph Smith. In *Latin America Writes Back: Postmodernity in the Periphery*, edited by Emil Volek, 217–224. *Hispanic Issues* 28. New York: Routledge. 2002.

Giménez, Hugo. "Palabras del director." *Malba*. 2019. https://www.malba.org.ar/estreno-matar-a-un-muerto.

Glantz, Margo. "La novela de la revolución mexicana y *La sombra del caudillo*." *Revista Iberoamericana* 55, no. 148–149 (1989): 869–878.

Goity, Elena, and David Oubiña. "El policial argentino." In *Cine argentino en democracia 1983–1993*, edited by Claudio España and Gabriela Fabbro, 208–229. Buenos Aires: Fondo Nacional de las Artes, 1994.

Goldman, Francisco. "Introduction." In *The Mongolian Conspiracy* by Rafael Bernal, translated by Katherine Silver, 116–134. New York: New Directions Books, 2013.

González Bombal, Inés. "Nunca más: el juicio más allá de los estrados." In *Juicio, castigo y memorias: derechos humanos y justicia en la política argentina*, edited by C. H. Acuña et al., 193–216. Buenos Aires: Nueva Visión, 1995.

González Bravo, Guadalupe. "Los carácteres psicológicos en el cine mexicano: *Canoa*." In *Anuario 1989*, edited by S. Millán, 131–137. Mexico City: Instituto Mexicano de Psicoanálisis, 1989.

González de Canales Carcereny, Júlia. "*Hamaca paraguaya*: poesía fílmica glocal." *DeSignis* 27 (2017): 77–84.

Green, Martin. *Seven Types of Adventure Tale: An Etiology of a Major Genre*. University Park: Pennsylvania State University Press, 1991.

Grindon, Leger. "Cycles and Clusters: The Shape of Film Genre History." In *Film Genre Reader IV*, edited by Barry Keith Grant, 42–59. Austin: University of Texas Press, 2012.

Guedes, Wallace Andrioli. "O filme *Reparação* e o debate sobre a luta armada como veículo para o antipetismo no cinema brasileiro contemporâneo." *Aniki: Revista Portuguesa da Imagem em Movimento* 5, no. 2 (2018): 400–418.

Guzmán, Martín Luis. *La sombra del caudillo*. Barcelona: Castalia, 2003.

Haddu, Miriam. *Contemporary Mexican Cinema 1989–1999: History, Space, and Identity*. Lewiston/Queenston/Lampeter, Wales: Edwin Meller Press, 2007.

Haddu, Miriam. "Political Violence and Fiction in Mexican Film: The Case of Carlos Bolado's *Colosio: el asesinato* (2012)." *Journal of Latin American Cultural Studies* 24, no. 4 (2019): 453–473.

Haddu, Miriam. *Violence, Conflict and Discourse in Mexican Cinema (2002–2015)*. New York: Palgrave Macmillan, 2021.

Halberstam, Jack. *Skin Shows: Gothic Horror and the Technology of Monsters*. Durham, NC: Duke University Press, 1995.

Hanisch, Carol. "The Personal Is Political: The Women's Liberation Movement Classic with a New Explanatory Introduction." 2006. https://www.carolhanisch.org/CHwritings/PIP.html.

Harvey, David. *A Brief History of Neoliberalism*. Oxford: Oxford University Press, 2007.

Hennebelle, Guy, and Renée Delforge. "Z Movies or What Hath Costa-Gavras Wrought?" *Cinéaste* 6, no. 2 (1974): 28–31.

Hepburn, Allan. *Intrigue: Espionage and Culture*. New Haven: Yale University Press, 2005.

Hernaiz, Sebastián. *Rodolfo Walsh no escribió* Operación masacre *y otros ensayos*. Buenos Aires, 17G Editora, 2012.

Hill, John. "The Political Thriller Debate." In *The Oxford Guide to Film Studies*, edited by John Hill and Pamela Church Gibson, 114–116. Oxford: Oxford University Press, 1998.

Hirsch, Marianne. "The Generation of Postmemory." *Poetics Today* 29, no. 1 (2008): 103–128.

Hoberman, Jim. "When *Dr. No* Met *Dr Strangelove*: Movies of the Cold War and Kennedy Era." *Sight and Sound* 3, no. 12 (1993): 16–21.

Hudson, William Henry. *The Purple Land*. London: Penguin Books, 1927.

Hutcheon, Linda. *A Theory of Parody: The Teachings of Twentieth-Century Art Forms*. Chicago: University of Illinois Press, 2001.

Huyssen, Andreas. "Present Pasts: Media, Politics, Amnesia." *Public Culture* 12, no. 1 (2000): 21–38.

Islas, Octavio. "Los primeros años de internet en América Latina." *Razón y Palabra* 76 (May–July 2011): n.p.

Jakobson, Roman. "La dominante." In *Huit questions de poétique*, 77–85. Paris: Seuil, 1977.

Jameson, Fredric. "Cognitive Mapping." In *Marxism and the Interpretation of Culture*, edited by Cary Nelson and Lawrence Grossberg, 347–360. Champaign: University of Illinois Press, 1988.

Jameson, Fredric. *Postmodernism, or the Cultural Logic of Late Capitalism*. Durham, NC: Duke University Press, 1991.

Janzen, Rebecca. *Unholy Trinity: State, Church, and Film in Mexico*. Albany, NY: SUNY Press, 2021.

Kant, Immanuel. *Perpetual Peace: A Philosophical Essay*. Translated by M. Campbell Smith. New York: Macmillan, 1903.

Kasmir, Sharryn. "Precarity." In *The Open Encyclopedia of Anthropology*, edited by Felix Stein, n.p. DOI: 10.29164/18precarity.

Klein, Naomi. *The Shock Doctrine: The Rise of Disaster Capitalism*. Toronto: Knopf Canada, 2007.

Klope-Santamaria, Gema. *In the Vortex of Violence: Lynching, Extralegal Justice, and the State in Post-revolutionary Mexico*. Oakland: University of California Press, 2020. DOI: 10.2307/j.ctv1503grz.14.

Kohan, Alexandra. "Feminismo y punitivismo: un debate en movimiento." Interviewed by Guillermina Huarte. *Enfant Terrible*. September 15, 2020. https://enfantterrible.com.ar/transfeminismos/feminismo-y-punitivismo-un-debate-en-movimiento.

Kraniauskas, John. *Capitalism and Its Discontents: Power and Accumulation in Latin-American Culture*. Cardiff: University of Wales Press, 2017.

Laclau, Ernesto. *Emancipation(s)*. New York: Verso, 1996.

Laje, Agustín, and Nicolás Márquez. *El libro negro de la nueva izquierda: ideología de género o subversión cultural*. Buenos Aires: Hojas del Sur, 2024.

Leal, Luis. "*La sombra del caudillo*: roman à clef." *Modern Language Journal* 36, no. 1 (1952): 16–21.

Lévi-Strauss, Claude. *Introduction to the Work of Marcel Mauss*. Translated by Felicity Baker. London: Routledge & Kegan Paul, 1987.

Link, Daniel. "Rethinking Past Present." *Review: Literature and Arts of the Americas* 40, no. 2 (2007): 218–230.

Locane, Jorge J. "Avatares de la fricción en el corpus *Operación Masacre* de Rodolfo Walsh, Julio Troxler y Jorge Cedrón." In *Literatura argentina y el cine: el cine argentino y la literatura*, edited by Matthias Hausmann and Jörg Türschmann, 327–341. Col. Nexos y Diferencias 53. Madrid: Iberoamericana Vervuert, 2019.

López C., Ana María. "De la figuración a la imagen ausente: memoria en el cine chileno." In *Panorama del cine iberoamericano en un contexto global: historias comunes, propuestas, futuro*, edited by Ana María Sedeño Valdellós, Pedro Matute Villaseñor, and María Jesús Ruiz Muñoz, 235–254. Madrid: Dykinson, 2015.

López Mazz, José. "The Concealment of Bodies during the Military Dictatorship in Uruguay (1973–84)." In *Human Remains and Identification: Mass Violence, Genocide, and the "Forensic Turn,"* edited by Élisabeth Anstett and Jean-Marc Dreyfus, 83–97. Manchester, UK: Manchester University Press, 2016.

Lundegaard, Erik. "The Manchurian Movie." *Today.com*, April 18, 2005. https://today.com/popculture/manchurian-movie-wbna7547900.

Lusnich, Ana Laura. "Resistencia política y ficción cinematográfica: Argentina 1976–1989." *Significação: Revista de Cultura Audiovisual* 42, no. 43 (2015): 96–113.

Lusnich, Ana Laura, and Pablo Piedras. *Una historia del cine político y social en Argentina: formas, estilos y registros, 1969–2009*. Buenos Aires: Nueva Librería, 2011.

Majfud, Jorge. *Cine político latinoamericano*. Jacksonville, FL: SJ Languages, 2014.

Malamud, Andrés, and Luis Schenoni. "Sobre la creciente irrelevancia de América Latina." *Nueva Sociedad* 291 (January–February 2021): 66–79.

Mandel, Ernst. *Delightful Murder: A Social History of the Crime Story*. London: Pluto Press, 1984.

Manuel, Juan. *The Book of Count Lucanor and Patronio*. Translated by John E. Keller and L. Clark Keating. Lexington: University Press of Kentucky, 1977.

Manuel, Juan. *El Conde Lucanor o libro de los enxiemplos del Conde Lucanor et de patronio*. Edited by José Manuel Blecua. Madrid: Castalia, 1979.

Margariños, Alejo. *La cámara sin ley:* Hamaca paraguaya *y la refundación globalizada del cine guaraní*. Buenos Aires: Elaleph.com, 2018.

Martin, Deborah. "The Child in Post-dictatorship Southern Cone Film." In *The Child in Contemporary Latin American Cinema*, 133–163. New York: Palgrave Macmillan, 2019.

Martin, Deborah. "Planeta Cinénaga: Lucrecia Martel and Contemporary Argentine Women's Filmmaking." In *Latin American Women Filmmakers: Production, Politics, Poetics*, edited by Deborah Martin and Deborah Shaw, 241–262. London: Bloomsbury, 2017.

Martínez Estrada, Ezequiel. *El mundo maravilloso de Guillermo Enrique Hudson*. Mexico City: Fondo de Cultura Económica, 1951.

Martínez Grijalva, Gustavo Ricardo, and Iván Mercado Ortega. "'Canoa' (1975): el cine y la memoria social." *Versión: Estudios de Comunicación y Política* 35 (2015): 193–196.

Masmun, Carla. "Raymundo Gleyzer y el Grupo Cine de la Base: compromiso, activismo y resistencia." In *Una historia del cine político y social en Argentina: formas, estilos y registros, 1969–2009*, edited by Ana Laura Lusnich and Pedro Piedras, 173–183. Buenos Aires: Nueva Librería, 2011.

Masmun, Carla, and Denise Mora. "La liberación está en la base." In *Una historia del cine político y social en Argentina: formas, estilos y registros, 1969–2009*, edited by Ana Laura Lusnich and Pablo Piedras, 89–96. Buenos Aires: Nueva Librería, 2011.

Maxwell, Richard, and Katie Trumpener. "The Romance of the Outlands: The *Fin-de-siècle* Adventure Story between History and Geography." *Yearbook of English Studies* 41, no. 2 (2011): 106–124.

Melo, Demian Bezerra de. "Ditadura 'civil-militar'?: controvérsias historiográficas sobre o processo político brasileiro no pós-1964 e os desafios do tempo presente." *Espaço Plural* 13, no. 27 (2012): 39–53.

Méndez Cota, Gabriela. "Feminismo, infrapolítica, extinción." *Pensamiento al Margen* (special issue of *Infrapolítica y democracia*) (2018): 120–141.

Mendieta Rodríguez, Elios. "Emplazamientos del terror tras la dictadura argentina: la importancia del espacio en la película *El Clan* (2015), de Pablo Trapero." In *Buenos Aires: escrituras y metáforas de un espacio plural*, edited by Carmen Mejía Ruiz, Eugenia Popeanga, Alba Diz, Rodrigo Guijarro, and Marta Iturmendi, 181–199. Madrid: Iberoamericana, 2020.

Mendoza, Angélica. "Guillermo Enrique Hudson (1841–1922)." *Revista Hispánica Moderna* 10, no. 3/4 (July–October 1944): 86–112.

Meyer, Adriana. *Desaparecer en democracia: cuatro décadas de desapariciones forzadas en Argentina*. Buenos Aires: Marea, 2021.

Miller, David A. *The Novel and the Police*. Berkeley: University of California Press, 1988.

Monroy Hernández, Argenis. "Moisés Naím, *Dos espías en Caracas:* reseña." *Letras* 60, no. 97 (2020): 187–192. http://historico.upel.edu.ve:81/revistas/index.php/letras/article/viewFile/9320/5813.

Monsiváis, Carlos. *Aires de familia: cultura y sociedad en América Latina*. Barcelona: Anagrama, 2000.

Monsiváis, Carlos. "South of the Border, Down Mexico's Way (El cine latinoamericano y Hollywood)." *Contratexto* 9 (1995): 29–41.

Monsiváis, Carlos. "Ustedes que jamás han sido asesinados." *Revista de la Universidad de México* 7 (1973): 1–11.

Montero, Ana Soledad. "Dictadura cívico-militar: ¿qué hay en el nombre? El debate sobre la participación civil en la última Dictadura argentina y sus ecos en el presente." *Estudios Sociales: Revista Universitaria Semestral* 62, no. 1 (2022): 1–19.

Mora, Carl J. *Mexican Cinema: Reflections of a Society.* Berkeley: University of California Press, 1982.

Moraña, Mabel. *El monstruo como máquina de guerra.* Madrid: Iberoamericana Vervuert, 2017.

Moreiras, Alberto. *Against Abstraction: Notes from an Ex-Latin Americanist.* Austin: University of Texas Press, 2020.

Moreiras, Alberto. *Infrapolítica.* Santiago de Chile: Palinodia, 2019.

Moreiras, Alberto. *Infrapolitics: A Handbook.* New York City: Fordham University Press, 2020.

Moreiras, Alberto. "Infrapolitics and the Thriller: A Prolegomenon to Every Possible Form of Antimoralist Literary Criticism. On Héctor Aguilar Camín's *La Guerra de Galio* and *Morir en el Golfo.*" In *The Ethics of Latin American Literary Criticism: Reading Otherwise,* edited by Erin Graff Zivin, 147–179. New York: Palgrave MacMillan, 2007.

Moreiras, Alberto. *Uncanny Rest: For Antiphilosophy.* Durham, NC: Duke University Press, 2022.

Moretti, Franco. *The Way of the World: The Bildungsroman in European Culture.* Translated by Albert Sbragia. New York: Verso, 1987.

Mouffe, Chantal. "Deliberative Democracy or Agonistic Pluralism?" *Social Research* 66, no. 3 (1999): 745–758. https://www.jstor.org/stable/40971349.

Mraz, John. "Mexican Cinema: Of *Churros* and *Charros.*" *Jump Cut* 29 (February 1984): 23–24.

Naishtat, Benjamín. "*Rojo* Cast and Crew Q&A, TIFF 2018." https://www.youtube.com/watch?v=h7V7JoMMVt8.

Nancy, Jean-Luc. "Is Everything Political? (A Brief Remark)." Translated by Philip M. Adamek. *CR: The New Centennial Review* 2, no. 3 (2002): 15–22.

Neruda, Pablo. *All the Odes: A Bilingual Edition.* Edited by Ilan Stavans. New York: Farrar, Straus & Giroux, 2017.

Neruda, Pablo. *Odas elementales.* Edited by Jaime Concha. Madrid: Cátedra, 1954.

Nogueira, Lisandro. "*Lúcio Flávio: o passageiro da agonia,* de Hector Babenco." *Comunicação & Informação* 7, no. 2 (2004): 212–217.

Noriega, Gustavo. "*Rojo*: un film que despolitiza la historia a través de una mirada terriblemente severa sobre la clase media." *Infobae,* October 30, 2018. https://www.infobae.com/cultura/2018/10/30/rojo-un-film-que-despolitiza-la-historia-a-traves-de-una-mirada-terriblemente-severa-sobre-la-clase-media.

Nunca más: Report of the Argentine National Commission on the Disappeared (Spanish original 1984). New York: Farrar Straus & Giroux, 1986.

Oricchio, Luiz Zanin. *Cinema de novo: um balanço crítico da retomada.* São Paulo: Estação Liberdade, 2003.

Orwell, George. "Why I Write." *Gangrel* (1946): n.p.

Oxandabarat, Rosalba. "La estafa menor." *Brecha,* September 4, 2014.

The Oxford Dictionary of Word Origins. Edited by Julia Cresswell. Oxford: Oxford University Press, 2010.

Page, Joanna. *Crisis and Capitalism in Contemporary Argentine Cinema*. Durham, NC: Duke University Press, 2009.

Palmer, Jerry. *Thrillers: Genesis and Structure of a Popular Genre*. New York: E. Arnold, 1978.

Parkinson, David. "*Rojo* Review." *Empire*, September 2, 2019.

Patán, Julio. "Conspiracionismo razonable." *Gente* (June 2012): 65–67.

Paz, Octavio. "The Other Mexico." In *The Labyrinth of Solitude and Other Writings*, translated by Lysander Kemp, Yara Milos, and Rachel Phillips Belash, 213–325. New York: Grove Press, 1985.

Pereira, Gustavo. "*Real—o plano por trás da história*." *Plano Aberto*, May 22, 2017. https://www.planoaberto.com.br/critica/real-o-plano-por-tras-da-historia.

Pick, Zuzana M. *The New Latin American Cinema: A Continental Project*. Austin: University of Texas Press, 1993.

Piglia, Ricardo. "Conversaciones en Princeton." In *Crítica y ficción*, 171–224. Barcelona: Anagrama, 2001.

Piglia, Ricardo. "La ficción paranoica." *Cultura y Nación Clarín*, October 10, 1991: 4–5.

Piglia, Ricardo. "La loca y el relato del crimen." In *Prisión perpetua*. 93–102. Madrid: Lengua de Trapo, 2000.

Piglia, Ricardo. "Teoría del complot." *Ramona: Revista de Artes Visuales* (2002): 4–15.

Pinto, Iván, and Luis Felipe Horta. "Vías no realizadas en el cine político chileno: parodia, extrañamiento y reflexividad." *Aisthesis* 47 (2010): 128–141.

Plager, Federico. *Diccionario integral del español de la Argentina*. Buenos Aires: Voz Activa, 2008.

Plenel, Edwy. "Cinéma et politique: Costa-Gavras ou l'espoir." *Mediapart*, November 8, 2016.

Podalsky, Laura. *The Politics of Affect and Emotion in Contemporary Latin American Cinema: Argentina, Brazil, Cuba, and Mexico*. New York: Palgrave Macmillan, 2011.

Punte, María José. "Más allá del vano de la puerta: infancia y dictadura en tres películas argentinas." *Toma Uno* 4 (2015): 177–190.

Raggio, Sandra. "*La noche de los lápices*: y los tiempos de la memoria." *Memoria Abierta* (2009): 1–10. https://memoriaabierta.org.ar/materiales/pdf/la_noche_de_los_lapices.pdf.

Rama, Ángel. "Rodolfo Walsh: la narrativa en el conflicto de las culturas." In *Literatura y clase social*, 261–302. Barcelona: Ediciones Folio, 1983.

Ramírez, Catherine S., Sylvanna M. Falcón, Juan Poblete, Steven C. McKay, and Felicity Amaya Schaeffer. *Precarity and Belonging: Labor, Migration and Noncitizenship*. New Brunswick, NJ: Rutgers University Press, 2021.

Ramírez Berg, Charles. *A Cinema of Solitude: A Critical Study of Mexican Film, 1967–1983*. Austin: University of Texas Press, 2010.

Ramírez Figueroa, Juan Carlos. "Pinochet's Ghost Still Haunts." *Index on Censorship* 52, no. 3 (2023): 18–20.

Real Academia Española. *Corpus de referencia del español actual* (*CREA*). https://corpus.rae.es/creanet.html.

Real Academia Española. *Corpus diacrónico del español* (*CORDE*). https://corpus.rae.es/cordenet.html.

Real Academia Española. *Diccionario de la lengua española*. 22nd ed. Madrid: Espasa-Calpe, 2001. https://rae.es/dhle.

Real Academia Española. *Diccionario de la lengua española*. 23rd ed. Madrid: Espasa-Calpe, 2014. https://dle.rae.es.

Real Academia Española. *Nuevo tesoro lexicográfico de la lengua española*. Madrid: RAE, 2002. https://apps2.rae.es/ntlle/SrvltGUISalirNtlle.

Rengifo, Alci. "Benjamin Naishtat's *Rojo* and a Region's Cinematic Reckoning." *Medium Film*, July 19, 2019.

Richard, Nelly. *Cultural Residues: Chile in Transition*. Translated by Theodore Quester and Alan West-Durán. Minneapolis: University of Minnesota Press, 2004.

Robbins, Hollis. "The Emperor's New Critique." *New Literary History* 34, no. 4 (2003): 659–675. doi:10.1353/nlh.2004.0010.

Rocha, Carolina. "National and Transnational Dimensions of Memory in *Matar a todos* and *Paisito*." *Hispanic Research Journal* 17, no. 1 (2016): 19–33.

Rockwood, Roy (pseudonym). *Jack North's Treasure Hunt: Or Daring Adventures in South America*. Cleveland: World Syndicate Publishing, 1907.

Rodrigues, Carla Daniela Rabelo. 2021. "Cinema regional peruano e políticas culturais da diferença: os casos de *La casa rosada e Wiñaypacha*." *Imagofagia: Revista de la Asociación Argentina de Estudios de Cine y Audiovisual* 20 (December): 395–411. https://www.asaeca.org/imagofagia/index.php/imagofagia/article/view/120.

Rodríguez Joulia Saint-Cyr, Carlos. *La novela de intriga: diccionario de autores, obras y personajes*. Madrid: ABBA, 1972.

Rojo, Juan J. "La memoria como 'espectro' en *Rojo amanecer* de Jorge Fons." *Arizona Journal of Hispanic Cultural Studies* 14 (2010): 49–64.

Roosevelt, Theodore. "An Introductory Note." In *The Purple Land* by W. H. Hudson, ix–x. New York: Dutton, 1916.

Royo, Amelia. "Rosas y Perón: representaciones convergentes en el sistema literario argentino." *Thesavrvs: Revista Digital del Instituto Caro y Cuervo* 54, no. 3 (1999): 860–881.

Rubin, Martin. *Thrillers*. Cambridge: Cambridge University Press, 1999.

Russell, Roberto, and Fabián Calle. "Periferias turbulentas y penetradas: su papel en la expansión de los intereses de seguridad de Estados Unidos en América Latina." *CEBRI* 1, no. 1 (2022): 167–189.

Sánchez, Fernando Fabio. "M for *Murder*: Mexico and Its *Democratic* State." In *Modern Mexican Culture: Critical Foundations*, edited by Stuart A. Day, 123–147. Tucson: University of Arizona Press, 2017.

Sánchez, María Antonia, and Luis Roniger. "El destierro paraguayo: aspectos transnacionales y generacionales." *Revista Mexicana de Ciencias Políticas* 52, no. 208 (2010): 135–158.

Sánchez Prado, Ignacio M. "Alegorías sin pueblo: el cine echeverrista y la crisis del contrato social de la cultura mexicana." *Chasqui* 44, no. 2 (2015): 50–67.

Sánchez Prado, Ignacio M. "Felipe Cazals: The Question of the Film Auteur in the Age of Cinematic Crisis." In *The Lost Cinema of Mexico*, edited by Olivia Cosentino and Brian Price, 192–219. Gainesville: University Press of Florida, 2022.

Sánchez Prado, Ignacio M. "Peripheral Noir, Mediation, and Capitalism: Noir Form, Noir Mediascape, Sociological Noir." In *Noir Affect*, edited by Christopher Breu and Elizabeth A. Hatmaker, 137–155. New York: Fordham University Press, 2020.

Sánchez Prado, Ignacio M. *Screening Neoliberalism: Transforming Mexican Cinema, 1988–2012*. Nashville, TN: Vanderbilt University Press, 2014.

Sands-O'Connor, Karen. "The Stratemeyer Chums Have Fun in the Caribbean: America and Empire in Children's Series." In *Internationalism in Children's Series*, edited by Karen Sands-O'Connor, 59–75. London: Palgrave Macmillan, 2014.

Santillán Buelna, José Ramón. "Un siglo de cine político mexicano." *Ámbitos: Revista Internacional de Comunicación* 33 (2016): 1–10.

Sarmento-Pantoja, Tânia. "Cinema e literatura: resistência política e representações do herói guerrilheiro em *Pessach, A Travessia* e *Cabra-cega*." *Nonada: Letras em Revista* 1, no. 22 (May–September 2014): n.p.

Sarmento-Pantoja, Tânia, and Veridiana Valente Pinheiro. "Resistência e paranóia no filme *Cabra-cega*." *Revista Margens Interdisciplinar* 5, no. 6 (2009): 353–365. DOI: 10.18542/rmi.v5i6.2932.

Sauerberg, Lars Ole. *Secret Agents in Fiction: Ian Fleming, John le Carré, and Len Deighton*. New York: St. Martin's Press, 1984.

Schatz, Thomas. *Hollywood Genres: Formulas, Filmmaking, and the Studio System*. New York: Random House, 1981.

Schein, Harry. "A Magnificent Fiasco?" *Quarterly of Film Radio and Television* 10, no. 4 (Summer 1956): 407–415.

Schelotto, Magdalena. "La dictadura cívico-militar uruguaya (1973–1985): la construcción de la noción de víctima y la figura del exiliado en el Uruguay post-dictatorial." *Nuevo Mundo Mundos Nuevos* (2015): n.p. DOI: 10.4000/nuevomundo.67888.

Schroeder Rodríguez, Paul A. *Latin American Cinema: A Comparative History*. Oakland: University of California Press, 2016. DOI: 10.1525/9780520963535.

Schwarzböck, Silvia. "Cómo se llega a ser peronista: sobre *Operación masacre*, de Rodolfo Walsh, y *Operación masacre*, de Jorge Cedrón." *El Matadero* 7 (2010): 183–207.

Scott, Ian. *American Politics in Hollywood Film* (2000). Edinburgh: Edinburgh University Press, 2011.

Segato, Rita. "La escritura en el cuerpo de las mujeres asesinadas en Ciudad Juárez: territorio, soberanía y crímenes de segundo estado." *Debate Feminista* 37, 2008: 78–102.

Segato, Rita. *La guerra contra las mujeres*. Madrid: Traficante de Sueños, 2016.
Semán, Ernesto. *Breve historia del antipopulismo: los intentos por domesticar a la Argentina plebeya, de 1810 a Macri*. Buenos Aires: Siglo XXI, 2021.
Serna, Mercedes. *Crónicas de Indias*. Madrid: Cátedra, 2000.
Simmel, Georg. "The Sociology of Secrecy and of Secret Societies." *American Journal of Sociology* 11, no. 4 (1906): 441–498.
Simpson, Amelia S. *Detective Fiction from Latin America*. Vancouver: Farleigh Dickinson University Press, 1990.
Sommer, Doris. "Irresistible Romance: The Foundational Fictions of Latin America." In *Nation and Narration*, edited by Homi K. Bhabha, 71–98. New York: Routledge, 1990.
Sorrentino, Fernando. "*Allá lejos y hace tiempo*: anglos nativos pájaros escuerzos." *Archipiélago: Revista Cultural de Nuestra América* 26, no. 101 (2018): 17–20.
Springer, Claudia. "Comprehension and Crisis: Report Films and the Third World." In *Unspeakable Images: Ethnicity and the American Cinema*, edited by Lester D. Friedman, 167–189. Urbana: University of Illinois Press, 1991.
Staiger, Janet. "Hybrid of Inbred: The Purity Hypothesis and Hollywood Genre History." *Film Criticism* 22, no. 1 (Fall 1997: special issue on genre): 5–20.
Stavans, Ilan. *Antiheroes: Mexico and Its Detective Novel*. Translated by Jesse H. Lytle and Jennifer A. Mattson. Cranbury, NJ: Associated University Press, 1997.
Stavans, Ilan. *Antihéroes: México y su novela policial*. Mexico City: Joaquín Mortiz, 1993.
Steinberg, Samuel. *Photopoetics at Tlatelolco: Afterimages of Mexico, 1968*. Austin: University of Texas Press, 2016.
Steinberg, Samuel. "Re-cinema: Hauntology of 1968." *Discourse* 33, no. 1 (2011): 3–26.
Stites Mor, Jessica L. *Transition Cinema: Political Filmmaking and the Argentine Left since 1968*. Pittsburgh, PA: University of Pittsburgh Press, 2012.
Streber Lee, Guilherme von. "Paraguay and the Complexities of a Bilingual Nation: The Contradiction of the Guarani Language as a National Symbol and Its Condition of Diglossia." *Encuentros* 16, no. 1 (2018): 107–119.
Taibo, Paco Ignacio, II. "La (otra) novela policíaca." *Los Cuadernos del Norte* 8, no. 41 (March–April 1987): 36–41.
Taussig, Michael. *Defacement: Public Secrecy and the Labor of the Negative*. Stanford, CA: Stanford University Press, 1999.
Tocco, Fabricio. "'A language not of this world': Depersonalization and Unintelligibility in Roberto Bolaño's 'The Part about the Crimes.'" *Journal of Latin American Cultural Studies* 30, no. 1 (2021): 91–105. DOI: 10.1080/13569325.2020.1798219.
Tocco, Fabricio. *Latin American Detectives against Power: Individualism, the State and Failure in Crime Fiction*. Lanham, MD: Lexington, 2022.
Tocco, Fabricio, and Iván Cherjovsky. *Secretos precarios: el thriller político en el Río de la Plata*. SBS On Demand, 2025.
Todorov, Tzvetan. "The Typology of Detective Fiction." In *The Poetics of Prose*, 42–52. Translated by Richard Howard. Ithaca, NY: Cornell University Press, 1977.

"Uruguay: la Fuerza Aérea admitió que hubo vuelos de la muerte." *Clarín*, August 11, 2005. https://www.clarin.com/ediciones-anteriores/uruguay-fuerza-aerea-admitio-vuelos-muerte_0_S1BlMZO1CYe.html.

Valdés, Chris. "The Changing Demographic Landscape of Chile: Crime and Recent Immigration Patterns." *Encrucijada Americana* 10, no. 2 (2018): 47–54.

Valdez Morgan, Jorge. "Cine peruano y violencia: realidad y representación: análisis histórico de *La boca del lobo*." *Contratexto* 14 (2006): 177–196.

Valdivia Ortiz De Zárate, Verónica. "Estatismo y neoliberalismo: un contrapunto militar, Chile 1973–1979." *Historia* (Santiago) 34 (2001): 167–226.

Valentino, Benjamin A. "Why We Kill: The Political Science of Political Violence against Civilians." *Annual Review of Political Science* 17, no. 1 (2014): 89–103.

Vázquez Mantecón, Álvaro. "No se olvida . . . *Rojo amanecer* [film review]." *Estudios Interdisciplinarios de América Latina y el Caribe* 9 (1998): 141–144.

Vázquez Pérez, Pablo. "*Araña* (Andrés Wood)." *Cinemaldito*, November 23, 2019. https://www.cinemaldito.com/arana-andres-wood.

Vázquez Prieto, Paula. "Llega *Araña* de Andrés Wood." *Página 12*, February 16, 2020. https://www.pagina12.com.ar/247623-llega-arana-de-andres-wood-la-historia-del-grupo-paramilitar.

Velazco, Salvador. "*Rojo amanecer* y *La ley de Herodes*: cine político de la transición mexicana." *Hispanic Research Journal* 6, no. 1 (2005): 67–80.

Veronese, Keith. "The Origins and Evolution of the Strategy Board Game RISK." *Gizmodo.com*, March 30, 2012. https://gizmodo.com/the-origins-and-evolution-of-the-strategy-board-game-ri-5897532.

Vich, Víctor. "El discurso sobre la sierra del Perú: la fantasía del atraso." In *Nuevos hispanismos interdisciplinarios y trasatlánticos*, edited by Julio Ortega, 253–265. Madrid: Iberoamericana, 2010.

Viñuela, Eduardo. "Rock in Spanish: A Field of Dispute and Convergence between Spain and Latin America." *Resonancias* 23, no. 45 (July–November 2019): 197–214. DOI: 10.7764/res.2019.45.8.

Waisbord, Silvio Ricardo. *Watchdog Journalism in South America: News, Accountability, and Democracy*. New York: Columbia University Press, 2000.

Walsh, Rodolfo. *Operation Massacre*. Translated by Daniella Gitlin. New York: Seven Stories Press, 2013.

Wenders, Wim. *The Logic of Images: Essays and Conversations*. Translated by Michael Hoffmann. Boston: Faber and Faber, 1991.

Wolf, William. "Costa-Gavras Goes to Hollywood." *New York*, February 1, 1982.

Wolfenzon, Carolyn. "'El pishtaco' y el conflicto entre la costa y la sierra en *Lituma en los Andes* y *Madeinusa*." *Latin American Literary Review* 38, no. 75 (2010): 24–45.

Woman Critiqued: Translated Essays on Japanese Women's Writing. Edited by Rebecca L. Copeland. Honolulu: University of Hawai'i Press, 2006.

Wood, David. "Playing by the Book: Football in Latin American Literature." *Soccer & Society* 12, no. 1 (2011): 27–41.

Young, Paul. "The *Land* That England Lost: W. H. Hudson's *The Purple Land*, Liebig's Extract of Meat Company, and the Romance of the Outlands." In *Victorian*

Sustainability in Literature and Culture, edited by Wendy Parkins, 180–203. New York: Routledge, 2017.

Zaracho Robertti, María Esther. "Cultura y Stronismo: memorias de la dictadura en una década del audiovisual paraguayo (2006–2016)." In *Stronismo: nuevas lupas*, edited by Paulo Silva and Lorena Soler, 141–157. Foz do Iguaçu: EDUNILA, 2021.

Zarco, Gloria Julieta. "Argentina: cine, censura y dictadura (1969–1983)." In *Saggi*, edited by Ada Agresi and Rosella Mamoli Zorza, 131–142. Venice: Cafoscarina, 2012.

Zilliacus, Konni. "The Cold War in the Balkans." *Political Quarterly* 22 (1951): 85–94. DOI: 10.1111/j.1467-923X.1951.tb00196.x.

Žižek, Slavoj. "Good Manners in the Age of WikiLeaks." *London Review of Books* 33, no. 2 (2011): n.p. https://www.lrb.co.uk/the-paper/v33/n02/slavoj-zizek/good-manners-in-the-age-of-wikileaks.

Žižek, Slavoj. "Ideology II: Competition Is a Sin." *Lacan.com*, 2008. https://www.lacan.com/zizdesolationroad.html.

Žižek, Slavoj. *The Sublime Object of Ideology*. New York: Verso, 1989.

Žižek, Slavoj. "'The Thing That Thinks': The Kantian Background of the *Noir* Subject." In *Shades of Noir*, edited by Joan Copjec, 199–226. New York: Verso, 1993.

Zorzo, Solange Salete Toccolini. "*Cabra-cega*: do roteiro às telas." *Revista de Estudios Brasileños* 4, no. 7 (2017): 102–109.

Index